Mrs. P. Jones
14 Ludlow Street
Penarth
South Glamorgan
CF64 1EW

PRINCE CHARLES

BREAKING THE CYCLE

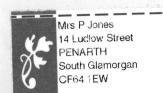

PRINCE CHARLES

BREAKING THE CYCLE

James Morton

Ebury Press

First published in Great Britain in 1998

1 3 5 7 9 10 8 6 4 2

Ebury Press
Random House, 20 Vauxhall Bridge Road, London SW1V 2SA

Random House Australia Pty Limited
20 Alfred Street, Milsons Point, Sydney, New South Wales 2061, Australia

Random House New Zealand Limited
18 Poland Road, Glenfield, Auckland 10, New Zealand

Random House South Africa (Pty) Limited
Endulini, 5A Jubilee Road, Parktown 2193, South Africa

Random House UK Limited Reg. No. 954009

www.randomhouse.co.uk

Papers used by Ebury Press are natural, recyclable products made from wood
grown in sustainable forests.

A CIP catalogue record for this book is available from the British Library.

ISBN 0 09 186571 9

Printed and bound in Great Britain by
Mackays of Chatham PLC, Chatham, Kent

CONTENTS

This book is dedicated to the over 600,000 young people
who have participated in one of the Prince's programmes
over the last 25 years, and to the more than 25,000 staff
and volunteers who have helped him during this period.
This book is their story too. I feel sure that the Prince of
Wales would want the dedication to go to those whose efforts
are his constant source of inspiration.

2 October 1998

ACKNOWLEDGEMENTS

A book like this requires enormous effort from a small army of people to help pull it all together. I have been given support from so many people that it is not possible to mention every one. At St. James's Palace, I particularly want to thank Sandy Henney, press officer to the Prince of Wales, who has been enormously helpful, Jonathan Skan, assistant private secretary, who gave me early encouragement and much valuable advice, and David Hutson, the Prince's archivist, who repeatedly returned to the archives to fill a stream of requests for documents.

Breaking the Cycle is an independent book. I received help, but no direction whatsoever, and no-one tried to influence the content. The original concept, research, analysis, conclusions and final text, are entirely my own. The Prince of Wales gave permission for his staff to co-operate, and consented to meet me. While he would agree with much of it – and of course it includes many of his own words – there are bound to be passages with which he disagrees, perhaps strongly in certain instances.

The help of Tom Shebbeare, chief executive of the Prince's Trust, has been invaluable. Over 20 years around the investment business I have met many top managers from many large and successful companies, and no-one has impressed me more as an inspirational leader.

Deborah Lincoln, head of press and communications at the Prince's Trust, was my principal contact. She has always made herself available, even while holding down the equivalent of two full-time jobs. I also want to thank Dr Neil Caldwell, director of the Prince's Trust – Bro; Elizabeth Crowther-Hunt, executive director of the Prince's Trust – Volunteers; Leslie Morphy, policy director; Richard Street, chief executive of the Prince's Youth Business Trust; and Arwyn Thomas, executive director of the Prince's Trust – Action.

Julia Cleverdon, chief executive of Business in the Community, deserves special thanks. She has been incredibly helpful, and a fund of fascinating stories. Other organisations also opened up their records. I am particularly grateful to Peter Holland, chief executive of the Disability Partnership, Robert Davies, chief executive of the Prince of Wales Business Leaders Forum, and Alan Smith, chief executive of Threshold.

Many more individuals in these organisations found time to talk or scrounged articles, information and photographs. Vivienne Bowen-Morgan, Amanda Bowman, Nicola Brentnall, David Cooper, Susie Creighton, John Gillingham,

Amanda Harvie, David Hiscocks, Rona Martin, Claire Mead, Nancy Haque, Hazel Mosienko, Brendan Mullen, Joe Naughton, Gill Osborne, Judith Roberts, David Tee, Josie Turtle and Clare Winterton are just a few of those who contributed.

Sarah Darling, manager of royal events at Business in the Community, and Caroline Jones, marketing director at the Prince's Youth Business Trust, both went the extra mile to assist with research. Jack Curtin, area manager for Walsall and Wolverhampton, deserves my heartfelt thanks. As a 13-year veteran of the Prince's Youth Business Trust, he was there when four people and the Prince of Wales formed the full complement of personnel, and his personal archives are a treasure trove. Annie Lycett, who looks after the Prince's Trust Ambassadors, has also gone out of her way to resurrect long-lost items, as has Vivien Cockburn, who has overall responsibility for target markets.

Many other people made themselves available, or dug into their attics and diaries to provide anecdotes, letters and personal photographs. I am grateful to them all. I would particularly like to thank Dr Eric Anderson, Richard Beckett, QC, Michael Bichard, the Rt Hon Virginia Bottomley, MP, John Bird, Roy Bristow, Rudi Bogni, Bill Castell, Michael Colburne, the Rev. Canon David Collyer, Sir Paul Condon, Sir Alcon Copisarow, David Cox, the Draper's Company, Rupert Fairfax, Sir Matthew Farrer, Harry Fitzgibbons, Jane Fulford, Derek Goldman, the Rt Hon John Gummer, MP, Sir Ernest Hall, Nick Hardwick, Sir Harold Haywood, Sally Hewell, Lord Hunt of Wirral, Field Marshall the Lord Inge, John Jarvis, Antony Kenney, Simon Livingstone, Brian Lymberry, Don MacDonald, Tony McGann, Sir George Martin, Richard Maudslay, the Rev Andrew Mawson, Sheila McKechnie, Hugh Merrill, Peter Mimpress, the Rev. Dr John Morgans, Sir Claus Moser, Archie Norman, MP, Stephen O'Brien, Sir Angus Ogilvie, Hilary Omissi, Elizabeth Paganussi, Dave Parker, Chief Superintendent Parry, Lord Patten, John Pervin, Melanie Phillips, Sir Jonathon Porritt, John Rae Price, Lord Remnant, Sir John Riddell, Sir David Rowand, Guy Salter, the Rt Hon Gillian Shephard, MP, Lord Sheppard, Jon Snow, the Earl of Snowdon, Sarabjeet Soar, Sir Dennis Stevenson, Kay Stratton, David Tilbury, Lakshmi V.Venkatesan, Lord Weatherill and Lord Young.

I must also thank those individuals whose stories are profiled, for allowing me to write about their personal experiences. Special thanks go to Bernard Adams, Manny Amran, Michael Anderson, Steve Balsamo, Mohammed Datoo, Huw Davies, Michael Dixon, Debbie Evershed, Leigh Goodsell, Julian Golding, Paul Gullick, Paul Mackie, Andrew McAllister, Lisa Metcalfe, Joanne Price, Fiona Rae, Ian Robertson, Lawrence Steele, Danny Stevens, and Helen Tilbury.

I am very grateful for the assistance of John Herbert, who carried out a great deal of research. Between us, we conducted hundreds of interviews and synthesised so many documents that I lost count long ago. Jackie George, my mole in Massachusetts, unearthed much material on visits Prince Charles made to the USA.

Claire Powell and Sylvia Nash, once again, took on the task of turning my scribbling into a manuscript with their customary efficiency. My secretary, Beverley Baker-Simms, has had to stretch her day even further than usual to accommodate additional work flow.

I want to thank everyone at Random House for sharing the vision behind this book, and for their constructive criticism and invaluable advice. This book is quite different and, in my opinion at least, much more interesting and rather more readable due to their ideas. In particular, Julian Shuckburgh was always available to give me guidance and good advice, and Susan Hill made major improvements to my early drafts.

Finally, and most important of all, I thank my wife, Ellen, who has had to exercise unusual tolerance this year. She remained a constant source of encouragement and support, even though sometimes feeling that the Prince of Wales had taken over our lives. No-one could have been a more caring or constructive critic.

Photograph Acknowledgements

The author and publishers are grateful to the following for supplying photographs, and for their permission to reproduce them: Sir Harold Haywood, 1; George Bodnar, 36; Doug McKenzie, 2, 3, 6, 7; Tim Graham, 4, 5, 19, 20, 24, 25, 34; Express & Star, Wolverhampton, 8; Leigh Goodsell (PYBT '94), 9; Graham Grieves, 10; Picture Link, 11 (Martin Potter), 15 (David Harris); Eastern Counties Newspapers, 12, 33; AIC, 13; South Wales Echo, 14; Colin Poole, 16; Colin Beere, 17; The Prince's Trust, 18; Williams Photography, 21; Financial Times, 22; Business in the Community - Wales, 23; Sir Ernest Hall, 26, 27; The News, Portsmouth, 28; Les Millar, 29; LWT Copyright, 30; Banbury Guardian, 31; Len Cross, 32; Stuart Colwill, 35; Lea Events, 37; Simon Livingstone, 38; Terry O'Neill, 39; Antonia Reeve, 40; The Herald and Evening Times, 41; Business Leaders Forum, 42.

INTRODUCTION

You are about to read a remarkable story. This is not another biography of the Prince of Wales – far from it. *Breaking the Cycle* is a profile of the Prince as a professional. Emphasis on his work distinguishes *Breaking the Cycle* from all previous books about him, or indeed about any other member of the royal family.

On 14 November 1998 Prince Charles celebrates his 50th birthday. Reaching 50 is a time for reflection, for taking stock of accomplishments and for setting new goals. When a public figure whose activities attract so much interest reaches such a milestone it is inevitable that the occasion will be marked by a critique of that person's life. Unlike most people who come and go on the public stage, the Prince has always had to live in the spotlight. Three photographers were skulking in the street outside Hill House on his second day at the school when he was only seven. Media attention has only increased since. Strange then, that so much of this attention has focused on his private life, when in many ways his public life is much more interesting.

The fashion among the chattering class has been to write the monarchy off as a tired symbol of past glory, a relic to be replaced during the Cool Britannia make-over. Reporting on the royal family has tended to dwell on the superficial or on personal problems, preferably with unflattering photographs attached. There has been a surfeit of the House of Windsor does *Dynasty*. Yet a great deal of hard work is going on – less glamorous and perhaps less easy to capture in a headline – but vital to the well-being of the nation. Somehow this story has been shunted into a siding.

Breaking the Cycle tells that untold story, capturing for the first time the side of his life that matters most. To appreciate Prince Charles you must understand two things: his passion for community service and his quest to redress disadvantage among the young. *Breaking the Cycle* covers his activities in pursuit of these aims. Starting with ideas – hazy and not well thought-out – with almost no backing and the princely sum of £3,000, he has built up an organisation over 20,000 strong which now helps over 80,000 disadvantaged young people a year in meaningful and measurable ways. This is the true story of the Prince of Wales.

Through the Prince's Trust, Business in the Community and other organisations in which he is active, Prince Charles has achieved an enormous amount since he embarked on work which effectively began on 1 December 1972. He has:

- set up a self-employment scheme which has started 39,000 businesses and created 52,000 jobs;

- helped over 60,000 other young people find work through his programmes;
- enabled nearly 30,000 young people to perform service which has benefited both them and their communities;
- pioneered an out-of-school hours programme, Study Support, which has enabled over 100,000 students to do homework in conducive surroundings with help at hand;
- encouraged over 400 of the largest companies in Britain to contribute to the regeneration of depressed communities all across the country;
- been the catalyst for improvements in the quality of life for disabled people in access, education, employment and healthcare.

His work has brought tangible improvement to the lives of over 600,000 disadvantaged young people and in the process generated benefits for the country with a value approaching £12 billion.

When the Prince first started to carve out a role for himself, his initial steps were hesitant. Early efforts were extensions of previous patronage the royal family customarily gave to good causes. The established pattern was by way of rather random grants. Even at the outset Prince Charles saw the need to do things differently. He was convinced of the importance of helping individuals as well as organisations and that it was vital that this help should be personal and given at a local level. He also wanted recipients to be part of the process, suggesting schemes which would help them, rather than being told what was good for them in the time-honoured manner.

In redefining his role, over the years, the Prince has run risks and created controversy. He has ignored advice and chosen to take on vested interests. At various times he has had to argue against the government of the day, the civil service, trade unions, voluntary organisations, courtiers at Buckingham Palace and even members of his own staff. It is hard to think of a constituency of any importance which at some point has not opposed something he was trying to do. It is amazing he did not pack his bags and go back to his rather comfortable home. Instead he stood his ground.

One might almost be tempted to characterise Prince Charles as an anti-establishment figure. Look at some of the company he keeps and some of the people he admires: George Pratt, a probation officer who helped him start his trust, the rock star Phil Collins, John Bird, co-founder of the *Big Issue* and Tony McGann of the Eldonians. He constantly advocates new ways of doing things and consistently challenges conventional wisdom, so he is bound to ruffle feathers; and he has occasionally crossed the line from constructive comment to direct criticism. And he has brought about measurable changes in Britain. Several current government programmes and recent legislation show signs of his influence, incorporating solutions he has been advocating to social problems over many years.

The Prince knows social problems do not fit into neat compartments which would make them easy to solve. The Prince does not see things in such simple terms. He has a holistic view of the community and of the individual, and of the responsibilities of each to the other. Without balance, the quality of life for everyone is adversely affected. Why are people poor? Lack of family, lack of education, a negative environment, suffering from a special handicap. The interconnection between unemployment and homelessness, or between truancy from school and crimes by young offenders, requires an integrated approach because there is no one root cause of poverty and so no one solution. Only public/private partnerships, which bring together all constituencies and create coalitions with people at the grass roots, can break the cycle.

The Prince of Wales has set in motion many programmes over the past 25 years, directly or indirectly, and all are designed to alleviate poverty in the broadest sense. His emphasis is on young people but in particular on the disadvantaged. Sometimes activities may not seem related and the sequence of events is not always neat and tidy so the overall pattern may not be obvious. But anyone who studies all the separate areas can see the interrelation. Each supports an unified approach that, taken as a whole, is designed to restore a sense of balance in the community and help each individual to rebuild a belief in their self-worth. The common theme throughout is his emphasis on helping disadvantaged young people.

Prince Charles uses the word 'disadvantaged' in almost every speech or conversation about his work. The Prince's Trust Network Manual of 1996 identifies 12 dimensions to be used in helping ascertain whether an individual is disadvantaged. They are: ex-offenders, broken families, unemployed, unable to gain access to training, educational failure, single parent families, physical, learning or secondary disability, discriminated against due to sex, race, religion or culture, living in an isolated or run-down area, homeless, history of care, and substance abuse. See also a list that he drew up in 1992: environmental protection, health care, education, homelessness, crime and unemployment were issues he identified as priorities. These categories encapsulate the issues which the Prince feels most deserve his greatest attention. Ask him for his own definition of disadvantage and the answer is simple but powerful: "When you see it, you recognise it."

These are the themes which *Breaking the Cycle* tackles in assessing the impact of the work of the Prince of Wales. In this book, the issues are examined through his eyes but also from the perspective of the people who have seen him in action. The problems are clear: the solutions less so. Most are designed to address one or more of these problems. One programme has the potential to be the most comprehensive solution of all: community service. That is so fundamental to his approach that no study of his work could be complete without a separate chapter devoted to it.

Coverage cannot be comprehensive. The Prince directs most of his attention to the problems of young people – but not to the exclusion of other important social issues. He has been increasingly active with problems related to ageing. As president of Age Concern and patron of Help the Aged, among other organisations, this is no token gesture. But these very real commitments are outside the scope of this book.

What is within it is an examination of how he operates. The Prince is rather like an executive chairman of an enormous charitable conglomerate. His management style has created a culture of risk taking, flexibility, innovation and trust. One part of this job is so huge as to deserve its own chapter: the key to growth in any enterprise is raising resources. Chapter 9 examines how the Prince has recruited people and found the funds to support and expand his initiatives. Chapter 10 adds another dimension: his international activities.

The final section looks at what the future holds. Chapter 11 summarises progress so far and Chapter 12 looks forward to what the Prince wants to achieve and his goals for the next 10 years. The institution of monarchy provides his family with an opportunity to think within a time scale which may seem irrelevant to everyday life but could matter a great deal to our grandchildren. He has a vision for the country he would like Britain to be today and also far into the future.

Once, when asked what he most wanted to do with his life, he answered: "I just want to put the Great back into Britain." The reply could have seemed trite but he really means it. No-one who has spent time with him can doubt his sincerity. He has chosen a hard road when there were plenty of soft options available. During interviews for this book, people associated with his work – particularly the young people – were unanimous: "He did not have to do this."

Can one person make a difference? When the final chapter on Prince Charles is written, what will he be remembered for? In my opinion he will be remembered as an advocate for the underprivileged, for the battles he fought on behalf of those who lacked the ability to make their own case and for highlighting the needs of sections of society which had somehow slipped between official cracks. He will be remembered because he chose to champion causes which often were unpopular or unfashionable and ventured where politicians feared to tread. He will be remembered as someone who changed the lives of hundreds of thousands of people in Britain, most especially those of the most disadvantaged and marginalised young people, by creating a safety net of last resort.

Each person whose life is improved will in turn pass hope on to those around them. If you are an unemployed head of household and you get a job through training, all your family will be better off. There is the money of course, but also, with self-esteem restored, the atmosphere at home improves. A positive mind set breeds better mental and physical health, and so on. It does not always work out this way exactly but often the virtuous cycle, once set in motion, can be extraordinarily powerful. I call this the percolating-up effect. If you could not read properly but now can manage more on your own, then you are less of a burden to others. On a broader level, if a young shoplifter is weaned away from delinquency then society as a whole is spared enormous social costs.

Newspapers are quick to point out that there are many readers for every copy sold. I am comfortable arguing that for every person who comes out of one of the Prince's programmes better able to cope with the challenges of life, at least two other people see improvement in their lives. That means 1.8 million people, or over three per cent of the entire population. If 1.8 million seems high, think again. I am certain that this number is an underestimate.

Nowhere in these numbers is there any allowance for the impact of his work with the environment or in any of the urban regeneration areas where he has contributed and often played a crucial part. Another way to look at his impact is to add up the benefits where it has been possible to assign a value to what has been accomplished. Job creation, higher education and crime prevention are all susceptible to economic analysis. The Prince of Wales has created benefits worth £12 billion for this country.

Read the material in *Breaking the Cycle* and decide for yourself to what extent my portrait presents a fair and balanced assessment. The material is based on actual events, supported by eyewitness accounts and the true stories of people who have been helped by, and worked with, Prince Charles. Interpretation is a separate issue. Reasonable people can and will disagree and draw different conclusions. The facts, however, are indisputable.

Some people will want to pick holes in this book because *Breaking the Cycle* is full of positives. I make no apology. There are many stories in these pages of how individuals have been able to improve their lives with help from one of his organisations but, in the main, through their own efforts and determination. The Prince often says how amazed he is at their level of achievement, particularly since so many start with the odds heavily stacked against success. "You don't want to talk about what I do. You should talk abut what these young people do. That is much more interesting."

I am also aware that a book devoting itself to the work of the Prince of Wales risks being called a hagiography. This is only because, when you look at what he has done with his life and then assess his impact on society, the result is impressive – especially considering that he has been doing things which no previous Prince of

Wales ever attempted. Prince Charles has made the role a catalyst for change in the country. Not content to be an heir in waiting, he has chosen to be an heir in action.

The cumulative impact of his work has been grossly underestimated before this book because no one has ever attempted to tell the full story, let alone measure the extent of his accomplishments. There have been scraps of information and isolated stories but piecemeal reporting could never give a true sense of the scale. It is a sad commentary on media priorities that so little received proper coverage, mainly because it has not been populist and lacked tabloid appeal. The prevailing wisdom is if it's good, it's dull or, as Volunteer team leader Simon Cole said, after being turned down by local TV for the third time, "They'd be down here like a shot if someone's granny had been mugged."

At 50 Prince Charles is in the prime of life. Each year he grows in confidence that his work is making a difference because he can see for himself a lasting and positive impact on the lives of people he has helped. The country too, is waking up to a realisation that he has not been wasting his time.

What is the Prince of Wales after? Nothing less than a better Britain – and to achieve that he needs all the help he can get. Your Prince needs you! If, at the end of this book, you feel you could contribute something, don't hold back. Prince Charles has accomplished an extraordinary amount; but he is far from complacent. He wants to do much, much more. Some of his ideas get a full airing here. Others are still germinating. All will require greater resources in both funding and time from people willing to help. A culture in which private individuals give their money, their time and their commitment to improving their communities would be the best 50th birthday present of all.

Chapter 1

IN THE
BEGINNING

"How can I help?"

The work of the Prince effectively began in 1972. He has always wanted to do what he can to help right social wrongs. Even at school he enjoyed community service, an experience which he recalls as one of the most satisfying in his life. He developed a belief that every person has something to contribute to society, but he could not see that everyone was being offered ways to make a contribution.

"I think it was this that led me to try and develop a way of dealing with the most disadvantaged, the most disaffected, the most alienated people in society, because I felt so often that all of us have some sort of potential which is often under-utilised or not used in the right way."

These were the sentiments that set him searching for something different. Until his early 20s Prince Charles had followed dutifully along the prescribed path: education, including spells at Timber Tops in Australia as well as a term at the University of Aberystwyth in Wales, followed and interspersed with Gordonstoun and Cambridge. Education over, he went into the armed forces with five years in the Navy.

So far so satisfactory, but what next? Precedents were not especially promising. Alan Bennett wrote in his drama *The Madness of King George* that "being the Prince of Wales is not a title: it's a predicament". It is interesting to speculate how Edward VII's lifestyle when Prince of Wales would have been perceived if subjected to the same level of scrutiny as prevails today. Edward VIII appeared to show a streak of compassion, but was found wanting when the crisis came. Given the age and health of the Queen, Prince Charles needed a role he could make his own and one wherein he could remain relevant to the country on into the next millennium.

As early as 1965 the Palace began to search for a solution, but with society in flux and the future opaque they were flying blind. Nothing substantive came of these discussions. Nor was it any clearer at Cambridge, where he said in a speech: "My great problem in life is that I do not really know what my role in life is." The issue was still festering years later. A number of well-meaning suggestions were made about interesting posts he might hold, most of which could have been disastrous. Among those allegedly on offer were Governor General of Australia and ambassador to France, neither of which would have dovetailed with his real interests: lots of ceremony and almost no substance.

By custom, heirs to the throne inherit the same organisations in which their parents were prominent. One obvious place for Prince Charles to cut his teeth was at the King George's Jubilee Trust, a well-established body with laudable aims, run along conservative lines, which funded conventional projects without a whiff of controversy; and so thoroughly suitable. In 1974 he was appointed president of its administrative council. Having been around since 1935, the Jubilee Trust was steeped in the practices of the past and not really what he was looking for. He would not feel satisfied being a figurehead. As he said in a June 1974 interview, "I couldn't stand being around if there didn't seem to be any point to it … I don't want to appear in public just for the sake of being in public. I only want to appear when I can really help."[1] His search took him in new directions and into making connections outside the court circle.

The trigger for action was a BBC Home Service radio interview in late 1972 in which George Pratt, a probation officer, described the depressing circumstances of the young people whom he met through his work. Discussion turned to the Criminal Justice Act of 1972 due to come into effect in January 1973 under which young people sent to borstal would be compelled to do 240 hours community work. The idea was to offer a character-building experience but the linkage often seemed like extra punishment.

The Prince of Wales was listening and was moved by hearing about young people with no jobs, no family, with no support of any sort, who were being failed by the state and discarded by society. Pratt made the appeal, "If only someone will befriend them, perhaps they would have a chance." Prince Charles decided that he would be that friend.

Squadron leader David Checketts, then his private secretary, tracked down Pratt, who received an unexpected invitation. Pratt took along three friends who also had expertise in the problems of young people. Another invitee was Jon Snow, now an ITN newscaster. In 1972 he was running a Covent Garden 'drop in' for teenagers with drug problems.

[1] *Observer*, 16 June 1974.

The five people at the gathering which led to the formation of the Prince's Trust were:

- Chief Superintendent J Collie   Metropolitan Police community relations
- Norman Ingram-Smith   Director, social service unit, St Martin's in the Field
- George Pratt   Deputy principal probation officer for the Inner London probation and aftercare service
- John Rea Price   Director of social services, London borough of Islington
- Jon Snow   Director, New Horizons Youth Centre

Not a title or a gong between them, yet these men all had firsthand experience of the problems which he wanted to understand more fully. The group assembled for what was billed as a 'discussion on youth' at 10.30 am on Friday, 1 December 1972, in the Chinese Room at Buckingham Palace. They were to become the Prince's unofficial think tank.

Several of the areas that are still his main priorities in 1998 feature prominently in the notes from this very first meeting: not so surprising, given the topic. Young people in trouble often share several characteristics: inadequate education, unemployment, lack of motivation and nothing constructive to do. Some were homeless. A disproportionate number of young in trouble had West Indian backgrounds.

Pratt's views on young offenders overlapped with the Prince's concern that, with compulsory National Service gone, something voluntary should be offered in its place. Prince Charles had in mind some form of community service, but was looking for guidance. Snow suggested a scheme run by Sally Trench where young people refurbished houses for the elderly and spastics. The need was to find useful activities for young people, especially in the transition period between school and work. The meeting was a cross between Q&A and a brainstorming session. Some of the ideas tossed around 26 years ago still remain at the heart of his work. As Rea Price remarked in 1998: "The Prince's Trust is doing today exactly what he had hoped it would do when we started all those years ago."

Snow remembers the flavour and general direction of their conversation. "The Prince of Wales struck me as being extraordinarily well informed about the problems. He asked very intelligent questions, all of which centred around 'What change could I help bring about using my position? What should I do?' He was looking to make some contribution which would give the poorer end of the young people in the community some extra chance. At this time he was still quite imprecise about what he was going to do."

So started a sort of royal skunk works which was kept strictly under wraps. It is clear that the Prince sees this meeting as the effective starting point of his work, even if his trust did not come into being for a further three and a half years. In the foreword to the ten year review, he referred to it and confirmed that the original culture and goals of the Trust remained central.

"The goal of the Prince's Trust, from its inception in 1972 and its official commencement ten years ago, has been to encourage disadvantaged young people who had not been motivated by more conventional methods. My original hope was to help them recognise their own potential by encouraging them to use their talents and energies to pursue self-help projects, some of which might enable them to help others."

The Prince wanted to meet some of these young characters in their own setting. Pratt suggested 'incognito' visits to Centrepoint, Islington and Huntercombe borstal at Henley, which was experimenting with community service as part of a rehabilitation programme. He was keen to go, but officials were against such unorthodox activity. Plenty of people regarded his enthusiasm with grave misgivings. When news of fact-finding in the field leaked out, the powers that be intervened. One such night visit was all set for the Harambee Project on Holloway Road, Islington, in January 1973. Collie checked the place out and concluded that there were no problems. But after the Home Office had been informed the day before as a matter of courtesy, the visit was suddenly cancelled on the alleged grounds of 'security'. This was only one example of the sort of opposition he faced.

"It was quite difficult to get many people to believe in what I wanted to do; and I needed help to find out what was going on, or I couldn't have started the Trust ..."

The December 1972 meeting and those that followed provided the Prince with insights into the problems of young people, as he searched for a way to give meaningful help, to prevent alienated youth from becoming young offenders. One idea was some form of compulsory national service, which would keep them off the streets and remove temptation; but he also wanted to explore the softer side of prevention. An informal advisory body evolved, led by Pratt, and subsequently bolstered by Peter Newsam, deputy education officer for the Inner London Authority. While Prince Charles was away on naval duties during most of 1973, Pratt was encouraged to keep this group alive, ready to make recommendations on his return. The first tangible output reached the Prince in early July, while he was attending the independence celebration of the Bahamas.

In his response to that draft proposal most of the core values which make the work of the Trust so relevant today can already be found in written form: a culture of community service, the need to consult and involve the people he wanted to help, and the need to take risks.

"The object of the overall strategy must always be a subtle attempt to make people aware of themselves as useful citizens with a more rational and responsible attitude to life ... The deprived groups must themselves be consulted and represented on any committee we might set up ... Risks must be taken and one or two disasters accepted if we are going to progress anywhere at all."

It was essential to keep any structure small: "Something like the Prince of Wales Committee seems too big as far as I am concerned." In terms of how to proceed, the Prince wanted to "concentrate first on one small area" with "a controlled experiment" in which "alienated" young people found their own level. He would provide equipment and training but they should take ownership and run the project.

1973 was not a high point of economic prosperity for Britain, and things were going to get worse, with the three-day week and other disruptions which led to rising unemployment and poverty, especially among young people. There was a sense of unreality about the progress of the group, which met at irregular intervals due to the Prince's naval commitments. Social workers were protesting in the streets of Islington while Rea Price was off to the Palace in a 20-seater ambulance – the sole form of transport available to him from the council pool.

Not all the initial ideas made sense. Prince Charles was keen on a volunteer fire brigade similar to Gordonstoun's. Fire brigade union militancy was at an all-time high, so suggesting that on a national scale could have been pouring petrol on flames. Community service continued as the common theme, along with the notion of providing small sums of money which kids could use to advance their own ideas. The next suggestion was to set up local committees to encourage young people to come up with proposals themselves. The thought that young people might propose things, rather than join established organisations and do what they were told, was radical 25 years ago. That a Prince of Wales should associate himself with such progressive notions shocked opponents into action.

Questions were raised as to whether this particular group were the right advisors for the heir to the throne. Certainly what he was hearing was at variance with prevailing wisdom. Arriving at Buckingham Palace one December day in 1973, Rea Price found Joan Cooper, director of social work service from the DHSS, waiting and wanting to have a quiet chat about precisely what was going on. There were grave concerns in Whitehall that the Prince might become a loose cannon. The Home Office did not like what they saw, but since Prince Charles had elicited experienced people who would not be easy to discredit, the decision had been made to co-opt rather than confront.

So, the next time everyone convened, five representatives of relevant government departments were inserted into the original group. There is a reference in Home Office correspondence to "that part of the report which concerned the carrying out of work in the community by unemployed youth would be politically sensitive." [2]

The report clearly implied that government was failing young people. It stated that "resources still remain quite inadequate in relation to needs" and "it is essential to examine the extent to which the nation is getting an efficient return from such resources"; and "considerable loss of impact arises from the failure of services to establish effective contact and communication with groups they seek to serve ... services are pursuing a policy of welfare colonialism ... and are trying to apply middle-class philosophies and aspirations to groups they seek to serve". Strong stuff for civil service stomachs. If the Prince were to go public with remarks like these, unscrupulous people might have tried to use his words to their own advantage in an already strained political environment.

Hence the arrival of the civil service contingent, bent on making sure no such commentary made its way into the public domain. Palace records suggest that at least one member of the Home Office team was under instructions either to discourage the whole exercise or, failing that, to try and hijack the project and take it back under the wing of government. From December 1973, each member of the informal group was shadowed by a senior civil servant, whose main function seemed to be looking over their shoulders to make sure nothing much happened.

The enlarged group did continue a lively debate. One point of agreement about 'alienated' young people was a sense that they could be stimulated to show concern for others. There was also evidence coming in from young offenders involved in community service that attitudes could change. That then became the starting point for a less controversial programme. Most of the minutes, however, refer to the importance of taking risks and that ideas for projects should come from the young themselves if they were to succeed.

At this point the Prince asked the Rt Rev. Launcelot Fleming, dean of Windsor, to add another view to an emerging consensus which took the form of a report presented on 26 May 1974 at St George's House. The report had been re-jigged and given a generous coating of civil service speak. Offending phrases had dematerialised between drafts, but the main intent remained intact. "The

2 Home Office to Checketts, 18 December 1973.

Prince of Wales has expressed the wish to be associated with a programme designed to reach out to disadvantaged young people. The aim would be to provide opportunities for the encouragement of self-help and community service activities to be carried out by such young people ... " So did the methodology: "Further initiatives and innovatory methods need to be devised to reach these young people ... unwilling or unable to make constructive use of the well-established educational and recreational routes to economic and personal autonomy. Given help to devise and carry through their own ideas and ambitions, their restless energy and talents may be canalised into constructive activities ... "; and the culture: "The fund should support innovatory and, at times, unorthodox ventures ... and accept the risk that a proportion of the projects would fail ... The executive committee should include a number of people in the younger age group." The conclusion was that the Prince of Wales should set up his own Trust to "enable young people to develop their own constructive programmes".

One prime concern was whether there was any constitutional barrier to the heir to the throne involving himself in matters which might be deemed political. He needed a green light from Westminster. The Home Secretary personally reviewed the request, and concluded that there was no objection, on the basis that "the scheme provides a degree of separation between the Prince as initiator and patron and the decision-making machinery."[3]

The next stage was to test public opinion, via an interview in the *Observer*. Around the same time, on 13 June 1974, the Prince of Wales made his maiden speech in the House of Lords. The occasion was a debate on sport and leisure. The speech shows that the Prince had grasped the crucial relationship between the problems he was discussing with his youth group and the productive use of leisure time. " ... If leisure time is employed anti-socially by some people, it is therefore well worthwhile trying to channel that anti-social recreation into more healthy pastimes." He wanted to take up "the challenge of removing the dead hand of boredom and frustration".

The third step was to get some pilot projects up and running, to see if their ideas would actually work. Prince Charles put up the first £200 from his personal settlement to get things under way.

First out of the box was the Haggerson Housing Estate in east London, aptly described as "Pentonville with the roof off". 19-year-old Pauline O'Haloran and a couple of her friends, none of whom had any formal training, had taken over a social club for residents from a youth worker. The club was the only place in the

3 Home Office letter, 23 April 1974.

area that offered anything to entice kids off the streets. The second grant went to two young offenders, aged 21, who ran a fishing club, again designed to keep people like themselves out of trouble. Also in London, a former borstal boy had set up a youth club, play group and a mother and toddler club in a nearby derelict building. From Cornwall came a scheme to train young trouble-makers as life-guards. Money was needed to hire the local swimming baths. These were the earliest applications to receive funding. They became the guinea pigs.

A total of 21 pilot projects received his support in this period, many of them involving groups of delinquents and drop-outs. The Prince personally reviewed every application, and asked for regular progress reports on each of the schemes he funded. Two 14-year-old boys who had been before the juvenile courts asked for assistance to go camping. They were given £37.50 to cover rail fares. Buckingham Palace obtained a tent and some pots and pans from the Army, and their teacher lent them a camera. A few weeks later an illustrated account of the expedition turned up on his desk. More to the point, the boys were back at school.

A south London gang of young bicycle thieves were given £100 to buy frames and parts to learn how to repair cycles and create their own. Feedback confirmed that he was on the right track. All this was carried out anonymously with Pratt as the front, so at first no-one knew the identify of the benefactor; but secrets about royal activity are hard to keep. After reading a number of these reports and letters of thanks Prince Charles decided to meet some of those involved.

Meanwhile, the group now had a name: the Prince of Wales Committee for Disadvantaged Young People. The next phase involved sharing ideas with a number of prominent voluntary organisations to gauge their interest; but the reaction of groups such as the British Red Cross, the RNLI and the Royal Life Saving Society was thoroughly discouraging, and can charitably be described as a polite "thanks, but no thanks". In one sense he had had a lucky escape. It was clear that trying to work within existing organisations was not the right route. He would be better off pursuing his own approach without compromise.

He faced similar difficulties at the King George's Jubilee Trust. Some concerns were shared, highly relevant and depressingly familiar. Its 1975 annual report highlights many of the issues the Prince would make his own:

"Slum clearance continues but high rise buildings have created new problems ... it is the Trust's duty to ensure that every effort is made to mitigate the potentially disastrous effect on young people unable to find jobs ... absenteeism from school is ... depriving thousands from having equal opportunities ... The Trust continued to support many excellent projects involving physically handicapped young people."

What bothered the Prince was the way money was distributed, with an emphasis on groups, doled out from the centre, far removed from the recipients or, if at the local level, usually through dignitaries such as lord lieutenants. Eminent as these people were, they were not perhaps best able to judge whether a potential grantee was either deserving or in need. At least Prince Charles was young himself, and better aware of the changes that were sweeping Britain in the early 1970s. He had also acquired a few unorthodox friends and advisors who encouraged him not to do everything by the book.

In June the Prince went public during his second speech to the House of Lords, revealing that he had already been conducting small-scale trials with some success. "I have decided to establish experimental schemes with the aid of a committee in areas with which I have a titular connection, and so far the response in each part of the country has been extraordinarily encouraging. It is obvious that many young people – and particularly those who are often categorised as amongst the most impossible and the most difficult – are only too keen to become involved in useful or imaginative schemes, but they lack the funds or the necessary equipment. Once an impetus has been provided it is most heartening to see how it is continued and developed by the young people themselves."

In December 1975 it was announced that the Prince would lead a national appeal in the Queen's Silver Jubilee year. This was a major commitment which would leave him little time to pursue existing plans but, in one respect, this appointment galvanised the group into a decision about a separate trust.

There continued to be reservations in certain quarters. Michael Colborne remembers politicians who were anxious to anchor the Prince to some good cause which would keep him out of the way. Staff at Buckingham Palace were asking questions about the wisdom of, and indeed the necessity for, a new vehicle specifically for the Prince of Wales. Memos from the Queen's private secretary, Martin Charteris, make plain that opposition was coming from somewhere. The Duke of Edinburgh remarked to Checketts in June that year that the Trusts seemed to have "a rather similar purpose". Another faction argued that the whole thing smacked of a Duke of Edinburgh's award scheme mark II, which was felt to be too personalised. Of course something personal was precisely what was required. In any case, his emphasis was on a section of youth entirely separate from his father's constituency, which emphasised achievers.

Prince Charles was not satisfied with his role at the King George's Silver Jubilee Trust, and could not see any immediate prospect of converting that body to his point of view. Prospects elsewhere were no more appealing. Voluntary work with young people was carried out primarily through youth or sports clubs, schools, uniformed groups, such as scouts or guides, or the church – and usually leisure-related. None of these was right for the young underclass which developed in the 1970s, as he had grasped. "The important thing is that the young people should run their own shows. They don't want to do things which are prescribed, planned and supervised by adults."[4]

The approach to charity can be described as moving through three questions: what can we do for them; what can they do for themselves, and what can they do for others? The Prince started with the third question. He saw the relevance of question two, and rejected outright the approach implicit in question one.

Sitting on the dockside in Rosyth, where his command *HMS Bronington* was based, Prince Charles jotted down on a brown envelope the key elements of his own approach:

- he did not just want to give out money for good causes;
- he wanted people to propose ideas and prove in advance that the money he gave them would help make a difference;
- the money itself should buy things like paint and tools to renovate a hall.

The Prince of Wales prevailed and the Queen gave her consent. The intention had been to call it the Springboard Trust, but somehow Community Service Volunteers nabbed that name just as they were going to press. The Prince's Trust did seem to fit the bill better. During a radio interview when asked about how his work got started, the Prince summarised the three-year gestation.

"I was thinking a great deal about the difficulties that so many young people must face, particularly being brought up in more deprived or disadvantaged circumstances, and I felt that the most important thing was to try and find a way of helping to reach the people who were the most difficult to reach because, obviously, there were lots of other organisations dealing with young people and their problems; but I felt the most important thing was to try and get at those who were the most difficult to reach. That's why I got a group of people together to talk about this whole question: people from the probation service, police and others."

Rea Price says: "He wanted to focus on the more disadvantaged and he wanted to encourage community service and get the two objectives to be satisfied simultaneously through the ideas of young people." Snow put the goal of the new trust in perspective. "The whole idea was to give young people a chance to live a life which does not end in conflict or tragedy."

The question of funding, however, continued to bedevil things. It had been abundantly clear from all the meetings that there would be no money from any

[4] *Observer*, 16 June 1974.

area of government. Prince Charles personally advanced £3,353 to fund the trials. The first outside money came from an unlikely source. He was initiated as the 705th Water Rat in December 1975. It was the custom of the order to present a cheque to the charity of choice of the new member. Prince Charles gave the majority of his donation to Atlantic College, but around £3,000 was retained in a suspense account pending creation of his Trust. This, then, was the starting capital with which he set up the Prince's Trust on 7 April 1976. The deed is an unimpressive, off-the-shelf document which reflects its low-budget origin. As he was to admit later. "When we began in 1976 we had an idea of what we wanted to do and how we wanted to do it, but little or nothing to do it with."

The first trustees were Fleming, Checketts, Richard Beckett and Pratt. His choice of confidants and advisors was unconventional. George Pratt, for one, might seem to have been an unlikely selection, but he had been key to the Trust's formation. Richard Beckett, a rising young barrister, brought legal expertise to the position, but he was there as a friend who shared the same concerns as the Prince and was active in Save the Children, among other charities. The same was true of his first local committees – all police and youth workers and most having some link to Pratt.

"A Trust is a trust." Prince Charles meant exactly what he said. "He wants to trust people," Pratt explained. "He believes that youngsters mature more when they feel they are trusted and that we should offer this trust, where, perhaps others don't."[5] As he said repeatedly, "If in doubt, pay out." Following that philosophy, the Prince gave express instructions that the young people given money should not be asked for a receipt. There could be no greater evidence of trust in a group grown used to suspicion. And as Beckett explains: "We had to take a view about supervision early on. We had neither the wherewithal nor the desire to sit over every recipient and dictate the way they spent the money. I don't think we ever regretted having settled on this approach."

He was also adamant that there should be a minimum of form filling – nothing to discourage potential applicants. "It seemed to me the most important thing to do was to ensure that there was as little red tape and bureaucratic delay as possible, because I think that's what really puts young people off. And there was nothing to join. You didn't have to be part of an organisation."

The Prince's Trust was different from all its royal predecessors. Now that he had his Trust, the next challenge for the Prince of Wales was to make it work. The days of talking and testing were over.

[5] *Daily Express*, 25 October 1985.

Chapter 2

FROM THERE TO HERE

*"I want to show everyone what the young can do,
given half a chance"*

The Prince now had his Trust. He had theories about how things should be done, some of which had received a partial airing. But he still had almost no money – and neither he nor anyone closely associated with the venture had any real experience of starting up new programmes on other than a pilot scale. In a 1986 interview with Alistair Burnet he explained his expectations. "I do not think I have a master plan, but basically I want to see the Prince's Trust as my fighting arm."

Early activity was restricted to small scale grants, and given the cash constraints the grants needed to be very small indeed. One of the trustees' main anxieties in the first couple of years was not to arouse public interest, for fear of attracting too many applications which they would have to turn away. The Trust struggled to make it past its first anniversary.

Prince Charles personally underwrote expenses. A £4,000 cheque for an American TV interview he gave about George III was the cornerstone of the first year. His own position was constrained by his role as fund-raiser-in-chief for the Queen's Silver Jubilee. Friends rallied round. Money came in from James Goldsmith, a property developer, Raymond Green and Andy Netro, a theatrical agent. Cliff Richard did a show. The actor Terry-Thomas contributed £105 after an abortive attempt to cross the English Channel on water skis. Harry Secombe sent a cheque for £2,000 along with a letter saying the money came from "selling my mother-in-law to an Arab, and for doing a special charity concert". One significant donation is alleged to have come from Paul Getty.

Richard Beckett remembers that "we were conscious that there was a fair degree of idealism behind the enterprise, and rather wondered if it would be a real runner in the long term". The first year's income came to £6,532.

Everything was effectively run from George Pratt's office, with the Drapers' Company providing an accommodation address and forwarding service. Nearly four years passed before the Trust had its own premises. The Drapers came to the rescue again, converting an upstairs bedroom, 15 by 10 feet, into the first headquarters. There was a desk, chair, table lamp, telephone and intercom. Pratt was the nearest thing to a full-time executive. As the Prince put it, "our principal asset was a tiny band of enthusiastic volunteers". It was not until April 1980 that help arrived with the secondment of Richard Shaw from NatWest Bank. In due course a small second room became available for daytime use.

The work of getting the Trust off the ground fell very much on Prince Charles's shoulders. Especially in the beginning, for any event to succeed he had to be present. This meant an awful lot of engagements. Fund-raising aside, he went around opening doors to establish a countrywide structure. Money and people began to trickle in.

The Trust's first grants are decidedly random, although there are clues about the focus to come. One grant of £300 went to purchase canoe-building kits. An informal club adapted canoes for use by the disabled. The club received 100 orders. Another £500 went to convert a disused cricket pavilion into a music practice room, while £300 purchased a second-hand printing machine for a group of unemployed young people who started to make money out of flyers and pamphlets. Two girls were given an award to set up a holiday sports club in an inner city recently torn by riots. This kept 100 or more children off the streets and led to the formation of several sports teams.

The Prince began to break away from his minders. He refused to be shielded from unpleasantness. Visits to the poorer parts of South London, Bradford and other areas were early indications of his agenda, and he would not let himself be misled. David Collyer recalls a 1977 visit to the Balsall Heath section of Birmingham, then a red light area in desperate disrepair. There was police advice that he shouldn't come, but the Prince would not be put off. Then the council hastily tidied up – even going so far as to rebuild the walls of houses along the planned route. When he heard this he promptly chose other streets to walk down – and he made sure he had half an hour to sit with an impoverished family and listen to their problems.

The Prince recalled these early days in a radio interview in 1995. "When I first established it, it was very difficult because we met with a great deal of scepticism and disbelief. And I remember having initial meetings where we did come up with a lot of obstacles ... we broke through these sometimes rather official obstacles as they began to see what we could do."

The occasion of the Queen's Silver Jubilee was an important milestone in raising his profile, and giving added impetus to his activities. Leading this appeal was his first 'real job', but the way arrangements were made put the whole exercise in jeopardy and was in danger of leaving him on the sidelines. He was still in the Navy when the council was formed, and had no input into initial plans. The average age of the inner circle was in excess of 60. The next generation was represented by Prince Charles and Dennis Stevenson, then chairman of the National Association of Youth Clubs, who was drafted in as the token young man.

No-one wanted to let the Prince assume command. Stevenson described the situation. "It was an unutterable shambles. There was this feel about it, that it was going to be a catastrophe. The committee was badly led and contained a heady brew of, by-and-large, really awful courtiers, mostly second and third rate, who were completely out of their depth. There was too much talking and not enough doing. When our leader arrived everyone was very condescending to him, even though they were making a terrible mess of things. There was the potential for a great national humiliation."

The Prince realised that he needed more and different people to help him. Fresh faces were added. Bill Chalmers, who had run the Imperial War Graves, arrived. Lord Windlesham energised the industry and commerce committee. Stevenson's youth involvement committee wrote to every single school in the country encouraging them to arrange events. Prince Charles made himself visible and began stirring up support.

In the end corporate UK came to the rescue, and the country chipped in with a fever of fêtes and fairs as well as less orthodox snail races, frog jumping competitions and a worm-eating contest. Lee Wilson, writing in the *Daily Telegraph* in January 1979, described it as "the biggest, largest, most successful tin-rattling exercise ever launched in the United Kingdom". Following completion of the £16.4 million appeal, the two Jubilee Trusts were to all intents and purposes combined into one.

The two traditional features of a royal Trust at this time were giving indirectly, and to safe organisations. Safe meant that no-one could criticise the grants. Indirect meant that, if anything did go wrong, the Trust would not get the blame. This was a risk-free approach and the Prince was having none of it. Not only did he intend to move grants into controversial areas, but he also wanted a much more direct personal involvement. He set out to change just about every aspect of the way royal charity had worked in the past.

Since there were millions sitting in the Jubilee Trusts and next to nothing in the coffers of the Prince's Trust, if he was to do anything other than tinker around the edges he had to get the Jubilee Trusts to line up behind his ideas. Given the conservative composition of the council, this was never going to be easy. The most sensible route would have been to nestle alongside the Jubilee Trusts and use their facilities and resources.

But Pratt wanted to make sure that the organisations remained separate. He was afraid the Jubilee Trusts would swamp the Prince's Trust and even contaminate the underlying approach. He felt it was essential that the Prince's Trust establish a clear and separate identity – starting with separate physical space – before any merger could be contemplated. This game plan called for a form of reverse takeover, where the dynamic newcomer with the ideas gains control of the much larger but sleepy organisation.

One promising development was the appointment of Harold Haywood as executive director of the Jubilee Trusts. His background as a youth worker, including a stint at the National Association of Youth Clubs, made him sympathetic to a new approach. But he reported to a group of trustees, most of whom leaned the other way.

Even as early as 1979 criticism – if muted – began to appear in the press. Haywood responded with "if there are any young people in a rage about their circumstances, about the rotten tower block they live in, about the lousy estate that is their home, and if they are prepared to do something to improve their own and other's situations, then come to us."[1]

Some of those few who did were weeded out. The small numbers left suggested a token gesture, by people intent on carrying on as before. Most of the grants continued to go to charities with strong links to the establishment. In part this obstruction was possible because the Prince was still formulating his own ideas. Whenever possible in the late 1970s he visited various parts of the country canvassing views. He also arranged meetings for groups such as probation officers and the police to come to Buckingham Palace to discuss youth issues.

What Prince Charles heard alarmed him. He was writing and talking about problems in the inner city, the underclass and racial discontent well in advance of Britain's 1981–82 riots. He could see that young people at the top had opportunities enough, but those at the bottom had nothing – and that their frustrations were ready to boil over. Those in power dismissed his observations as inaccurate or inappropriate, but the Prince was not wrong.

Where he could, he began to make changes. At his insistence much of the power of the purse strings began to devolve down to local committees. At his urging the composition of committees began to change. The people needed to organise grants were seldom the same people who could raise money. Many local members of the great and the good came on primarily to help with the Silver Jubilee Appeal, but stayed on. Prince Charles was keen to add people who knew more about the types of young people he wanted to reach.Some of his new ideas worked. Some did not.

[1] *Daily Telegraph*, 18 January 1979.

The Glasgow Youth Action Research investigated the needs of residents living in a tenement area under notice of demolition. A panel investigated the value of residential courses for preparing pupils moving from a small to a larger school by giving teachers and incoming pupils the opportunity to get to know each other. That went down well with participants. No Particular Place to Go put a community worker into a housing estate in Scotland to try to build up indigenous leadership which might break up anti-social behaviour. Project Latchkey ran an alternative education scheme in London's Docklands. The Prince's Trust began research, in co-operation with Brunel University, to evaluate the effectiveness of community service projects.

These tests gave him feedback on several ideas: the value of residency, ways to influence behaviour among truant groups, and the benefit of unorthodox out-of-school educational methods. All were to show up later as features of much larger scale programmes, once he had refined the original concepts and been able to gather greater resources. At this point results were often inconclusive and qualitative, and little more than research was done in the first few years.

In 1979 the Jubilee Trust's administrative council concluded that to give out more than 75 per cent of the income to the same 50 organisations every year was wrong. The process was opened up, the size of grants varied and the money spread more widely. The annual report that year stated: "The Trust particularly welcomes applications concerned with meeting the needs of young people in ethnic minorities, on housing estates in situations in which they may become involved in vandalism and violence or among the increasing number of young single homeless."

10,000 leaflets were distributed to schools, youth organisations and libraries to try and get the message across to young people that the Trust "can help you to help others … If you are aged 25 or under and have a suggestion for a scheme that could help the community you live in, we in turn can help you to get it off the ground and to keep it moving."

In 1980 BBC Radio 1 invited young people to "have a go" helping others. DJs Kid Jensen and Andy Peebles visited trust projects and broadcast their stories. The Trust also helped to fund the BBC television roadshow which offered advice to young people. All this activity stimulated some increase in applications, particularly from groups who were not in the traditional mould.

Prince Charles had identified his priorities: unemployment, and channelling disadvantaged young people into more productive activities. By 1981 it was clear that his intentions were beginning to get through, at least to some local committees. Both in implementation and selection of projects, young people were more involved. Haywood recalls the Prince buttonholing him after one meeting and asking, "Why don't we have young people in the age of benefit in the grant-making process? Surely they know better than anyone what young people want?" No-one could raise any sensible objection. So a mandate went out that two members on every committee should be under 25. Most regions responded. London created a committee consisting entirely of young people.

But even this could cause confusion. Two young black assessors went to Brixton to find the red carpet rolled out, but they themselves were shunted aside. Intense conversation convinced the receiving line that they *were* the VIPs and, after that hiccup, things did not get better.

Unlike many benefactors the Prince likes to get his hands dirty, so the process was still not satisfactory. Giving money out to these groups was better than before – but what actually happened once the money left the Trusts was to a very large extent unknown. Implementation was all a bit haphazard. For the most part money at the local level continued to go to 'deserving' causes, and the left hand had only the vaguest idea what the right hand was doing. Too many grant committee members were in the old mould, and there was no proper control at the centre.

Prince Charles must share some of the blame here, because his attitude was unequivocal. His favoured saying, "if in doubt, pay out", set the tone for the way in which the Trust helped the most marginal young people: very appealing in the sense of giving them maximum freedom of action to develop themselves, but also open to abuse. For many years there were no checks of any sort, and the Prince continued to be adamant that young people should not even sign a receipt. "Trust them," he would say constantly. "Give them the money and don't start accounting." But he wanted to do more than just hand out money and hope. One of his suggestions was that applicants should not be given the entire sum requested. Giving only part provided an incentive to raise the rest elsewhere, which required grantees to use their initiative.

His Trust was still considered very much a junior cousin in the league of royal organisations. Suspicion over his intentions often translated into tension. The old guard sensed he might be going beyond "appropriate" boundaries. They were in favour of helping the disadvantaged at a distance, or in carefully controlled surroundings such as special camps, but the idea of the Prince of Wales mixing one on one with "undesirable" individuals did not go down at all well.

In 1981, riots erupted in cities all across the country. Some were extremely serious, several lasted for days, extensive damage was done to buildings, looting occurred, a large number of people were injured and hundreds were arrested.

The most notorious took place in Toxteth. The Toxteth Team Ministry had received a grant in 1977, and the Prince knew the area to be particularly troubled. But the scale of the outbreaks was a shock. In Sydney, when he first heard the news, Prince Charles felt the pain of people there and was determined to do something.

If there was any one event which increased his determination to take a direct personal role, it was the riots in Toxteth that year.

What was wrong? Too much unemployment; a lack of suitable skills; a belief that government did not want to know? The country was in a state of economic and social transition. Modernisation had been made all the more necessary due to decades of political neglect. However urgent and overdue, economic transition is a painful process. Side effects included inflation and unemployment, both at double digit levels. The burden of unemployment fell mostly on young people. A frightening 35 per cent of people of working age were out of work, over 50 per cent of them in the 16–24 age group.

Racial discontent was also a feature of that dismal summer. Black communities in particular were disproportionately represented in the riots, both because of general economic grievances and specific claims of discrimination. Protestors on the street had little or nothing to lose. Many were homeless or living in slum conditions. Run-down housing estates long overdue for renovation contributed to general frustration and the lowest living standards. Trying to solve these problems was going to be central to the Prince of Wales for the rest of his life.

He began to steer more money to some of the worst affected areas. Grants were given to organisations active in depressed inner city neighbourhoods such as Brixton, Castletown and Moss Side. He asked Haywood and Colburne to provide him with unfiltered intelligence, and they visited most of the major trouble spots, including Brixton, Toxteth and Bristol St Pauls. In April 1982 he wrote to Haywood, inviting him on "some of my expeditions round the country ... For instance, I am going to Southall on 29 April, Newark etc on 19 May (ethnic minorities in particular), and badly hit unemployment areas in South Wales on 3 June." Later the same year he went to Handsworth, a mere five miles from Birmingham centre which had also been hard hit. This private visit hammered home the ghastly cycle of unemployment and poverty.

He hosted a lunch with Lord Scarman, whose report on the riots had aired some of the problems. The Prince found himself in agreement with much of that report, specifically Scarman's emphasis on local regeneration and his statement that "inner-city areas are not human deserts". But fine sentiments are no substitute for bare necessities, and tangible action was in short supply.

A whole mosaic of causes underpinned the unrest, but unemployment stood out. It has all sorts of negative consequences for both the unemployed individual and those around: erosion of self-confidence, a culture of blame, boredom, frustration and alienation, often leading to vandalism or worse. Any programme had to focus on finding work. This was never going to be easy during a period of high unemployment, especially when your aim was to help those with the least attractive profile as potential employees.

The Prince adopted a two-pronged approach. One was to prepare people better through training. The Prince's Trust got behind a project in Birmingham. The West Midlands Training Initiative was the first practical response. The second idea was to try and attract young people into self-employment by starting their own businesses. The Youth Business Initiative got going in 1982 to see if a "hobby" could be turned into a paying proposition. That concept, of a young person going out on their own and setting up a business, is accepted in 1998 in part because of the success of the Prince's Trust.

Prince Charles described the reaction seven years later:
"In those days I remember there was a great deal of scepticism and a certain amount of disbelief amongst quite a large number of people about the ideas that I was putting forward and, in particular, about making grants of money to people who were in the sort of areas which I particularly wanted to get at – those which were most alienated and disadvantaged, who were in the kinds of places which others, perhaps, found difficulty in reaching. And this is why I felt very strongly about the importance of taking risks that you have to take in order to make sure that you were reaching the sort of people who normally were not reached. It didn't mean to say, of course, that lots of people ran off with the money, because that hasn't happened." [2]

The Prince soon discovered that people you set out to assist may be resentful or suspicious. Union leaders took an immediate dislike to his ideas. Ministers interpreted his actions as an implied criticism that their policies were not working. Social workers found the idea alien. Their stock answer to any problem was to demand more money, with all assistance sent through a larger network of designated social workers.

The arrival of rock galas signalled a major step forward for the Prince's activities. They provided a significant source of recurring revenues, and they made a monumental difference to the Trust's ability to function in the mid-1980s.

In early 1982 Prince Charles floated the idea of a competition for 30 rock bands that had been aided by the Trust. Tony Stratton-Smith, then president of Charisma Records, took charge. Whittling 30 down to 12, a panel listened to two demo songs from each group. The Prince took the chair, and other members included Pete Townshend and George Martin. Having selected the best, Stratton-Smith then suggested a fund-raising gig, with the winner opening the show: proceeds, of

---

[2] Address accompanying release of the 1989 Prince's Trust annual report, Livingstone,
  4 September 1989.

course, to go to the Trust. This was to be the rock industry's equivalent of the Royal Variety Show.

The response was very positive. Madness topped the bill. The first Prince's Trust Rock Gala All Stars included Joan Armatrading, Ian Anderson, Phil Collins, Robert Plant and Pete Townshend. Suggs of Madness – whose first single, ironically, was "The Prince", spoke for all: "The Prince's Trust helps groups and youth clubs, particularly on the musical side. If you can give money to help young people make music it's got to be a good thing."

The Prince of Wales played a leading part. Stratton-Smith made a point of revealing his role. "The Prince himself saw very quickly the relationship between rock and roll and the work of his Trust … If it hadn't been for his presence and encouragement, things would not have moved so quickly, if at all."[3]

Once rock concerts became regular events, money started to roll in. Suddenly he was in a position to start doing something meaningful. Income was all the more necessary because new business start-ups went from next to nothing to over 1,000 in just three years.

This was fantastic progress. With over £1 million in his trust, the Prince could start to do more: more training, more new business start-ups, more residential camps and, even more importantly, he could start formal programmes that could have continuity and provide proper outlets for the disadvantaged young.

The one activity that was clearly achieving its goals by the mid-1980s was the Youth Business Initiative. Unemployed young people were starting viable businesses. With careful culling of applicants, over 80 per cent were making it through to the second year. Meanwhile, over at the National Association of Youth Clubs, Sir Angus Ogilvy had set up a similar organisation called the Youth Enterprise Scheme, where the main difference lay in the fact that entrepreneurs got loans, not grants. Both approaches seemed to work. The Prince and Sir Angus met from time to time to share ideas and report on progress.

But without substantial sums of money there was a limit to how far these schemes could go. The break-through came when Ogilvy persuaded David Young, then Secretary of State for Employment, to commit the government to matching funds. The Trust was thinking of £3 million to be raised in conjunction with the 1986 Lord Mayor's appeal. Would he double that? Young agree that he would – on the condition that the Youth Business Initiative and the Youth Enterprise Scheme merged.

Young duly attended a lunch at the Mansion House where the appeal was to be launched, but speakers ran on, as they sometimes do. Young had a question in the

[3] Programme notes, 1983 Rock Gala.

House to answer at 2.35 pm, so when his turn came time was short and he cut to the chase. "The one thing you all want to hear," he said, "is that we will match whatever you raise." Young hurried off, to a hearty round of applause. In pledging government commitment Young had made no mention of a cap. Young gave the matter no further thought and the 1986 fund-raising rather fizzled out.

But the question of money was back on the table soon enough. This time they decided to go for £40 million, tied to the Prince's 40th birthday. Having had the omission of a cap pointed out, Young, who was in general supportive of the self-employment solution, was willing to agree to the higher limit. No-one felt £40 million was anything other than a quixotic dream. The Prince of Wales recalls the outcome with a degree of understatement: "I suppose Lord Young thought we'd raise a million or two at most. When we did raise nearly £40 million it didn't go down all that well at the Treasury."

The appeal was also remarkable for the posters that appeared with a somewhat controversial message. Captions featured: "Help us to encourage him to create wealth, not aggro", accompanying a tough-looking young man. "Help us set her up in business. Before someone else does" showed a vulnerable young girl and an unmistakable *double entendre*. Terse press advertisements accompanied the posters. "Sean Todd had the perfect credentials. A UB40 card. A complete lack of social graces. And an outright refusal from just about every bank in town ..." The Prince was after the transformation of some pretty rough young types.

The Trusts were not his only route. In 1981 he became patron of the British end of the UN International Year of the Disabled. He was delighted to take up that post and worked alongside the president, Lord Snowdon. This brought a new dimension to work which continued for 16 years through the Prince of Wales's Advisory Group on Disability. This panel of experts has made advances in areas such as housing, employment, medicine and education.

In 1985 the Prince became president of Business in the Community. Business in the Community gave him a constituency which made him more difficult to ignore. Its mission was to pressure companies into seeing that community projects could be a form of enlightened self-interest: a role it still plays today. The agenda had been created by former financier Stephen O'Brien. First contact had come about through a shared interest in the problems of ethnic minorities in business. O'Brien was at the helm, and saw in Prince Charles a like-minded individual who could bring enormous kudos to the organisation.

When Prince Charles began talking about public/private partnerships in the mid-1980s there was a Conservative Government which was doing its best to keep the two apart, and a Labour opposition which could not accept the idea of business making a positive contribution to social problems. The Prince was pioneering a third way at a time when the ideological climate was chilly and unreceptive. As he used this platform to advance his agenda, and as important corporations became active members, even government began to pay attention.

Business in the Community has come a long way since he climbed on board. Over 400 companies are now on the register, compared to 128 in 1985. Eighty per cent of the *Financial Times* 100 are members. As of 1998 there is a staff of 214, up from only four. Looking back over the past 13 years the Prince takes great pleasure in the progress made since he got involved. "It is encouraging to realise how much has been achieved in persuading companies to see the benefits of community investment. Many of the original and, at the time, unorthodox ideas have since become an accepted part of corporate wisdom – such as building partnerships between the public and private sectors, backing community entrepreneurs and encouraging companies to devote a percentage of pre-tax profits towards community investment."

Under the aegis of Business in the Community the Prince was able to pursue several important initiatives, particularly in the area of urban regeneration and education. It provided him with the infrastructure to introduce new ideas about business involvement in schools, and to develop a range of support services – including mentoring – which drew on member personnel.

Another of the Prince's concerns was about urban regeneration. He was conscious that at the community level a deteriorating environment contributed directly to the cycle of disadvantage and disillusionment. But this was a global problem, requiring solutions that would only work with co-operation across counties. Prince Charles became deeply involved in promoting a range of environmental initiatives.

Scepticism was rife about this and other aspects of his work that had political overtones. For the Prince, field expeditions were a vital part of the learning process. One of the most notorious was an October 1985 visit to the Centrepoint night shelter in Dean Street, Soho, and the Rufford Street, King's Cross hostel. Accompanied by Haywood, the Prince then proceeded to the Embankment, where he saw homeless people asleep under the arches. He acquired something of a reputation for these voyages of exploration: so much so that JAK published a cartoon in December 1985 where a policeman on a seedy street warned a group of scruffy youths, "Straighten up, you lot. I think it's the Prince of Wales."

It was not only people on the outside who were sceptical about his activities. In the mid-to late 1980s people at Kensington Palace were raising questions about whether all this Prince's Trust stuff mattered or was it perhaps a distraction, even a waste of his time? His answer was to take his staff along to see the projects. That usually did the trick. Slowly he was starting to tie the various strands of his work together. One thing he never lost sight of was the potential of community service to transform lives. In 1985 he was finally able to organise a pilot that would test his theory. Community Venture was very much a Prince of Wales special, incorporating a bundle of features that created a unique and powerful programme. A 43-week course combining team building, skill training, personal development, work experience and community service, instilled self-confidence and a sense of service and made graduates more employable. The concept was new, untried and expensive, so not everyone at the Trust was in favour.

It started in Sunderland with two teams, ten in each. Prince Charles set the ball rolling and was able to return to present the first graduates with their Prince of Wales certificate ten months later. Similar schemes followed in Birmingham, Llanelli and Pembroke, to see whether the same approach would work in very different communities. After a few teething troubles, somewhat reluctant Venturers settled in and soon started to enjoy their experience. People who had previously done nothing but take, and could have expected to rely on handouts for life, were motivated to give something back. Better still, over 75 per cent of the early graduates found a job. The Venture was an unqualified success.

By then the Prince could point to a range of activities that had arisen largely through his efforts, many of which had been his idea. A 40th birthday celebration seemed to be called for, and was duly organised in the old tram depot in Birmingham. Though derelict for over 40 years the depot was renovated by trainees from Task Undertakings. The guest list was made up of nearly 1,500 young people who had been helped by the Prince's Trust. The Prince of Wales made a humorous speech and a good time was had by all.

Prince Charles was now keen to expand, especially in community service, but ran into a brick wall. The cost per Venturer was prohibitive. The Prince's Trust was still living a hand-to-mouth existence with no capital to speak of, and relying on constant fund-raising. No-one was really sure whether there would be enough money to maintain outgoings. In one respect matters were made worse by the £40 million campaign for his 40th birthday. This was the task which prompted Prince Charles to say, "Thank God I'm not any older." The campaign was a success for the Youth Business Trust, but bad news for everyone else. Many donors gave to the special appeal and did not see the need to write two cheques.

Something had to be done. One priority had long been to merge all the royal Trusts. In asking Jim Gardner to become chairman of the Prince's Trust trustees in August 1986, Prince Charles had charged him with making that his main mission.

The merger took the better part of three years, but once done the Prince's Trust had a sound capital base and the Youth Business Trust, with £80 million pledged, had enough financial firepower to keep growing for several years.

More ambitious programmes also meant changes in personnel. Prince Charles recognised the need for a new breed of professional manager. John Pervin from Unilever became the first full-time director of the Youth Business Trust. The arrival of Tom Shebbeare in February 1988 was another milestone. In Shebbeare he found someone who could take his work to the next level: more management, more control, more systems – in short everything that would make the organisation more efficient. The changing of the guard went on at director and trustee level too. Jim Gardner brought a new professionalism to the way the Trusts operated. Tough but fair businessmen like Alan Sheppard and John Jarvis strengthened the upper echelons.

But the Prince's Trust has never lost touch with its roots and never lost sight of its mission. The process might get tighter, but if anything the focus of the work was looser. "I think it is important to be professional, but not too slick – that, I think, is the balance that has to be found." [4]

By the late 1980s progress was being made on a wide range of fronts: in inner city schemes, at education with the Compact (where businesses pledged job opportunities to students), and with many more self-employment start-ups and Community Ventures also up and running. Higher profile and higher levels of activity brought new problems. Not least of these was that the Prince was criticised in the press and even by some supporters for lacking in focus. The problem lay not in his vision, which was comprehensive and consistent, but in the way it was being carried out. This perception was compounded by the proliferation of organisations and programmes which included the Prince somewhere on the letterhead.

For someone who values so highly the virtues of inclusion and sharing, it must have been irritating in the extreme to learn about the rivalry that had arisen between what, effectively, were internal arms of his own organisation. Fund-raisers from separate entities were not co-operating and some found themselves soliciting the same targets, sowing doubts in the minds of contributors. The Prince himself contributed inadvertently to internal confusion, because he might ring up executives on a point which was perhaps more pertinent to another person. As activities began to grow in scope and scale, the potential for problems and duplication in effort grew.

[4] Address accompanying release of the 1989 Prince's Trust annual report, Livingstone,
4 September 1989.

The Prince called a meeting at Sandringham in November 1992 to try and ensure greater cohesion among all concerned. The solution which emerged was a co-ordination committee that would meet three times a year to report on activities, deal with areas of possible overlap and resolve differences. The Prince undertook to try to attend all meetings.

More strenuous and systematic efforts were made to achieve greater integration. Business in the Community included Trust businesses in their extensive field trips. A more integrated approach to finding voluntary helpers was adopted. To reinforce the message, a house magazine entitled *Working Together* was launched in 1993. Joint events became commonplace. In July 1993, Business in the Community and the Prince's Trust Volunteers teamed up in Wales to host a recruiting session at Cardiff Airport. The Prince stressed to member companies that sending their employees to Volunteers made sense. Attendees responded by doubling the level of employed people on courses in Wales in 1994 on top of their existing commitments to Business in the Community.

No sooner was one problem solved than another needed attention. It was time to revisit grants. Arwyn Thomas, Chief Executive of Prince's Trust (Action) recalls: "By 1993 all sorts of myths had grown up about what the Prince of Wales did or did not want. You had 60-odd committees out there all interpreting things their own way and, in some cases, making claims to be representing the Prince of Wales. There was also this feeling we were doing good by doling out money, but where was the evidence?" This was a familiar question.

After consultation with John Jarvis, who was trying to force business disciplines on a rather unwieldy network, the Prince requested a full review together with recommendations on how to make the process more effective. In July 1994 Thomas presented a board paper. The Prince was in the chair. The meeting reaffirmed the focus on making these programmes accessible to the most disadvantaged and marginalised groups. Prince Charles also insisted that the selection and administration process needed to pay more attention to the suggestions of the young people themselves.

To listen to these debates 16 years into the life of the Trust must have been something of a disappointment, since he had been clear from the outset. To make sure the message gets across he sometimes has to bang on until people get sick of hearing him saying the same old thing over and over again. The July 1994 board meeting should have been the last time he needed to make this particular point. That year, on the 25th anniversary of his investiture, he wrote an open letter to the Prince of Wales' co-ordinating committee. "I thought it might be helpful if I were to restate the philosophy behind the work of my trusts; the common threads, if you like, which bind them together.

"In my travels around this country it has become more and more apparent to me that, when people feel excluded from their community and unable to make a contribution, the whole fabric of those communities is at serious risk. When that fabric starts to disintegrate then we all suffer – whatever our position. It seems to me that the best way of starting to tackle the problems is to provide practical help which will encourage people to do something for themselves to regain their self-belief and once again feel part of their community.

"The solutions are not primarily down to government. In fact I would go further and suggest that there are many things that simply cannot be done by governments alone. However, government can be a key partner in helping to co-ordinate what is being done and in encouraging local action.

"In my experience the best way of tackling many of the problems that we face is through developing partnerships. Different interest groups, when brought together in the right way, can achieve far more than they could possibly do by themselves. As I go around the country I am constantly struck by the goodwill which exists. People do want to tackle the problems that beset their communities but too often all their efforts come to nothing because different groups cannot see the benefit of working together, or simply do not have the chance to do so.

"I hope that I may have been able to play a role in bringing people together and in creating partnerships with government. But it struck me that, until quite recently, there were a large number of businesses that had failed to see the important role they could play. Hence the need for Business in the Community and I was delighted when they invited me to become their president in 1985. Now we are really starting to engage the private sector. Encouraging partnership is one key part of the work of my trusts. Another is that the Trusts often act as effective catalysts enabling people to find their own local solutions.

"From time to time in this country there has been a tendency to try and impose solutions on communities, at best alienating local people and at worst, with disastrous consequences. In truth, not only will the answers vary from place to place but it also occurs to me that different regions are often trying to answer different questions in the first place. Superficial similarities often hide profound differences. Consultation and involvement at a local level are crucial. We can assist that process.

"Finally, I believe my trusts are about providing long-term help. I have always been deeply suspicious of the 'quick fix', particularly when so many of the challenges that we face have been with us for years."

A strategic plan was formulated in 1995 and the Prince's activities were brought more sharply into focus. Sharing ideas and resources was the order of the day: and externally the message was starting to get across unencumbered by a host of conflicting labels. In 1996 unity of purpose as well as efficiency in execution lay behind the integration of the central functions of four of the main organisations under one roof at Park Square East in London.

One measure of growth is money. Cash inflows at the Prince's Trust show a dramatic increase over the years:

Another measure is staffing and salaries. There were no salaries for anyone until 1983, when the sum of £1,160 was reluctantly released. The first full-time employee for whom the Prince's Trust picked up the tab was Tom Shebbeare, who arrived in February 1988. Today there are 482 paid personnel. When the Trust started Prince Charles could call on his Youth Council, trustees and a handful of others elsewhere: all volunteers. There were 16 names on the first circulation sheet in June 1976. During 1998 over 20,000 people will give some of their time to one or more of his programmes.

1977:	£35,411	1989:	£10,030198
1980:	£31,374	1992:	£12,534,839
1983:	£242,446	1995:	£13,290,639
1986:	£459,923	1998:	£25,000,000 +

So the stream of new initiatives goes on. The Prince prods and pushes. His constant drive to innovate and move the frontier forward infects people at every level in his organisations. He has been able to offer his solutions to other countries, and the formation of the Prince of Wales Business Leaders Forum in 1991 provided an international organisation with high level contacts around the world who share some of his concerns.

1997 alone gave birth to a wide range of new initiatives, all linked to breaking the cycle of disadvantage:

- En Route, an opportunity for disadvantaged young people to carry out community service in Europe;
- 'Mapping Hidden Talent', designed to uncover hidden musical talent in partnership with the National Youth Agency;
- The 'Network' club, to harness ex-Volunteers in spreading knowledge about the programmes;
- The Prince's Trust M-Power Awards, a special grant programme funded by the Millennium Commission, for 14- to 25-year-olds to help people in their community;

- 'Off-Road Motorcycle' for 14- to 18-year-olds to take part in the sport of motor-cross;
- 'One on One', a peer support scheme for disadvantaged young people in rural areas.

Today the Prince's Trust is at the leading edge of social progress: so much so that nearly every established programme has been picked up by the current government with a tweak or two. This seems to be true in education, in employment and in community service. Volunteers play a key role in the New Deal, and the government's Millennium Volunteers is a carbon copy of it. Extending Opportunity, a national framework for study support, looks rather like the Prince's Trust's Study Support.

The Prince of Wales is a pioneer with the ability to plan ahead. He can look at ideas that will work beyond the next election. He is willing to take risks and accept failure, and when something is successful to offer his solution to anyone with greater resources. So the role of the Prince's Trust may be akin to a research and development laboratory for social problems, while Business in the Community involves corporate UK in the implementation of solutions that work. The benefits are already impressive: through the Youth Business Trust, through Volunteers, the Compact, Study Support and a host of smaller programmes. Prince Charles has already done an amazing amount to break the cycle of disadvantage for young people in Britain.

Chapter 3

UNEMPLOYMENT

"I felt strongly we should do something to tackle this"

T he biggest single demarcation in society is between people with work and those without. People with jobs are OK. Some choose not to work but many have no choice. Most of the unemployed tend to have low self-esteem, live below or close to the poverty line, have poor health and other problems, and generally are among the most disadvantaged groups in society. Unemployment is a serious form of social exclusion. The Prince of Wales is determined to break this negative cycle.

Unemployment had been on the agenda since the December 1972 meeting, but measures to help young people find work tended to be confused with other objectives. Fellow travellers came primarily from the ranks of social workers with different priorities. A few grants helped someone find work or make small sums out of developing a hobby, but it was all hit or miss.

Over the years Prince Charles has tried to tackle unemployment in a variety of ways. His methods have included:

- grants;
- training;
- residential courses;
- business links to schools;
- community service;
- entrepreneurship.

All have helped. The greatest impact has come from setting young people up in self-employment. Not that most mind much how they get a job. Many are likely to agree with this assessment, since during his time the Prince has been instrumental in helping over 110,000 young people into work.

Grants for Work
By 1980 the Prince was determined to make unemployment a higher priority in the grant hierarchy. He talked at length with Haywood about how they could help

young people break free of that awful cycle of poverty and unemployment. One difficulty was that the Jubilee charter and charitable status was deemed to limit support to voluntary initiatives on behalf of young unemployed, meaning the Trusts could not create jobs. Even so £100,000 was set aside specifically to address unemployment. A compromise evolved. Groups got money to keep young people busy, without crossing the line into job creation.

So £270 went to St George's Youth Club, Merseyside, to buy tools and materials for volunteers, mostly unemployed, who cleared out the basement of a church crypt and converted it for use as a day centre. Groby Community College Jobshop in Leicestershire got £1,000 to fund non-paying tasks useful to the community, such as tree pruning and bicycle repairs, for the young unemployed. The goal was businesses that would be self-sufficient but non-profit. Other recipients were groups like:

- Art on the Dole, in Edinburgh;
- The Camden Unemployed Young Women's Project;
- Hartlepool Music Workshop for Unemployed;
- Not the Job Hunter of Coventry;
- The Newry Unemployed Action Group in County Down.

Some of these grants could well have helped some young people find work, but no-one had a clue as to their effectiveness or whether value for money was being delivered at the local level. Something more systematic was needed.

The riots in the early 1980s underlined how critical unemployment was in igniting social tensions. When the Prince was in Handsworth shortly after gangs there had gone on the rampage, a group of young men gave him their explanation for the violence: no jobs. Almost one in three under-25s in the area were unemployed. They had ideas about things they might like to try but no-one was willing to give them a leg up. This more than anything hit home with the Prince of Wales. He was immediately sympathetic to their situation.

"A lot of these people had very good ideas but could never get them off the ground, because there was a great lack of seed-corn finance and too few others who believed in what they had to offer."[1]

The quickest way forward was to give more individuals the wherewithal to find work. The Trusts started to consider more applications with an employment angle, gingerly feeling their way into an arena which, given the political climate, could be seen as both encroaching on a government function and criticising its economic policies.

[1] 14 November 1988.

In 1982 grants continued to be cautious, essentially traditional charity with a concession to a practical economic outcome. The Longridge Unemployed Group in Lancashire received £1,000 to buy a badge-making machine. Their idea was to use the machines for training, but also to sell badges to other clubs and groups to make the group (not the members) self-supporting. Another grant went to a music collective, which provided an inexpensive place for young people to make music, to purchase equipment.

Committees were asked to go after people who had the chance of employment but were unable to take up the job for some reason, if things could be fixed by a small sum of money. One Friday Tom Williams (PT Grant '92) was feeling frustrated. He had just been offered work as a carpenter starting the following week. He should have been feeling great, but there was a drawback: he had to provide his own tools and the DHSS would not help. Williams was broke. There was no way he could buy the required items. Clutching at straws, he contacted his local Trust committee. Later the same day he was able to purchase everything he needed and turned up for work on Monday morning raring to go.

Buying trade tools is routine. The Prince uses the example of a microphone so someone could sing in pubs and clubs and make a bit of money that way. Providing bicycles and second-hand cars enabled people to get to work. Paying fares means they can attend auditions and interviews. Paying for special courses such as off-shore sea survival and for exam fees enables them to qualify. Applicants have come up with imaginative requests. In order to place people in employment the Trust has purchased:

• a sword box for a magician;
• an electronic milking machine for a young Guernsey farmer;
• a spear for a martial arts instructor;
• special equipment to manufacture didgeridoos.

Buying equipment is just one way in which grants can help the unemployed land jobs. The Trust has paid for haircuts, new clothes and tattoo removal, all to make sure an interview candidate would be presentable. Whatever it takes to get people into work.

The grants process has been re-jigged over the years to make it more consistent with the Prince's overall objectives: more practical, more concerned with tangible results and, above all, going to the people who need help most. Employment remains one of the main priorities, directly accounting for about ten per cent of a recent sample and, indirectly, for over 50 per cent. Between 25 per cent and 30 per cent of all recipients went on to get a job, and in most cases the grant made the difference.

Grants ensured that people like Paul Whelan, a joiner who was given £230 for driving lessons, was able to get a job which depended upon him being mobile. Joanne Quincy, a former shop assistant, received £299 towards a knitting machine and Matthew Reilly, a student bricklayer, got £169 to buy building tools. Both were able to find work once they had the necessary kit, courtesy of the Trust. Chris Harrisford used his grant to buy an eight-foot unicycle and print colour brochures to advertise his act. Moving up in the world, he was able to go from a street busker to a cabaret artist. Wasiat Ladimeji was planning to become a model, but needed to pay her way to the finals of the Miss Afro-Caribbean beauty pageant. The Trust stepped in to make sure she got there. Over the years grants have been responsible for helping about 12,500 people find jobs, a number now increasing at well over 1,000 each year.

Training to Enter Employment

The West Midlands Training Initiative (Training) provided a practical laboratory in which to test some of Prince Charles's ideas on a larger scale. This was a Birmingham backed idea, with some money raised locally but significant support from the Prince's Trust. The Prince came to cut the ribbon and help raise funds. Training came into existence in a matter of weeks, because Prince Charles was so appalled by what he encountered in Handsworth that he was not willing to wait around for the perfect solution. He wanted to get on with something right away. A small-scale programme was already operating under the chairmanship of Reverend David Collyer, who was also the regional chair of the Trust. The simple solution was to fold that into a new entity and ramp up the numbers.

The initial emphasis was on building skills, and the first project was to refurbish the Curzon Street Railway Station in Birmingham, a Grade I listed building that subsequently became the head office for the Training operation.

Bricklaying, painting, electrical and woodworking were the main skills taught. Once skills had been learned, the students put them into practice in the real world. Training acquired old properties, primarily derelict terraces, and refurbished them as homes for the elderly and the homeless. Training even restored the Birmingham Tram Depot in time for the Prince to hold his 40th birthday party there. Old workshops in central Birmingham were acquired, along with machine tools to teach metal work, and even some basic computers, and professional trainers who taught a variety of skills including elementary information technology.

Two things made this Training different. Some trainees learned about community care in nursery schools or homes for the disabled. Perhaps more importantly, Training took on almost all comers, even giving preference to people who were, on the face of it, 'no hopers'. Most other schemes were selective. This difference is even more pronounced today, when jobs and vocational qualifications are the measurements of success. Less selectivity results in low scores, which suggests poor performance. Budget-conscious groups weed out ill-suited applicants. Training will work with almost anyone on the basis that everyone gets something out of what they offer, even those unable to achieve a grade at the end.

In Training Prince Charles had his first real response to the problem of unemployment. Within a year nearly 4,000 unemployed young people had completed some course. But it has not been an unmitigated success. Local unions were suspicious, despite being consulted. Employers were not entirely convinced of its merits. There was a quasi-governmental air to the proceedings which set it apart from all the Prince's other ideas. The company suffered a severe financial crisis in the late 1980s and nearly went under.

But a large number of unemployed young people did acquire skills. Today, out of every 100 Training graduates, about 20 get jobs right away. Another 40 obtain an NVQ or similar qualification to show for their efforts. Some of those will also find work later. Percentages were slightly lower in earlier years. All told, about 75,000 people have received training – and for a disadvantaged young person that alone has been a plus.

The Prince has also encouraged Business in the Community members to support special training programmes. Most link back to their own businesses, such as a Lloyds initiative to train people in insurance, and a Welcome Break course that concentrated on catering. Grand Met converted a disused pub, the *Crown and Leek*, into a centre for learning construction skills. A number of people found work through these schemes. They are, however, individual initiatives rather than part of any overall programme. Business in the Community acts as a sponsor or catalyst. Most programmes are small scale, with about 20 to 30 trainees. Anywhere from 10 to 15 schemes have been active each year. The placement rate suggests that over 60 per cent of those who passed through went on to work.

Residential Courses

Residential courses have also helped. Some of the hardest nuts have been cracked after an intensive week away. The idea evolved out of earlier *ad hoc* camps. The Prince's visits to run-down inner city areas, where he saw people standing around with nothing to do, spurred him on to run a regular residential programme that would take these people off the streets, even if only for a short time. The man who translated this idea into action in spring 1985 was Antony Kenney, deputy principal at St Mary's University College, who came on board when the course was only 12 weeks away. The site, the 1830 Club at Middleton-on-Sea, was undergoing refurbishment and workers were still laying concrete the week before.

The idea was to take 250 rather tricky characters, many of whom had not left home before – and most of whom were only turning up because they had nothing better to do – and make them employable in seven days. The task sounded impossible, but that was the Prince's expectation and Kenney did not intend to disappoint. First off, the experience had to be fun, which for a group of 18–25s meant alcohol on site. Then he had to find trainers and equipment. It was a minor miracle that Middleton took place at all, and given the mood of the crowd, by the third night Pratt and Kenney may well have wished they had shelved the scheme. They were close to a riot. What deterred them from calling in the police was the vision of the next day's headlines. The Prince was constantly urging people to take risks, but for a few hours this was looking like a risk too far. If his charges went on the rampage, the result would not have done a lot for the royal reputation or the credibility of the Prince's Trust. Fortunately Pratt managed to defuse the situation, though tensions were rising high again when the Prince put in his appearance on the final Friday.

Kenney had feared the worst. "I was proved absolutely wrong. He had this wonderful ability to take everyone he met at their level. He talked to every person and responded to every question asked, and in a sensible way which was not at all patronising."

So the course could be chalked up as a success, though in need of revision. The experience may not have been perfect, but a lot of participants went home if not different, at least with a different attitude, having looked at life from a new perspective. Enough found work or went to college to justify a regular event. Kenney continued as course director, juggling two jobs. Work, Sport and Leisure had arrived.

The course was a cocktail. Sport was there to energise, leisure because many of these young kids were likely to have plenty of enforced leisure time in their lives, and workshops to learn skills that would help in finding a job, the whole object of the exercise. One of the ways that residential courses connect is by pulling in big names, who add an air of excitement and encourage young people to come. Phil Collins is a veteran, coming to Caister camp almost every year, in one case chartering a private plane from Florida. Others who have helped make residential courses come alive include world snooker champion Stephen Hendry, WBC heavyweight world champion boxer Frank Bruno, actress Sarah Miles, DJ Annie Nightingale and singer Jazzie B from Soul to Soul.

Residential courses were not without problems. Physical exercise sometimes took its toll. In 1990 there were 150 visits to the local hospital inside the week. Inevitably there have been incidents. In 1986 the course at Caister got off to an inauspicious start. Within 15 minutes of the arrival of a train load of attendees in nearby Great Yarmouth, the chief constable was on the telephone complaining of broken windows in houses near the station. One year a group of four youths who might have been participants, or perhaps outsiders attending a nearby soul concert, smashed 30 windows around the swimming pool. A headline in the *Sun* ran: '400 Youths Go On Drunken Rampage'. The Prince's response: "Now you know why it is not always worth believing what you read in the newspapers." The response inside Caister was a whip round, raising £500 from kids with no cash. Then there was minor arson on a caravan, but the police were convinced that no-one at Caister was to blame. So in spite of taking substantial risks with a volatile clientele, these residential programmes have gone surprisingly well.

The Prince makes a point of coming, and always joins in the fun. Over the years he has played billiards, driven a forklift truck, received a shoulder massage, bobbed for apples and walked on tin cans. He has even taken to the floor of the disco, for which he got an eight out of ten from Kim Dixon (Caister '86).

The Prince did not just go walkabout. He had a message to deliver, encouraging everyone there to carry on after the course was over. In 1990 his message was: "I hope that when you get home you can put these skills into practice and maybe some of you can even set up your own business."[2]

People come out pumped up with renewed determination to change their life. The impact on individual campers like Andy Clark (Caister '90) is so important. "I know more about how to get a job." Elizabeth Merritt (Caister '93) said, "I now feel that I have the confidence to go for a job and get it." Kevin Washington (Ayr '95): "If it wasn't for the Prince's Trust I'd be sitting around doing absolutely nothing and drowning in my own self-pity."

The experience of Danny Stevens (Ayr '97) illustrates the difference the course can make. Danny's parents split when he was four, which did not help his attitude in school. He was also dyslexic. On leaving school without any qualifications Danny got in with a bad crowd. "I was out of work and didn't know what to do. Took too many drugs because I was bored."

After drifting for a while he passed five GCSEs, but his confidence received a massive blow as he searched for a job. He was rejected by a manager who told him he was too short. Danny is four feet eleven inches. This and other setbacks sent him on a downward spiral. He finally landed the most menial job as a kitchen assistant at a nursing home in Seaford. With his self-esteem at rock bottom, it did not occur to Danny he might do more.

[2] *Eastern Daily Press*, 29 March 1990.

Persuaded to go to a Prince's Trust residential course, Danny was transformed. "I hated it at first, but in the end I didn't want to come home." He made friends with a heroin addict who was trying to stay off the drug, and two alcoholics who have kept dry ever since. In Danny's case he discovered an ability to listen and be supportive of others' problems. Realising he could help others changed his whole outlook. "It's down to the Prince's Trust that I am now confident and outgoing."

The first day back at work, he asked to become a carer rather than remain in the kitchen – something he had wanted to do for a while but had kept quiet, unwilling to risk another rejection. To his surprise the manager was delighted. He was promoted on the spot and has never been happier or more fulfilled. Danny is quite clear on who gets the credit. "If I ever meet the Prince of Wales, I'll shake his hand and thank him. I don't care what other people say about him. He's the one who started all this off."

As the employment emphasis increased, sessions such as writing a CV and the art of being interviewed were added to the programmes. When combined with a supportive environment which shouts out "you can do it", this sort of tailored training really works. One of the workshop leaders at the 1995 Recharge course held at Ayr was Peta Clifton, head of personnel at Carphone Warehouse. She was so impressed by the attitude and commitment of some of the young people she met that she interviewed several for jobs. Two were hired. Those kids from Ayr '95 are not there today: one worked for a while before leaving to have a baby, and the other departed under somewhat suspicious circumstances. Even so the company is still hiring out of Recharge in 1998.

Records indicate that over 3,000 participants who were not the most promising employment material did in fact find work following their course, and the success rate seems to be rising. Informed estimates from the late 1980s and early 1990s suggest that between 55 and 65 per cent found a job or went into formal training within six months. In March 1997 the Prince's Trust was able to report that 70 per cent of the nearly 1,500 young people who had been on residential courses during the prior period were in employment or further training. This was the best result ever.

Music is one area where grant activity and residential programmes complement the Prince's efforts to combat unemployment. Grants to both individuals and bands allow purchase of musical instruments and equipment. Special awards enable musicians to participate in events which may be just the break they need to launch a professional career. For example, the Trust paid for The Chosen Ones, a five-member rap group, to take part in the world's biggest international music fair, the New Music Seminar in New York. Subsequently they signed a recording contract with Virgin Records. Rupert Parks, aka Photek, who also signed with

Virgin, made *Modus Operandi* which sold over 100,000 copies. He later received a grant to set up his own record label.

In 1993 Stereophonics, from Aberdare in South Wales, got £500 to buy equipment. They were awarded another £800 to replace speakers that had been stolen and without which no-one would have booked the band. Later, lead singer and song writer Kelly Jones received a separate grant to buy a word processor so he could tune up his lyrics. Stereophonics won Best Newcomers at the 1998 Brit Awards and their recent album reached number six in the charts.

Almost from the outset residential programmes have contained music workshops. In due course that split out to become a separate employment initiative: the Rock School, recently renamed Sounds Live. There are now six sessions each year, with course composition which includes new technologies, and increased time given to film and video production as well as creating and playing music.

Many graduates end up with work, even if the income flow was uneven – near inevitable in the music business. Some, like Damien Keyes (Rock School '96), went on to teach – in his case at the Guildford School of Music. Gary Lewis (Rock School '96) became lead guitar for Passion Star. Bands were formed that went on tour or played live for a living at their local. Three bands in the competition for the 1982 Rock Gala went on to record, including Unity and Cry Wolf.

Schools to Jobs
Creating employable graduates is one measure of a successful education system. Of all Prince Charles's education programmes the one that has had a direct effect on employment is the Compact, which seeks to link local businesses to schools. The Prince played a pivotal role in introducing the Compact to Britain and Compacts have facilitated the transition into employment for thousands of school leavers. This and other education activities are described in Chapter 5.

I Serve Therefore I Work
Another approach to tackling unemployment is via voluntary work. The results of the first Community Ventures were spectacular. An external evaluation at the end of three years found that 231 out of the 238 unemployed people who completed the programme had gone on to jobs or further education. Nearly 65 per cent had been on government training schemes before coming to Ventures – and were *still* unemployed. So the success rate was phenomenal and often with people the system had already failed – but so too was the cost per person, working out at £3,800 in 1988, or nearly £6,000 in today's terms. Ventures metamorphosed into Volunteers as a much cheaper route to most of the same benefits. These activities will be

examined in more detail in Chapter 4. Suffice it to say here that, by my estimate, Volunteers has put nearly 15,000 people back to work in less than eight years.

There's No Employment Like Self-employment

Not everyone who wants a job will be able to find one. There are also many people who are not suited to traditional employment, but who do want to work. The Prince had observed how some grants contained the germ of a viable living. The group which manufactured canoes for the disabled, for example, or the individual who developed a new fishing fly, might have the basis of their own business should they so desire. Some did. Most lacked access to capital with which to start, but they did have the get up and go attitude which was more valuable than money.

The Prince of Wales sees the self-employment option as a scheme for job makers rather than job seekers. That was why he started the Youth Business Initiative, though with limited expectations about what could be accomplished. As he ruefully explained to a group of visiting Americans from Jobs for Youths in Boston, "one of the things we find in this country is that in the north of England there's no tradition at all of individual enterprise". John Pervin, the first managing director, put their objective in perspective. "He never had any pretensions about helping to solve the youth unemployment problem single-handed. He wanted to be a beacon in the dark and so encourage others to emulate his contribution."

The Prince's Trust did not just give entrepreneurs seed capital. Every bit as important was advice and education. Steering someone elsewhere could be equally helpful. A directory was published, "Want to be Your Own Boss? Start Here". It listed hundreds of agencies throughout the country who provided such help.

The very first bursaries for self-employment came out of the Jubilee Trusts in January 1982: 34 applicants, ten acceptances. Initial bursaries supported a range of ventures, including car valeting, a fish and chip shop, knitwear design and production, sewing of soft toys, secretarial services, catering and painting and decorating – sensible small-scale ventures. It was all very much trial and error, and there were errors. The amount of money was small, not more than £1,000, and the number of trials was small, too, about 50 over the first 12 months.

Sixteen years on, the Prince recalls how it all began: "I think, perhaps, it came out as a result of discussing ways in which we could take the work of the Prince's Trust further, which was taking risks with people. At that stage it was providing people with a little bit of money to achieve their particular ambition, whether it was setting up as a band, or whatever. So it was a natural step, perhaps, to move to 'hang on a minute – perhaps we could help them set up in a business' and really, I think, what led to that was the background of growing unemployment in the early '80s, which more than anything else, led us to try and see if we could encourage people to start up in business because all these traditional industries were being shut down all over the shop. What on earth were people to do? It did seem to us at the time that self-employment was an option."

And again, the riots created a catalyst which added a sense of urgency. "I started the Youth Business Initiative as a result of those very unfortunate riots in various cities in 1980 and 1981. I remember talking to the people in my trust about this and saying we must find ways, even small ways, in which we as a trust could perhaps help prevent those sorts of situations arising again in the future. Although we could only do a very small amount, as a result of the discussions we had produced this idea to try and start off by helping people in their own businesses.

"And it was a crying need, I think, because so many of the banks simply didn't want to know about some person who wanted £1,800 or whatever. We wanted to enable people who were in disadvantaged or deprived circumstances and, inevitably, found it incredibly hard to achieve their own particular ambitions because of lack of financial resources and good advice, but providing them, in a small way, with what they lacked to begin their own enterprises. That was the genesis of the Youth Business Trust."

When survival rates in the early years exceeded 80 per cent, and some start-ups were growing way beyond one man bands, there was a rapid reappraisal of the whole scheme. Prince Charles has remarked that the self-employment programme has been "more successful than I dared hope … to my absolute astonishment it has flourished, surpassing all expectations." He recalls, with a wry smile, "at the time, the concept of self-employment was not a very common thing. I mean it was really only for the people who either had some sort of collateral, or I suppose, a very supportive family or were just born entrepreneurs. The idea that it could be expanded on to this extent was not at all thought of."

But at the time, he came in for criticism for showing excess naïvety. The conventional wisdom was that backing people under the age of 25 would not work. He did not waste time rebutting these charges. He just got on with setting up businesses, quietly confident that even if some failed enough would work to make the exercise worthwhile.

One big plus was that this activity proved attractive to corporate supporters. In the first year American Express donated £15,000. P&O, GKN, Sears, Cadbury Schweppes and Bass all put pen to cheque book. The Jubilee Trusts stumped up £92,000 in seed capital for this "joint venture" with the Prince's Trust, but after that it was on its own. Much more money was needed if the programme was ever to be more than an experiment. The first stop was the clearing banks, but they were sceptical. The concept was worthy, so they lent manpower but kept their hands firmly in their pockets until much later.

The Youth Business Initiative was more people-intensive than grant giving. "Then we realised that you could not do that without providing people with a helping hand and the necessary advice." One feature was in place from the outset. "Each recipient of an award receives on-going help from an experienced adult." The young entrepreneurs were also asked – though initially not required – to accept two "tutors", normally one with financial expertise and, in practice, often a local bank manager; and another knowledgeable about the relevant business field.

So human resources were every bit as necessary as financial ones. Here again, many of the larger companies pitched in. Secondees came from Abbey National, ICI, NatWest, Thorn EMI and Marks & Spencer, which enabled pilots to start in eight regions. Sir Alcon Copisarow, the first chairman, was cautious. "How the scheme progresses rests both on the donations and resources provided by industry and commerce, and on being able to demonstrate that they were being used profitably."

From day one, regional co-ordinators focused on two areas crucial to long-term success. Time and effort went into producing a realistic business plan before any money changed hands. Many of the businesses had to rewrite and amend plans several times before receiving financial aid. The interviews were no walkover either, often lasting up to one hour as the panel probed to test whether an idea was really viable. The guiding principle was only to back business plans that truly had "a reasonable chance of success". There was charitable intent, but leavened with business nous.

Less than 25 per cent of the initial applications were approved in each of the first four years. This policy was deliberate, to try and ensure that the experiment had a fair chance to prove itself. Weeding out continues to be vital to its success. After all, no-one benefits in the long run if money is given out indiscriminately. Failure might only confirm their fear that they were useless, which could be worse than earlier rejections.

The Prince has attended a couple of these panels. Paul Mackie (PSYBT '95) was unemployed and decided to try running his own show; he was young and without experience. His previous employer, the Royal Bank of Scotland, was not able to help but the manager did have a suggestion. Try the Prince's Trust. They set him up as Firstdrive, with £2,000, in a business buying old bangers which he refurbished and sold. The first months were hard, but in spite of making mistakes Paul persevered. Then he applied for an expansion loan, and found Prince Charles was part of his second approval. "He asked me a lot of questions, more than other panel members: not just about the business but about how I got the idea, why I wanted to go on my own and whether the decision had been hard."

The Prince had been given a crib sheet which he apparently ignored, instead asking whether Paul had taken in the enterprise allowance scheme in calculating cash flow. He also asked: "Why should people trust a second-hand car salesperson?" Paul survived his ordeal. Firstdrive seems to be surviving too, and in its third year is set to top £100,000 in turnover, validating Prince Charles's credit decision.

There was one vital change that had to happen before self-employment could take off: a separate structure. People with a business orientation had to evaluate applications. Distinct regional committees were set up. A separate annexe, at the central office, also emphasised that it was to be run along different lines.

When in March 1986 the Prince took stock of how self-employment was doing, he was encouraged. Of the first 1,167 businesses set up, nearly 950 had survived through their crucial first year. It was too early to say for sure whether he had hit upon a sound, long-term solution, but the concept was past the experimental stage.

Charity with an Edge

A year or so after the Youth Business Initiative started the Youth Enterprise Scheme emerged out of the National Association of Youth Clubs, headed by Sir Angus Ogilvy. The rallying cry for the new programme was, "You can't say No to YES." The organisations went about their business in parallel, with a couple of important distinctions. The Prince's initiative evolved out of what was effectively a charitable activity and gave money to people to start a business. YES used loans, soft loans to be sure, and with low expectations as to whether they would ever be paid back – but the subtle psychological difference can be important in providing an extra incentive in the struggle for survival. And a remarkable number of these early businesses did not merely survive: they prospered. In one respect they were lucky to be there at all. Their very existence could have been illegal.

Charity law was enshrined in an act of 1602 and had only evolved through legal precedent. Loans to set up a new business did not qualify under existing exemptions. Education – no; religion – definitely no; purpose of benefit to the community – at a stretch, maybe; relief of poverty – that held out some hope, but to be on the safe side it made sense to get prior approval, which meant persuading both the Charity Commission and the Treasury to agree to a definition which was possibly broader than the Tudors had in mind. The key turned out to be the condition that an applicant could not find finance by any other means, and the interpretation still enshrined in policy to this day was that two financial institutions should have turned down the proposal before the Trust gave a loan. On that basis a special ruling was obtained to sanction the activity.

The other difference emerged later. The value of an adult advisor to help the fledging entrepreneur avoid obvious potholes was agreed. This idea stemmed from unpleasant personal experience. In his entrepreneurial days Ogilvy numbered a seemingly successful disco amongst his operations – until he found out about crooked bar staff. When you are new in business, repeating old mistakes is inevitable unless you have someone who has been there before to show you the ropes.

The Youth Enterprise Scheme followed the requirement of appointing advisors religiously, and made sure their advisors had solid business experience. The emphasis at the Youth Business Initiative was more on the personal, of having someone involved who cared and on making the entrepreneur feel they were not on their own. Many tutors came from local government or were social workers. And the rule about having two advisors was more honoured in the breach than the observance.

Between 1983 and 1986 the Prince and Ogilvy held numerous conversations, often at Windsor where they spent Christmas together, or at St James's Palace where both men had an office. They were in agreement that their effectiveness could be enhanced if the two organisations merged, but not on these philosophical differences. Prince Charles leant towards bursaries, concerned that loan pressure might prove too much on top of all the other problems, and worried that people might be put off applying altogether. Ogilvy recalls deeply felt disputes over this issue. "People were saying it was totally unfair to load young businesses with loans, and that the entrepreneurs would worry too much."

During a reception at Kensington Palace in 1987 concerns were raised about whether the organisation would become too commercial and only able to help those with proven abilities. Absolutely not, the Prince of Wales assured them. "As long as I am there, we'll still have bursaries for the really needy. The Trust will never go down the road of being loans only." So bursaries stayed, regardless of whether that was a bad financial decision and irrespective of whether it meant a higher failure rate.

In the end the two agreed that in some cases a bursary would be right, while in others a loan would make more sense and the most sensible solution was to allow the local committee to use discretion. A balanced approach may seem obvious now, but it was something of a compromise at the time.

The Prince is still convinced that, on balance, in most instances a loan is the better way. "There is a sense of responsibility that it gives and for some people, at least where a loan is involved, they may try that little bit harder. We also find that many applicants like to feel someone has faith in them. After all, they came to us after having been turned down elsewhere. Giving a bursary suggests less confidence in their ability to succeed. When we make a loan, that is more of a business decision and there is an obligation to pay it back. From our standpoint it is incredibly helpful to get repaid, because that is our capital and the more we get back the more new businesses we can fund." The current mix is about 80 per cent loan and 20 per cent bursary, though loans remain semi-rigid and the Trust writes off sizeable sums each year: £2.3 million in 1997.

Even after all the operating technicalities were resolved, the birth of the Youth Business Trust was not without its pangs. As one private secretary remarked, "Lord Hanson has an easier time of it putting two businesses together. That just takes money." In the end the Prince of Wales lost patience. Young people were losing out on opportunities, due to internal wrangling. He got both sets of trustees around one table in a private meeting, prepared if necessary to knock a few heads together. He made it clear that he would only consent to be president if he got to select the chairman. After he left there was no more argument.

The merged organisation, complete with new name, also started to take on a new personality. Professional management took control in the shape of John Pervin from Unilever, whose good work on the 50th celebration of the King George Jubilee Trust had attracted the Prince's attention. As in any start-up there was a fair degree of chaos and muddling through. Handing out bursaries was relatively straightforward, but monitoring loans was another matter. As for cash flow, a crisis erupted just after the merger. In theory there were ample resources, but pledges did not always arrive on time, or came in instalments which did not match outgoings. So money in the kitty could be very different from the book entries, which was the problem about four months after Pervin took over. Commitments appeared covered, but there was not going to be enough cash to pay wages at the end of the month.

Pervin's contacts at B&Q and Reader's Digest came to the rescue. The mini crisis sparked a realisation that an increasing degree of professionalism was essential – and this was true for both the Trust and its entrepreneurs, for whom managing cash flow always was the biggest problem.

At this juncture Pervin sat down to calculate the financial requirement for the following five years. It came out at £80 million. Pervin checked the numbers several times to make sure he had not misplaced a decimal point. Unfortunately not. A daunting proposition for an organisation which had accumulated funds, at the end of 1986, of precisely £195,146.

Aim high has always been part of the Prince's philosophy. Even so finding £80 million seemed insuperable until someone pointed out that the Prince of Wales was to be 40 the following year. So if they could raise say, £40 million, and if the Government would match the funds … There were some rather large ifs in that, but there was David Young's Mansion House promise.

Why not try and claim that the commitment, which had inadvertently been open-ended, still applied, even though the goal was now much more ambitious? Young stood by his pledge, even though he knew full well that everyone had only £3 million in mind at the time. Young admires the Trust's audacity: "They had no right at all to claim our agreement to double any amount of money, as it was related only to the £3 million pledge – but when I heard they had already raised over £30 million, my reaction was 'good'. I didn't mean to give them more but I was delighted."

And of course it was all in a very good cause, even if it did get up the Treasury's nose. The Treasury, who were always dismissive of anything associated with the Prince of Wales, kicked up a a stink and forced the issue in front of Margaret Thatcher. "What idiot did this?" she asked, and on being told that David Young was the culprit, relented. "Oh, well – I suppose we'd better do it."

Merger complete, management in place, money in the bank: at last they could get back to helping young entrepreneurs. Prince Charles was an active president. Pervin was required to report every other Friday. Conversations never concluded without some new suggestion on how to move things forward. Pervin recalls, "He was always available when required. Even when there were things we asked for which I could tell he did not really want to do, if it would help us he would agree."

He involved himself fully in organising the first few Youth Business Trust exhibitions, went over proposals as to which businesses should attend, worked on the structure of the show and even altered the layout of stands. His level of interest showed in the time he would spend with the businesses, invariably – to the despair of his staff – running over the specified time-slot. There were a lot of these visits in the mid-1980s, as he hugely enjoyed meeting people who had beaten the odds and proved the sceptics wrong.

Entrepreneurs like Fiona Rae, who graduated with first class honours in jewellery design from St Martin's in 1988. Fiona fancied the idea of going into business for herself but the cost of getting a workshop together was beyond her. The only work she found was part-time and that disappeared when business turned down, leaving her with only ten hours of work a week teaching, which paid next to nothing.

Fiona may not have had a job, but she had talent and a good idea. She saw that there was very little enamel men's jewellery, especially with a more contemporary design. She believed she could fill this gap. As part of her search for work, she took a course at the City of London Business School, where she heard about the Prince's Youth Business Trust. She drew up a business plan to produce contemporary cufflinks. She was awarded £2,500, sufficient to equip a studio in Soho with minimum tooling and buy the special kiln needed to fire enamel.

Fiona started with just four designs, which she tried to sell herself. Not far from her studio, Paul Smith was building a successful men's clothing business in his Covent Garden store. Fiona wandered in, and the next thing she knew she had landed her first proper customer – and a very prestigious account at that.

She first met Prince Charles when she won the Prince's Youth Business Trust gold medal at the international giftware exhibition in September 1992. He presented her with the prize. The encounter was brief. Fiona remembers him as "very approachable, surprisingly so". In December the same year, hers was one of ten businesses selected to represent North London at an event in the presence of the Prince of Wales. She decided to give him a gift to show her appreciation. What could be more appropriate than the piece that had won in Birmingham?

Fiona describes the presentation: "They were a pair of silver and enamel cufflinks in a long oval shape. The pattern was a chequer board, with one black and white enamel and the other black and red. When it came to my turn I handed him the box. He seemed very pleased. He showed me the cufflinks he had on which were also enamel, saying he particularly liked enamel cufflinks. His had the Union Jack and had been made by Garrards. He seemed to like my present."

Fiona received an invitation to bring her products to St James's Palace for a special showing, as they were felt suitable to be given as Christmas presents. In 1993 she supplied the Prince with 15 pairs of cufflinks. Next, she was commissioned to do an exclusive design incorporating his feathers. That too passed muster. Further orders followed, including pairs in colours of claret and Eton blue. Fiona has now moved on to silver enamel pill boxes also incorporating the feathers.

This patronage was not some charitable gesture. Prince Charles is a customer because Fiona's products are excellent. She currently sells to some of the most exclusive stores in the world, including Joyce Ma in Hong Kong, Bergdorf Goodman in New York, Holt Renfrew in Canada and Liberty's of London. The Prince remembers how St James's Palace helped add another name to a distinguished client list. "There is a girl called Fiona Rae who does these marvellous enamel cufflinks. Through my people she was put in touch with one of the buying staff at Aspreys, and now she supplies them. They are very happy with her work. There's a lot of wheels within wheels helping in this way and passing people along."

Fiona does not advertise that she has a royal client, but word got around and gives her a cachet which is very helpful, as she is targeting the top retail outlets. Business is booming. Fiona now employs a team of eight outworkers. Her turnover has doubled each year since 1991. She would not have been able to start at all without the help of the Trust.

Since it started, the self-employment programme has gone from strength to strength. The original ceiling per person was set at £1,000, but that rose to £3,000. In the right hands such a sum can go a long way. The top 100 businesses funded by the Prince's Trust now turn over in excess of £100 million, up from only half that three years ago. Growing in confidence, the Trust began to give out larger sums and became more creative in the mix of bursaries, initial loans, test marketing, expansion loans – of up to £5,000 – and other refinements. At the time of writing I calculate over 23,000 businesses are active, most of them a credit to the programme and to themselves.

Leigh Goodsell had always intended to be a professional photographer like his grandfather and great-great-grandfather. As a young child he used to spend time in the darkroom watching pictures emerge, as if by magic, out of the developing tray. When only four he was given a battered old box camera which he took to school, and by the age of 13 his grandfather gave him an old Agfa Rangefinder on the condition he took 12 good photos and showed himself capable of developing them properly.

In his late teens Leigh rebelled and went to work at a riding school. That was fun for a while but realising after several years that he had a limited future in horses, Leigh tried to resurrect his photographic interest. He landed a job as in-house photographer at an advertising agency, and so seemed set for a successful transition. But the 1992 recession led to his employer filing for bankruptcy. Leigh was out of work at a bad time.

He knew by then that photography was right for him. He also knew a few clients who were willing to give him assignments – but his capabilities were limited by a camera that was almost an antique. He secured the odd job, but not nearly enough to make a living, or to raise funds to upgrade his camera. His family could not help, and no bank would lend. After two years unemployed, and going more or less nowhere, Leigh was stuck at home with no money or prospects when a friend who had started a business encouraged him to approach the Trust.

In due course he secured a low interest rate loan of £4,000, supplemented by £3,000 from Barclay's Bank. This £7,000 was enough to buy a full suite of modern equipment. Leigh knows that he only got the bank loan because the Prince's Trust was willing to back him, and the bank believed that with their support he was a reasonable risk.

Leigh's big break came in 1997 when the King's Fund, a medical charity of which Prince Charles is president, wished to commission a portrait photograph of him for their centenary. It was suggested that they might want to use a Prince's Trust photographer. Sample portfolios were sent in. Leigh's was selected, giving great satisfaction to the entire Goodsell family because Leigh's great-great-grandfather, William Anckorn of Arbroath, had photographed Edward VII on several occasions during the 1890s when he was the Prince of Wales.

Leigh was allotted a 15-minute session at St James's Palace, which put the pressure on because his usual sitting ran for well over an hour. "It was a rather surreal experience and I was very nervous. He put me quite at ease, which is normally my job. He asked me about my business and how I got along with the Trust. Then he complimented me on my cameras, which he obviously knew a bit about. I told him he owned most of them, as they were all bought with his money. He came across as a very humorous and accessible man. It struck me how lousy his press was, and in person he was entirely different from what you read about him."

Leigh took 36 photographs, and the one chosen by the King's Fund and approved by the Palace now graces the reception area.

Leigh is allowed to mention on promotional material that he has photographed the Prince of Wales. He can point to assignments received because of that. People say, "If I'm good enough for His Royal Highness, I must be good enough for them." Leigh's studio in Brancaster is busier now, and he has been able to pay back most of the loan. Self-employment is never a bed of roses, but he loves his work. "Not many people get the opportunity to do something they enjoy with their life. That is what the Prince's Trust has done for me."

The life of an entrepreneur is often a roller-coaster ride. The transformation from despair to elation can be rapid. On 13 May 1997 Lesley Cooper and Tracey Cunningham arrived at work to find that their boss was not there and they were out of a job. With help from the Prince's Scottish Youth Business Trust they set up the Sorbie Hayes Hair Company to take over, as owners, the premises where only a few weeks before, they had been employees. They now have four people working for them. On 13 March 1998 they were voted Outstanding Young Businesswomen of the Year by the Association of Scottish Businesswomen.

All told, over 39,000 new businesses have emerged since self-employment started in 1982. Several have become medium-sized employers. There was a period when the image was one of crafts and gardening, but those days are long past. The 10,000th person to be helped, Derek Coffey, set up as a cattle chiropodist. In its time the Trust has backed businesses which range from aquafit classes to flint-knapping demonstrations, from a pedigree ram bank for servicing ewes to making reproduction 1920s wind-up gramophones, and from charcoal burning to breeding exotic insects, such as the praying mantis and scorpion.

The Trust will not support businesses that could bring the Prince into disrepute. Examples of unacceptable businesses include amusement arcades, sex shops, model agencies, debt collecting, pyramid selling and palmists. On the whole, the Prince remains relaxed, though on one occasion he expressed concern over a seller of comics because of the violence contained in the publications. And giving money out for bad ideas does no-one a favour. He has been known to express concern that "we are in danger of doing too many T shirts". He also makes the distinction between an interest which can become a viable business and something which could never be more than a hobby. After reviewing one group of entrepreneurs, he once took Pervin on one side and, pointing to a landscape painter of moderate quality, said, "That is not a business. We shouldn't be helping that sort of thing." That story did the rounds of the approval committees. No more pastimes masquerading as professions.

When you set up 4,000 businesses a year, there is scope for mistakes. The one that collects the booby prize caused the *Sun* to run a story headed 'Prince and the Hooker'. The Trust funded an apparently kosher telephone answering service, which took on an escort agency as a customer which proved to be a front for a prostitution ring. That aside, it is remarkable how few embarrassing episodes have interfered with progress.

The top ten by turnover today include a milk testing business, a language school, a Just in Time expediter and a computer games distributor. That Trust businesses constantly win prizes proves that they meet real economic needs. Aardvark (PYBT '90), a Sheffield-based woodworking business, won Yorkshire Television's competition "Enterprise 92" and £10,000. Lee Brearley (PYBT '94) won the 1997 *Yorkshire Post* competition for Growing Business of the Year. Brearley's installs and repairs draught-dispensing equipment for breweries and soft drink companies. Solo entrepreneurs are also providing a remarkable range of services, with great success. Alison Rogers (PYBT '95) came second in the 1998 British Dog Grooming Championships. Julie McDonagh (PYBT '96) won a 1997 Giftware Industry Award for Excellence.

The evolution of the annual exhibition parallels the development of the Trust. Prince Charles pushed the idea as a showcase, and to attract buyers. Hanger No. 6 at Manchester Airport was probably not the ideal venue. Four years of disuse had left debris littering the floor and a pool of water the size of a small lake. Somehow, on 29 October 1986, it all came together with display boards borrowed from Marks & Spencer. A total of 108 businesses offered their wares to about 200 people who were served tasteless packaged meals. Not much business was transacted. Even so, from an unpromising beginning, the exhibition has gone from strength to strength.

It led a peripatetic existence for its first few years, popping up in Cardiff, Liverpool, and even for one summer in Hyde Park, before settling into a permanent slot as an annexe of the Autumn International trade fair in Birmingham. In 1997 over 200 businesses presented a much more polished product range, and over 6,500 visitors attended the Trust's hall. Buyers came from top department stores in Britain, including Harvey Nichols and Liberty's, as well as from abroad.

The profile in 1998 is very different from the pilot of 1982. There has always been enormous enthusiasm, but the degree of professionalism has grown, along with the scope of the programme. As one of the longest serving area managers, Jack Curtin, explained: "We have moved on from the days of mops and buckets, but we have not forgotten our roots. Saving jobs by helping the local pro buy the golf shop is the new face of the Prince's Youth Business Trust, but we still have plenty of people who can make a decent living cleaning windows."

The Prince patronises many of the businesses he has helped. Over the years he has bought shawls from Ulrike Textiles, plates from JD Ceramics and glass sculptures from Artisan Crystal, and uses caterer Inn or Out for meals at Highgrove and St James's Palace. Many associated with the work follow his example. Perhaps the ultimate example is Khalid Aziz, chairman of Southern Counties Board. His company employs a Youth Business Trust car valet, a Youth Business Trust gardener and a Youth Business Trust caterer. The company brochure was produced by a Youth Business Trust graphic designer and even his house was thatched by a Youth Business Trust business.

People who want to give the Prince of Wales a present sometimes go out of their way to select an item from a Trust business, knowing their thoughtfulness will be appreciated. The 1990 exhibitors sent him a book of messages on special marbled paper from Victoria Hall of Norwich, and a flower arrangement from Flowerbox Design in Swansea. He provides commissions. Animal portrait artist Aron Gadd received permission to paint the royal polo pony. Hilary Shedel of Dollis Hill took the official photograph for his 42nd birthday. Richard Adam and John Foyle, two stonemasons, won a restoration contract at the Royal Pavilion at Brighton.

The Prince can now take pleasure in watching an increasing number of success stories.

"The thing that has really encouraged me more than anything else is the letters I receive from so many of the people who we've set up in business or helped in other ways to say what a difference it has made in their lives. Even if it was only one, that would give me the satisfaction that it was all worthwhile. The knowledge that some of them are now actually turning over very large amounts of money and employing substantial numbers of people is hugely encouraging.

"We have, I think, demonstrated that people who have been written off as unreasonable risks have the energy and commitment to succeed and have demonstrated to those that have the financial resources, the banks and others, that they are worthwhile risks."[3]

[3] Address accompanying release of the 1989 Prince's Trust annual report, Livingstone,
   4 September 1989.

Tina Adams (PYBT '96) of the Little Angels Play Group is his ideal entrepreneur. Tina could not hold a permanent position because of constant attacks of asthma, made worse by worrying about whether she would lose her job – which, of course, she did. Once out on her own, those worries ceased. Not only has her business taken off, going from eight to 35 children, but her health has never been better. Oh, and now she is successful, with a two-year waiting list, the Midland Bank is looking at lending her the money to buy a Portakabin so she can expand to two classes.

There are several stories that Prince Charles enjoys recounting.

"Julie Dedman is a great example. She had been made redundant – from a dairy, I think. Instead of sitting around doing nothing she decided she would start her own business and it's been an incredible story. Last time I saw her she modestly stated that her turnover was in excess of £1 million. She now employs a number of people, including her husband. Isis is another. David Brown does English courses for foreign students, and he has come a long way in a short time. There are so many now. There is Uwe up in Newcastle, which makes very lovely washed cotton garments."

Prince Charles is well aware that vigilance in all aspects of the programme is essential. He constantly returns to the need to maintain the quality of the businesses.

"Although there is a huge temptation to want to help everyone, one has to be realistic that not everybody is going to be able to cope with self-employment. There was a time when I noted that there were an awful lot of T-shirt businesses springing up. You could see that some just weren't going to survive, and it was clear that some local committees were obviously trying, almost too hard, to help. Quite understandably, but I couldn't help thinking in the end that it wasn't going to do them any good either. I said, 'We have to be careful that we build up the quality of the business and that quality doesn't get forgotten about, as they have to be competitive.'"

No discussion of the success of the self-employment programme can be complete without recognition of the role played by the business advisors. The Prince always makes the point that they are vital.

"I've often said that anyone could hand out money to people who can't get it from the banks and say, 'Go on, start up your own business' – but a lot of those people would collapse by the wayside very quickly. The secret of our success has been this hand-holding operation, which does make a stupendous difference. The really critical part of the whole exercise is having this network of advisors."

Typical of the sort of advisor who makes it all work is Bill Lowe. He started as an errand boy at 15. The Prince was four when Bill began his own business, a newsagent in Sutton Coldfield. Now he has a chain of ten convenience stores. So far he has mentored three new businesses past that crucial first year. Explaining why he got involved and still stays active at 68, Bill captures the spirit of thousands of other advisors:

"I'm now virtually semi-retired, so working voluntarily for the Prince's Youth Business Trust is ideal," he said. "To help these young people in the early stages of building up a business, it seemed to me it was also an ideal way I could put something back into the community. There is tremendous satisfaction to be gained from helping today's young people put their business ideas into practice and make a success of them. You share their sense of achievement and at the same time you are making a positive contribution to helping fight problems of youth unemployment."

What a Difference a Prince Makes

Has all this activity had a meaningful effect on employment in Britain? In calculating the number of jobs created, I have drawn on research at the Prince's Trust as well as on an external survey carried out in 1997 by the Department of Education and Employment. This was an audit to satisfy the DfEE that it was getting value for money from supporting the Trust. No complaints were forthcoming once the numbers were in. Out of every 100 businesses helped to get off the ground, 60 are still going three years from formation. A 1991 study by PE International came out at 67 per cent. So 60 per cent seems safe. Other points to note are that a business which survives past the first two years seems to have good prospects for longevity, and that the average business employs just over two people by its third year.

This survival rate is actually above the national average for all new businesses. So the Prince's Trust, working with people who have all been turned down elsewhere – young and inexperienced as they are – appears to beat the average on a consistent basis. And even if the business itself did not work out, almost everyone emerged more employable. Many chose to go on to jobs elsewhere, like Suzy Cooper (PYBT '94) who set up her own design company but was enticed away by a customer and is now product development executive at Compton & Woodhouse, a mail-order collectibles company. Even those who simply ground to a halt had learned new skills and done something useful. In that sense it is fair to say that the failure rate is close to zero.

About half of the 40 no longer in business have moved on to other employment or education. So the success rate for the primary objective, which is to create employment, seems to be a staggering 70 per cent! This last statistic is the hardest to verify. I contacted over 100 entrepreneurs and found several had ceased trading – but in every case the individual had a job.

Back to the tally. As we have seen, since 1982 the Youth Business Trust and predecessor organisations have started around 39,000 new businesses. Adjusting for the survival rate of 60 per cent, and average employment a shade over two per business, this translates to nearly 52,000 jobs: very big numbers. As far as I can tell the Prince's Trust is by far the largest and most successful provider of seed corn capital anywhere. In Scotland it believes it is the largest lender of unsecured finance to young people. For the most part these are new jobs.

The impact of all the Prince's programmes on helping individuals to find employment is less clear cut. Employment could be the prime goal of a programme, but equally may be an incidental benefit. That alone makes it hard to identify every beneficiary. Cause and effect may not be direct. The degree of accuracy varies, depending upon which programme comes under the microscope. We can be reasonably confident about the number at the Youth Business Trust, because that is based on tracking businesses which ceased to trade.

Residential courses and Volunteers are also monitored fairly closely, with follow-up questionnaires and surveys comprehensive enough to satisfy the most demanding statisticians. While there are no hard numbers before 1991, we now know that 12 months after completing these courses 40 per cent and 60 per cent respectively are employed. Surveys also exist for other programmes with employment objectives.

But cataloguing the impact of the Compact calls for more art than analysis. First of all, you have to decide who gets credit for what. The Prince of Wales introduced the idea and set the ball rolling, so at least success at the original schools is down to him. In 1988, the first full year, the original London Compact had 300 jobs to its credit. In north London they created a pool of 600 jobs. What followed is more complex. With the Government launching a Compact that was similar but not the same, and the Prince out there promoting the concept at every opportunity, who deserves credit for the proliferation of school/business partnerships and the jobs that resulted? Then you have a new generation of Compact Plus and Compact Plus for Jobs. School-leavers who got a job may not care, but for the purposes of this computation I am including only the original four London Compacts and one outside, which represent less than ten per cent of the national total, and recent extensions managed by the Prince's organisations.

Training has decent records, and Trust programmes are supplemented by special courses run by Business in the Community members. Urban regeneration, covered in Chapter 6, can improve unemployment rates in a local community, especially when that community has a multitude of social problems which tend to put potential employers off the area. Again, it is hard to say who should get the credit, but credit-seeking has not driven the exercise. To simplify matters I only allow for 2,000, though that is a massive understatement.

This analysis is summarised below to show the number helped into a job, as opposed to self-employment:

Grants to individuals	50,000 x 0.25	=	12,500
Training	75,000 x 0.20 + 3,125 x 0.60	=	16,900
Residential programmes	9,000 x 0.35	=	3,200
The Compacts		=	5,500
Volunteers	27,000 x 0.65 x 0.85	=	14,900
PYBT (follow-on jobs)	39,000 x 0.12	=	4,700
Urban regeneration		=	2,000
Others	3,000 x 0.20	=	600

So the number of people who seem to have found employment through the primary programmes comes to a grand total of 60,300.

This is where we wander into more contentious territory. How many of these young people would have found work anyway; and what about of the degree of displacement – how many others elsewhere have been *deprived* of jobs? But these questions miss the main point. Most of these people are those with the least prospect of any kind of career. Successful students usually get sorted sooner or later, but we are talking here about individuals who for one reason or another might never have got a job.

The accepted statistic is that about 50 per cent of the unemployed find a job within six months, but that is hardly relevant. This is the other 50 per cent, the bottom of the barrel, often people with severe attitude problems and/or skill defects. To get on Volunteers as unemployed, a person has to be out of work for over six months. If you want to be picky, perhaps only 75 per cent are truly "new" positions. From anecdotal evidence I believe the number to be higher, but even at only 75 per cent the current tally of new jobs created comes to 45,200. Whether it's 60,000 or 45,000, either way the Prince's work is worth an enormous amount to the country and to the Exchequer.

How much precisely? This employment may not be well paid, but when you start out with nothing almost anything can seem an awfully big improvement. Here is a simple calculation: economic value = taxes paid + benefits not paid x number of years.

Now to put in numbers. Taxes paid includes VAT, national insurance, income tax, business charges and a whole host of other unpleasant items which most of us do not have to deal with. My accountant suggests a typical small business with two employees generating £22,000 of gross profit before wages would face an annual tax bill of almost £4,000. Since the entrepreneurs are young, I have assumed 85 per cent are single in arriving at this sum. So £22,000 may be on the low side. A March 1997 DfEE study put the 1996 turnover of a Prince's Trust sole trader at over £20,000. In Scotland, where data are maintained with scrupulous accuracy, the average three-year-old business has a turnover of £56,000.

Benefits not paid include job seeker's allowance and housing where applicable. Over a year the total derived from DoSS tables would seem to be about £4,900 for each young jobless person. The number of years is the most subjective of these variables. This calculation will use a working life of 20. I have to pick a discount rate to get the present value of future savings. Economists use the 30-year Treasury rate. That seems fair. So seven per cent it is. Bear in mind that this calculation goes backwards as well as forwards. To adjust for that, the discount is being applied for 14 years. We're nearly there. Seven per cent gives a current value to the Exchequer for each job of £83,000, rounded to the nearest thousand.

Contrast benefit with cost. The cost has always been monitored closely. The initial 1,000 jobs required a cash outlay of around £750 each during the first half of the 1980s. There was somewhat greater selectivity in screening, and the survival rate was correspondingly higher. The cash cost in 1998 is still very low at about £1,800. With annual start-ups ten times higher, and increased emphasis on more disadvantaged young people who will have a higher failure rate, this represents a massive victory.

Based on 52,000 jobs, the Prince's Youth Business Trust has created value to the tune of £4.3 billion in today's terms, which benefits all of Britain. This computation assigns no value at all to any of the businesses, which cannot be the case – but we should not get carried away.

The economic benefit of each person placed in employment is harder to measure. Assuming mostly low paying positions and an average wage not much above the proposed minimum, say £4 per hour, or £8,300 over the year, then the annual tax take including National Insurance employer's contribution would work out to not very much at all – about £800. Benefits no longer paid does not change at £4,900. Using the same discount gives a value to these jobs of £53,000. Note that in both these calculations I assume no increase in current earnings, another conservative assumption, since most people do make more as they get older. With over 45,000 new jobs arising out of the Prince's programmes, that makes another £2.4 billion.

Bear in mind that these are first order cash numbers only. There is nothing anywhere in these calculations for the multiplier effect. My assumption that all these jobs have no other benefit to the economy is plainly another understatement of what has been achieved. I am only going to include what can be measured with some degree of confidence.

It is instructive to compare this performance with the amount the Government spends on jobs. There are two types of expenditure. The first relates to job maintenance, with subsidies to keep people employed. A recent example might be coal miners, where the annual cost to the taxpayer could run to £26,000, or 19 times the cost of a Youth Business entrepreneur. Then there is job creation, where the Government, at both national and local level, provides special initiatives to employers to hire people. Here you can find all sorts, from tax holidays to salary contributions to training allowances. Governments in Britain and elsewhere have an appalling record of paying over the odds, both to preserve positions long past their sell by date and to create completely artificial posts. In contrast, the cash cost of job creation by the Prince's Trust, at £1,800, is a fraction of the sort of sum successive governments of both political persuasions have shelled out. Clearly you have to be careful how you use these numbers. They are not absolutely accurate. But what is indisputable is that the outcome is a huge benefit for all concerned: the individual, the economy and the Exchequer.

Clearly, the single best use of employment subsidies should be to hand all the money earmarked for that purpose over to the Prince's Trust and similar organisations, and let them get on with it. This is my view and not the opinion of the Palace, but at the very least it would make sense to up the current contribution. Where else can the Treasury hope to find a 40-times return?

Not Just about Setting Up Businesses but about Changing Lives

Numbers do not mean much set beside the incalculable value of helping turn a life around. "What I want to see above all is someone being able to achieve their potential and, very often, having their life transformed," says the Prince. It's about individuals, but also about whole communities. In a 1988 interview for *Reader's Digest*, he made this point. "These people represent larger operations which will do a great deal towards providing the employment and regeneration of economic activity we badly need." He has the bigger picture in mind. New businesses should have a wider impact in their community. Seed enough and you start to rebuild whole areas.

He has also, indirectly, become one of the biggest employment agencies in the country – only there is no fee. In 1998, if all goes to plan, the Prince will mark his 50th birthday by finding work, one way or another, for a further 14,500 young people. What's more he eschews the easy targets. It was not always so. In the 1980s the goal was more general: help young people find employment one way or another. Anyone out of work was in the frame, regardless of personal abilities or resources. Over time the test has become more demanding. Now Prince Charles sets his sights on the long-term unemployed, those with the biggest problems and the fewest skills. These are the people the "system" has failed. He seeks out those most likely to fall between bureaucratic cracks, or who are so alienated that they actively avoid any contact with the formal social safety net. The failure rate may rise, but if so that is a risk he will take. He has grown accustomed to having experts tell him that what he is doing won't work.

The fact is that 52,000 young people in new businesses are all the answer he needs. Another 60,000 who found jobs underlines just how effective his programmes have been across the board in helping break the poverty cycle for the disadvantaged young in this country. That makes 112,000 lives changed for the better.

Chapter 4

COMMUNITY SERVICE

"Let's inspire young people to create better communities"

People close to Prince Charles say it would be hard to overestimate the importance to him of community service. This passion stems in part from his school days.

"At Gordonstoun there was a great accent on service to the community. It was one of Dr Hahn's best ideas ... We had different things like the fire service, a coastguard service and a mountain rescue service, and all of us had to get involved ... It taught me an awful lot and I think it did a lot for the other boys as well. More than anything else, I think it helped to develop self-confidence – not that I have that in abundant quantities, but it made one feel one was actually somebody who could contribute something.

"Based purely on my own experience, which I think is the only thing I can go on, I greatly appreciate what my particular experience of service to the community as a coastguard, when I was at school, did for me ... A lot of us when we're in our teens and that difficult transition from boyhood to manhood, very often need to be given a sense of self-discovery and self-confidence which can lead to so many other worthwhile things later in life. I also felt that, and I'm speaking again from my own experience in a way, this sort of activity – of coming together, working as a team and getting involved in effective projects and so on – is enormously beneficial in terms of developing self-confidence and a good approach to life."[1]

The Prince found his belief confirmed by experiences at sea. "When I was in the Navy I came across people who I always felt could face life much more enthusiastically, perhaps, if they were given a chance to develop self-confidence and self-esteem, to realise there were people worse off, sometimes, than themselves and by giving service, particularly within a team situation."

[1] The Prince's Volunteers, LWT, 25 April 1990.

The Prince has a sense of duty which is almost spiritual. Speaking to the Cambridge Union in November 1978, he talked about the concept of a nation of individuals "modelled on the example set by the greatest expression of an individual life in service in Palestine some 2,000 years ago. This example … challenged the human being to recognise that he had within himself a personal obligation towards the life of his time which was peculiarly his own and in the service of which he found a meaning that made his life, no matter how hard or cruel, more than worthwhile."

There were echoes here of remarks he had made in a 1975 speech to the House of Lords. "Voluntary service is an essential element in any society that calls itself civilised. It is, in many ways, a measure of people's concern for each other as human beings, and the only way in which concern, compassion, a sense of duty or service can be properly expressed."[2]

On a more prosaic plain, when young people perform community service it should be enlightened self-interest. They benefit and the community benefits. "There is so much to contribute to. So much that needs doing, so many people that need helping and so much service that could be given … By bringing young people face to face with the community, with their peers and above all with themselves, we are helping to create a more cohesive, tolerant and, hopefully, more understanding society."

This last point goes to the heart of his belief that community service can bring people together. As he said in 1996, "the Trust's Volunteers are having enormous success helping all the participants realise … that everyone, employed and unemployed, is part of the same society". Young people who mingle with others of similar age but from a different background usually emerge more understanding, more tolerant, more self-confident and more capable of being a solid citizen. Often it is the toughest nuts who change most. "So often you would find at Gordonstoun that the most difficult and unco-operative of boys underwent an astonishing transformation, subordinating any selfish attitudes to the overall requirements of the team."[3]

In serving others, we serve ourselves

In 1977 the Prince of Wales launched the Queen's Silver Jubilee Appeal: "The purpose of this appeal is to encourage service, adventurous or otherwise, by young people to the community in which they live. The Queen has specifically asked that the money contributed will be used 'to help young people help others'." A liaison

2 House of Lords, 25 June 1975.

3 House of Lords, 25 June 1975.

committee was set up in 1978, (a) to ask industry and commerce to consider how young people in employment might be more strongly encouraged to interest themselves in voluntary services; and (b) to consider whether industry can be mobilised to help the less advantaged young (including the unemployed) by enabling them to become involved in adventures and challenging opportunities through community commitment.

Research into how to attract employed young people began in York and Swindon in 1979. Pilot projects were run in conjunction with Community Service Volunteers. The end result was a report, 'Young Volunteers from Industry', whose findings were to re-emerge in the structure of the Prince's first community service teams.

By the early 1980s community service was the largest beneficiary of the Jubilee Trusts. Grants for community work remain important. About 30 per cent of funding is set aside for such projects.

The Prince was not satisfied doing things at one remove. Regardless of opposition, he wanted to try out new ideas directly. He was itching to have a go himself, in part because he felt that no existing organisation offered what young people really wanted.

In June 1975 he had called on the Government to promote voluntary service. "The Government has a duty to ensure that as many people as possible are able to offer themselves for voluntary service in a wide range of fields – if necessary making helpful concessions (financial or otherwise) in order to enable organisations to continue to provide a valuable service to the community – both morally and physically."[4]

Ten years later, both Labour and Conservative administrations had ducked the issue, which left the field wide open. Prince Charles had a clear idea of what he wanted to achieve when he piloted the first Prince of Wales Community Venture in September 1985. Where he was less sure was whether the particular programme he had devised along with George Thurston, director of the Drake Fellowship, would do the trick. There was a risk that the whole thing could go horribly wrong since it had been cobbled together in typical fashion under cover of the Drake. But he was determined to take personal ownership. This was his venture, and he left no-one in any doubt about why he wanted to develop the programme.

"We should all have the opportunity at one stage in our lives to give service to our country … It is vital that we find ways in which people from all walks of life and backgrounds can operate together."

A typical team could consist of three people in work, someone in the year between school and university, a disabled person, possibly someone who suffered

4 House of Lords, 25 June 1975.

from epilepsy, a young offender on probation and half a dozen unemployed young people who may have mustered six GCSEs between them. In all likelihood they would never have worked in a team before, were short on self-confidence and, come day one, wondered why they were there.

An unconventional approach was needed to keep participants stimulated: a blend of physical and mental activities, and constant new challenges. Community Venture came close to the perfect package. There was personal supervision over a long period, combined with intensive activity. Participants completed community service, both in small groups and individually. A ten-week period of outdoor pursuits led to a spell at the emergency services, three work-experience placements and help in job application techniques. Venturers were 'adopted' by a local business, with mentors who helped prepare them for work. It is hard to imagine any programme better balanced or more comprehensive.

The aims of the new programme were clear and concise: to motivate young people who want to give service, to train them to do so, to provide opportunities, and then to give them personal guidance and training throughout the programme.

But the Prince's ambitions went further. "If you can fire their interest and enthusiasm, for whatever type of service may appeal to their interests and talents, then you will have laid not only the cornerstones of the Community Venture but also the foundations of a much wider form of service – for who knows what interests their own enthusiasm may in turn awaken amongst families and friends within the community."

The aims were clear but implementation was not easy. Every organisation in the Prince's ambit was roped in. A secondee at the Trust provided administrative back-up. Business in the Community helped in the planning, and with business contacts. The Jubilee Trusts put their hands in their pockets. Then came the hard part: how and where to go public. Sunderland got the nod, largely through the efforts of Jim Gardner, who had excellent contacts in government and industry and was able to rally resources. It helped when councillor Baxter made the Community Venture his favoured charity for his year as mayor.

Sunderland was on his side, but wider enthusiasm was in shorter supply. The Prince was used to this. Scepticism not only came from 'experts' and officials but there was also suspicion from the constituency which really mattered to him – the young people he hoped to reach.

"The difficulty is, of course, to persuade people that this is something worth volunteering for, because so often I find that you don't want to do things when you're at that age ... It seems a pretty silly idea until you actually do it, and then you find that it's better than you thought it would be."[5]

5 The Prince's Volunteers, LWT, 25 April 1990.

The first project was to clean up the seashore at Seaburn. Then the team went on to Maiden Castle for conservation work. Tasks became more varied, with assignments in homes for the disabled and elderly. Three years into the experiment, Community Ventures showed good results despite some pretty unpromising material. Nearly everyone who went the distance found full-time work. Prince Charles asked for an external appraisal by the independent Economic and Social Research Council. "I then suggested that we ought to have this pilot scheme written up and examined by outsiders, to see whether it actually had any relevance or was worthwhile and was not just duplicating what everybody else was doing."

This was a risky business, as Tom Shebbeare pointed out in a 1988 interview with the *Observer*. "It was asking an outside government-sponsored, but objective, body to come in and see whether he had designed it right."

The risk paid off. Research carried out by Martin Shipman, professor of education at the University of Surrey, concluded that "inside and outside the Venturers, those interviewed were convinced that this was a simple idea with a powerful impact. Venturers were developing as persons, while serving their communities." Venturers came out much more self-confident, better able to work as a team and so more employable. As a bonus they were also more aware of the needs of others and more prepared to help. Anyone tempted to dismiss this assessment as cheer-leading need only look at the numbers. Of the first 137 to finish during the initial two years, 94 found jobs.

Almost all attributed this to the course. Venturing showed potential employers that an individual had not just stayed home and watched TV. People emerged more positive, and made a much better impression at an interview. Now more than 137 volunteers graduate every week, and the success rate in finding work is still over 50 per cent.

Not everyone was impressed. Unions were suspicious of the Prince's intentions. Rodney Bickerstaffe of the National Union of Public Employees feared that Venturers could substitute for existing jobs. Even a private lunch could not bring him round. Although he could not win over everyone, Prince Charles had a convincing case. Four pilots with very different characteristics confirmed its worth in Sunderland, Birmingham, Llanelli and Pembroke.

Some early graduates were profiled in a report commissioned by the Trust and written by Chris Lightbown of the *Sunday Times*. Greg Vaddey (Venturer '88) had a troubled background, as Lightbown's notes reveal. "Hated school. Hit his PE teacher. Locked elderly teacher, allergic to oranges, into cupboard stacked with oranges. Unemployed for two years. Hung around amusement arcades, getting money from old ladies for helping them on machines. Constant niggles with police. From mining family. Uncle first man in County Durham to be arrested in miners' strike. Father flying picket. All strongly anti-police. When badly hurt in pub fight, gave police vague description of assailant. Amazed when police managed to trace man. (He got nine months.) So impressed by police success after pub incident, asked to do Venture placement with them. Father stopped talking to him. When police car picked him up in the morning, neighbours assumed he was being arrested. Biggest surprise: 'The police talk about normal things – where did you go last night, how much did you drink?' Told police how to talk to offenders. 'You start with the hard lads first, then the others have got to talk to you.' Father so impressed with new self-discipline, has begun talking to him again. Standard question: 'Seen any of your mates arrested today?'"

If the Community Venture was the Rolls Royce of programmes, there was as we have seen one drawback: it was very expensive. The time was right to step up several gears, but any meaningful acceleration was too costly to contemplate. The Prince asked Shebbeare to devise a programme which could cope with 100,000 young people a year by 2001, and give each person a meaningful community service experience. No small task.

A team was formed co-ordinated by Hilary Omissi, seconded from the Department of Employment. She soon realised that one – perhaps the main – reason for the Venture's success was the people, like Vivienne Bowen-Morgan and Dave Parker, who ran the local teams. That the young people realised there are always people less fortunate than yourself also helped. When a drug addict from a slum area got to work with mentally retarded children, this realisation could cause a material change. But Ventures had flaws. There was the length: nearly 40 per cent failed to finish. Employed people were put off. Finding top team leaders to do 43 weeks was difficult. Potential employers want to see evidence of achievement, and the composition of the new course had to reflect that. Some formal qualification was needed.

In January 1990 Prince Charles met his key advisors at Sandringham to decide on the future shape of the project. Present were Sir John Cassells, David Baker from the advertising agency J. Walter Thompson, Frances Morrell, Sir Richard O'Brien, Hilary Omissi, Sir John Riddell and Tom Shebbeare. He waa in broad agreement with the draft plan, but he asked a large number of questions and concluded that the goal was too ambitious. So the target was trimmed to a pilot of 10,000. He wanted environmental and social projects to have equal status. He also hoped that the ultimate structure would enable young people to tap the experience of retired people as mentors or project advisors. Much of the discussion revolved around how to brand the new programme. The name on which all agreed was simply the Prince's Trust Volunteers.

Once he had given the green light, Prince Charles was insistent that they should solicit as much feedback as possible before the final version was unveiled. Such a quantum leap in his community service programme would put his credibility and that of the Trust on the line. There was even anxiety in the family about possible overlap with the Duke of Edinburgh's Award Scheme. Five hundred copies of a consultation document were distributed to voluntary organisations, government departments and politicians.

Omissi went through the proposals with the Duke of Edinburgh's Award people in person. The Commission on Citizenship was canvassed, as was the Shadow Employment Secretary, one Tony Blair, and John Monks of the TUC. Margaret Thatcher was kept informed by the Prince in person. The only slightly sour note came from voluntary groups concerned that their budgets could suffer, submerged in a tidal wave of Prince's Volunteers. Elizabeth Hoodless, head of Community Service Volunteers, became the focal point of these concerns; particularly since CSV and Volunteers seemed to some to be as alike as two peas. They were missing a key distinction. The Prince was after the young people least likely to volunteer. In the end there was a sort of fudge about focus, which left honour intact. The emphasis at Volunteers on the most disadvantaged was accepted as a sufficient point of difference.

Meanwhile, the Prince went to work on his launch speech, recognising its importance. He was taking no chances: right down to sending a draft to Sir Jimmy Savile for comment. Savile wrote back a lengthy letter suggesting changes in style and tone. He thought the Prince should make the point that Volunteers was not "'just a good idea I've had over breakfast,' but 'something where I've had months of consultation'" – which has not always been the perception of the Prince and how he operates. The other question was how to make Volunteers more attractive to young people. Savile wrote that "to make the scheme more fashionable and glamorous, something to put on the wall in a frame is always acceptable to the majority of young people". So a special Prince of Wales certificate for those who completed the course was duly incorporated.

In introducing his new initiative Prince Charles emphasised several aspects which were of fundamental importance to him. "Volunteers is not a new organisation but a way of enabling young people to join a team and, with their peers, undertake an intensive period of voluntary work – challenging themselves and helping others in their community. To succeed, this initiative will need to involve a great variety of individuals and organisations from all sections of our society – especially the young. So it must appeal to their enthusiasm, idealism, sense of fun and adventure."

When Volunteers was officially launched on 25 April 1990, Michael Aspel said: "Fifty years after the Battle of Britain, the Prince is looking for volunteers for what he regards as the Battle for Britain."[6] Volunteers was welcomed by a broad cross-section of society; perhaps the first occasion on which the Prince was not on the receiving end of a barrage of criticism for sounding off on a social issue.

This was encouraging, since on previous occasions the reaction to comments he had made about community service had, in his own words, "received a gigantic raspberry, which you could hear echoing from one end of the land to another".[7] As he said only the other day, "you can easily criticise any of these sorts of ideas if you want to be negative. I've always seen it as a positive way of trying to enable more people to discover their own abilities and talents, which so often don't come out in school." He also used the launch to give the most complete exposition as to why he felt so strongly about community service:

"I was a volunteer myself at school. It was felt that this was good for your character and development ... that it took you out of yourself and gave you a challenge. I was young when I started – 12 or 13 – and felt enthusiastic about it from the beginning: anything to get out of the classroom!

"The point about being a coastguard was that it was adventurous and exciting. We went out on rough, stormy nights to watch from the lookout tower on the cliffs overlooking the Moray Firth. Everything was up to you. Here we were, schoolboys, entirely responsible for the safety of ships passing that piece of coast. What more could you want? We had to stay there, fill out the log and, of course, we were trained in what to do – how to fire Verey lights, work a breeches buoy and get in touch with the ships at sea. It gave you a sense of responsibility and you were going solo, so to speak, drawing on yourself and your own resources.

"The man who founded the school I went to, Kurt Hahn, believed that adventure and service should be combined 'to make the brave gentle, and the gentle brave'. There is a basic instinct in young people to get out and use their energy and aggression. But it is also very important to offer the chance to help people in need because that can often provide young people who are apparently tough with the opportunity to discover and test themselves in a different way. On the Community Venture many of these 'tough characters' have found that they are good at work with handicapped children or with elderly people.

"For those young people who are less outgoing than others, to be challenged as an individual within a team is enormously beneficial as a way of gaining confidence and it is useful for the outgoing ones, too, in that it gives them a chance to try gentler occupations. Very often the young people who are most aggressive and

6 The Prince's Volunteers, LWT, 25 April 1990.

7 Address accompanying the release of the Prince's Trust 1989 annual report at Livingstone, 4 September 1989.

anti-social are the ones who lack self-confidence but who have the most energy to turn into something constructive, if they are given the opportunity. They may suddenly find they have talents in areas they have not realised; leadership talents, for example, and the ability to organise and encourage other people.

"I believe very strongly that there are not enough means in this country by which people from all walks of life and from all backgrounds can work together for a common purpose; for their own country. Without such means there tends to be polarisation between different groups. I believe that there should be means by which people can come together and find out about each other and do something constructive for their country. So I would like to see as many young people as possible having the chance to work together as volunteers, even if it is only for a short period; for 12 or 18 weeks of their lives. I hope it will be something on which they will look back as having made a difference, both to themselves and to their communities."

This was the challenge that Elizabeth Crowther-Hunt inherited. The launch had gone off all guns blazing on the back of success at the Community Venture. But there was no staff, and no support structure on which to hang anything. Starting from scratch, a field organisation had to be found. Given the proposed scale, the immediate requirement was to lock in voluntary help at the local level, so resources from the centre could be conserved. The solution was a franchise model, with existing organisations becoming local franchisees and receiving a small amount of seed funding. Local partners could be anything: voluntary organisations, government agencies, companies or schools.

The programme was a stripped-down version of Ventures, which included the bare minimum of the residential, and most expensive, element with community service carried out in the local area. A typical 60-day programme is mapped out in Appendix 3. The team approach, and the goal to complete a project which the team itself would identify as being of benefit to its community, and for which it would find all required resources, remained intact. The aim was more modest and the transition into employment at the end less certain than in the much longer and more intense experience which had characterised the Community Venture; but there was no question that the new format did its main job.

Fund-raising can be unusual. Try tugging a Jaguar jet 100 metres down the runway of RAF Cottishall, which raised £600 to build an obstacle course in a children's playground, or cleaning a double decker bus with a toothbrush, or being locked in a theatre said to be haunted by 18 ghosts.

Why does the programme achieve such good results? Like a good recipe, it is a matter of the right blend and proportions. A bit of team building, something outdoors, a mix of work, problem solving and a project, topped off with certificates and awards. The week away, the sharing and caring, the dedication of a team leader and the emphasis on taking personal responsibility. Perhaps most of all, the trust and belief in each individual to contribute. For the overwhelming majority it is an experience which changes lives.

Rob Carr (Venturer '85) was unemployed, bored and just sitting around at home when he decided to give it a go. "I worked with the police at Gill Bridge and also with the Tyne and Wear fire brigade ... It was while doing this that I realised I'd like to do this kind of work." So much so that Rob is still doing it – at Fulwell fire station in Sunderland. He found his niche in life, something he does so well that last year he got a commendation for bravery.

Then there is Nicola Quigley (Venturer '85), who had been unemployed for about a year. "I was unable to find a job. I was in the depths of depression." These days she is a trainer in customer services for BT, who poached her from the course mid-way, starting her as a clerical assistant. Several promotions later she is a 12-year veteran.

Coming right up to date, there is Michael Anderson (Volunteer '97), whose history proves the course can work even for people with serious problems. Michael had made a mess of his life by the time he drifted into the Darlington programme, a recovering heroin addict with a record. His father died when he was young, he and his mum had a bust up, and Michael moved on. He left school without qualifications. All in all Michael was an easy mark. The heroin took hold when he was living on a housing estate in Barnsley, an area notorious for criminals and addicts. To feed his habit he started out stealing car stereos and then graduated to cars. Then Michael began to sell the stuff himself.

By the time the police caught up with him, Michael was facing no less than nine court charges for possession of heroin, as well as multiple charges for theft and shoplifting, and with driving a car without insurance thrown in for good measure. As a first offender he got off with probation and a community service order. But Michael was soon up to his old tricks, breaking into garden sheds. "In my mind, it wasn't as bad as burgling houses."

Second time around he was sentenced to six months, but got a reprieve to allow him one last shot at salvaging himself. Michael moved into a homeless shelter and went cold turkey. He was still there, attempting to kick drugs, when he started with the Volunteers.

Michael says the Prince's Trust has been critical in his rehabilitation. "It was the first course I ever started and finished. Before going I had no direction. Now I've got much more confidence and I'm getting myself together. I'm thinking maybe of being an outward bound instructor." He hopes to use his experience to help others avoid making the same mistakes.

Michael is still a long way from being out of the woods. He has yet to find paid employment, and is still living at a hostel. But he has made real progress in setting himself straight: no more drugs, no more crime and some serious thinking about his future. Michael now has a conditional discharge and recently won an award from an adult learning centre. This is a million miles away from where he was two years ago.

Community Service and the Community are Intertwined

Performing community service is a sort of apprenticeship for the model citizen, a rite of passage into adulthood. "I think that there are similarities for all of us in the sense of the problems we face at certain ages. We go through phases in our lives and it is interesting to see how so-called primitive societies always mark those phases in a ritual way. Modern societies no longer do that, which is a pity. We need, I believe, the contemporary equivalents of initiation rituals to mark the passage from childhood to adulthood."[8]

Community service takes Volunteers all over the shop, from renovating crofters' cottages in the outer Hebrides to helping in soup kitchens in inner city Birmingham. In Wales, community service work has always had a strong environmental slant. A few completed schemes show what gets done:

- building wheelchair ramps and gardens at the Neuromuscular Centre in Chester;
- refurbishing a clothing store for the WRVS;
- pond balancing at the Slimbridge Wildlife and Wetlands Trust;
- caring for guests on holiday at Winged Fellowship Holiday Homes;
- staging a 'Cockney Carnival' for members of Age Concern.

Some schemes come in handy sooner than expected. During 1993, a team from Barrowfield, Glasgow, fitted smoke detectors in homes and gave advice to residents on fire prevention. Only a week later a fire started in a chip pan at one of the homes, but thanks to the new alarm the family were alerted early enough to deal with the fire, and damage was minimal.

Through schemes like these Volunteers build links to the community. Individuals, on their own or as part of a team, focus on a manageable project at the local level where they can see that they have achieved something and may even enjoy the fruits of their own labours. Llanelli may be the model for what the Prince would like to see happen everywhere. Nowhere else has a whole community come together so completely, to work in a co-operative way on projects that improve the

[8] Launch of Volunteers, 25 April 1990.

local quality of life. Community service could be said to be embedded in the culture. Housed in the basement of the town hall, the Llanelli Centre is led by Vivienne Bowen-Morgan.

What has happened at Llanelli over the past ten years is extraordinarily impressive:

- 1,380 Volunteers have graduated from the Llanelli Centre;
- 130 environmental projects have been completed;
- 160 new businesses employing 300 people have been started;
- 170 young people have created their own employment, thanks to the Foothold Youth Enterprise Agency and Business in the Community;
- 59 young people have been to residential courses at Caister and Ayr;
- 102 small grants have been given out, totalling nearly £20,000.

... and all in a town with a catchment area of only 60,000 people. Assume an average family of four, and over 13 per cent of the total population has come into contact with the Prince of Wales's activities. Completed projects, such as converting an outside toilet block into a library, and creating a butterfly garden at Pentip Junior School, improve the quality of life for everyone in Llanelli. Former mayor, Sefton Coslett, said: "they have become part of the life of Llanelli. This value to our community has been immense. They have always brought great credit and distinction to our Borough."

Everyone's a Winner

One measure of success is the proliferation of activity. There were six Community Ventures in existence when Prince Charles started Volunteers. Only 80 enrolled in 1990. As of April 1998, there were 213 active locations. Over 7,000 young people have completed community service projects during the past 12 months. The target for 1998 is 9,000.

At the launch Tom Shebbeare said: "One of the ways which we must judge success is whether this initiative effectively brings much larger numbers of people into a field in which they never believed they could make a contribution. If we're just recycling people who volunteered in one way to volunteering with our scheme, that will not have achieved anything. What we hope to do is to involve much greater numbers and, after all, those in the age group 16 to 24 are the least likely, statistically, to volunteer to do anything."

In June 1996 the Prince invited Mary Robinson, at the time President of Ireland and now Commissioner for Human Rights at the United Nations, to join him for a special celebration for the Volunteers at St James' Palace. Three other political figures also chose to put in an appearance: John Major, then Prime Minister, Tony

Blair, leader of the opposition, and Paddy Ashdown, leader of the Liberal Democrats.

John Major: "The motto of the Prince of Wales is Ich Dien – I serve, and at the heart of all volunteering is the concept of service … The Prince's Trust Volunteers do much for their communities … But they also do something for themselves."

Tony Blair: "I am pleased to celebrate its achievements in developing the skills and self-esteem of our young people – employed and unemployed – through voluntary service in the community."

Paddy Ashdown: "The programme has an impressive track record and I strongly support its expansion plans. Initiatives like the Prince's Trust Volunteers have cross-party backing because they make such good sense."

So it's unanimous. The Prince of Wales has a model that works, and everyone across the political spectrum accepts its validity. Once again, as with the Youth Business Trust in 1987, Prince Charles has support from every major political leader in the country. Proponents of community service like Prince Charles had long been derided as old fogies, trying to revive a concept whose worth had passed. But the concept now seems to command new respect, as government starts to take it seriously.

The influence of Volunteers on the New Deal has been profound. Its intensity to start with. One-on-one assignment for the entire experience for another. The New Deal appears to be the very first time that someone on a government programme can be sure that they will start and finish with the same person as their point of contact. The central role of the mentoring is a third legacy. Volunteers is an official sub-contractor, already administering 200 young people in July 1998, with expectations of managing thousands next year.

There is one element in the entire equation which remains controversial. Should community service be compulsory? The Prince thinks so. During an interview with Jonathan Dimbleby, he said: "We had been the only country in Europe which abandoned National Service and I felt that some form of national service is something which can be of enormous benefit in providing people with at least some sort of basis in life, and also a chance to meet people from all sorts of backgrounds at one point in their life, while doing something for the country. It does not have to be military service. I felt that what was a real worry in this country was that so many people were becoming polarised and ghettoised to different social groups. There was no cohesion of any kind. I have always felt that that's a problem for a nation if there isn't any sense of cohesion."

He knows this is not a popular point of view. "I remember once standing up and making a speech about this and getting, 'Yah, boo! Shut up! Don't be so bloody stupid,' all the usual stuff. I have never forgotten it. I have had endless arguments with my Trust about it. I still believe that it should be compulsory. I still believe that there should be national community service. There should be options, but even a three-month stint would be better than nothing.

"I can see from what happens with the Volunteers. It has proved the point. We have a 70 per cent success rate in terms of people whose whole lives have been turned round by somebody seeing that they can do something in life for other people, very often through working with disabled or handicapped young people and discovering a talent that they did not know they had. But they would never, ever have if they hadn't taken part in this scheme ... As several Volunteers have told me over the years, the only fault with the programme is that it isn't compulsory for everyone!" The Prince is in the minority for now.

Perhaps the most pleasing statistic comes from the evaluation every person gives on completion, in which attitudes to voluntary work score highly. A total of 82 per cent stated they felt more inclined to do voluntary work in the future, owing to their experience. Follow-up surveys show that 50 per cent continue with some form of community service. Since most had other priorities when they began, such as getting some qualification or finding a job, the high percentage converted to the cause is testimony to the effectiveness of Volunteers.

More Than One Way to Serve

Ventures and Volunteers were custom-built courses with community service as their raison d'être. The Prince hopes other parts of his organisations will be sensitive to the same issues. At the Prince's Trust businesses are encouraged to consider community issues and get involved. To promote participation a special prize will be awarded for the first time this year. The Best Contribution to the Local Community Award recognises Trust businesses who also give something back to the community.

The Trust can also contribute by backing the right sort of business: one which combines benefits to the community with economic returns to the entrepreneur: businesses like CAM Rider Training, run by Bernard Adams (PYBT '92). Adams had been made redundant, and was filling in time by volunteering at a motorcycle training centre. The centre was run, rather badly, by Cambridge City Council; so badly in fact, that it was losing around £80,000 and the council decided to shut it down.

Adams did not want to see the centre close, so he offered to take charge. Financial backing was needed to tide him over, but a loss-making proposition presented by a 24-year-old with no experience received the thumbs down from local banks. Adams decided to try the Prince's Trust as a last resort. The maximum amount was his in a matter of days. Then the struggle started. Adams had to cut costs to the bone, converting his garage to an office. The first few months were hairy, with only three paying customers a week, but he hung on and survived. Six years later CAM Rider averages 65 clients a week. The company is flourishing, with 14 full-time and 36 part-time staff.

Adams attributes his success to a decision not to compromise on quality and to focus on road safety as the selling point rather than price. He limited class size to four, and only operated with fully qualified instructors. Strange as this may seem, for anything except compulsory basic training neither of these restrictions is required by law. So any cowboy can enter this business. Adams also guaranteed training until you pass. When people complete his course, they can handle their machines properly.

This approach has made such an impression that Cambridgeshire chose CAM Rider to run a Drivesafe programme. Motorcyclists charged with driving offences may be sent to retraining in lieu of a penalty. Adams hopes to extend this option to other areas. He has also campaigned for more control over trainers, and was behind 1994 legislation which limited class size for basic 125cc instruction. No surprise that CAM Rider won the 1996 tenth anniversary award from the Prince's Trust, which Prince Charles personally presented to Adams. The resulting publicity boosted bookings, as association with the Trust and the structure of the programme both attracted favourable attention. Running CAM Rider along lines which were good for the community turned out to be good for the company.

Anyone Can Have a Go

Community service need not be restricted to young people. Business in the Community is a catalyst for encouraging business in Britain to contribute to community activities. Of the 100 largest public companies, 81 now have some involvement, along with most government departments. This number has been rising every year since records have been kept. Member companies have nearly 4,300,000 employees. It is estimated that around 300,000, or seven per cent, volunteer each year. Much of this activity has been stimulated by Business in the Community, which directly brokered close to 27,000 person days of volunteer service in 1997.

The Prince of Wales has used Business in the Community as his prime entry point to access corporate UK and involve it in his vision. Businesses can play a vital role. Individual companies can facilitate projects providing resources – money, materials, equipment and supplies that may be surplus to commercial requirements. They are also a route to employee volunteers. Community service is important not just for individuals. It is also, thinks the Prince, an essential element in the make-up of responsible corporations.

"Leading edge companies are beginning to recognise this fact, and to view their employees not just as workers but as individuals with something to contribute and as members of the community. More broadly, more and more companies recognise that what happens to business matters to the rest of society and that what happens to society matters to business."[9]

The initial contact for many comes when the Prince of Wales invites a member of top management to a 'Seeing is Believing' visit. These evolved out of the Halifax urban regeneration, which confirmed his suspicion that the best and possibly the only way to co-opt busy people whose priorities lay elsewhere was to confront them directly with a social problem.

In 1990 Business in the Community formalised a programme where Prince Charles would go walkabout in the company of a dozen or so senior executives. Latterly he rarely goes into the field, but receives reports from groups at follow-up meetings. There can be complications when he is part of Seeing is Believing. As one business leader put it, "When the Prince arrives, everything else stops. All eyes are on him, so the real purpose of the meeting gets shoved to the side. Then every local dignitary wants to show up to shake his hand. It can all become a bit of a circus." The revised arrangement tends to be more effective in galvanising business into a more active role in the community.

Volunteers are the Spice of Life

If you really want to win the respect of the Prince, the short cut is to volunteer. He has spoken frequently and eloquently on the merits of the volunteer. In July 1994 when addressing the TEC conference, he said, "I never forget that you are volunteers which, to me, is the remarkable thing about you – and one of your greatest strengths". If Prince Charles were to rank society, the upper echelon would be made up of volunteers who give part of their time to serve their community. No-one would argue against the proposition that volunteers are more enthusiastic, but to equate enthusiasm with effectiveness may be a leap of logic too far. This caveat notwithstanding, the Prince has a point. Professionals climb mountains, but volunteers have been known to move them.

A fresh opportunity opened up with the conjunction of lottery money and millennium activities. The Prince has endorsed a special programme administered by the Prince's Trust which gives grants to young people for community service projects.

And here we go again with the Millennium Volunteers, just announced by the Government, which bears a striking resemblance to the Prince's Trust – Volunteers,

[9] TEC Conference, Birmingham, 14 July 1994.

16 to 25-year-olds, "attracting young people from a wide variety of backgrounds …
experiencing what it is like to be part of a team … themselves identifying and
developing their own projects … with the opportunity for learning and personal
development … and receiving a certificate on completion." Prince Charles is on to
a good thing; and his reception now is 180 degrees from a raspberry all round, with
adoption of his approach by the government of the day.

Community Service Creates Value

Volunteers seems to have a positive effect on almost any individual who sees it
through. The Prince of Wales is constantly making this point – especially to
employers. "Just try one" was his constant refrain to sceptical companies, confident
that once one went more would follow. Community service cuts both ways.
Employees should return with enhanced personal skills and be more effective at
their work.

Employers confirm the course can make a difference. Martin Gray, chief
executive of NatWest UK, is a believer. He has seen 150 young employees go
through Volunteers. "I feel sure that people who have been on the programme will
have a greater appeal to employers than those who have not. They come back with
a better understanding, more tolerance and a greater sensitivity, better developed
and with more skills."

Sir Paul Condon also sees both sides. Under his guidance the police became a
significant source of team leaders, a role which exposes them to the challenges that
many young people face and – at the same time – gives hard cases a new look at
the police. "It shows them the human side to policing and their commitment to
society."

Fred Marks from KPMG Peat Marwick stresses a slightly different angle: "The
programme offers us a unique opportunity to be able to give something back to
the area in which we work."[10]

According to Michael Bichard, former chief executive of the Benefits Agency,
"This wasn't just one of those schemes where it was good to put something back
into the community. It had tangible benefits for us as an employer. We were getting
more benefit from the PTV programmes than from sending them on traditional
civil service training. They were coming back with more confidence, better
communication skills and showing more leadership skills. In that environment you
learn to take responsibility, not to pass it."

Bichard likes Volunteers because it brings the unemployed and employed
together in a team, and forms a contact which would be unthinkable in normal

[10] *Evening Standard*, 26 March 1996.

circumstances. The Benefits Agency started off in 1992 with a couple of people to test the concept. Now over 750 have participated, and they have done so in such large numbers because Volunteers works for them and is a quality experience.

That benefits are not confined to boosting the unemployed is a big plus; but the main focal point has to be the disadvantaged young who want to use the course to get their life back on track. Any improvement is a victory.

"I feel strongly that if you're going to try and bring long-term unemployed people back into work, it's going to be very, very difficult to expect people suddenly to get into work and hold a job down. Many of the Volunteers admit to me that just the business of getting up out of bed in the morning is half the problem. So I believe the answer is going through, first of all, a character building, confidence building process which brings people back into the basic framework of life again. I don't know how you suddenly switch. Many of these people are terribly damaged. They may be on drugs and goodness knows what else."

It is hard to measure the value of enhanced skills to society, though anecdotes abound of people who got promoted shortly after returning. Helen O'Neill (Volunteer '93), went out as assistant manager of a pub and came back to a promotion to full licensee. Paul Workman, of Mitchells and Butlers Taverns, explained. "Her achievement in coming through the tough Prince's Trust Volunteers course has served to underline that she had the right qualities for the job."

Volunteers has been keeping tabs on its graduates almost since inception, so there are now seven years of data, although the information is not complete. The 1996 Mori survey provides independent confirmation. Follow-up reports found that 80 per cent of unemployed team members were working or had gone on to further education or training. Of those unemployed at the start, over 50 per cent were in work 12 months on. Many credit this transformation to the communication and other skills acquired as a Volunteer.

The cost benefit equation is also instructive. The cost side is relatively easy to nail down. The outlay for each young person was around £1,000 in 1997, so the cash cost per person put back to work is less than £2,000. Assuming an estimated annual value of these jobs to the Exchequer of £5,700, the pay back period is a mere four months.

We should not lose track of the second store of value created. Communities also benefit.

"The Spastics Society festival of sport could not be run without a large number of Volunteers, so I am especially grateful to them all." *Cathy Lowe, event organiser*.

"Volunteers are extremely important, we couldn't run the sessions without the voluntary help." *Sheila Hynes, Estherow Riding for the Disabled Centre*.

"If it had not been for them, we would have closed down. They did lots of fund-raising to buy new toys for us, and provided the best Christmas party we've ever had." *Jane Darby, organiser, mother and toddler group, Middlewood, Sheffield.*

The diversity of projects makes any assessment a massive challenge. What is a new footpath worth? What is the value of converting a rubbish dump into a playground? How much should be assigned to a mobile library for remote rural areas, or replacing crude graffiti in the garage of a tower block with pleasing murals or making a woodland area accessible to people in wheelchairs?

One approach is to use a baseline wage rate and apply that figure to the number of full-time equivalent weeks of work spent at a project site (normally nine). The equation is pretty simple: total participants (1990–98) x average productive hours x hourly rate = value.

For Volunteers, that translates to 31,761 x 205 x £4 for participants and 3,894 x 360 x £20 for team leaders. So around £54 million. The build-up is rapid. Based on this methodology, 1999 should add a further £20 million.

It is possible to calculate for 1997, and then extrapolate backwards across all the organisations to get a grand total. Everyone who works for free counts. Team leaders running Recharge perform a variety of community service, as do business advisors and mentors in schools. For the sake of simplicity, I am only going to cover the largest concentrations of voluntary helpers. Apply the same formula, and for 1997 alone time in kind was £43 million.

Value of free hours for 1997
(£ million)

1.	Business advisors	7,089 x 42 x £80	23.8
2.	Volunteer team leaders	1,280 x 360 x £20	9.2
3.	School mentors	3,500 x 39 x £30	4.1
4.	The Professional Partnership		2.0
5.	Grant committees	1,586 x 12 x £50	1.0
6.	Seeing is Believing	180 x 6 x £200	0.6
7.	BITC other		1.0
8.	All other, (Disability Forum, Threshold, Residential)		1.0

A certain amount of guesstimation is called for. I shall not bore you with the back-up, but go straight to the bottom line. Through his programmes over the past ten years the Prince of Wales has marshalled volunteers whose combined efforts must aggregate well over £300 million.

To the value of voluntary work should be added some allowance for gifts in kind, materials for building, computer equipment for schools, even food distributed to the homeless. This would add up to tens of million more. Prince Charles does not think of community service in these terms. For him it is the contribution to the community and the impact on the individual which matters most. "One of the factors of overriding importance is that voluntary service is as beneficial to the volunteer as one hopes it is to the recipients of that service. To be frank it is quite simply 'good for the soul'."[11]

How does the Prince himself measure the success of community service programmes? "There's a difference in outlook, attitude and their whole approach to life. That's the great thing for me. Just to enable one person to develop as a rounded human being who may not have had the chance to do so in the past." The ultimate evaluation has to come from Volunteers.

"My tolerance has improved and I'm more confident talking to people and meeting people." *Joanne Baker (Volunteer '97).*

"I was made redundant. You can imagine how I felt – so low and direction-less. Volunteers transformed my outlook … made me feel positive … What happened to me is typical." *Andrew Davies (Volunteer '93).*

"I didn't realise now much I could do, and I wish I'd known a heck of a lot earlier." *Scott Ellison (Volunteer '94).*

"I think my personality changed altogether. I'm more caring. Now I'd go out of my way to help most people …" *Justin Evans (Venturer '90).*

"There's not one person who hasn't changed. People say I've grown up a lot." *Julie Ferguson (Venturer '89).*

Looking ahead, the Prince hopes for even more. "Down the road, quite a lot of these characters, if we can get a lot more volunteering as they get older, may realise this is something that perhaps their children would benefit from. You see what I mean: it may feed back into the system in 20 or 30 years' time."

[11] House of Lords, 25 June 1975.

Chapter 5

EDUCATION

"We've all got some particular talent"

I f you want to see the Prince of Wales in full flow, get him on the subject of education. Education provides the foundation for life. In Britain the foundation looks wobbly.

"Here in Britain we seem to get it wrong almost before we have begun. In Italy and Belgium every child under five receives nursery education from the state. Here less than half our children have that right. There is much that we can learn from the experience of countries like France and Germany.

"We will never realise our full economic potential in this country until standards of education and training match those of our competitors. It appears to be an increasingly common impression that standards of handwriting, spelling, punctuation and numeracy are not at all what they should be.

"Perhaps most alarming of all, only a third of our 16- to 18-year-olds are still in full-time education … 40 per cent of our children leave full-time schooling with no significant educational qualifications at all. As many as 15 per cent are truant or disruptive, and five per cent have effectively dropped out of school altogether. This can hardly be the trademark of a civilised society."

Education in Britain in the eyes of Prince Charles must rate somewhere around a C+. Where children with most difficulties are concerned, the grade is even lower. The current system is failing too many young people. Six million people in the UK are considered to fall below the basic standard of literacy and numeracy. Who would argue that these two skills should not be the bare minimum that children learn in school? Yet one in five leave without even a 'G' GCSE in English and maths. He is not wrong to shine the spotlight on this subject, even if the sight revealed makes some squirm. Recent statistics confirm that results remain unsatisfactory. A 1998 survey by Nationwide concluded that two thirds of Britons cannot add up.

The Prince is in no doubt about the magnitude of the task: "The challenge facing us is therefore to take action now to secure the best possible education and training for every young person in this country, so that we will be better able to compete and to create jobs in the future ... If the United Kingdom is to thrive in the next millennium, it will need committed, imaginative and, above all, well-educated citizens.[1]

He has produced a depressingly long list of areas in need of improvement.

"We need the right package of support measures: attainable but creditable qualifications, appropriate courses, good schools, enlightened partnerships between education, business and the wider community supported by the Training Enterprise Councils and by local and national government."

What are "appropriate courses"? The Prince has never put forward proposals for a comprehensive overhaul in content and methodology, but he stresses:

- the need to strengthen the core curriculum and make sure every student masters basic literacy and numeracy;
- the need to tailor education for those less academically inclined, to give them other skills, both vocational and personal, which will make them more employable once they leave school;
- the importance of supplementing in-school education with out-of-school programmes, especially for those children perceived to be failing or at risk of exclusion.

He has also has put forward practical steps to be taken by his own organisations and by others.

1. More time should be spent on English and maths. "There is no doubt that the failure of so many of our young people to learn the basic skills of reading, writing and numeracy puts them at the greatest possible disadvantage for the rest of their lives."[2]

2. One size does not fit all. For those who cannot find a good match in the current curriculum, alternatives should be offered – especially vocational training. "The move towards jobs which require ever higher qualifications and skill levels is continuing. As society becomes more complex and the technology more advanced, our standards and aspirations will have to continue to rise ... The introduction of the new Vocational Qualifications is, I believe, a welcome indication of the importance of giving due weight to the achievements of everyone undergoing education and training or, put another way, of giving parity of esteem to all broadly equivalent qualifications, be they academic, vocational or a combination of the two."[3]

[1] 'Opportunity Through Partnership', Aim High Launch, Salford, 28 October 1992.

[2] Aim High Awards, 11 July 1996.

[3] 'Opportunity Through Partnership', Aim High Launch, Salford, 28 October 1992.

1. *An early recruiting poster for the Trusts.*

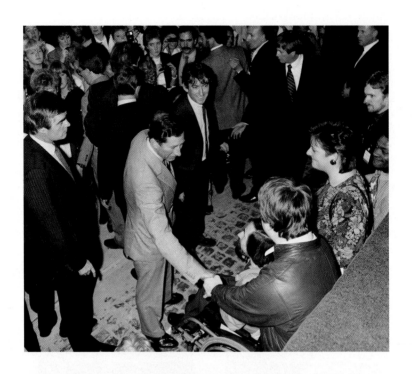

2 & 3. Celebrating his 40th birthday with 1,500 of the Prince's Trust graduates in 1988.

4. *Marking the creation of 25,000 jobs by the Youth Business Trust, 1996.*

5. *Opening the Trust shop in King's Walk, Chelsea.*

6. *With Tom Shebbeare, Chief Executive of the Prince's Trust, 1997.*

7. *An autograph for Unity winners of the music competition at the first Rock Gala, 1982.*

8. *The Prince mimes eating a 12-inch sandwich at the Philadelphia Flyer, a Youth Business Trust business in Wolverhampton.*

9. Leigh Goodsell's portrait photograph for the King's Fund centenary.

10. *Fiona Rae (PYBT '90), jewellery designer, presents a pair of her prize-winning cuff-links.*

11. A new dress code for Prince William, courtesy of the Prince's Youth Business Trust.

12. Joining Phil Collins' band at Caister in 1988.

13. Grilling Paul Mackie of Firstdrive (PSYBT '96) during a loan application.

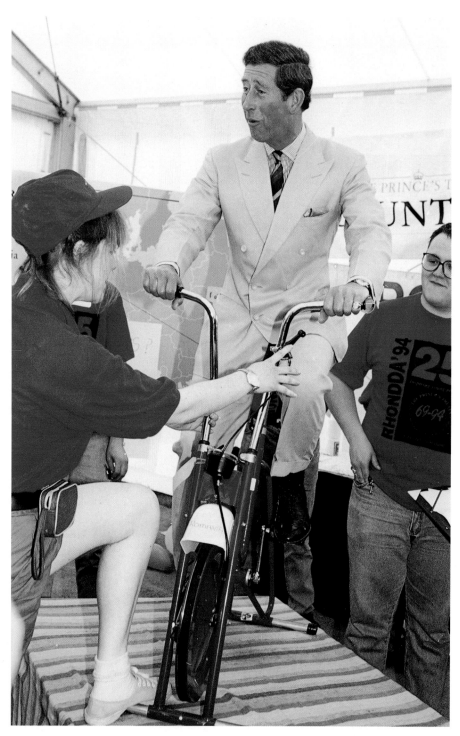

14. Biking for Newport Volunteers, 1994.

15. *All political leaders in England and Ireland agree in 1996 that everyone is a Volunteer. Among them are the Irish President Mary Robinson, Tony Blair, John Major and Paddy Ashdown.*

16. Kick-off at the Aim High Campaign in Education, Salford, 1992.

17. *At Winton Primary School in King's Cross, London, a showcase for BITC activity.*

18. Reviewing a record of achievement, with a mentor at Acton High School, 1998.

3. The burden of creating productive young people should not rest solely on the shoulders of schools and teachers. "We all have a role to play in winning over hearts and minds: teachers, trainers, mentors, business people, politicians – and above all, parents. For if they don't take the training of their children seriously, giving them full backing for their studies ... they have no right to ask others to do it on their behalf."[4]

Education, he believes, should be more holistic, enhancing those skills best taught in schools, reinforcing classroom progress and adding other training – including personal development – which might take place in another setting altogether. That can only happen if the whole community helps. Prince Charles sees the need for a broad coalition that goes way beyond the teaching profession.

4. Education has to be inclusive, making more allowance for students who lag behind. "Young people – not just the most able, but everyone – need to aim higher and achieve more; and we must make them want to do so."[5] "He always takes the view that education matters for everybody, not just the few." Dr Eric Anderson, who was once one of the Prince's teachers, recognises this component of the campaign. Including everyone, whatever their ability, may require extra schooling over and above what is usually on offer in the classroom. The key is not to force feed though detention, which does not do the trick, but to make extra effort attractive.

Balance matters in education, just as it does in making sure community service achieves an holistic outcome for young Volunteers. The Prince knows that both technical and personal skills are needed to succeed in life. One without the other produces an incomplete person.

A Holistic Education

I have developed a simple schematic. It does not do justice to the subject's complexity, but seeks to highlight the interrelation between what could otherwise be seen as a host of separate initiatives. At the top of the chart is the overall goal: raise results. The Prince of Wales wants to help improve the standard of education for every student, though he is most concerned with those disadvantaged and not doing well. Different sub-groups within the student body have different needs, so over the years he has supported different solutions. This chapter takes a look at all the major initiatives where he has been instrumental in forcing the pace, how he got involved and the impact he has had.

[4] 'Opportunity Through Partnership', Aim High Launch, Salford, 28 October 1992.
[5] 'Opportunity Through Partnership', Aim High Launch, Salford, 28 October 1992.

Raise Results

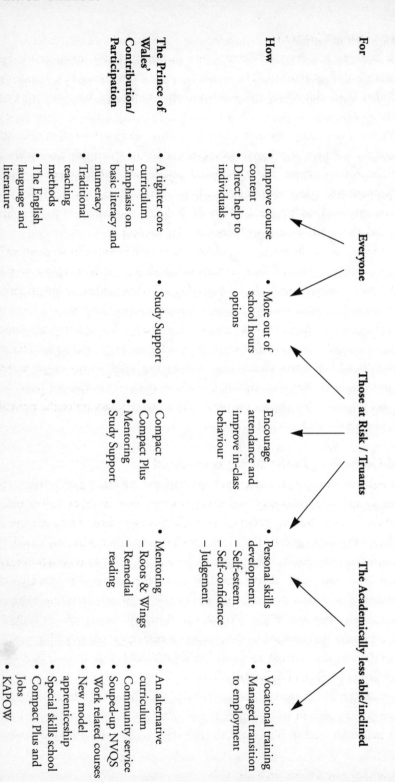

	Everyone	**Those at Risk / Truants**	**The Academically less able/inclined**
For			

How	• Improve course content
	• Direct help to individuals
	• More out of school hours options
		• Encourage attendance and improve in-class behaviour
		• Personal skills development
		  – Self-esteem
		  – Self-confidence
		  – Judgement
			• Vocational training
			• Managed transition to employment

The Prince of Wales' Contribution/ Participation	• A tighter core curriculum
	• Emphasis on basic literacy and numeracy
	• Traditional teaching methods
	• The English language and literature
		• Study Support
		• Compact
		• Compact Plus
		• Mentoring
		• Study Support
		• Mentoring
		  – Roots & Wings
		  – Remedial reading
			• An alternative curriculum
			• Community service
			• Souped-up NVQS
			• Work related courses
			• New model apprenticeship
			• Special skills school
			• Compact Plus and Jobs
			• KAPOW

Improve Course Content

The link between low levels of literacy and numeracy and poor prospects for employment is well established. The Business in the Community target team on education has made this area the number one priority for member firms working in schools.

The Prince has strong views on the way English should be taught. He has denounced the false use of progress as a justification to undermine basic literacy skills. His reported outburst in 1989 against people who cannot speak or write English properly was taken out of context, but was nonetheless heartfelt. He used his tercentenary address to the College of William and Mary to express his concern, and also to draw on other authorities for support.

"Basic literacy is the bedrock, and without this as a foundation students will struggle to make progress ... People have not been taught how to use words properly. I do not merely mean the inability to spell or punctuate – though these obviously matter. I mean that there is a real problem in the poverty of many people's ability to express themselves. Winston Churchill was, I believe, one of the greatest and most effective practitioners of the English language. But he too had to learn his craft and knew how important it was to do so: 'By being so long in the lowest form at school, I gained an immense advantage over the cleverer boys', he wrote in his memoirs. 'I got into my bones the essential structure of the normal English sentence – which is a noble thing.'"

A Good Grounding in the Basics is Essential

"I do think that ... as you get older you appreciate the importance of having been taught real grammar. I had a very frightening teacher who was an ex-Indian army officer believe it or not, but, my goodness he taught good grammar. It may not sound it to you now but I am so grateful to that man for having taught me the way he did."[6]

His stance was considered controversial by certain "experts". Their reaction only confirmed his suspicions that something was rotten in the educational establishment. Frustration that teaching policy-makers were not taking matters seriously enough came out in the Shakespeare Birthday Lecture of April 1991, when he expressed concerns about deficiencies in education, along with a robust critique of the way the curriculum seemed to detach children from their heritage, and in particular from the English language.

"There are terrible dangers ... in so following fashionable trends in education ... that we end up with an entire generation of culturally disinherited people ... It is almost incredible that in Shakespeare's land one child in seven leaves primary

6 Brno English Language Conference, 8 May 1991.

school functionally illiterate ... When they reach secondary level, what awaits them? Certainly a great many devoted and committed teachers, many no doubt inspirational, but as often as not, too great an emphasis on the child-centred approach, the open-ended learning situation and too much stress on process rather than content. Of course, this can engender enthusiasm and interest in the classroom, but seems correspondingly less likely to instil fundamental standards of accuracy in the basic skills."

This was hard-hitting stuff, which provoked charges of interference from the National Association for Teachers of English.

His concern for a framework for learning had surfaced early in a 1974 interview with the *Observer*. "I think that discipline, not in the sense of taking your bath in cold water, but in the Latin sense – giving shape, form and tidiness to your life – is the most important thing your education can do." Or again in the introduction to his *A Vision of Britain*. "I remember thinking in the 1960s, how crazy it was to destroy much of value and, by obeying the dictates of fashion, to throw the baby out with the bath water. This frenzied attack on long-established principles and values affected not only architecture but also ... education."

According to Dr Anderson, "the Prince of Wales believes that rigorous teaching is better than letting people find out for themselves". Letters of support for his stance poured in, and most teachers were in agreement. Indeed, his initiatives explicitly set out to involve teachers at the local level and work closely with schools to help them do what they always wanted to do.

The guilty parties were a small band of self-styled progressive educationists, who had managed to hijack the education agenda and taken control of the curriculum. Also at fault were civil servants who had either connived in or failed to fight ideas they often knew were barmy, and government ministers who he felt had not taken a strong enough stand in favour of the fundamentals. Today his approach seems to be in the ascendant, as leading experts come back to his side.

The Dearing report of March 1996 – "Review of Qualifications for 16–19 Year Olds" says: "The need to improve standards in the skills of communication and the application of numbers amongst young people was the most frequently expressed concern during the extensive consultation undertaken for this review." No wonder the Government has set ambitious targets for attainment levels by 11-year-olds. The Prince would approve of the added emphasis, but that still leaves an educational underclass which will be left behind even if the new standards are achieved.

"I do feel the schools have rather come full circle now from where they were 25 years ago, to seeing all the damage that has been done by progressive ideas and, perhaps, taking another look at a more disciplined approach. It's not always popular. Make any mention of anything disciplined and there are people who will go berserk. That's the origin of the battle in education, but it's discipline that gives a framework for life … "

The Prince has always expressed the view that traditional teaching methods should be restored. And not only in literacy. The Numeracy Hour, launched by the Secretary of State for Education and Employment, David Blunkett, in 1998, looks like a step in the right direction. The hour will involve kicking out calculators until students have mastered their tables. By going backwards sometimes we go forwards.

Prince Charles has come in for criticism for banging on about the need to master English. His reasons are not nationalistic or nostalgic but thoroughly pragmatic, as this extract from a 1991 speech in Brno in the Czech Republic makes plain:

"It remains, I believe, essential to preserve standards in English language teaching so that those who learn English are able not only to communicate functionally but also to enjoy the cultural heritage … It is important to guard against the danger of such distortions being introduced into the language so that so-called English speakers in different parts of the world can no longer communicate. Pandit Nehru, who was the first Prime Minister of India and himself a master of the language, is said to have expressed the fear more than once that the English spoken in Bombay could one day so differ from the English of Madras that the inhabitants of both would be unable to communicate with one another in any language at all."

But it goes even further than that, because English is a key competitive advantage. The Prince underlined its importance in his Williamsburg address. "We are heirs to what I believe to be one of the richest languages the world has ever known, and which now dominates that world. In diplomacy and law, business and the arts, sport and academia, English rules. But it will not rule and will have no right to do so if we do not guard it and guide it, fight for the highest standards and see it as our shared responsibility to do so."

Another concern about English relates to the integration of ethnic minority communities. His instincts had been confirmed by research in the early 1980s. Limited fluency in English was identified as one of the prime reasons some ethnic minorities failed to find employment. Here he saw what seemed like discrimination in schools which set the tone for later life. He wants a more inclusive education, which gives everyone the same base and therefore a more equal opportunity.

"I do believe passionately that a proper knowledge and understanding of our history and of the best of our wonderful literature play a key role in helping us to understand our national and cultural identity."[7]

[7] Aim High Awards, 11 July 1996.

So he did not stop at basic literacy in his critique of the curriculum. In February 1993 he was talking to students at Williamsburg, Virginia, but his message was for the teaching establishment back in Britain. "If we can be accused of neglecting our incomparable common language – and I think we can – we are equally in danger ... of failing to give due importance to our incomparable literature. This process has been made worse by well-meaning but misguided attempts to counter what is seen as elitism in our schools. There are those who say that children from poorer backgrounds should not have the work of writers from past ages thrust upon them. Such writers, it is said, merely indoctrinate their readers in the habits of a hierarchical society, clothed in a language with which they are not familiar.

"It is this approach which strikes me as real elitism. It amounts to telling these children that, because they live in ghettos or slums, because they come from varying ethnic backgrounds, because they are poor or parentless, they must be deprived of much of the greatness of human thought and the beauty of human expression.

"We are not as open as we should be to our history and our heritage as they are expressed in our literature, or to the wisdom that literature contains. So we become shallow-rooted, bereft of a sense of direction. It is said that the past is another country. If so, we have become xenophobic. Literature is for everybody because it is about everybody. Access to it is, in my view, one of the fundamental human rights which it is the duty of a civilised society to safeguard.

"What is so special about literature, some people may ask? I will try to provide my own, rather personal answer. All great literature has a strong sense of place and time, a wonderful precision of detail and a cultural particularity. And yet paradoxically, all great literature is also timeless. It may describe only a single moment or a unique scene. Yet as it does so, it speaks about all people, and all time and all places."[8]

The high profile of his utterances and the generally positive reaction has had a real influence on policy. He has been instrumental in raising the tempo of the debate about what should be at the heart of a modern education. There has been a refocusing of resources and some changes in the curriculum which lean back to the basics. There is always a danger in attributing specific results to one person. Prince Charles never claims any credit for himself. But it is not unreasonable to say that he has had an influence on a number of developments, including the final version of a new national curriculum.

Lord Patten, when he was Education Secretary, publicly endorsed many of the Prince's views in the final recommendations. "The Prince of Wales had an enormously powerful impact on the state and flavour of the national curriculum,

[8] Tercentenary celebration of the College of William and Mary, Williamsburg, 13 February 1993.

particularly in respect of English, and to a lesser extent history ... He raised the quality of the debate by stressing the importance of proper English, proper literature, and a proper understanding of our national heritage. He also realised how our language and our history go to the heart of our nationhood and our national culture. I suspect that he also sensed how both had been debauched by politically correct classroom methods, when they should have been taught not discovered."

Sir Claus Moser, who had a distinguished career in education, confirms that "Prince Charles is regarded by all my friends and colleagues in education as one of the key influences. His interventions had a key effect in raising the status and priority of education as a public concern."

Curriculum development is not dull and worthy. For school leavers getting it right can mean the difference between a job and no job, which is why the Prince has taken a personal interest in trying to align the curriculum more closely to the needs of employers. Employers speak from experience of school leavers who have not acquired the skills to fill available employment. Too often, course content lags behind changing conditions in industry. A better educated workforce, and in particular one with the right skill mix, is high on the wish list of employers.

Prince Charles asks employers: "What are you doing to help schools get it right?" The standard response used to be that this was the Government's job. The second excuse was, "We don't know what to do." The Prince would rather businesses came up with answers themselves, so they could take ownership. What he needed was a vehicle to bring business leaders together with education professionals and the students themselves. The first one he found was the Compact.

Encourage Attendance and Improve In-class Behaviour/ Transition to Employment

In September 1986 Prince Charles attended a 'Futures for Youth' conference in Boston, Massachusetts, on youth unemployment. Partnerships between business, public entities and schools featured prominently. The central discussion was attended by the Prince and the state governor, Michael Dukakis. A separate seminar was devoted to the Compact, and delegates spent part of the afternoon visiting Compact schools.

The Boston Compact was an innovative programme launched against the background of a 47 per cent drop-out rate in a city system where two-thirds of the students were from racial minorities. The main aim was to encourage children to stay in school. When the Prince came across the Compact, it had been going for four years, a kind of bargain between teachers, kids, their parents and local employers.

The kids entered into undertakings, including a 90 per cent attendance record and achieving a basic level of literacy and maths. Their parents promised to do everything in their power to provide a supportive home environment. Teachers agreed to assist. Businesses undertook to offer first crack at summer and full-time jobs on graduation to kids who stuck to the Compact. Colleges joined in too, offering priority admission, as did unions setting aside apprenticeships. In 1985 Compact companies placed 2,600 students in summer jobs, and found employment for 800 graduates.

Prince Charles saw the relevance at once. Here was a classic case of private sector leadership. The Compact encapsulated many of the themes he wanted to pull together himself – better school attendance, higher maths scores, greater literacy – with a hook which made it work: priority in jobs. He came back to Britain determined to set up something similar.

The Compact was different and, as Kay Stratton, head of the Office of Training and Employment Policy in Massachusetts says, "The thing that the Prince grasped immediately was that it was about a bargain. It wasn't a fuzzy, unaccountable partnership."

The first step was to pick the right place to start, and nail down companies who would provide the essential employment element. The Prince instructed Business in the Community to come up with a British version and to find a place to test it. He also invited Dr Laval Wilson, the superintendent of Boston's schools, to come to London that December.

Heading into Compact territory was not without risk. Organising business/school partnerships took him dangerously close to areas traditionally reserved for politicians, who tend to get nervous if they are not calling the shots; and corporations are not accountable to any electorate. So not everyone was thrilled when the Prince promoted this new concept.

The London 'Docklands Compact' was an experiment, with Business in the Community as midwife, that brought together the Inner London Education Authority and the London Enterprise Agency, and created the London Education Business Partnership. The original partnership had an impressive list of backers: BP, 3i, Whitbread and the TUC. The sum of £100,000 was raised through a special Trust.

It would have been hard to have created a tougher challenge than Docklands, Hackney and Tower Hamlets, the areas chosen for the experiment. All had more than their share of racial problems and children from difficult backgrounds. If it worked there, the Compact would work anywhere. Complications came in the form of a raging political conflict between the Conservative Government and an education authority run by a group which was well to the left of left and unable to accept that businesses could do anything good.

The very first guinea pig was Mulberry School in east London, soon joined by three others. Forty firms signed the letter of intent, and agreed to offer around 500 full-time jobs. In the first year nearly 1,200 students went through a two-week summer work experience. Attendance levels began to rise, and there was a marked increase in the number staying on for further education. These results were sufficiently encouraging for Prince Charles to launch a concerted campaign for Compacts all over the country.

In 1988 the Rt Hon Norman Fowler MP, Secretary of State for Employment, also went to Boston, came back impressed and proposed an official scheme called the Government Compact. The link between this initiative and what Prince Charles had already pioneered is not entirely clear. What was clear was that the Government was not willing to give any credit to the Prince for having spotted the idea first.

Having the same origin, there were strong similarities between the two Compacts. There was, however, one very fundamental difference: the method of funding. The Prince found his in the usual way, as and when with no strings attached. The Treasury at that time refused to countenance full funding without guaranteed jobs, which was not on. Companies that were comfortable signing up on a voluntary basis, and with every intention of fulfilling their obligations, were altogether less enthusiastic about entering into formal guarantees with the Government. So the Government scheme never caught on properly.

Prince Charles meanwhile continued to promote the idea. He made connecting companies to schools a priority at Business in the Community. His enthusiasm and unstinting support kept the Compact flag flying. By the early 1990s, the programme had achieved critical mass, with over 700 schools covering 140,000 students and nearly 10,000 companies making some commitment. The intersection between education and employment is at its closest with Compacts. Local variations abound, and the next generation has begun to emerge. Compact Plus clubs provide guidance and personal support, with full-time advisors and volunteers. 'Members', often Compact students who have not honoured the original agreement, are reminded of the value of school qualifications in obtaining employment and given fresh incentives. A further extension is Compact Plus with Jobs.

Government involvement in the debate over employment and education links brought one enormously important bonus. High on the agenda for the Prince was more skills training, an objective he shared with Stephen O'Brien who was attempting to insert Business in the Community as a catalyst. One thought was to link training to the Compact. When the Government joined the party, Prince Charles asked Fowler to dinner with O'Brien and Hector Laing. The conversation that evening was one of the more influential in persuading Fowler to put his full weight behind the creation of Training and Education Councils. TECs' main mission is to effect the very linkage the Prince of Wales was promoting; TECs, in turn, play a vital role in the Trust's star educational performer – Study Support.

Compact schools reported mixed results, but in almost every case there was something to show, and in the worst areas improvement could be material. After three years Tower Hamlets recorded 15 per cent more pupils staying on for further education. The programme can be extremely cost-effective. A nation-wide evaluation in 1996 found the most expensive Compacts spent about £275 per pupil, against costs of remedial training in excess of £5,000. Even if only one in ten of those at risk who enrolled saw improvements, the economics would be attractive. Available results from a sample of 17 schools came in comfortably above that. Completion of course options, and Record of Achievement portfolios by students, are 20 per cent higher than those not in the Compact. On the jobs front the news has been even better. Two in ten more school leavers found jobs than had been predicted.

The enhanced Compact Plus has helped students like Stuart Brown, labelled by teachers as "an aggressive, unco-operative young man with no people skills and an antipathy to teachers and authority". The different approach gave him his first experience of achievement and self-worth. He joined in activities such as sponsored runs and sponsored silences, so that by the end of the year he wrote to his student advisor, "I've learned more on Compact Plus than any other lesson. Debbie, you're the best teacher I've had." His marks improved and teachers recognised his more co-operative approach in class. He is now able to work with his peer group without resorting to violence. Stuart himself feels different. "I used to be in trouble at school. I didn't have much confidence in what I was doing and always wanted to be the centre of attention. Compact Plus helped me build confidence and understand different people." He has found a job at the Wheatsheaf pub in Stockport. He also went through a mock interview with the Royal Marines as part of his programme, which aroused his interest to such an extent that Stuart is applying to join the army.

The Prince has lent his support to other organisations which emphasise the link between education and employment. Kids and the Power of Work runs a special module in the curriculum that helps children in primary schools see a connection between what they learn in the classroom and skills they will need to succeed in a career. By understanding what goes on in the workplace they should recognise the need to attend school and do well in exams. KAPOW, which originated in the US, saw the light of day at the John Keble School in Harlesden. 2,000 students in Britain have been involved so far. Schools report an increase in interest from parents, though it is too early to measure the impact on students.

Out of School Hours Options

The programme in the Prince's stable which has had the greatest direct impact on educational performance is Study Support. The Trust played a pivotal role, even though it has a mixed pedigree. Elements derive from what Prince Charles learned in Boston and also in Japan, where he had seen a concept which, translated into English, means 'Homework Havens'. Touring schools all around Britain to sell the Compact, he sensed that students needed more than a disciplined study framework in school. There were also fundamental failings after school, where homework went by the wayside.

John Bowerman, senior teacher at Preston Manor School, Wembley, summed up the problem succinctly. "Many of our pupils go home to a one-bedroom flat where they have nowhere to work." The Prince was aware of the efforts of teachers who had struggled to introduce additional after-hours activities. Here was the germ of Study Support as something separate from the Compact, which stressed attendance and in-school behaviour.

The trigger was a conversation between the Rt Hon Virginia Bottomley MP and the Prince at a conference on the environment early in 1990. What was a new junior environment minister up to, pushing an education project, and why approach Prince Charles? On 14 November 1988, Bottomley had been in Birmingham where Prince Charles was celebrating his 40th birthday. "I remember thinking that here was the Prince of Wales not playing polo or at Balmoral, but in Birmingham identifying himself with the underprivileged. This is a man with a real sense of the issues which matter." His choice of venue and companions made a deep impression.

Subsequently Bottomley had been to Asia, where she saw a homework centre in Hong Kong and a *juku* or crammer in Japan. She concluded that what was missing in Britain were facilities for students wanting to study but lacking a suitable place at home; but environment was her brief, not education. Colleagues were not convinced of the virtues of her 'Swot Shops', and Mrs Thatcher's response was "Look after litter, Virginia."

It took no more than a few minutes for Prince Charles to agree to provide leadership. The requirement for something extra which took place outside the classroom would from that moment be central to all his pronouncements on education. Three days later Tom Shebbeare was in Bottomley's office writing the brief, and Study Support moved from paper to pilot in short order.

A mere year or so down the road, the Prince wrote to Bottomley enclosing a copy of the 1991 Trust annual report. "You may remember that you once button-holed me about 'Swot-Centres' … I thought you might like to see the progress we've made over the past year, which is summarised on page 11. Perhaps you were right when you said that maybe it is sometimes true that we can get things moving more quickly than government!"

He was referring to this: "During the year the Trusts have initiated support for a programme of Study Support Centres aiming to provide facilities for young people who come from homes that cannot provide the right circumstances in which they can study. This new project shows all the signs of developing into a major new initiative."

Sarah Bonnell was the perfect pilot school. The 1,200 girls there speak 76 languages between them. Some have learning disabilities. Others come from difficult backgrounds, including asylum seekers, and live in conditions not conducive to home study.

By the time Prince Charles came to call in December 1993, Study Support had made its mark. The number of students achieving five GCSE A-C grades had risen from 23 per cent to 54 per cent; 98 per cent now achieve five GCSEs. Head teacher Carolyn Brown attributes a large part of that remarkable rise to the programme. "Study Support has been integral to the way the school has improved ... "

Study Support came a long way in a short time. From four experimental sites in 1990, two in London and two in Belfast, the programme has mushroomed. In 1998 the Prince's Trust will be actively involved with 429 centres, and there are over 400 others which now stand on their own. This year around 100,000 students are expected to attend a centre, students like Sonay Aydugan of Elizabeth Garrett Anderson School. Fifteen-year-old Sonay comes from a Kurdish-speaking family which arrived in Britain in 1994. Studying at home is difficult. Sonay shares her room with one sibling and a three-year-old brother constantly interrupts her. As she said, "It's quieter in the library. I was able to catch up on my course work." So much quieter that not only has her English improved but also she has become hooked on the equipment. "I am studying GCSE information technology and so I need to use the computer a lot. I go to the centre after school and at lunch times." The Study Support programme has 10 aims:

- to give students a place to study;
- to give students access to resources;
- to provide opportunities for students to study and learn together;
- to provide students with tutor/teacher support;
- to tackle student under-achievement;
- to offer quality time to a specific group;
- to enhance learning and teaching through improved study skills;
- to improve student-teacher relationships;
- to improve examination performance;
- to help students develop greater self-confidence and self-esteem.

Study Support has succeeded in a mere eight years because it works so well. It has made a difference in better exam results and lower truancy rates. Pupils and teachers have nothing but good things to say. Professor John MacBeath of

Strathclyde University says it works because "the atmosphere is relaxed, the young people feel teachers are taking an interest in them and they are doing it voluntarily. The children and teachers both want to be there."[9] The atmosphere is the key, and an added trick is to find something each child can do well, emphasise that and go from there. Positive feedback often sets off a change of attitude that spills over into school and grades. Macbeath has called Study Support "possibly the most significant development in recent years in tackling low achievement".

Derek Goldman of Bellshills Academy emphasises the improvement in personal skills which he saw in students who participated. "They have better communication skills. They have better relationship skills, working with other people and coming up with better ideas in a group than they could on their own. I have noticed a greater ability to see another person's perspective. Best of all they are better at listening. These are the soft skills that employers really want." That will be vital in a former steel community just to the north of Glasgow where there is fierce competition for jobs among school leavers. Certainly it helped Andrew McAllister (Study Support '95).

Andrew's situation is different from most of those who participate because he was there not to study but to supervise; but he was also there to learn. His teachers felt sure he was bright, but he was not doing as well as he should in part because he did not seem to concentrate in class and was easily frustrated. Helping younger students who were slower seemed a good way for him to acquire a better approach to his own learning. After an intensive weekend of training his new role began. For three terms he helped the 11–13 bracket with their homework and in the process developed his own skills, as he now recognises.

"I'm a better listener now; and I've got more patience. Previously I used to hurry and lose my temper if I couldn't understand something immediately. Now I take my time, look things over, understand them better. I've learned to plan more. The responsibility was good. Helped my confidence."

Helped his grades too, which were good enough to get him a place at Glasgow College of Building and Printing. He wants to illustrate children's books and CDs, and is confident he will do well when he gets his first job. With stronger personal skills and more confidence in himself, there is every likelihood.

Once the pioneer, the Trust's present role is to provide strategic leadership, monitor quality control at all centres and make sure that the network continues to develop in the most disadvantaged areas where students and schools are most in need. Business in the Community has pitched in too, adapting its Aim High campaign to encourage more businesses to take an active role. Business can bring plenty to this particular

[9] *Sunday Express*, December 1993.

table, with financial sponsorship and volunteers to staff centres. These days even the educational establishment, which has not always seen eye to eye with the Prince, embraces this programme. Jonathan Petre, education correspondent of the *Sunday Telegraph*, is one of those who has noticed what is happening and is giving credit where it is due. "A new phenomenon is sweeping school which reverses the age-old image of children being dragged unwillingly to lessons ..."

Like so much of what the Prince supports, Study Support helps level the playing field. May Marsh, head teacher at Holland Park in London, sees this as its great strength:

"Giving students the opportunity to learn outside the school day is the easiest way of balancing up disadvantaged children with more well-off children."

The students are less analytical. Like Loretta Shoderu of Elizabeth Garrett Anderson School (Study Support '97), they just want a place to study. "I can get on with my work. If I go home I have to look after my brother, get his tea and clean the house."

Loretta is sure the centre has helped her. "I used to be a very bad reader but now with the aid of Sally and fiction I've improved my English."

Her teachers agree. Janet Goss, her maths teacher, was able to report: "Loretta is now not afraid to try more challenging work. She can research a topic on her own ... She has used this resource to improve her maths skill."

There are tens of thousands of Lorettas who can look forward to better results at school and more fulfilling jobs because of the extra dimension Study Support adds to their education.

Personal Skills Development

Self-confidence, self-esteem, regain confidence: these are the buzz words that constantly recur in conversations with the Prince, in his speeches and through his organisations. Remember what he took away from Gordonstoun was "an education which tried to balance the physical and mental with the emphasis on self-reliance to develop a rounded human being". These soft skills are relevant requirements which need explicit development. All the learning in the world will not do much good without the personal skills to make use of the knowledge. Many have natural abilities and require no special assistance, but others are less lucky.

"It's very important, obviously, that a great deal of effort should go into enabling people to get the right kind of skills but at the same time, another aspect – another side to the equation – is that it's very important to develop the personal skills as well, because it's no good being well versed in a particular technical skill without, at the same time, having the kind of human skills which make such a difference."

The Prince believes that with the right environment and the right level of encouragement, it is possible to improve personal skills just as structured exam performance can be improved. Self-confidence is the starting point.

Talk to any individual working for Prince Charles, and at some point the conversation will come around to the importance of self-confidence. Pick up brochures, watch a video, visit the Web site. The word appears everywhere. This value is central to every educational initiative, regardless of whether the overt aim is to raise basic standards, supplement the school curriculum or extend the learning cycle beyond school; and not just in education. Raising self-confidence is an explicit objective of every programme that the Prince supports.

This emphasis is linked with his belief that everyone is intelligent in at least one way, even if it is not always immediately apparent. Self-confidence is the key to unlocking that potential. Mentoring can help develop self-confidence.

Having seen mentoring work so well at the Youth Business Trust, the Prince began to wonder if that sort of personal attention would have the same impact in an educational environment. Parental involvement is usually a plus. When parents are not around, an adult substitute might suffice. In some cases the child might be better off with the substitute. There were elements of mentoring in the Compact. By the time Prince Charles launched Study Support, mentoring had moved centre stage. "Mentoring is one of the great secrets for making schools get better results with students."

Mentoring is now standard procedure in almost every educational activity involving the Prince's organisations. Someone showing a personal interest in the young person is generally accepted as a critical success factor. It is interesting to recall that the original Mentor was the wise and trusted friend of Odysseus, and tutor to his son, Telemachus. In the context of Study Support, many students who could benefit most need not only help with their studies but also a wise friend to give them good general advice.

Overcoming the challenges inherent in mentoring also can help employees develop personal skills, a feature that has attracted considerable business support as a form of staff training. Swiss Bank Corp/UBS has a very active programme following a Seeing is Believing visit which Rudi Bogni, the chief executive of private banking at UBS, made to Deptford Green School. Bogni was concerned about the limited perspective of new recruits. "The City gives a distorted view of the world. This [mentoring] helps keep their feet on the ground so they appreciate what life is all about." Currently, 54 UBS employees mentor in schools, each taking responsibility for one student. A relationship this intense can have a very positive impact. Deptford Green has seen significant grade improvement, especially at higher levels. Historically only three per cent of pupils achieved four A-Cs at GCSE, but that percentage has risen to over 20 per cent. Analysis of the

1997 results found that mentees averaged a one point improvement in GCSEs.

Mentoring can be very powerful. Combine it with a window on the world of work, and you have a winning formula. In New Cross, south east London, there are 74 mentors. Pupils also visit the offices of IPC Publishing twice a month – a sort of student Seeing is Believing. This exposure to a business environment seems to have helped; not only have more than 80 per cent of the mentored pupils remained in full-time education – compared with 50 per cent of non-mentored pupils – they have also achieved GCSE grades 10 per cent higher than those of comparable non-mentored pupils.

Francis Combe in Watford, where BT is active, has seen the number of students staying on to the sixth form double since mentoring started. Geoffrey Carr, head of community links at the school, is a believer. "A very substantial part of the reason for that is to do with the mentoring. It really works. The whole concept of external mentors greatly influences pupils."

Mentoring works. That is the bottom line, although Keith Ajebo, head teacher at Deptford Green, is careful in his choice of words. "The grades at GCSE of those pupils who were mentored were better than would have been predicted. The mentoring helps build that sense of self-confidence that they can achieve." Attitudes do change and mentors such as George Rea, of KPMG, see the difference. "My mentee used to think that school was just something you had to do, but now she feels there's a real purpose to it."

Personal skills are not just about having sufficient self-confidence to face the world. Students also have to understand how to use that confidence in making value judgements. For Prince Charles, a complete education must cover the tricky and intangible, but ever so vital, issue of how to live life. One school of thought holds that education at school and morality do not mix. That responsibility should rest with the parents. The Prince is in the other camp.

Perhaps his most powerful exposition on this subject was reserved for the celebration of 350 years of Harvard in 1986. Delivering the address to more than 18,000 celebrants, he called for renewed emphasis on moral education. "We should never lose sight ... that, to avert disaster, we have not only to teach men to make things but also produce people who have complete moral control over the things they make." Morality does not come down the chimney with Santa Claus. "Children have to be taught that to live in this world is no easy matter without standards to live by ... It would appear that we may have forgotten that when all is said and done, a good man, as the Greeks would say, is a nobler work than a good technologist." Which is not to disparage the invaluable contribution technologists make; merely to say there is something higher. Understanding this need for judgement is important, whether school leads to higher education or not.

Vocational Training

In this as in other areas of education, the Prince has looked across the channel. "We do ourselves no service if we ignore that greater value is attached to technical and vocational training, staying on rates are higher, and better apprenticeship arrangements prevail in some of our European partner countries."[10]

Not everyone is academically inclined. Prince Charles feels strongly that where a young person is not responding to a formal education, the answer is not to give up and label that child a failure. The right reaction is to look for alternative training which can provide practical skills.

He wants to encourage more students to stay on for further education but in a 1991 speech he showed some sympathy with those who pack it in at 16. "On reflection it is not all that surprising that so many leave school as soon as they can. Sixth form education is, after all, geared mainly to preparing pupils for universities ... or other forms of higher education. This inevitably frightens off those who are less academically-minded, if it does not simply disqualify those who would like to do so from staying on ... It would be encouraging to think that an attractive programme of vocational training was available for the large numbers of our young people coming out of full-time education at 16."

The Prince has also set up specialist vehicles to address specific needs. Developing musical talent has long been one of his particular interests. Seminars with professional musicians have been integral to the residential courses, including Recharge and Work, Sport & Leisure. In 1996 Rock School split off to become a separate entity whose sole purpose is to provide education for people seeking a career in the entertainment industry.

Ian Robertson had always wanted a career in music. On the dole for two years of increasing frustration, he had very little to show for his efforts: the odd gig, but nothing steady. He heard about Rock School where top session players taught. Ian managed to get on two courses, in August 1996 and March 1997. He started out playing a trumpet at the age of 11. Now he is a drummer. He credits Rock School with helping him reach a new level. "I was able to develop new styles and try out more diverse things, not just sticking with one rhythm. I went in a drummer and came out a more confident and more accomplished drummer." Ian was selected to go to South Africa and play in the concert fronted by the Spice Girls. He found a home in a band called New Rising, which plays atmospheric space rock. New Rising was signed to Jealous Records, part of Virgin, last November. Their first single, Drowning Reason, was released in April 1998. The band has a nation-wide tour of Firkin Breweries lined up. Ian may

[10] 'Opportunity Through Partnership', Aim High Launch, Salford, 28 October 1992.

still be reaching for stardom, but today he is getting by when before he had been getting nothing.

Alternative learning is a key concept. The Prince constantly harps on the need to bring young people back into the mainstream through developing skills outside the classroom. The message permeates the approach now followed by his organisations. Implementation can take many forms. In Stapleford the Prince's Trust supports the 'Chase Project', enabling students to purchase dilapidated bicycles and refurbish them. The British School of Motoring, a member of Business in the Community, has supported classroom teaching of road safety and off-road driving.

Teaching is not an academic exercise because education, whether good or bad, is all most people ever get to equip them to earn a living. Prince Charles feels that the very direct link between education and employment has not received enough attention, and particularly in the case of students who score below average in tests. There is an assumption that better students will find jobs. But what about the rest? That is where the Prince wants to focus.

"You could look at where the shortages of skills are and some of the craftsmanship skills. There are huge gaps here … We are going to have a skills festival because the other area is actually the people who have never set up, who I come across all the time: adolescents who have failed at school academically and yet have technical talent, which never seems to get developed. Even where somebody found out about these NVQs and modern apprenticeships. In somewhere like Germany they have always had these. The point is to make it equal status, as it were, for those who are technically talented and those who are academically talented. Not everybody is the same but there are an awful lot of the young out there going to school who are never going to succeed because they are not being able to put their real talents into practice."

It was this line of thought that he applied to the structure of the New Modern Apprenticeship. The Prince was actively involved in helping shape both the concept and the detail. Gillian Shephard worked assiduously to get the programme off the ground, and David Hunt saw it through. The Prince was the loudest voice championing the need to make apprenticeships, which had traditionally been so heavily male dominated, become much more accessible to females. He was also critical of the deficiencies of previous schemes, which had taken people on for three or four or even 12 months and then put them back on the street scarcely better prepared and without work. He had seen the results in many of the young people who find their way to the Prince's Trust. The four-year programme differed from prior models in content and length. Here was a cause which could legitimately claim the mantle University of Industry, and comes close to providing the sort of proper vocational training that he had been hoping for. According to Shephard,

"With the Dearing reform, and the building in of fundamental qualifications with NVQs, the Prince of Wales's principles have been incorporated into the system."

Even so, the Prince feels the jury is still out on whether what is available is really right for the students who need that sort of development. "They've introduced this NVQ system, but I am not so certain that it does provide necessarily what's required." He is watching to decide whether further action on his part is appropriate.

There is an additional element that he would like to see included in the education of every person. His absolute belief that everyone benefits from volunteering leads him to conclude that community service should be part of the curriculum. In a piece in the February 1998 *Big Issue*, he wrote: "It is worth considering making volunteering an integral part of every young person's education, as is already happening in some schools." That is the public position, though it represents one of the more restrained royal utterances on the topic. Schools could be the ideal conduit to a national programme of community service. Prince Charles knows that, for now, a revamped version of National Service is not on the cards, which does not stop him dreaming of a day when every school will provide every student with the opportunity to volunteer.

Direct Grant Support

One activity that will continue outside the school system is giving grants to young people, aiming to raise their education level. Some grants are multifaceted. A St Neot's job club for out-of-work teenagers received money to buy word processors. They were used to improve the quality of application letters and CVs, and for training so users acquired a new skill which made them more employable.

It is wonderful how even a small sum, at the right time for the right purpose, can change lives, such as the £200 given to Joanna Price (PT Grant '90). Joanna came from a broken home and struggled at school, mostly because she had to take on a series of part-time jobs while still only 14, since her mother was barely able to support her. She ended up with average GCSEs, but was sure she could have done better had she been able to devote herself to her studies, and longed to continue her education. At 18 Joanna decided to leave home, solely so she could apply for grants and not be labelled as a dependant. She moved into a single room above a bakery. "I was not well equipped for the outside world. I missed my family and was completely undomesticated. To cut down on fat in my diet I fried sausages in water!" Joanna got her grants, but they were not enough to pay for all the required text books and exam fees – which was where the Prince's Trust came in. Their money made up the difference, enabling her to take her A levels.

She passed in all three subjects, with grades sufficiently strong to secure a place reading sociology at the University of Sussex. Joanna has never looked back. Even while studying for her degree, she had to work part-time. But she emerged with a BSc, and is now a training and development officer at Medway Council. Of the help she received she says, "the Prince's Trust helped me to achieve my aim in life".

The Trust's involvement does not stop when students leave school. Grants help with further education, and specialist training. About 30 per cent of awards during the 1990s went this way, the majority for fees, books, computers or other educational aids. Occasionally requests can be more unusual. Katie Lowe, studying for GCSEs at a Cambridgeshire college, was hampered by the cost of the bus going to and from the childminder for her four-year-old son. She got £80 to buy a bike with a child seat, and a safety helmet for Craig.

Grants are also made to groups involved with education or training. The Prince's Trust supported the Terence Higgins Trust Roadshow, which visited young people's venues nationwide to raise awareness of HIV and Aids. Project Fullemploy, with its concentration on training in inner city areas, is another favourite.

Teachers Train Too

If education is going to improve, it is not only students who need help. Teachers are often overworked and lack adequate support. The Prince sees this area as one where the business community can help. KPMG runs a programme which provides senior managers to act as mentors to head teachers, the chief executive equivalents. Monthly meetings discuss how schools can be better run using business methods. This programme only started in 1995, when 25 professionals from KPMG tested the idea in Southwark and Tower Hamlets. There are now over 700 active pairings. Those involved must think the time well spent since this mentor relationship has been developed by the Teacher Training Agency into a national head teacher programme.

The Prince gives this programme high marks. "I have seen remarkable results from employees of KPMG, who mentor head teachers. They have so many tasks to perform with planning and budgets, as well as the everyday management, and have done all sorts of useful things to make their time more productive."

Making It All Happen

There are many activities going on in schools all over the country where companies have made commitments as a result of being introduced to the issues by the Prince or through Business in the Community. This all falls under the umbrella of the Aim High campaign. There are four main areas of activity:

• spending time in a primary school once a week to help pupils with reading and numeracy;

- mentoring young people at risk in secondary schools under the 'Roots and Wings' programme;
- mentoring a head teacher;
- providing equipment or helping with Study Support and IT Learning Centres at schools serving disadvantaged communities.

There is a package of services that Business in the Community member firms can provide. Winton Primary is making the most of it. The head teacher, Jane Fulford, enjoys an excellent relationship with Jude Chinn of KPMG, who started as her personal mentor in 1996 and is now a school governor. Among topics discussed were the appraisal system, matching personnel to positions and cutting down on administration. NatWest has been sending volunteers since 1990. Nearly 200 members of staff have helped children learn to read at Winton, putting in an average of one hour per week during term time. Others come from Business in the Community itself, and Walkers Foods. As a result of three Seeing is Believing visits, the school has received donations from several firms, including books and stationery. Valuable services have been provided by the 'Professional Firms Group'. Winton got free legal advice about converting into a charity, and architectural assistance when they renovated a derelict building on the school site to create a parents' centre.

Fulford feels this support has made a great difference. "Everyone at Winton – pupils, parents and staff – has benefited from our links with business. Volunteer readers raise children's self-confidence and levels of achievement, and give them experience of the world of work. Teachers appreciate the interest and support from people from outside the school, which helps their pupils to progress faster. Our business links are a breath of fresh air and a personal source of support and encouragement, particularly the head teacher mentoring partnership. Business in the Community's Professional Firms' Group has also given me the opportunity to develop a range of projects in the school that would otherwise have been impossible."

Ofsted seems to agree. "An additional and important strength of the school is its continuing relationship with up to 50 volunteers from local industry through 'Winton and Co'. These visitors regularly hear readers and also offer skills such as art and craft, book making and information technology and therefore enhance and extend existing activities."

Winton is an excellent example of a comprehensive education/business partnership, and it attracted Prince Charles's interest. He had a second reason to visit, since Fulford had debated teaching methods with him at Highgrove after a meeting to discuss head teacher mentoring. She invited him to "come and see what we do". The Prince was impressed to learn how a holistic approach by Business in the Community members could work. Fulford assured him there was two-way traffic. Many mentors got satisfaction from working with the children, returning to the office refreshed and with renewed application to their own work.

Winton is not the easiest of educational environments. Its 320 pupils aged from three to 11 speak 27 different languages. Ethnic minorities make up 75 per cent of each class. Seventy per cent are on free school meals. Yet the results are encouraging. Pupils like eight-year-old Nahom Getu, who arrived from Ethiopia three years ago and whose first language is Amharic, has made an 18 per cent improvement on standardised scores in his English since he started reading with mentor Michelle Astley. "Most of the time I'm having a little bit of fun with books. Now I'm starting to read better and I read harder books. I stop when there's a full stop. I didn't used to do that. I like Julian the Crimebuster story. We read it together – that makes it fun."

Benefits and Values

What is all this improvement worth? First off, there is a benefit when costly and counter-productive activity like truancy is reduced through more effective education. Truancy is a major factor among youngsters who drift into crime. Police estimate that over 40 per cent of domestic burglaries, muggings and acts of vandalism in Britain in 1997 were committed by truants aged between 10 and 16. So the social costs of not fixing the problem run far higher than the loss of education.

The aggregate impact of the Prince of Wales is hard to measure. The place to start is better exam results. Improvement has been seen time and again at schools with Study Support. First a quick disclaimer: I am about to use data in ways which were not intended by the researchers.

Regular attendance can raise the number of students achieving bands 1 to 4, especially in maths, by over 50 per cent. One Shropshire school recorded an increase in maths passes from 39 per cent to 62 per cent following the introduction of Study Support, with even more impressive improvements in science pass rates. Improvement has been logged in other subjects, including history, geography and modern studies. Pilot schools, as a whole, have seen increases of 10 to 15 per cent in the number achieving five A-Cs at GCSE and a similar rise in D-Es. At Elizabeth Garrett Anderson, 30 per cent more students gained five GCSE passes in 1997 compared with 1994. Doon Academy in Ayrshire recorded increases ranging from 23 per cent in maths to 40 per cent in science. Whether it is a stretch to extrapolate these results across the wider school population is open to debate.

I contend that the pilot results represent a sufficient sample so that extrapolation is unlikely to be wildly wrong, and since information was collated over a three-year period the analysis has credibility. Not every student experiences the same success. Results vary, as one would expect. There are examples of no change at all, but also plenty of instances of significant improvement.

The second difficulty comes in placing the right monetary value on better exam results. A better educated workforce will create more national wealth. Research has demonstrated that a worker with higher education will on average earn more, over a working life, than one with less. In a paper entitled 'Education, Training and the Youth Labour Market', Peter Robinson of the London School of Economics pulls together surveys showing the 'value' of differing levels of education. There are marked differences. At the lowest level, an employee 20 years into a career with one to four O levels or GCSEs can expect to earn 31 per cent more than someone without any qualifications. Those with five or more are 47 per cent above. Any improvement in education performance as measured by exam results, therefore, should be very valuable, particularly by students who look likely to drop out before they pass in a single subject. For every potential drop-out who ends up with qualifications, annual income could be higher by £3,000 or so, maybe more. Over a 40-year working life that would be worth £41,000 in today's terms, pre-tax.

There were 580 Study Support centres in May 1998, with around 70,000 students enrolled. Over 105,000 students have been involved so far. If all those were to match the improvements logged in the pilot centres, that would mean 105,000 school leavers with the potential to achieve an academic performance which should give them a higher standard of living. Slightly over one in three do seem to score better. On that basis Study Support could have created over £1.6 billion of incremental value, based on the increased earning power of the current group alone. I acknowledge that this is a crude measure, of course, but £1.6 billion and counting does give a good sense of the power of the programme.

Enormous lasting value is created when effective investment is made in improving the quality of education, whether by teachers, government or businesses, or by the Prince of Wales. The actual value created is much, much higher than my number. Study Support is only one programme. Around 15,000 young people have received financial assistance from the Trust for educational purposes, and many of these will have done better.

The data do not exist that would enable me to quantify adequately the educational benefit from the Compacts. Recent results at Compact Plus for Jobs suggest the impact is getting stronger. Business in the Community has also made a valuable contribution. In 1997 more than 500 schools with almost 500,000 students saw some benefit. At the individual level the impact may be small, but if maths and science really is more fun because of the Powergen 'Weather Reports' project, which provides weather measuring equipment and workshops, including tours of power stations, then that is of enormous importance as well as of real value to the nation. These efforts have eased the passage of more schoolchildren into employment, directly or indirectly via further education with training.

Intensive one-to-one relationships between students and mentors can aid performance as well as attitudes. Preliminary research on GCSE results suggests a 23 per cent improvement compared to a control group, though with the caveat of wide variations. One student assessment using the Cognitive Abilities Test found that 72 per cent of pupils who got additional support made greater than anticipated gains in reading levels. These programmes are still small, with the current annual run rate of mentoring close to 3,500, but they are set to expand rapidly.

Cumulative total of Student Mentors through Business in the Community Member Companies (to June 1998)

Compact Plus for Jobs	3,000
Local links	2,500
Reading schemes	4,500
Roots and Wings	1,500

The figure of 11,500 is relatively modest, but not all local efforts are tracked so these figures understate mentoring activity. If pupils who receive intensive mentoring go up half a notch in the value of their education, it seems reasonable to assign over £200 million in value to this group of affiliated activities operating under the Prince's umbrella. The reach goes much broader. Over 60,000 students have taken part in the programmes where mentors were active.

But who really cares whether we are talking about £2 billion or £10 billion? The really important testimonies come from the kids who have benefited from a programme and know about the impact Prince Charles has had on their lives; kids like Jerome Saunders (Mentoring '98). "Meeting the Prince makes me want to behave better." You cannot measure this in economic terms.

The public now understands that the Prince has made an impression. He is widely recognised for his contribution. When the *Evening Standard* was looking for candidates to compere an Oscars-style television awards ceremony to honour the nation's best teachers, the two names mooted were Tony Blair and Prince Charles. Whether or not this is something suitable remains to be seen, but what is clear is that education will remain one of his top priorities. He has said so himself. "The prospect is one of more and more young people joining the sad ranks of the under-educated, untrained and virtually unemployable. There are few battles which it is more important that we fight – and win." [11]

[11] 'Opportunity Through Partnership', Aim High Launch, Salford, 28 October 1992.

Chapter 6

THE
ENVIRONMENT

"We are the community we live in"

T he fourth broad theme with which the Prince of Wales identifies is the environment. When he began to show a strong interest in matters environmental in the late 1960s such concerns were considered to be on the fringe. Mainstream public opinion tended to scoff, as if this preoccupation was merely a flight of royal fancy. Later organic gardening seemed quaint, if not out of touch.

The Prince has been at the forefront of many of the most vital environmental debates, and often as an early advocate of change in the face of general scepticism. Today it is hard to think of any issue more mainstream. There are global conferences, environmental treaties and regulations proliferating almost as fast as the rain forest shrinks. Organic vegetables meanwhile have become one of the highest growth products at supermarkets such as Sainsbury and Tesco.

Prince Charles has pursued improvement in the environment regardless of whether his agenda has been in or out of fashion. His work has encompassed not only preservation of the countryside but also broadly based anti-pollution initiatives, and improving the urban environment through community regeneration.

Green is as Green Does

Ask the average person how to improve the environment and one likely answer is "plant a tree". The Prince of Wales' Committee has been giving grants for tree and shrub planting since 1971; but environmental issues are broad. Even in rural areas there is a place for a lick of paint, a wall repaired, graffiti removed or a cycle path restored. The Prince supports all such improvements.

Many members of the royal family have associations with maintaining the beauty of rural areas. The Duke of Edinburgh's awards for wildlife and conservation, and the Queen's affinity for the Scottish Highlands, are both part of this. The Prince of Wales inherited his parents' love of nature, and has actively campaigned to preserve the countryside. In *Highgrove: Portrait of an Estate*, he wrote:

"I have put my heart and soul into Highgrove. I have also put my back into Highgrove and, as a result, have probably rendered myself prematurely decrepit. All the things I have tried to do in this small corner of Gloucestershire have been the physical expression of a personal philosophy. When I was younger, I recall, I felt the nascent stirrings of such a philosophy; I felt a strong attachment to the soil of those places I loved best – Balmoral in Scotland and Sandringham in Norfolk. As far as I was concerned, every tree, every hedgerow, every wet place, every mountain and river had a special, almost sacred, character of its own."

His love of natural beauty has led to clashes with the agribusiness lobby. Intensive farming methods may achieve high yields, but at a cost to the diversity of the countryside and an as yet indeterminate impact on the purity of the harvest. In early 1998 he argued against genetic crops because of his concerns about mutation and other dangers yet unknown.

Prince Charles has developed the largest and most successful organic farm in Britain. He hopes that by leading the way, and showing that it is possible to be profitable employing environmentally friendly technologies, others will follow. Again writing in *Highgrove: Portrait of an Estate* with Charles Clover, he explained what organic farming meant to him:

"In farming, as in gardening, I believe that, if you treat the land with love and respect, it will repay you in kind ... Farming has a cultural significance which distinguishes it from any other activity. It is a way of life that is, or should be, intimately associated with the long-term health of the soil ... I see it as a means by which we can rediscover the rashly abandoned traditional principles which, for thousands of years, have helped to preserve the health and fertility of the soil and the essential diversity of species on which we ultimately depend ... I am searching for the most successful – and widely profitable – way of adopting a longer-term perspective in terms of management of the land, enhancement of wildlife, adding value to the primary products we produce, developing better energy efficiency and more effective waste utilisation. In this way I hope we can develop a model which could be used to explain, in a practical way, how it might be possible to live more effectively off the 'income' produced from nature's 'capital assets', rather than exploiting those capital assets in the short-term."

The 1,087 organic acres at Highgrove produced a profit of around £750,000 in 1997. It may not work for everyone, but the Prince has proved it is possible to farm organically and still make a good living.

His ban on the use of peat at Highgrove and on Duchy of Cornwall land also demonstrates his commitment to preserving the countryside as far as possible in its natural state. In a message read to the 1989 Conference of the Royal Society for Nature he said: "If we would like other countries to stop regarding the rain forests as 'useless jungles' we would do well to set an example by not treating our peat-land habitat as a useless bog ..." In the Duchy of Cornwall a number of old practices such as stone walling, pond clearance, tree planting and wildlife corridors have been revitalised.

This philosophy extends into all his organisations. The Youth Business Trust was asked to use recycled paper. The Prince also thinks entrepreneurs should be more conscious of the environment in the way they run their businesses. 'Green' businesses include Lasertech of Widnes, which remanufactures toner cartridges. Green can be good business. Nine-year-old Lasertech recently moved into bigger premises and added staff to cope with demand.

Wales is where Prince Charles has had most influence on environmental practices. When only 20, he agreed to become chairman of the Welsh steering committee for the forthcoming European Conservation Year. The first public speech he ever made was on the environment. One of his earliest articles, published in the Town Planning Institute Annual Conference Handbook, warned that Wales faced "the horrifying effects of pollution in all its cancerous forms ... The cost of many conservation exercises is a problem although the cost of inaction will be even greater." In this 1970 contribution he wrote about facing the least palatable part of the solution up front:

"Are we all prepared to accept these price increases to see our environment improved? A recent *Sunday Times* opinion poll indicated that a surprisingly large proportion of people might be. Are we also prepared to discipline ourselves to restrictions and regulations that we feel we ought to impose for our own good?"

Twenty years later he was making more or less the same point, though this time he was prepared to give an answer and his audience was in agreement. "The problem is, it seems to me, that you can't get something for nothing and this is always the stumbling block that one comes up against. Cost is always being cited as the difficulty. The consumer won't stand the price increases that are necessary in order to achieve this kind of preventive approach ... But my guess is through talking to people in different parts of the country that more people would accept price increases than maybe some would realise."[1]

One of his first tangible steps was been the announcement in 1968 of the Prince of Wales Countryside Award, green and white metal plaques to mark individual enterprise in protecting the environment: "They had great trouble trying to design

[1] 1987 Annual Countryside Award.

something which is vandal-proof. I am told that if anyone tries to shoot air gun pellets or .22 bullets at this, they will ricochet back and clobber them."[2]

Throughout the European Conservation Year Prince Charles was active visiting sites and raising funds. "There was much that needed to be done to improve the Welsh environment. The landscape was scarred with the relics of our industrial heritage. Many public buildings were no longer required for their original purposes and were falling into decay and public support for *conversation* and the environment was, to say the least, tepid."[3]

To make sure activity did not peter out he formed the Prince of Wales' Committee, or in deference to the Welsh language, Pwyllgor Tywysog Cymru, and remained as its chairman, Ei Uchelder Brenhinol Tywysog Cymru. As he remarked with pleasure in 1975, "we in Wales are the only people to continue functioning four years later".

The Committee, operating autonomously, raised money and awarded grants to conservation schemes around the principality. Prince Charles selected many himself. Most were small-scale local projects. Schoolboys marked out a town trail through the urban wasteland of Splott, in Cardiff; a historic oak tree was saved from encroaching tides by a new sea wall at Picton Ferry, near Haverfordwest; duck boards were laid across a marshy footpath by children from a Pontypridd comprehensive school; the Great Western Railway signal box at Penmaenpool was converted into an observation post for the Royal Society for the Protection of Birds. A group of secondary-school children built a carriage for a Napoleonic cannon, after the Prince had it airlifted by helicopter from a hilltop. In Aberfan the Prince of Wales Committee joined forces with the World Council of Churches to landscape sites left derelict by the disaster. The Prince's environmental work had an immediate if limited impact. The Jubilee Trusts provided grants, though these were never a priority. In 1980 conservation attracted a mere three per cent. Still, some money found its way to interesting projects. In 1980 Friends of the Earth in Birmingham received £1,500 to pilot a collection scheme and evaluate recycling plastics. Canal clearance remained popular, as did tree planting. Grants went to groups such as the Snowdonia Conservation Project, the Ecological Parks Trust and the British Trust Conservation Volunteers.

Wales has been the engine room of trust activity in innovative and thoughtful projects such as Dare Valley County Park, built on the site of three former collieries using stone salvaged from demolished chapels; and the renovation of the Gadlys Iron Works. One favourite was Dan-Y-Castell farm, outside Merthyr Tydfil, where

[2] Anthony Holden, *Prince Charles*.

[3] 1984 Annual Countryside Award.

youngsters in the Youth Training Scheme learned animal husbandry and market gardening. Grant giving went not just to projects that were concerned with visible improvements but for information services and education, especially of young people, so awareness of environmental issues became more widespread. Education was a specific goal which the Prince gave his Committee in Wales. They developed a GCSE Mode 2 exam, which some schools set.

Protection Through Legislation

We take the need to protect the environment for granted in 1998, though finding the right balance with economic growth remains tricky. Most politicians these days are keen to display green credentials. This was not so 30 years ago. Popular opinion then was either indifferent or hostile. For Prince Charles to line up alongside environmentalists was certainly risky. But he has a way of putting things, cutting through technical jargon and relying on common sense, to get his point across.

"We can't pretend that we aren't aware of the potential long-term dangers to the intricate balance of Nature. Since the Industrial Revolution human beings have been upsetting that balance, persistently choosing the short-term options and to hell with the long-term repercussions. Until we have managed to discover somewhere else in some other galaxy which has a comparable set of atmospheric conditions, it makes absolutely no sense to me at any rate to mess about unnecessarily with the fragile and delicate chemical compositions which perpetuate life on this globe."[4]

He has pointed to areas where the threat to our quality of life is greatest and most immediate. "The ozone layer is only one environmental question among many. The seas are fast becoming sewers. We make poisons so powerful we don't know where to put them. The rain forests are being turned into deserts. If we can stop the sky turning into a microwave oven we will still face the prospect of living in a garbage dump."

On these issues the Prince has been labelled a crank, eccentric, Luddite, even loony. His preoccupations definitely went down porrly with much of the media, and seemed remote from most of the population. Even the *Guardian* was moved to scepticism about the bottle bank he set up at Buckingham Palace in 1980. There is no doubt that during the late 1970s and most of the 1980s this contributed to his poor public image. The Prince himself realised that the cause could be a struggle. "Care for the environment is often hard to put across to people who are unemployed and see little hope in the future."[5]

[4] 'Saving the Ozone Layer', British Museum, 6 March 1989.
[5] 15th Anniversary of the Prince of Wales Committee, St David's Day, 1 March 1986.

But he was undeterred. One of his most eloquent appeals was when, as the United Kingdom's patron of the European Year of the Environment, he opened the North Sea Conference in November 1987. He pulled no punches.

"Over the past century," he began, " we have made it into a rubbish dump ... Some argue that we do not have enough proof of danger to justify stricter controls on dumping or to warrant the extra expenditure involved. They say that we must wait for science to provide that proof. If science has taught us anything, however, it is that the environment is full of uncertainty. It makes no sense to test it to destruction. While we wait for the doctor's diagnosis, the patient may easily die!

"We are right to cut dangerous substances, like heavy metals and organic chemicals. We are right to take measures to protect shallow, landlocked areas that are often both at greatest risk and richest in wildlife. We are right to take steps to tackle the garbage that lines some of our beaches with a ribbon of filth. We are also right to look at ways of controlling inputs of dangerous substances into our rivers and estuaries ... "

The North Sea Conference signalled a new line of attack as he articulated 'the Precautionary Principle'. The idea was not new, but this was one of the first times it received a high-profile public airing. There seems little doubt that the subsequent UK decision to ratify the sewage sludge dumping phase-out was made based on this principle. Even now officials will say scientific evidence is not conclusive, but Prince Charles made such a compelling and popular case that pressure built on the government to take action. According to people present, Nicholas Ridley, the relevant minister, looked progressively more horrified with each new remark. The Prince of Wales had already shown the speech to senior civil servants in the department beforehand, in accordance with accepted practice but, according to Jonathan Dimbleby, refused to make requested amendments. Furious rows allegedly ensued, but by then the Prince had made his point.

At various times he has pleaded for improved public transport to lower car emissions, argued for urban villages which would reduce transport requirements, commended manufacturers of pollution control equipment and castigated companies who evade their responsibility. And individuals everywhere should be concerned to reduce the mess the world is in.

"One of the trends which has so degraded our cities is that the communal values upon which cities were founded are now being overturned by the unthinking action of individuals ... There often seems to be a refusal to accept responsibility for our own actions – a refusal to recognise that each of our actions bears a cost. One example is litter. Don't you feel a particular sadness to see the amount of litter in our cities, not just because of the social and economic costs involved in clearing up the beastly stuff, but because of what it says about the attitude of those who contribute to the general mess? For what it's worth, I don't believe we have a hope in hell of protecting the global environment if we can't first persuade ourselves to respect and enhance our local surroundings."[6]

Recycling is one well accepted contribution individuals and businesses can make towards a cleaner planet. It is also the easiest to justify for corporations, since the expense may be offset elsewhere. Alastair Eperon, director of group corporate affairs at Boots, stated the case: "We save money on landfill costs and we become environmentally friendly as a result – something valued by both customers and staff."

Eighteen years after Prince Charles started a bottle bank, we have one on almost every street corner. Recycling is part of the weekly routine. Organic farming is close to becoming mainstream. People who argue against the use of renewable materials are now the cranks. And as for the press, the *Sunday Mirror* of 27 May 1990 said: "Prince Charles could be forgiven for adopting an air of quiet self-satisfaction these days. For the years of sneers and cheap jokes are over. The causes and enthusiasms that earned him taunts ... have suddenly become everyone's concern. Now it's his bandwagon everyone wants to jump on."

It would be wrong to attribute too much of the progress on environmental policy or the sea change in popular perception to the Prince of Wales; but there is no doubt his contribution to raising awareness and stimulating debate was very helpful. Jonathon Porritt said that "he makes it much harder for government to do what comes naturally, which is to continue with business as usual until it becomes impossible". The Prince generates added pressure to act, and so accelerates change. In certain instances he could be said to have instigated change.

Changing harmful environmental practices can only begin by increasing people's awareness, changing attitudes, coming up with alternatives. This is where the Prince is in his element. Former ministers recall meetings in which he led brainstorming sessions, with lists of ideas ending up on napkins. How these sessions translate to policy is more tenuous, and people who took part are reluctant to divulge details; but former ministers certainly give him credit for having a profound influence. The Rt Hon John Gummer MP, who was Secretary of State for the Environment for four years, says: "He has moulded our views about the total environment. The Prince of Wales Environment programmes have transformed the attitudes of business executives and their perceptions about what is possible."

The Prince's position allows him to say things when ministers are constrained. Recent Secretaries of State for Agriculture seem to have been in agreement with some of his positions, but unable to voice support publicly, and senior civil servants at the Environment department have been frustrated at the attitude of

[6] EC Conference on the Urban Environment, Madrid, 30 April 1991.

their counterparts at Agriculture but have been unable to say so. The Prince's critique of modern farming methods and agribusiness may infuriate the NFU and MAFF officials, but it finds supporters elsewhere in Whitehall. There have even been suggestions that some sympathetic civil servants fed information to him which their ministers would rather have suppressed, enabling him to be especially effective in forcing the pace of change.

Sandringham has been the venue for many discussions. The Prince brought together not only British politicians and civil servants but also key figures from Brussels such as Ripa di Mena and Ray MacSharry, European Commissioners for the Environment and Agriculture. He knows that an improved environment requires co-operation not just from different departments and areas of government, but also across countries.

The most high-profile event was a two-day seminar on *Britannia* to air some of the most contentious issues in advance of the 1992 UN Rio Summit. Prince Charles made the point that he was not "an economist, banker or statistician, and I didn't have to be re-elected ... but as an individual I believe in paying a premium for a sensible insurance policy, even if I don't make any claim on it". In the confines of *Britannia* discussions were relatively confidential, which allowed for the venting of deeply felt feelings. As he reminded the audience, there is "an apparently limitless capacity for hot air from world leaders of every conceivable denomination, with green words massively outnumbering green deeds".[7]

He had a real impact in the campaign to eliminate chloroflurocarbon gases. Arresting depletion of the ozone layer required radical and costly changes in business processes and lifestyle. CFC gases are present in many products, ranging from car radiators to domestic appliances. The Prince went on the offensive, calling for a complete ban, at the 'Saving the Ozone Layer' World Conference in 1989. "There is surely an overwhelming scientific case to change the treaty from a reduction to complete elimination." He was not the first person to call for a ban, but his unambiguous demands triggered widespread and mostly favourable coverage. His throwaway line about banning aerosols in his household caught popular interest. The Prince certainly ruffled feathers with *this* remark. BAMA, the aerosol industry group, were livid. The Government was already shifting its stance though the aerosol industry was still fighting. Suddenly the papers had their story. A campaign which had been building steam since late 1984 exploded. As Porritt put it, "it needed something like that to tip it over to unstoppable momentum".

He can also claim to have contributed to the passage of environmentally friendly legislation and rules, such as:

7 Personal speaking notes.

- the ban on straw burning announced in 1990 (seven million tons were being burned each year);
- a decision in 1993 by the Ministry of Agriculture to introduce a five-year incentive scheme to compensate farmers for the transitional costs of converting from current practices to organic farming;
- a phase-out of the disposal of sewage sludge in the North Sea.

All the regulations in the world will not bring back a green and pleasant land unless the parties most prone to pollute are willing. The Prince goes after businesses on three grounds these days. In addition to the moral argument, which has validity of its own, he tries to reposition the environmental proposition:

1. Preserving the environment can be good business.

2. 'Green' consumers will reward businesses which have a good record on the environment.

3. Shareholders will support corporate activity.

He made all these points in one place for the first time in a speech at the Environment Awards to Industry in February 1988: "There are a growing number for instance of what you might refer to as 'green consumers' nowadays, who do mind about what happens and what is done to the environment generally. Businesses always say the shareholders wouldn't like it, but I don't believe anybody has actually bothered to ask the shareholders whether they would like it or not."

On the third point he may have been naïve because, even if some shareholders agree, institutions who control most of the votes do not. On the second point the Prince is proving more right each passing year. Businesses who make profits from pollution control technology prove the first point valid. As he said to business leaders at Davos in 1992: "To the more sceptical among you, I would add that business should be involved because there is money in it. Fortunes are already being made from new, environmentally sensitive technology. Consumers care about these issues, and about what they buy. Companies which have already found ways of cutting pollution and using resources in a more sustainable fashion will find themselves ahead of the competition when these measures start to take greater effect."

The Urban Environment

While the word 'environment' conjures up the countryside, the reality of everyday life for most people is the city. Prince Charles is just as concerned to regenerate urban areas as to ensure the survival of rural ones. But effecting urban improvement means more time and effort. In cities there are more opportunities to make mistakes, and if things go wrong they are harder to put right.

The interest of the Prince in inner city communities was stimulated at the same time as his determination to do something about unemployment. The 1981 riots and his subsequent visits to blighted urban areas led him to take up the cause of community architecture. He understood that only urban renewal could give hope to people who lived in often squalid and depressing places, and that the chances of securing work for the long-term unemployed would be improved if their environment could be improved, by increasing their self-confidence and reducing their sense of alienation. Older inner city areas were run down, but they could be resuscitated. "The social consequences of this are all around us if we care to look. I have seen them in places such as the Penrhys Estate in South Wales, in Easterhouse in Glasgow and in some of our run down inner cities in England. What I have seen makes me somewhat relieved that at least my trusts are active in these situations."[8]

It must have been frustrating for him that the media missed the main point and preferred to pick up on a few emotive images. As the Prince lamented, "Carbuncles, I'm afraid, make better headlines than communities."[9]

Prince Charles has studied urban environmental problems first hand. During an interview in 1996 he said: "I've made it my business to go around a lot of those peripheral housing estates, in particular in the last few years. Real problems exist there. A lot of it, I think, is to do with the breakdown of communities or ... resulting from the design or planning of these areas in the first place, which makes it very difficult for people to manage their lives."

He began helping individuals through the Trust, but his experience in visiting some of the most depressed areas in Britain in the early 1980s moved the emphasis away from the individual and on to communities. By 1985 he had realised that something on a much grander scale was required. His speech to the Institute of Directors in February that year shows the effect of direct exposure to these problems.

"The desperate plight of the inner city areas is, I am sure, well known to you all, with the cycle of economic decline leading to physical deterioration and countless social problems. It is only when you visit these areas, as I do from time to time, that you begin to wonder how it is possible that people are able to live in such inhuman conditions ... the problems being greatest, of course, in those areas which were over-dependent on single industries where changes in demand or

[8] Prince's Trust conference, Towards the Millennium, Manchester, 11 March 1996.
[9] *The Times*, 6 June 1986.

technology have made the original communities redundant, leaving behind vacant buildings and contaminated, damaged or polluted land. The hopelessness felt in such communities is compounded by the decay all around, the vandalism and the inability to control their own lives."

Slum clearance programmes had not worked, and the tower blocks which replaced them made matters worse. The Prince believed a better solution lay in locally based initiatives, even though he was well aware of the problems involved. He described the barriers:

"I was electrified by the atmosphere I encountered in three communities I visited ... In the case of the Liverpool co-operative the residents ... with the help and expert advice of their own architect, fought their way through the seemingly impenetrable entanglements of red tape and official opposition until they finally succeeded in building the houses they wanted in the kind of lay-out they liked. The result ... was what amounted to a very attractive village, containing the whole of the original slum street community, nestling like an oasis in the midst of a barren, urban desert. The residents of the houses I visited all told me that their new situation was like a dream come true. They were now responsible for the maintenance of their properties, and that fact alone had virtually eliminated the vandalism that was previously so rife in the area.

"There is much resistance that stems from the inertia and conservatism of the financial institutions and developers that control the bulk of the resources, while the main obstacles to the type of initiatives I have been speaking about are to be found in the paternalism of central and local government, general bureaucratic inertia and the lack of effective management."

The solution lay in drawing local people, government and business together; starting with national government. "It would be very encouraging if we could see a more coherent approach to inner city problems through the programmes of the departments of the Environment, Trade and Industry and the Manpower Services Commission being made to work more closely together." Meanwhile, at the local government level, "there is an urgent need for a liberal interpretation of the rules by city authorities to allow for a mixture of use in inner cities which could help restore a sense of community". And "directors of private businesses also have a vital role to play. Retired managers could make valuable contributions to trusts by providing managerial skills while companies which still have commitments in inner city areas could join 'task forces'."

The need for urban regeneration is essential to breaking the cycle of disadvantage, because where you live and how you live is part and parcel of the problem. The Prince has made the link explicit on several occasions, as he did in September 1986 at the 'Futures for Youth' conference. "The problems of unemployment and our inner cities will only be resolved if young people who do not feel part of the system can be offered some stake." Regeneration has become one of his watchwords, but he defines it more broadly than many. David Cox, a former director of the Prince of Wales' Committee, stressed this point. "He never got away from the fact that it was all about people."

His environmental disaster has a broken community at its core, so he starts by trying to resuscitate the community as a whole. The logic is that if you give people back their self-respect they start to take pride in their surroundings. Graffiti suddenly seem an eyesore and must be washed away. Broken windows are no longer acceptable and get repaired. Each tiny token adds up. The Prince made this point to me in June:

"I believe strongly that the environment has a powerful effect on our psychological health. I would like to see the majority of these appalling inner city developments, so badly planned, so destructive to people's lives and I believe to their souls over the last 60 years or so, regenerated so that people have defensible space and a garden of some kind and rediscover the nature of our humanity."

The problem in 1985 was how he could help. He needed an organisation through which he could translate his ideas into action and a more general model which went beyond the successful but small examples he had seen. The organisation was to be Business in the Community. After taking the chair Prince Charles visited many depressed areas. During 1985 and 1986 he went from Brixton to Carlisle, from Tower Hamlets to Skelmersdale, learning about the process.

He believed that significant change could only come about through partnerships. He wanted to encourage an enterprise culture at the grass roots level, but recognised that on its own pushing up hill could only take things so far. The big battalions were on the side of business and government. They had to be brought onside, rather than being portrayed as the 'enemy'. A community architect or entrepreneur working with the local community *and* business involvement *and* governmental support was needed.

"The fundamental point to stress is the urgent need for partnership between the public and private sector, between local politicians, community groups and non-public sources of finances. We must sink our differences and cut great swathes through the cat's cradle of red tape which chokes this country from end to end."[10]

In September 1986 he found his model in Lowell, Massachusetts. He had heard about resurgence there at a seminar organised by the American Institute of Architects in Washington the previous November. He wanted to see for himself

---

[10] Speech at the *Times*/Royal Institute of British Architects Community Enterprise Awards, June 1986.

how a town hit by exactly the same sort of economic hardship as the old industrial centres in the north of England had bounced back. Lowell had been a thriving mill town until the decline of the textile industry in the 1960s and 1970s. In the early 1980s it had undergone a remarkable renaissance. Derelict buildings had been transformed through a combination of small business start-ups and attracting artists and artisans into the town centre. Fifteen per cent unemployment had fallen to three per cent.

Prince Charles saw how Lowell had got a new lease of life through a comprehensive programme of urban renovation suitable for high-tech industry. In addition to a tour of Wang Towers, he spent time at the restored Market Mills, a complex containing a visitors' centre, a gift shop and restaurants, which was the focal point for a mixed-use community. The experience set him thinking that many urban areas in Britain were facing similar problems and perhaps some of the same solutions would work. What was needed was a suitable mill town in which to pilot a project.

Two factors particularly impressed him. "They told me that for every $1 from the public sector, $16 or $17 are put in by the private sector." And the other point was the importance of focus sing on one place. "The trouble was that I felt that we were dissipating our energies too much all over the place trying to do too many things. It becomes hopeless because nobody can see anything except pin pricks. I said choose one place and concentrate all our efforts."

For his British Lowell the Prince turned to Stephen O'Brien, the chief executive at Business in the Community. A supportive local government was vital. Did O'Brien have a place in mind? He did not, but since there was an opening on the calendar only three weeks away when the Prince was to be in Yorkshire, O'Brien went to work to find the right spot. He and Robert Davies alighted upon Halifax, where they were aware of a major renovation at Dean Clough Mill. They put a proposition to the leader of the council. How would he feel about having the Prince of Wales take a special interest in the town?

Halifax came with all the right characteristics. The traditional textile industry had all but disappeared, abandoned buildings abounded and the community was in recession. Unemployment locally stood at 13 per cent in 1986 – high, but too low to qualify for priority grants from government. There was a local initiative, the Inheritance Project, which was trying to bring life back to the town but which confined its efforts to giving a face lift to public buildings. A supportive council chief executive was a clincher. Michael Ellison's view was that: "We want to see buildings being used not derelict."[11] And there was Sir Ernest Hall, the first community entrepreneur to work closely with the Prince of Wales.

[11] *Financial Times*, 17 July 1987.

Hall had a number of ideas. Many were similar to those that had worked in Lowell. He was active in mill conversions. Dean Clough lay right at the heart of Halifax. Once one of the world's largest carpet factories, employing over 5,000 at the turn of the century, by 1982 one million square feet lay vacant and deteriorating. Hall's approach encouraged arts, education and enterprise to create a 'practical Utopia'. His other idea was low cost incubators for small start-up companies of every ilk. Business brought jobs and demand for other services. New businesses were an essential precondition to revitalising the area, but were not on their own sufficient to complete the process.

Dean Clough could be the anchor. The Prince persuaded the mayor of Lowell to come over and give a few pointers. He also suggested that the mayor of Halifax go to Lowell and take a look. The Calderdale Partnership was launched by the Prince in February 1987. The area covered was a 140-square-mile district containing a population of 192,000, so if he could make an impact here no-one would be able to dismiss the project as small scale.

Halifax was an excellent choice, but not without problems. The local council contained members from the unreconstructed hard left who felt they should take charge and make all the decisions. Some actively opposed many of the partnership's proposals to bring life back to the community. In part due to the ability of the council to block improvements, the Halifax development took time to demonstrate progress.

The Prince went to Calderdale six times in 1987 and 1988. His most visible contribution took the form of bringing business leaders to see the work, and he was remarkably successful in dragging his rather reluctant guests to Halifax. He led one group along the high street, pointing out shabby store fronts. Confronted with evidence of eyesores and overdue renovations several companies, including Sears and the Burton Group, promptly smartened up their sites.

Companies began to co-operate on a series of schemes covering a wider range of activity. JCB lent a digger and trained two lads to create a riverside walk by Hebden Bridge. Bradford Pennine Insurance expanded its computer centre within Calderdale. Hambro Venture Capital was persuaded to open an office in Dean Clough following a lunch between the managing partner, Harry Fitzgibbons, and the Prince. Rowntree's set up a fund to make low interest loans to help people do up shops, houses or public buildings. British Rail agreed to clean up Halifax railway station. Several local firms sponsored the Hedben Bridge Festival Theatre. Derelict town centre sites such as Upper George Yard were converted, with funding from the local authority, into retail, restaurants and offices. Tetley's completely refurbished the five-storey Brass Cat Public House, helped by an English Heritage grant.

By March 1988 a total of £350,000 had been invested in the area, with a similar sum pledged for the following year. But something even more substantial was needed: specifically something which would create new jobs.

In 1987 the philanthropist Vivien Duffield visited the Children's Museum in Boston and decided to open something similar in Britain. She had in mind a Kensington site near many other museums, and approached the Prince to see if he would be willing to open her project. The Prince agreed, but with the condition that he was only available if the new museum was located in Halifax. This was not the venue Duffield had in mind but Prince Charles put the case convincingly, painting a broader picture of the potential contribution of her museum to the community. He took her to Calderdale that December. Duffield was persuaded. An £8 million investment followed, transforming a nine-acre site which up until that point had been a derelict eyesore. The Prince recalls how importance this was.

"One useful element of the regeneration process in a place like Halifax, which had all it's traditional industries knocked on the head, is to try and create a cultural focus. It would mean it would have something which other towns didn't have which would act as a sort of draw or would give the place a reputation for being the centre for something. In this case I suggested what about a children's museum. There isn't one anywhere else and it will give a reason to go to Halifax and help to create other things around that."

Eureka opened in 1992, and is now one of the top ten visitor destinations in the north west, attracting 400,000 visitors annually. It employs 80 people, and services contracted out probably create close to the same number of jobs again. Spending by visitors runs to millions of pounds. Dean Clough, the business, arts and education complex, has become a classic symbol of regeneration. By 1991 it housed 200 companies and organisations, employing around 2,500 people. Major firms like the Halifax Building Society moved there, as has the area's HM Customs and Excise. Hall calculated that the rates paid to the council are now 30 times greater than they were when the carpet factory was in existence.

No other programme has had such a direct impact on so many people as the Calderdale One Town Partnership. The Prince changed the whole climate towards regeneration. He got people together who had been at loggerheads. Then he stimulated a sense of shared purpose and local ownership. This was not some expert from London popping in to tell the local half-wits how to do things. Here was the Prince of Wales saying, look, you can do this yourselves if you just agree to work together, and I will do what I can to be helpful. Here are a few ideas to consider and names of other people who you might like to talk with. By the way, this is Richard Wade from Business in the Community, who can lend a hand. And as for me I'll look forward to stopping by in six months or so to see how you have got on.

People noticed, and it was not just the jobs – though the number employed at Dean Clough rose from 500 in 1986 to 2,500 by 1991. The place took on a different atmosphere, which was picked up in a late 1990 visit by business leaders, such as Victoria Mitchell, executive director of Savill's, the estate agents.

"I had preconceived ideas of Halifax being a bleak, dark, cold, unwelcoming, industrial town with mill chimneys belching soot. The reality in 1990 was the exact opposite. Everywhere we went was clean. There was space, room to breathe, an elegance, sense of prosperity and well-being, confidence and pride that I had not imagined would be there."

The Prince always stresses that regeneration requires a local community architect or entrepreneur. "Community architecture has 'shown' ordinary people that their views are worth having." Also critical is the involvement of the community as a whole. Urban regeneration will not work one house at a time. This is the horny old problem of 'who benefits if I do up my house?' Mostly me, but in part my next door neighbours. And if they do nothing I do not get the full enjoyment or uplift in value my improvements deserve. I have never heard Prince Charles articulate the economic theory known as the Landlord's Dilemma, but he understands the nub of the matter. Thus his emphasis on whole streets or areas as integrated communities, where the rising tide lifts all boats.

One drawback to a holistic approach is that nothing gets done without a community entrepreneur as catalyst, a potentially serious limitation. The Prince wanted to test the theory that if you can find the right place an entrepreneur will follow. The right place turned out to be a run-down London neighbourhood in Finsbury which straddled three boroughs: a classic case of slipping between the cracks, as each council shoved responsibility for the area on to the other in an endless round of pass the problem. Business in the Community assisted in the creation of the Finsbury Park Community Trust, and then set out to find someone. Amobi Modu, formerly a community officer at Lambeth, took charge and built a centre which turns over £800,000 annually and has found 200 jobs for local unemployed people.

So you could begin at either end, with a place or a person, allowing selection of areas most in need regardless of whether there was a local entrepreneur already active. This is fortunate since such people can be unlikely characters and not always the easiest of allies. Prince Charles has met several. Get him on the subject and he will wax lyrical about community architects such as Ernest Hall in Halifax or Paddy Doherty in Londonderry. One name which constantly crops up is that of Tony McGann of the Eldonians, where there have been three Seeing is Believing visits.

Prince Charles's support for the community architect or entrepreneur strengthened after his experience in Halifax. Another programme started in Blackburn in 1987. Newcastle, Bristol and Teeside all benefited from the involvement of Business in the Cities, which became the umbrella for several separate but similar initiatives. The CBI added its firepower to local business action teams that were starting to sprout up.

Thinking on a much grander scale required a more systematic approach. The Prince decided to institutionalise what had worked at Halifax. In the 1991 annual report for Business in the Community he wrote:

"I have seen first hand how their companies play a positive role in building strong local communities, both here and abroad. By inviting business leaders to visit the inner cities with me I have found that seeing the problems first hand is a powerful stimulus to action. I have launched a programme [Seeing is Believing] which takes business leaders out to examine different examples of business involvement in local communities."

The Prince's contribution varies from place to place, but one constant is that he always tries to overcome obstacles. I saw him in action on the Marsh Farm estate in Luton, gently cajoling local business leaders. "I've just been handed this marvellous proposal for a people's launderette, and asked if I could help. It seems that water doesn't seem to want to get to the higher floors in some of these flats, and it would make a huge difference if there could be a launderette on the ground floor. Now I wonder if there might be a few spare washing machines lying about anywhere?" Jim Ratcliffe, managing director of Granada Home Technology, knew exactly where to lay his hands on some.

The urban regeneration model advocated today by Prince Charles contains several elements which were new when introduced. One underlying premise is that what happens in the community could be the responsibility of someone other than the local authority. But then who is responsible? The Prince has two answers. First, the community itself has to be galvanised into action, which is where community entrepreneurs come in. There needs to be a strong local leader, usually outside any formal hierarchy, who is willing to take on entrenched interests and force through change. He identified this as the key ingredient. "Whenever regeneration worked, you would always find a community entrepreneur who was in it not for profit but for social objectives."

Secondly, outside parties have to be marshalled to help provide the resources that the community lacked. Here the Prince can encourage, exhort and persuade. The primary target is local businesses who should recognise a degree of self-interest in revitalising their community. They are also the most likely source of manpower, money and gifts or loans of materials and equipment. The phrase "prosperous back streets lead to prosperous high streets" became a watchword.

Urban regeneration is a hard slog, not least because progress often means reconciling opposing interests as well as conflicting ideas as to what should be done. He recognised this in a speech at a Building Communities Conference in December 1989. "There are often, as you will know, very deep underlying conflicts within inner cities communities. There are a multitude of different organisations and voluntary groups that need to be brought in and consulted and that obviously leads to several frustrating moments. Actually working together in partnership is an extraordinarily difficult task, and nobody is claiming that it is in any way easy." These partnerships are difficult to form and even more difficult to maintain but absolutely essential.

Another programme of urban renewal which attracted his attention and where he was able to nudge things along, is the Bromley-by-Bow Centre, an area where few people would choose to live. A corner of Tower Hamlets, London's poorest borough, it has the highest population density of any urban area of similar size in the country. With more of its surface area occupied by roads than any other municipality in Britain, it has the lowest proportion of car owners among residents, and one of the highest turnovers, as residents who can move out as quickly as possible.

The Centre grew around a church. When the Reverend Andrew Mawson arrived 14 years ago, the building was more or less derelict and he was advised not to switch on the lights or he might be electrocuted. The congregation consisted of 12 elderly people. Within a radius of a 10-minute walk over 50 different languages and dialects are spoken. Ethnic tension was high. Not long after he arrived Mawson saw a white woman dragging a pregnant Bengali along the street by her hair.

He realised his challenge was not confined to religion. The traditional role of the church and the voluntary sector in this community was irrelevant. He needed to rebuild a sense of community and improve the local quality of life. So he set about building partnerships with local people who were interested in running activities. Hearing Mawson describe how he goes about getting things done at Bromley-by-Bow, you could almost be listening to the Prince of Wales. "Start with people ... get people together and mix them up ... Sharing food is pragmatic. There's no point holding seminars on racism ... Build partnerships between the business community, statutory and voluntary sector ... Integrate and bring things together ... we are the environments we live in ... "

At Bromley-by-Bow strides have been made providing jobs in an area of high unemployment. There are now 100 people on the payroll and 35 volunteers. There is still a church, though totally surrounded by a nursery. There is a café, play area, garden, art areas and toy library. Rooms in the complex serve as bases for local support groups, including a very active Bengali outreach project serving over 300 families. There is a health centre – a remarkable place where the doctor could just as easily suggest a change in diet, a massage or even joining an art class (conveniently located in the next building) for a better social life, as valium. Opened by Tessa Jowell in March 1998, the new health centre is the model for a potential 500 'Healthy Living Centres' proposed in a government white paper. Its integrated approach has already attracted interest from the chief medical officer, Sir Kenneth Calman.

Development nearly came to a halt in December 1995. Second stage expansion, featuring the health complex, needed much more money. Mawson had put in for a £2.7 million grant from the Single Regeneration Budget, with £1 million in private sector support contingent on this grant. After two years the Department of Health confirmed all the necessary approvals to proceed – but two days later a letter arrived nixing the grant application. The problem was that the SRB was designed to fund job creation or training and enterprise projects, and what did a health centre have to do with employment? "For government, it's all about which box you are in: is it an employment problem or an environmental problem or a health problem? For us it's all about individuals and it's just Billy, whatever the problem."

This was Wednesday. On Friday Prince Charles came to call. "The good thing about the Prince of Wales is that he understood what is going on here and what this project is all about. He took a real interest in what we are doing. This was not just another event he had to do." The Prince liked what he saw, but not what he heard about a bureaucratic tangle which threatened to derail their plans. A personal, hand-written letter went to John Gummer at Environment asking him to see Mawson. Mawson got his meeting the very next month, followed by resumption of a dialogue with officials who made suggestions about how to amend the bid: specifically, remove any reference to the health centre, even though this money would create jobs there. Honour satisfied, the application was duly approved. Mawson gives full credit to the Prince. "You should not need to have the Prince of Wales intervene to make sure an integrated project like ours happens, but his intervention enabled us to have a direct discussion with the Secretary of State which got the officials to re-look at our funding."

Schemes like Bromley-by-Bow have to attract both business support and help from various areas of government if they are to succeed. "He has given legitimacy to something which in the early years was seen as fringe. The Prince of Wales has facilitated relationships between the social sector and the market sector."

The Prince inadvertently helped in another way. Mawson met an executive from Tesco during a reception at St James's Palace, and thus established a dialogue with the most important company in his neighbourhood. The first link was a trolley return scheme, which built a bridge. Subsequently Tesco stumped up money for renovation at the centre.

Bromley-by-Bow is a study in excellence of urban regeneration. The centre has taken huge strides in integrating different racial groups and different cultures, to such an extent that local Hindu and Jewish residents attended a recent celebration of the Muslim Eid in the Christian church. High on the agenda is an emphasis on getting people into employment, which often starts by restoring them to full mental and physical health. Many people have found work through the centre, and others have volunteered to do community service which has led to jobs. The garden attendant is an epileptic who originally came in as a patient. There have been programmes in association with the school across the road. With a philosophy which gives pride of place to holistic medical practice, the Prince of Wales might have designed it himself.

It is not necessary to convert a whole community every time. John Laing took the lead in a group working to convert a damaged building in Thanet into a centre for affordable child care. Practical programmes that have direct impact on the local community are proliferating. Tarmac led a spring clean in Birmingham's Balsall Heath, to remove 300 tons of rubbish from the area. These are typical of the ideas that surface from discussion groups and which individual companies can comfortably take on. Each activity on its own may not amount to much, but when you add it all up you can see how much the Prince has helped to achieve. Many opportunities to improve the environment are just waiting for someone to do the right thing, and it makes the Prince impatient that more people do not yet see how easy and attractive some schemes can be.

"If you've got all these redundant buildings from the past you've got already something to build on … You've got the material to regenerate with and people would then want to relocate there, businesses want to come because the environments are so much better. It is only now, when its almost too late, that people are beginning to realise that this is possible. I set up the Phoenix Trust two years ago for regeneration through Heritage for those mill buildings. I had been trying for years and couldn't get anywhere. None of these councils – nobody – could see the value in these old buildings, and yet they convert infinitely better to other uses, including residential use, than any modernist building does."

Urban regeneration finds its purest form of expression in the urban village concept, the community of the 21st century. The Prince is keen on expanding their numbers. "I am hoping we can encourage the development of 'urban villages' in order to re-introduce human scale, intimacy and a vibrant street life. These factors can help to restore to people this sense of belonging and pride in their own particular surroundings."[12]

[12] Address accompanying the release of the 1989 Prince's Trust annual report, Livingstone, 4 September 1989.

Housing is at the centre of any community, since the home is where people spend most time. "The debate about housing density must clearly be re-opened in response to the challenge of sustainability. In city after city soulless high-rise blocks have brutalised communities, reinforcing alienation, encouraging crime. But high-density does *not* necessarily mean high-rise; I have seen a number of new housing schemes specifically designed to rebuild the spirit of *community*, encouraging face-to-face interactions, ensuring that delicate balance between private space and shared or communal space."[13]

The concept of urban regeneration is now accepted, but plenty of communities around the country still have awful environments. In April 1998 Prince Charles named 47 action areas where he wanted to focus his future efforts, and where he hoped business would join him. The initial response in the press was reassuring, even though, as the *Birmingham Evening Mail* pointed out, "it is believed to be the first time any royal has taken the risk of courting political controversy so openly by singling out Britain's most poverty-hit communities".

The Prince is used to being pilloried. This time he was pleasantly surprised to receive comments like those of Jan Stebbens, senior cook at the Ladywood Health and Community Centre, who said: "Prince Charles's name will carry enough weight to get people involved and invest in the area." Councillor Pat Roberts of Bristol said: "Anything that raises the profile of Knowle West is a good thing ... " A government source quoted in the *Express* claimed the Prince's stance was backed by Tony Blair.

Everyone Can Make a Contribution

The Prince's position has been constant over 30 years. "If we and future generations are to continue to enjoy a comfortable lifestyle we need to learn to respect the environmental consequences of everything we do."[14]

Cross-pollination between programmes is encouraged by the Prince. The Youth Business Trust might seem to have objectives which are separate from environmental activities, yet there is much overlap. The environment, broadly defined, is improved when more people are employed. People with purpose are more conscious of their surroundings and more likely to do something to improve them. Young people tend to be more environmentally aware because they have grown up with the issue. There are no formal requirements to consider environmental issues in evaluating plans, but people working with the Prince are often encouraged by him to support more such businesses.

The Trust has backed garden and tree services, horticultural centres and

[13] EC Conference on the Urban Environment, Madrid, 30 April 1991.

[14] The 1998 Annual Report of the Prince's Trust – Bro.

companies which renovate buildings. Several are involved with recycling materials such as old cable and metal. One of the first businesses to receive a bursary in 1982 made fire logs out of old newspapers. Others emphasise repair, restoration and reuse of almost anything from wooden pallets to supermarket trolleys and electrical equipment. He encourages his Trust to help young people interested in keeping alive traditional skills and trades, such as dry stonewalling, thatching and making paints from hand ground natural pigments. Clive Muir, a dry stonewaller from Clywd, had been trained by the National Trust in this age-old skill. Such walls done right will last for 200 years or more without cement or mortar, often without attention. Clive was a natural to receive funding.

Especially creative, even idiosyncratic, ideas can be ecologically helpful and economically viable. One unlikely business, One Foot Taller, set up by Will White and Katarino Barac (PYBT '95), got its start by taking old washing machines and using their parts to make glassware such as fruit bowls and lamps. The Conran Shop and Heals have already stocked them. They now make the environment part of their design brief and use recycled plastic in their furniture. Wacky Artists, run by Suzanne Mcgrail (PYBT '97), uses discarded car wheel hubs as the basis for clocks. The Inner Tube, set up by Julie McDonagh (PYBT '96), makes handbags, luggage and other accessories, as well as sculptured seating, out of recycled inner tyre tubes. She has already won a Millennium Products Award, and exports as far afield as Australia and Hong Kong. Dan Hedges makes models out of scrap metal. The Prince is a paying customer, and Hedges' dinosaurs attracted other high profile clients, including the science fiction writer Arthur C. Clarke and actor David Jason.

There is probably no organisation that manages to combine more of these separate elements than Reclaim. Based in Sheffield, it recycles about 1,000 tonnes of plastic waste each year, as well as metal cans, foil and textiles. The business also acts as a feeder by employing young people, up to 75 at a time, many of whom have learning disabilities. Working at Reclaim helps disadvantaged young people acquire specific skills and boosts their self-confidence: many move on to work elsewhere. Here is an organisation which improves the environment through recycling and also creates jobs for unemployed disabled young people. The Prince's Trust helps fund it.

One initiative of the Business Leaders' Forum ties back to what the Prince had been saying at Cambridge 30 years ago. This relates to an ongoing search for suitable exploitation of renewable resources – be they timber, fish, or energy. British companies are also getting the message. Retailers B&Q and Do It All are looking for certified suppliers of hemlock and cedar. These days Sainsbury and Tesco try to buy fish only from suppliers that do not condone over-fishing. Eastern Electricity has committed to raising the proportion of electricity to be generated from renewable energy sources from zero to ten per cent.

Business in the Community members are also encouraged to consider environmental projects. A special target team – Business in the Environment – has developed an 'index of corporate environmental engagement', a check list which motivates companies to measure their progress in meeting environmental goals. Many of the projects carried out by Community Ventures and Volunteers were tailored to improve the environment. Where projects involve construction, the use of renewable materials is encouraged. Examples abound, from creating a bicycle path to restoring a water mill to planting a garden on a derelict lot.

Quantifying environmental benefits is an academic minefield. Whether it is reclaimed canals or graffiti-free walls, there is no common ground on how to translate benefits into pounds and pence.

Take the environmental work which took place in Wales over 30 years. Around £8 million was injected directly over the years, with much more alongside where the Prince of Wales Committee was the catalyst for something larger. That works out at about £16 million in today's terms, or £80 million assembled in total. What that money produced was certainly a great deal more when all the free labour and materials are added in. Woodlands and hedgerows are more 'valuable' 20 years on than the day they were planted. How can we account for several million daffodil bulbs planted during this period?

The Prince is reluctant to be drawn on the subject of the impact his influence may have had on improving the quality of environmental action by the Government. His role has been behind the scenes, low key and subtle, but evidence of former ministers and others confirm its impact. Evaluating improvement in communities where he has contributed to their regeneration is also tricky. It can be tangible, such as a new community centre, sports or garden equipment, or intangible, such as safer, cleaner streets. What is indisputable is that hundreds of thousands of people are better off, and the whole community benefits.

An interesting example of how the Seeing is Believing programme can contribute arose out of a December 1994 feedback session at St James's Palace. Chris Trotman, director at SKF, remembers that in the middle of a fairly humdrum speech Prince Charles said: "Why on earth can't you people get your act together and recycle your used equipment?"

Chatting over tea, Trotman asked the Prince, "Why can't we?"
He replied, "I want someone to tell me."
Trotman took the bait. "I'll find out."

And the answer was that there was no middle man, at least none capable of coping with the specific issues involved in recycling specialist equipment. Companies were happy to contribute, but not willing to make any special effort. Trotman formed Recycle IT, now part of Bytes Twice, a network which channels donations to suitable recipients. Recycle IT alone has processed over 2,000 computers which had an original cost of over £4 million. As a side benefit, the required refurbishment provides training places and part-time work for 20 people.

This is just one businessman who went on one Seeing is Believing visit four years ago. His response has been exceptional. Many people who see and even believe still do nothing or make a token gesture; but there are others who go the mile, senior business executives like Charles Allen, Bill Castell, Rudi Bogni, and Peter George, all of whom are active themselves and have encouraged many people who work for them to contribute to regeneration activities.

Since Seeing is Believing began there have been 134 visits similar to the one that inspired Trotman. David Thomas, chief executive of Whitbread, set up a hotline and developed a company-wide programme to recycle goods after a 1994 visit. In three years Whitbread donated 2,000 beds, 4,500 pillows, 850 chairs, carpets and curtains for over 1,000 rooms and more, worth £500,000 second hand and much more new. If each visit only spawned £2.5 million of incremental benefits, which does not seem too much given the resources available to those involved, that would work out at £335 million. Many projects develop a life of their own. Recycle IT alone should process nearly £2 million of additional equipment in 1998.

To summarise the environmental impact of the Prince one can reasonably claim that he has:

- influenced important legislation in the UK, and even elsewhere;
- encouraged through exhortation and his own example more eco-friendly behaviour, particularly through recycling;
- brought help to over 70 urban and rural communities, from Finsbury Park to Balsall Heath, covering more than 750,000 inhabitants;
- established urban regeneration as an accepted approach to development. Former Heritage Secretary Virginia Bottomley volunteered that "the concepts around urban regeneration come as much from the Prince of Wales as from anyone else";
- been the catalyst for at least £80 million of improvements in the countryside; stimulated business donations in excess of £335 million in goods and services directed to improving the quality of life in depressed communities.

These can only be a sample; but it is safe to say that the quality of the environment in Britain in 1998 is a lot healthier thanks to the efforts of the Prince of Wales.

Chapter 7

SPECIAL CONSTITUENCIES

"When people feel excluded we all suffer"

T he Prince of Wales has been associated with four specific groups in much of his work. These are people he feels need extra support.

PEOPLE WITH DISABILITIES

He starts with the premise that everyone can do something positive. This underlies the objectives of every organisation in which he is involved. Perhaps no area bears stronger testimony to it than his work with disabled people.

Grants to the disadvantaged and physically disabled were identified as a special category for the Trust at the outset. The initial focus was on making life more enjoyable through a holiday or special expedition. These short-term palliatives had limited impact, however welcome, and made little permanent improvement. There is a limit to what could be done when the average grant was only £100.

He became patron of the British Wheelchair Sports Foundation in 1978. In 1980 he agreed to help with the United Nations International Year of Disabled People. The UN Charter emphasises the importance of allowing disabled people to make decisions about their own lives. Traditional practice had been based on doing things *for* disabled people. Prince Charles favoured a movement designed to *empower* people with disabilities.

The Prince of Wales became patron for the UK and Lord Snowdon, president. Snowdon was the perfect choice. Ever since recovering from polio he had campaigned on behalf of disabled people. He was determined that 1981 should not just be a token interlude, but the start of a whole new way of thinking. When he said "there is no point climbing on the International Year of Disabled People bandwagon if it will be taken off the road on December 31st," Prince Charles was in total agreement, not least because of the way Snowdon stated the case. "It's not sympathy we want – it's understanding. It's not charity – it's action."

The Prince and Snowdon made several joint appearances, such as one at a June rally for disabled drivers at Silverstone. One solo visit to a purpose-built home made a deep impression. A young wheelchair user showed him the new and specially designed bathroom, where he was unable to use any of the facilities by himself because nothing was at the right height. Prince Charles was horrified. "Why hadn't anyone consulted the people who would be living here before it was built?" This seems such a simple question and he was not the only person asking it – but his concern made more people pay attention.

During 1981 all the Trusts intensified their activities in support of people with disabilities, and more projects received money. There was the 'Groomsmobile', a caravan fitted with specialised aids for physically impaired people, to give everyone a chance to experience the problems of disability. In Coventry there was support for a hostel for 'educationally subnormal' school leavers; and in Cardiff, a grant to publish a 'day out' access guide for the disabled, covering sites within a 100-mile radius of the city. But not much changed, and only two per cent of grants went to disabled groups. But by 1983 the number and percentage had been given a boost by another milestone event.

The Prince's marriage in 1981 proved just the opportunity to provide resources for this work. The Royal Wedding Fund had received money from a variety of sources, such as the Hyde Park fireworks, which raised £43,000, and the display of presents which produced £86,000. A further £636,000 came from the sale of two booklets on the wedding; all to be set aside specifically to help disabled people.

The royal wedding appeal attracted over 2,000 applications requesting funds. The Prince specified the approval guidelines. He wanted to make sure awards went to organisations giving direct and practical help to disabled people, or to groups providing self- and mutual help. This approach paralleled the way he was steering the Trust. He personally vetted every one of the 65 grants of £2,000 or more.

Giving out money was all very well, but Prince Charles felt that he could do much more than fund-raising. After the flurry of activity generated by the high profile campaign slowed down, his office was still inundated with calls and letters suggesting he should "stick with it". These requests, along with Snowdon's suggestion, confirmed his inclination to continue the work.

A meeting was convened for 1 December 1982, with Prince Charles in the chair, to thrash out his questions:

- is a new organisation really needed?
- would it overlap with existing organisations?
- where is the greatest need?
- how could a new organisation be funded?

The last proved easiest to answer. There was more than £300,000 left in the Royal Wedding Fund. As to the other questions, there was agreement that some new body was appropriate subject to resolving several sensitive issues. Specifically he did not want to appear to be diverting resources or duplicating established activities. It was also important not to be seen to take political stances. The new body was set a mandate restricting it to advising existing organisations. No financial role was envisaged, to ensure money stayed in the field rather than being recycled through the new group.

The Prince recapped the reason for its formation. "After the International Year of Disabled People when I was patron, it was felt it was silly to just end at the end of 1981. We thought it would be a good idea if we could continue the work that was done in that year, bringing in more people and trying to make them more aware of what the problems were which disabled people faced."[1]

Snowdon feels it was "wildly important that the Prince of Wales decided to get involved, because he is not political and so can fight for equal rights. When the Prince of Wales goes on a visit around a factory he can point out problems for people with disabilities."

In July 1983 the Prince of Wales Advisory Group on Disability (POWAGOD) officially met for the first time. The Snowdon working party, set up in early 1982 to keep things ticking over, was subsumed into POWAGOD.

The original advisors were distinguished in the field of disability service, and many were themselves disabled. Bill Buchanan, the second chairman, was a businessman who had been paralysed late in life as the result of falling out of an apple tree. Other wheelchair users in the group were Anne Davies and Stephen Bradshaw, who was also CEO of the Spinal Injuries Association. The vice chairman, lawyer Colin Low, was blind. Every member had something special to contribute, with designated experts in complementary areas such as leisure, media and religion. More significant, they were not representing any group or organisation.

There was no formal charter, but written into the culture was an explicit understanding that consultation with disabled people would come before anything else. As to his own role, that would be on an *ad hoc* basis once the group was ready to recommend specific activity. The group would seek to be a catalyst, to bridge gaps and bring together groups already active so they could be more effective.

The Prince was aware that many professionals talked down to people with disabilities, as if a problem that affected one part of their faculties reduced all their abilities. He wanted to eradicate condescension and empower disabled people – and then get out of the way and let them get on with it. These ideas sound so

[1] NHBC Design Award launch, 29 October 1987.

sensible that it is hard now to grasp that they were new and necessary, but people who were involved have described the community of charities working in the disabled arena in the early 1980s as engaged in internecine guerrilla warfare. The disability community rarely spoke with a united voice. The Prince realised that as a single constituency, people with disabilities could carry much more weight, whether as consumers, voters or activists. He wanted to harness all the major organisations and, at least on pan-disability issues, persuade them to sing from the same hymn sheet. He was determined to avoid arguments over terminology and language, and the ranking of degrees of disability.

The priorities for the group and for the Prince were summarised in a February 1985 publication entitled *Living Options*, in which the most important problems facing *all* disabled people were identified. The principles which Prince Charles wanted to govern any initiatives were choice, consultation, information, participation, recognition and autonomy. Over 30 separate organisations were involved in the consultation process, and all gave *Living Options* their approval.

Living Options was so well received that the DHSS allocated nearly £1 million in sponsorship, for staffing to support further development work into the key areas of concern. The three greatest concerns of disabled people are not very different from those of people without disabilities: employment, healthcare and education. There is a fourth which is specific to them and that is the whole area of access. The Prince has been supportive in seeking improvements in all four areas. As Professor Anthony Clare said: "He continually emphasised the practical needs of the disabled. He only wanted to seek practical advances in the fields that matter."

Employment Options

In Britain there are nearly six million people of working age who have some form of disability, or who suffer from a health problem so serious that it affects their ability to hold down a regular job. Less than 10 per cent of disabled people in Britain are in wheelchairs. Disability comes in many forms, physical, sensory, hidden and mental. The Prince has been known to say that nearly everyone is disabled in at least one way. Nearly 60 per cent of them do not work and are likely to remain unemployed. Most firms are reluctant to take on people with problems which are perceived as affecting their ability to perform.

Discrimination in employment persists in 1998. A recent DfEE survey found that people with disabilities are twice as likely to be unemployed as able-bodied people, and those who are employed are likely to be in lower-level jobs. Yet in the same survey 93 per cent of employers claimed to believe that people with disabilities at their firms performed at least as well as everyone else. So if performance is not the problem, the problem must be prejudice.

POWAGOD targeted employment as the place to push first. The Prince felt that only a top-down approach was likely to yield substantive results. The first of what was to be a series of meetings took place in Kensington Palace in November 1983, when the chairmen of 12 of the largest companies received an invitation to lunch followed by a letter setting out the topic for discussion: "What is your company doing to ensure disabled people get a fair shake?"

Among those in attendance were British Rail and BT. Corporate policies on disability were rare in 1983. Prince Charles's prompt sheet for the lunch emphasises two points that many businesses miss. Employees with disabilities can be equally competent, and disabled people represent a large market. The points were made, and the meal ended in the usual way: "I'd so like an update. Someone will be in touch. Can I have a progress report in 12 months?"

So no-one was to be let off the hook, and while in some cases there was reluctance to take concrete action, others become converts. Dialogue led to the creation of a separate organisation, the Employers' Forum on Disability, which exists to promote the employment of more disabled people. Set up in 1990 with £36,000, it has grown by 1998 to 280 members covering four million employees, about 15 per cent of the workforce. The new organisation stayed under the umbrella of the POWAGOD until 1993, when it received separate charitable status.

The Forum also co-ordinated with Business in the Community to raise awareness among executives by including organisations working with disabled people on Seeing is Believing schedules. What happened on 6 June 1996 in south-east London is illustrative of a day devoted to the disabled. Executives spent time at:
- the Blackfriars Settlement, a project providing work-related opportunities for those with learning disabilities or mental health problems;
- Action for Blind People; and
- Sabre Employment, which specialises in the placement of people with disabilities.

The Forum aims to promote best practices among employers, and increase positive attitudes towards disabled employees. It organises career fairs, conferences, publications and research, and special schemes such as Supported Employment for People With Autism. The Forum also gets involved in lobbying. It was one of the parties that helped trigger the Disability Discrimination Act of 1996, and was instrumental in securing several amendments to that legislation.

One of the most recent ideas to surface was the formation of the Leadership Consortium. As employment barriers began to come down, the glass ceiling on disabled employees seemed to move lower. The idea was to take a disabled person with particular promise and arrange leadership and management training, to enhance their ability to get ahead on the corporate ladder or elsewhere. The Leadership Consortium started in a small way in 1992. Sponsorship has risen to 52. The Prince of Wales held a private reception for the first 50 in May 1998, where he met bursary holders and heard stories of people who had overcome serious impairments to achieve something special. He also invited ministers and senior civil servants. Impressed by what they heard and encouraged by the Prince's support, seven more government departments have since signed up to the programme.

The idea of helping disabled people become self-employed is an important contribution Prince Charles has made to the debate. Self-employment overcomes many, though by no means all, of the problems facing disabled people who want to work. There is more flexibility as to where to work, when and even how.

Evergreen Horticultural Services shows how well this can work. Michael Dixon had qualified in horticulture at Sparsholt College of Agriculture, intending to go into gardening. Those plans were scuppered as he sat in a parked car outside the local job centre and was rammed from behind. The accident caused severe whiplash. Back problems meant that Michael could no longer do heavy gardening work. Many other career options were also closed off. He had been on incapacity benefit for several months when he turned to Lesley Roddick-Harris, a disability employment advisor.

Huw Davies was also having difficulty holding down a job. His problem was a learning disability, dyspraxia, which makes it hard to remember things. He also arrived at Roddick-Harris's office that same morning. Huw and Michael had been friends for many years, but this encounter came as a surprise. They put their heads together and came up with a perfect solution. Both were having difficulties finding work, but were willing to consider self-employment. Neither Michael nor Huw could run a gardening business on their own, but a partnership might succeed. Michael needed someone to do the hard grafting. Huw needed someone who would tolerate his lapses. Roddick-Harris steered them to the Prince's Trust, which came up with a £1,500 bursary to buy gardening tools, supplies and pay for the insurance on a car and trailer. A further £1,500, by way of a loan, was promised for later.

The loan was never needed. The combination has been a winner. Evergreen Horticultural Services started on 1 August 1997 with ten clients, mostly introduced through the Youth Business Trust. Now there are over 100. Huw and Michael are working 12 hours a day seven days a week, and expect to hire their first employee this year to cope with the overload; and they will be looking to hire a person who, like them, experiences some form of disability which makes it hard to find regular employment.

Both Huw and Michael know they only have a successful business today because the Prince's Trust was willing to back them. The royal connection has not done any harm either. Michael explained, "When people heard we were meeting the Prince, we had customers calling up wanting to see if we were on the TV, and the local media coverage helped in recommending our service, so we should get some new customers that way." "Not that we need any more work," Huw added, not looking entirely happy at the prospect. "Still, maybe we can hire *two* more people."

Another success story is that of Stuart Dunne, who as a teenager was involved in an accident which confined him to hospital for five months and left him in a wheelchair. Stuart began to tinker with designs for wheelchairs to make them more useful for sports. Having made modifications that worked for him, Stuart decided to set up in business as a manufacturer and distributor of sports equipment for the disabled. The Youth Business Trust provided an initial bursary of £1,500 and a loan of £3,500 to help start CJS Custom in 1989.

Stuart has never looked back. Today CJS, appropriately renamed Cyclone, is one of the fastest growing small companies in the country. Turnover should top £750,000 this year. Stuart employs his own brother as well as nine other people, five of whom are also disabled. The product range has kept pace, and now includes quad bikes and freedom buggies which can be operated on a suck and blow system. Exports go all over Europe. He has turned an awful accident into a productive and profitable life.

Progress is being made, but not as fast as the Prince would like. The BOOST project (Building on our Strengths Together) was set up within the Youth Business Trust to devise ways to access disabled people and so stimulate more of them to think about self-employment. In 1995 the disabled accounted for 149 new businesses. In the most recent 12-month period, the number had risen to 261. The Trust has engaged in a range of activities to encourage this trend, starting with staff training. There has been a programme of national and specialist media coverage, such as the Spinal Injuries Association's *Forward* magazine, and presentations to specialist schools like Portland College. Access has been improved, through preparation of special material in braille, and via Minicom text phones.

This encourages more entrepreneurs like Helen Tilbury, who will be 25 the day after the Prince of Wales passes 50. Helen was born with cerebral palsy, so she spends much of her time in an electric wheelchair. She also has a speech impediment and limited co-ordination, especially in her arms and hands.

But Helen has no wish to be treated differently from any other young person of her age. What she wants is a chance to make her own way in the world. She has come a long way already, having gained six GCSEs and a diploma in business studies and information technology at Lord Mayor Treloar College in Alton,

Hampshire. She scores well above average in intelligence and educational qualifications, and with a modified keyboard she is completely versatile on her computer. But firms were reluctant to employ her because of her very obvious disabilities. She secured a few temporary assignments and some voluntary work, but seemed destined to be unemployed for most of her life – extremely frustrating when you are intelligent and motivated.

The idea of becoming self-employed came to Helen after a disabled employment officer put her in touch with the BOOST project. Working from home made sense, but there was a problem. "I only had an Archimedes computer with an extremely old word processing package called 1st Word Plus, and a very old DTP package. If I was to work for myself I knew I needed to upgrade, which would involve very specialised equipment. An off-the-shelf PC would be no use to me."

Helen has crossed paths with the Prince of Wales on three occasions. While she was a student in Alton he came to open the Trail Centre for sixth-form students. In April 1998 she was able to show him exactly how she expected to make her business a success, even though she faces difficulties unimaginable to most of us. "Our conversation focused on my business intentions. I showed him a brief outline of my educational background and my plans for the future, which I had word processed on to a computer screen." Helen now produces items such as invitations, calendars and birthday cards from her own home office. "The Prince's Trust has opened doors for me. I didn't feel I was given the appropriate kind of help anywhere else but now I feel there are new opportunities for me. Instead of listening to people emphasise what I can't do, thanks to the Trust, I finally have a chance to show what I can do."

- The list of people with disabilities who have started successful businesses with help from the Youth Business Trust is remarkable. Here are a few:
- Andrea Denne (PYBT '87) did not let a congenital foot problem stop her starting dog kennels;
- Stephen Cobb (PYBT '97) started a business as a remedial therapist, even though he is almost blind;
- Neil Gummery (PYBT '93), who was paralysed from the waist down when a wall fell on him, runs Lynx Hand Controls, manufacturing a portable device which allows disabled drivers to drive any automatic car with one hand.

Many disabled people are not suited to starting a business, just as many people without disabilities are not natural entrepreneurs. So the Prince also tried to find routes to regular *employment* for disabled people. Grants sometimes go part of the way to helping, while stopping one step short of a full business.

- Mark Wellington (PT Grant '91), paralysed from the neck down after a motorbike accident, needed £500 towards a computer which could be operated with a headset;
- Michael Prendergast (PT Grant '87), who was born with spina bifida, got a grant to buy a portable keyboard so he could work at a shopping complex.

Prince Charles has also encouraged partnering other organisations with similar objectives. The work of the Trust with Reclaim is one of the more successful ventures helping disabled people find regular work. Chief executive Mark Powell also works as a volunteer for the Trust. He sees employment in the context of a total plan for life, which reintegrates disabled people into the mainstream of society: "Many young people with learning disabilities have little social contact with other members of society. However, with the Trust's help, we believe we can give such people opportunities they wouldn't otherwise have."

Healthcare Options

The Prince of Wales has been especially supportive in raising awareness of the problems disabled people face in receiving the right healthcare. Priorities included emphasis on care at home, setting up a network of care attendants, wider use of special equipment both at home and at work, and the need to have more centres for Independent Living.

Bill Buchanan, ex-chairman of POWAGOD, described how the process worked from his perspective. "We see ourselves in the role of a catalyst. His Royal Highness is there to make things happen even though he cannot be involved on a day-to-day basis. He highlights a matter that needs attention and then brings together those who can actually move things along."

One broad area stood out as a suitable case for this treatment: the difficulties the disabled encountered dealing with doctors. Two solutions made sense. A rethink of hospital policy and specific education for healthcare professionals. People with disabilities are likely to have more encounters with doctors and hospitals than most. Feedback suggested that healthcare workers were not as knowledgeable or as well attuned to their needs as they should be. In July 1986, acting on advice from POWAGOD, the Prince invited deans of medical schools as well as tutors from nursing colleges to a meeting. He asked them about what they were doing to ensure medical students were educated in the needs of disabled people. The answer was not a lot and, in some cases, nothing at all. One dean, Sir William Slack, was sufficiently embarrassed that he left determined to rectify the situation.

What followed was a new training module that entered the curriculum of medical students in their fifth year at the then University College in Middlesex

Hospital Medical School, with the use of a medical lecturer working with a disabled person to teach the course. Technical aspects were covered, but also awareness and sensitivity training.

After a conference on the subject in 1990, which brought together over 30 experts in the field, a working group studied ways to change the curriculum which would fill the void, and three years later issued a set of recommendations. The last chapter was written in 1997, with the publication of 'Medical Education in Relation to Disability and Rehabilitation'. This was a set of best practices covering every aspect, and setting out recommendations endorsed by the education committee of the General Medical Council. What began as one teaching module ended up changing the national approach. Today around 70 per cent of degrees in medicine include some training in respect of patients with disabilities.

Another step was taken in 1992, with the preparation of 'A Charter for Disabled People Using Hospitals', formalising a partnership with the Royal College of Physicians, whose support was vital in winning acceptance for it. Prince Charles said: "I warmly recommend this charter, which deserves the widest possible circulation and recognition. As hospitals strive ever harder to achieve the highest standards, the charter will help to ensure that meeting the specific needs of disabled people is part of that process." The charter incorporated as a key principle a point he had been trying to get across for a long time. "A person who has learned to live with a disability is usually much better informed about it than anyone else".

Education Options

Education for people with disabilities fell short of aspirations in several respects. The Advisory Group decided to focus on the needs of the disabled who want to continue education after school. Many people were put off because there was no one place to go to get information, let alone solutions: an issue tailor-made for POWAGOD, with its cross-organisation approach to problem solving.

The Prince invited a group of college principals, education specialists from the voluntary sector and representatives of government – notably the relevant minister, the Rt Hon Kenneth Baker MP, Nicholas Scott MP, Minister for Social Security and the Disabled and Baroness Hooper, along with selected senior civil servants – to Kensington Palace in December 1987. He had heard too many stories of people who had drive and ability but encountered so many problems that they had been forced to abandon their plans. He felt strongly about this injustice. "While most people are able to take advantage of opportunities for continuing [the learning process] after leaving full-time secondary education, disabled young people and adults are often frustrated by the difficulties which they experience in gaining admission to colleges and courses ... Given the opportunity to learn, these students have much to contribute – both to their peers and to society."[2]

Research was done to assess the extent of the problem, which was exacerbated by the number of government departments responsible for different areas. The Department of Education was notoriously bad about consulting with the Health and Transport departments, or indeed anyone else who could have helped. In July 1993 the Prince hosted a lunch to discuss progress. It had been somewhere between slow and non-existent. Around the table were Nicholas Scott from the DHSS, Viscount Ullswater from Employment and senior representatives from other relevant departments.

What was already known to the Prince soon became apparent to everyone else. These departments were still not talking to each other. Jan Leschly of Smith-Kline Beecham was so astonished that he was reported as saying, "If I ran my company the way these civil servants operate we'd be broke in a month." Following this revelation, an interdepartmental task force was formed, with senior civil servants reporting to Scott. Four and a half years later, and fully ten years after the initial meeting, a definitive set of guidelines finally emerged. It was signed by four Secretaries of State: Education and Employment, Health, Environment and Wales, as well as by the Minister for Disabled People. The ministerial foreword goes out of its way to stress the key role played by the Prince of Wales.

Access Options

Initial efforts were directed at transport, but these soon faltered. POWAGOD does not always turn up trumps. Early hopes for improvement ran up against economic realities. A 1985 investigation carried out with British Rail looked at how to make platforms safe for visually impaired people. The estimated cost of putting in a strip of separate material to alert the foot of someone who cannot see the edge was £850 million, so a non-starter. Attitudes at least have improved. People in wheelchairs are no longer required to travel in the baggage compartment. In most other respects the train has yet to leave the station.

The next area where access was a huge issue was housing. Progress had to happen here because, as the Prince put it, "Above anything else, people with disabilities need to feel that they belong and are part of their own neighbourhood and their own community. I suspect that people don't really want special provision because they are less mobile, but what they really want is a house which is

[2] *Learning Options,* June 1988.

convenient and secure, and many of them would like to have access to other people's homes so they can visit."[3]

He hoped that private builders could be encouraged to provide housing suitable for everyone, including those with mobility problems. Lunches were arranged for architects, planners, commissioners and private sector builders. Meetings were held with the National House Building Council. Early conversations tended to conclude with little more than pious expressions of good intent. Anxious to put teeth into the dialogue, and to provide some incentive to encourage action, the Prince launched a design award in October 1987 for higher standards of accessibility and security.

He couched the concept in general terms. "It would not just be disabled people who would benefit from the various additions and improvements to houses, such as having level entrances and entrance level WCs and wider passages. Most of us, I suspect, will end up with one kind of problem or another as we get older, and would appreciate such facilities."

If you build better houses with the disabled in mind, everyone benefits. Barratts at Bracknell, selected as the first model development, incorporated in its standard design both the flat entry and downstairs lavatory. Royal recognition managed to stimulate some of the concrete improvements for disabled people, even if it was a case of one small step at a time.

Many builders listened and made changes. In the longer term this campaign had influence at national level when the Government amended Part M of the Building Regulations on accessibility, bringing them into line with some of the standards POWAGOD had advocated.

The same struggle went on in the hospitality area. The Prince used an estimate by Deloitte Touche that disabled visitors across Europe would spend an additional £17 billion annually if accessibility improved, to make top executives take notice. Following a lunch in February 1991 and a conference in October 1992, a special sub-group was formed to study this subject. The hotel industry has since developed a code of practice. Members began to make changes before the latest legislation.

Robert Peel, former managing director of Thistle Hotels, was one of the first to accept there was commercial logic to making improvements. "I get a better return from my adapted bedrooms than I do from putting in a gym or swimming pool." Hotel chains, especially Thistle and Mount Charlotte, have modified rooms to meet the needs of disabled customers. Some Holiday Inns include information on access in their literature, while Novotel has a special hot line advising staff on how to meet the needs of guests with disabilities. Ramada has produced registration

[3] NHBC Design Award launch, 29 October 1987.

forms, menus and fire instructions in Braille. The process of raising awareness fed back into employment practices, with Choice and Hilton among those making sure disabled applicants have equal opportunities for work.

POWAGOD's activity in the area of access has been an uphill battle, with frustration and failure more frequent than success; but in key areas progress has been marked. Housing and hotels stand out.

The Prince's Options

Prince Charles tries to relate personally to the problems encountered by disabled people. He makes practical points about the design of everything from forms to buildings. Documents should be easy to read, easy to understand and easy to fill out. He does not like small print for this reason. Older people increasingly face mobility problems. In these ways the Prince points out that a disabled person is still a person first and disabled second.

People with disabilities have a keenly developed sense of whether someone's concern is genuine or false. In my observation, their assessment of Prince Charles is favourable. He wants to help the disadvantaged in this country to help themselves, and whether they have a disability is only relevant to the extent that it may accentuate the degree of disadvantage. "Whether or not we are affected by disability, we are all individuals."[4]

His sincerity and the commitment to his work in this area shows up in small but significant ways. He insisted that the premises of the Prince's Trust should have wheelchair access long before legislation made that mandatory. He instructed the selection committee at POWAGOD to hire senior employees with disabilities. Peter Holland, the current chief executive of POWAGOD, now called the Disability Partnership, has good reason to remember his interview for the job. Right at the end, the chairman remarked, "As far as we're concerned you have all the right experience and expertise. It's a pity that you're not disabled, because HRH is keen that a disabled person should be given this role." Holland was able to help them make the right decision when he revealed that he had epilepsy, and so was eminently qualified.

Measuring the Options

It is not possible to quantify the Prince's impact in the area of disability, partly because his contribution has been subtle and some of the critical issues intangible, such as improved awareness and attitudes towards people with disabilities. POWAGOD does not provide physical services or financial assistance.

[4] Foreword to *Living Options*, February 1985.

Summarising its key achievements:

- Since *Living Options'* launch in 1985, over 80 per cent of all healthcare districts in England and Wales have set up partnership planning arrangements using its guidelines.
- There are now 280 corporate members of the Employers' Forum on Disability, all committed to equal opportunities for disabled people.
- Over 200 hospitals and hospital trusts are using part or all of the procedures proposed in 'A Charter for Disabled People Using Hospitals'.
- Medical student training now incorporates modules on disability in 70 per cent of all colleges nationwide. A booklet is being prepared to be distributed to every medical student starting at college over the next ten years.
- Further education is now a reality for more people with disabilities, thanks to the cross-departmental programme in the civil service stimulated by POWAGOD.
- Housing has been modified in several ways to become more user-friendly, particularly with flat thresholds and downstairs lavatories.
- The Hoteliers' Forum has become a focal point for making hotels more user-friendly to disabled people, with plans to make 500,000 beds around Europe more accessible.

Some of the things that happened may have occurred without the Prince's involvement but many would not or not in the same way. All these problems were recognised and the subject of much debate before he came on the scene as a catalyst. He has also intervened at critical junctions to keep initiatives moving forward, when some were in danger of getting stuck. And, if there is still much to be done, at least there has been progress since he began his interventions.

HOMELESS PEOPLE

It is hard to talk about homework to a young person who is crashing on a friend's floor because there is nowhere else to go. How can any exam seem important when you have no home? Why worry about a job in ten years' time, when you are wondering where to sleep at night?

The Prince of Wales has long been aware that homelessness is one social problem that defies straightforward solutions. To help a young person who is homeless you have to start by removing the cause. Before you can begin to do that you have to understand the cause, often parental problems or some other extreme form of unpleasantness in the home. A Centrepoint study found that 86 per cent of young homeless people had not left home of their own accord.

Homeless people may not be a popular cause, but as he said: "Homelessness is not well understood. There is a tendency, for example, to believe people 'bring it on themselves'. I believe that this a grotesque over-simplification. Few homeless people actually want to be homeless. On the other hand their needs are complex. Many of them are quite gravely damaged by their experiences. They are often not easy to help."[5]

The Prince understands the complexity. In the February 1998 *Big Issue*, he cited various difficulties, any one of which can complicate finding a solution. "The lack of a home is one of the dreadful problems facing many of our young people today but, all too often, homelessness tends to be a symptom rather than a cause. Unemployment, lack of suitable adult role models, low educational achievement and drug or drink problems all take their toll, and prevent many people from fulfilling their potential."

There are also people homeless due to mental health problems. "Housing, for example, is a vital ingredient which regrettably is often lacking at present ... At the moment I know there are times when patients have to be discharged into poor accommodation without supervision, often in a deprived area, in the certain knowledge that this is going to aggravate their illnesses and result in their return to hospital."[6] One in three street people have mental problems, and their suicide rate is 35 times the national average.

And then there are people who have been in care. These young people often have a miserable background of abuse and tragedy which demands urgent attention. People usually leave care before the age of 18, while the national average age for leaving home is 22. At 17 or 18 you are a lot less able to look after yourself.

Anything is preferable to doing nothing. The quickest way to bring relief to the homeless, even if the least effective, is via a grant. Since none of the Trusts had the capacity to help directly, that meant working through other organisations. Not knowing much about how best to help, the Prince held discussions with those who did. Between 1981 and 1983 he and his advisors met with the National Association for the Care and Resettlement of Offenders (NACRO), Shelter, the Cyrenians, and other bodies active in the area. These conversations led to more focused grants, joint activity and to the Prince's decision to set aside properties on Duchy of Cornwall land in Kennington, south London, for homeless youngsters.

Before becoming more directly involved, the Prince wanted to understand the problem. By the mid-1980s he got to grips with homelessness first hand, starting

[5] Notes for Merchant Taylors meeting on Homelessness, 8 November 1990.
[6] Lecture to the Royal College of Psychiatrists, 5 July 1991.

with Centrepoint. The original concept in the 1960s had been to save young runaways from being corrupted by Soho and send them home, but most of them either had no home or did not want to go back. So Centrepoint became a refuge. A crowded, scruffy place with barely room for 32 to stay, the clientele were just the sort of struggling young people Prince Charles wanted to help.

In October 1985 interest in the homeless was not high. Most voluntary organisations working with homeless people struggled to keep going. When the Prince went to Centrepoint there was no fuss, no ceremony and no cameras. This was a private visit by someone who wanted to listen and learn from the homeless themselves. Inevitably news leaked out later, along with headlines about Prince Charles down among the dossers; not what he had in mind but there was a bonus. Just by turning up and taking an interest he started a subtle shift in the climate.

Nick Hardwick, who ran Centrepoint for over nine years, saw the difference one royal visit could make. "There was a ripple effect. People were saying if the Prince of Wales is concerned maybe we should be too. What he did opened doors for us. Suddenly it was easier to get in to see Westminster Council about a grant. Not that he was pulling strings. He just shone a spotlight on us, and we found more people wanted to know what we were up to and were willing to help."

Which Comes First – the Home or the Job?

So how to help? The best way is to make homeless people more employable, which in most cases means more training before they can handle regular work. Even if no training is required the homeless still face a classic Catch 22 symptomatic of the poverty trap: no money, no deposit; no home, no job; no money. Most firms will not hire people of no fixed abode. Even the Youth Business Trust is leery of helping those without a permanent address. The homeless cycle is aggravated by the way the social services operate. Money is available to provide deposits for rented accommodation for those who qualify. But a young person cannot apply for the money until they have an address. That Catch 22 again. Step one has to be to break this self-defeating cycle.

The Trust has a history of helping with this first step. In 1988, working with the National Association for Voluntary Hostels, it established Lodgers, which aimed to put young people in touch with households able to provide lodgings. A Trust scheme in Watford supplies deposits for young people so they can secure proper accommodation, as the first step towards finding employment. Another similar scheme in Edinburgh gives guarantees to landlords, to encourage them to rent to young homeless people. Initial results are promising.

Anyone in doubt as to whether these programmes are important should listen to people who are forced to live in hostels because they have nowhere else to go: people such as 16-year-old Jeni Wainwright (PT Grant '97). "Do you know what it's like to go to bed at night and put your wardrobe against the door because you're scared, and listen to the girl in the next room crying; and the one in the room after that crying? And you're crying too because no-one wanted to help me, no-one cared for me. I was stuck in a hostel with no employment, no family and no hope. Every time I went for a job, they took one look at my address and wanted to know what I'd done wrong."

Most employers are not interested. There are a couple of exceptions that not only hire homeless people but go out of their way to do so. The most visible, if only because of its street sellers, is the *Big Issue* magazine. To sell it you have to be homeless. From one office and a few vendors, it has grown to 30 offices with 2,000 people – all in seven years. Readership is over one million, and the paper makes a profit which is ploughed back into the business.

Co-founder John Bird met Prince Charles for the first time in 1997. The Prince had read the paper, and wanted to learn more about it. The initial contact with his work came through a Seeing is Believing visit, after which Express Newspapers sent ten employees to acts as volunteers and mentors to *Big Issue* staff, and donated office equipment. GGT Advertising gave free poster sites for the magazine.

The *Big Issue* is about helping the homeless help themselves, and giving street people an alternative to begging. Bird sees homelessness as a manifestation of a social crisis, because there is always a heap of other things that have gone wrong before you become homeless. Restoring self-confidence, giving back a sense of purpose and responsibility and dealing with the personal problems underneath, requires a holistic solution.

Bird speaks of the similarity between the Prince's Trust and the *Big Issue*: "We have looked at a social problem and tried to create a business that can answer that problem. The Prince's Youth Business Trust is giving loans to people who have been refused by the bank. That's getting right down to the people who have no voice and no economic profile." Self-help is the core philosophy, and both the *Big Issue* and the Prince's Trust avoid making value judgements about those they assist.

The Prince visited the offices of the *Big Issue* in December 1997, and bumped into Clive Harold, who had been at Hill House school with him over 40 years ago. Harold was down on his luck. As the Prince pointed out, this unexpected encounter "was a vivid reminder that homelessness can happen to almost anyone" – even people whose parents could afford to send them to expensive schools where members of the royal family are educated. Harold is not the only old acquaintance who became homeless. When the Prince visited the Norwich Foyer in January 1994, he came across Rod Perman, who had served under him in the Navy.

Home is Where a Foyer Is

The Prince has played a key role in the development of one programme that has now become a front-line weapon in the struggle to reintegrate homeless people into the community. Foyers were originally French. They began in the 1930s to help young people from rural areas with no place to stay make the transition to an urban environment. Integration was assisted by facilities on the premises, where members of the local community could befriend newcomers. In the French model this facility was invariably a restaurant. The earliest Foyers were designed exclusively for people who had employment.

Integration with the community is still the primary task, but today Foyers deal with a much more challenging constituency. Many of the current generation of young people who stay in Foyers have a history of trauma, possibly abuse, or could be leaving care. About 35 per cent have had a run-in with the law. Most, though not all, are unemployed when they arrive.

Foyers provide much more than just a bed. Foyers aim to equip a homeless and troubled young person with the personal and professional skills to make the transition to a stable adulthood. During their stay residents receive training and counselling on the premises. By the time someone leaves they should have acquired sufficient independence to survive on their own. When a resident is ready to move on, help is provided in finding a place of their own.

The Prince heard about Foyers not in France but in Spain. At the Madrid Conference on the Urban Environment in April 1991, he was introduced to the director general, Charles Antoine Arnaud, who gave him material on Foyers. Letters were exchanged, and Arnaud advanced the possibility of starting something similar in Britain.

Prince Charles was impressed by the integrated approach, which seemed to offer a solution to several different problems simultaneously, and which formed a link between homelessness and welfare to work. Foyers are not just about soup and a roof, but about taking back control of one's life. They give people affordable accommodation, plus vocational and other guidance, and a controlled environment which allowed them to build self-esteem and reduce any anti-social tendencies.

Arnaud had already put out feelers to Shelter about linking to a pan-national organisation, which would make it easier to get funding from Brussels. The Madrid speech convinced Arnaud that Prince Charles would be the perfect person to provide leadership in Britain. By November 1991, when Richard Mann of Grand Met went to St James's Palace for a review of results arising from the 1990 Homeless Seminar, he was able to tell the Prince that plans were well advanced. The British Foyer federation started life in February 1992.

The Prince's interest drew attention to Foyers and their potential. The press dutifully turned out, and their profile rose. He was also critical in attracting support from corporations and other voluntary groups. In the early years, when the movement needed exposure most, he personally opened several Foyers, among them those in Camberwell, Norwich and the Gateway in Southwark. Don MacDonald, the first chief executive of the Foyer Federation, saw the results that followed from his visit to the Gateway: "The fact that the Prince of Wales was going to open it galvanised lots of companies to give time and resources for free."

He also encouraged his organisations to work with Foyers. Business in the Community arranged Seeing is Believing visits. Sir Christopher Harding of BET was so impressed by what he saw on a visit to the Gateway in October 1993 that he joined the board of the Federation. He in turn got BPB involved, and persuaded them to fund more Foyers. Other member companies have joined in. Whitbread has helped 14 Foyers with donations in kind. Luton alone received around £100,000 worth of furniture for residents' rooms and common areas.

You can see why the Prince likes Foyers. "The holistic approach to young people's needs offered by Foyers is both essential and successful. The transition from childhood dependence to adult independence can be a daunting experience for those who have the support of family and friends. Foyers offer a stepping stone to disadvantaged young people in an environment where their hopes can be sympathetically channelled towards achievable targets, and where their skills can be enhanced by training and work experience."[7]

Foyers hit another of the Prince's hot buttons. The movement has given thought to how atmosphere and environment affect residents. Where consistent with cost and design, builders have recycled materials to create a sense of space far removed from the institutional style that characterises most accommodation for homeless people. The Swansea Foyer is a 'green' building which used renewable materials and conserves heat. Some of these places were converted old buildings. The Foyer he visited in Fife had once been a mill.

Foyers epitomise the precise corporate structure that Prince Charles is trying to encourage at many similar institutions, not just those for the homeless. "I saw an excellent example of partnership between the local community, business and local government when I opened the new Salford Foyer this morning."[8]

Former assistant private secretary Matthew Butler sums up the attraction. "What he found so encouraging was that they were helping homeless young people in a practical way; and that they were an example of public/private partnerships

[7] Message to National Foyer Federation Conference, 29 November 1995.

[8] Prince's Trust conference, Towards the Millennium, Manchester, 11 March 1996.

where you got different people coming together to make these places happen."

If you are homeless it can be quite helpful if the Prince pops in. Arriving at the Swale Foyer in September 1995, he was greeted by Lawrence Steele. Lawrence never took school seriously, but music was another matter. He says playing in pubs was his education. At 11 he went on stage with his uncle's band, and was hooked. But music did not pay the rent. After a couple of years unemployed, Lawrence decided to have another go at education. Again the call of music proved irresistible. He took off for a blues festival in Germany, and on his return found he had been dropped from his college course.

Life at home was difficult. There were constant arguments about education. His mother's second marriage was collapsing. She was rowing all the time with his stepfather. He needed to get out, to clear his head and think about his future. His father did not want to know, so with nowhere else to go Lawrence checked in to the Foyer.

When the Prince reached his room, Lawrence played an electric version of God Save the Queen. Prince Charles noticed that the guitar was not plugged in. The amplifier was failing and Lawrence could not afford a new one. The Prince was not going to miss a cue like that. "I know just the place for you," Lawrence recalls him saying, "the Prince's Trust. We give money to support musicians." Lawrence followed his suggestion and applied for a grant. Two months and £800 later he was the proud owner of a Twin Fender Reverb.

On the back of that, a three-man group was formed. "Without the new amp it would have been practically impossible to get a band together. The old one used to break down. I'd get up on stage and it would conk out." Now the Lawrence Steele Band does regular gigs, and is recording a demo tape at a studio in Bethnall Green. Lawrence has been able to leave the Foyer, and has his own rented accommodation.

In five years, 60 Foyers have opened, offering accommodation to over 3,200 homeless people. Over 12,000 have already benefited from their stay. The Chancellor has called for a Foyer in every town during the lifetime of this parliament. So by 2003 there should be 400 all across Britain. This display of enthusiasm by the Exchequer is no charitable whim. Foyers work. Follow-up surveys of the first 1,800 residents showed that 55 per cent found jobs. The cost per person to support someone at a Foyer has been calculated at only about £1,500, against the annual cost to government for a young person in care of anywhere from £10,000 up to £50,000. But it gets better. The effective cost for getting someone into employment works out at less than £3,000; and the pay back period to the Exchequer is a mere seven months. No wonder Prince Charles sees Foyers as "one of the great success stories" in the struggle against homelessness.

There are other ways that the Prince can help more homeless people help themselves. One, obviously, is by individual grants. A total of 16 per cent of 1997 grants went to people classified as homeless or living in hostels. Interview clothing or travel costs help homeless people in the same way as other grantees, even a former *Big Issue* vendor. Phil Clover (PT Grant '96) had been homeless for five years and selling the magazine for 12 months when he applied. He had trained as a house painter but getting to jobs was a problem. The sum of £300 was enough to pay for driving lessons so he could get his licence.

Robin Goodburn (PT Grant '94) was a homeless drifter before he turned to the Prince's Trust. They sent him on a three-week Outward Bound course in Aberdovey in Wales. This led to him working for the Trust as a team leader, helping jobless youngsters in Newcastle upon Tyne. "I agreed to go because I thought it would be a free holiday. With my board and lodging paid I'd be able to collect three weeks Giro when I left. Instead I left with a new attitude. When you're on the dole you regard something as simple as signing on as a major headache. Going for a job interview is a nightmare. But after you have climbed a sheer rock face or hiked for 50 miles, you have the confidence to face anything and everything. I decided that it was time I stopped drifting. If I had not been there I would have kept on settling for the easiest option. Now I have a job I love and the chance to go up the career ladder."[9]

Then there are the Prince's Trust residential courses, which offer places to people who are homeless or living in hostels, around 13 per cent of the attendees over the past three years. The Mary Seacole Housing Association has been sending boys and girls on Trust courses, and has seen them come back much more optimistic about their prospects. Richard Wyatt, chief executive, was encouraged by the degree to which they had changed. "They were a lot more self-confident. They tend to be able to take authority a bit better. There is also a noticeable increase in their self-esteem."

Volunteers have also developed links with more than half the Foyers nationwide on their courses. Last year four residents from Southend enrolled. According to Foyer co-ordinator Maureen Glynne, "they became transformed. It was brilliant. Because they had released skills they didn't know they had, they were able to apply for jobs with confidence. They had really moved on." Their team leader, Chris Skeet, struck up a relationship with PGL Travel, Britain's largest provider of activity courses for children. This company has been around for 41 years, and handles holidays for 112,000 customers aged six to 18. When Skeet showed the boys PGL's literature, their eyes lit up. All they wanted to know was, "how could we do this?"

In February 1998, Skeet successfully submitted four applications. Before going

[9] The *Sun*, 1 July 1995.

on the course they were an unhappy bunch, homeless and out of work. Three now have seasonal positions, two as instructors and one as a catering assistant. A great start, which seems to be working so well that another eight former Foyer residents, graduating via Volunteers, are now in the apprenticeship phase at PGL.

The Prince has asked Business in the Community to investigate innovative ways to make more businesses active in the area of homelessness. A 1995 Seeing is Believing day to Knowle West in Bristol was one of the most productive. Executives at NatWest Life Assurance visited the Julian House Night Shelter and the Bristol Cyrenians. The Cyrenians, which provides day care, supported housing, and a resettlement service for single homeless men and women, got £225,000. The Julian Trust received money from a staff casual-wear day.

Corporate donations can be particularly helpful in furnishing institutions that are always desperately short of almost everything. Their gratitude can be almost embarrassing. Cynthia Vanstone, director of Lionel House Trust, a charity providing homes for homeless youngsters aged 18-25, wrote to Whitbread after their help:

"... it was furniture that we could never, ever have afforded to buy; in particular the beds for which we were desperate ... I wish you could have seen our youngsters' faces when they saw the size of the lorries and the amount of furniture you had given ... there are no words that can say thank you enough."

The Executive Forum, set up in July 1998, should make the process of tapping corporate members for support in this area more systematic and efficient in the future.

Individual initiatives all over the country have support from the Prince, where they can make a meaningful impact on alleviating homelessness. In December 1992 he opened the Homeground Centre in Merseyside. Homeground is impressive. It owes its existence to one 1991 Seeing is Believing visit which took in several homelessness organisations: the Passage Day Centre, the St Mungo Mission and the Spitalfield Job Club. The lunch speaker was Nick Hardwick, then still at Centrepoint. Business leaders from companies best placed to help with accommodation were heavily represented on that itinerary.

Peter George, managing director of Ladbroke (Hilton) thought about how his company could contribute. "We can examine unused property ... As a major hotelier regularly disposing of used linen and other materials we should look at ways in which these can be put to better use ... " George was as good as his word. He looked around his company and hit upon converting a large, empty building on Scotland Road in Liverpool, which had been the old Vernon Pools headquarters.

Assembling a group of companies to help, including Forte Hotels, Ideal Homes and McAlpines, George transformed it into a special centre with 30 beds. Every requirement came free, from Business in the Community members. The building is worth £260,000. The value of the refurbishment would have been around

£250,000 if done on a commercial basis. Over the past three years Homeground has seen 592 people pass through. One hundred and fifty five have subsequently found their own accommodation, and a further 39 were reconciled with their families. One hundred and sixty-three have found work with firms such as Butlins, the Post Office, and even the Department of Employment, or went on to further education.

A new initiative that should bring significant resources to the field is Invest in Futures. Lack of effective co-ordination between voluntary agencies not only reduced their effectiveness, but could create a sense of competition. Homeless organisations did not seem immune from this problem. The Trust began a process of teaching local offices how to tap local businesses more efficiently so as to attract more resources.

This concept convinced Centrepoint, the De Paul Trust, the National Homeless Alliance and Shelter to combine with the Prince's Trust and test new approaches in six regions. Lessons learned over the past two years are being analysed to create a best practices model. In Dorset, eight companies were persuaded not just to donate computers and make homeless groups their charity of the year, but to take a much more active approach, providing interview clothing, lending meeting rooms for preparation and arranging mock interviews. Nottingham companies helped with funding applications, and set up a jobs advertising system to reach homeless people in the area. These pilots proved sufficiently successful for the DoETR to agree to fund a three-year roll out to many more regions, hoping to replicate these results across much more of the country.

Paying Down the Mortgage

Records for the past few years give an approximate percentage of homeless young people who benefited from the Prince's programmes. Extrapolation indicates that slightly over 11,000 have received help.

Did this help enable these people to stand on their own sufficiently to find somewhere to live? If the local authority no longer has to pay accommodation costs, that is a saving. Allowing for a lower success rate here than for participants, it is reasonable to assume around 3,200 homeless young people got a fresh start, saving on average £25,000 a year for 2G years, or £180 million. Add contributions from Business in the Community members such as Homeground, and the incremental benefit in this area tops £200 million. This is direct assistance only. I am assigning no value to the the Prince's part at Foyers, where 12,000 have received help, nor to his influence behind the scenes in encouraging government to do more.

There are an estimated 200,000 floaters in Britain, though the hard core make up a fairly small percentage and those who actually sleep in the streets number a few thousand. The Prince is currently reaching only about one per cent directly. Foyers should top three per cent in 1998, but that could rise to 20 per cent by

2001. Of course accommodation is only the first step. Prince Charles wants to take more homeless young people all the way back into the mainstream. That is the next challenge.

ETHNIC MINORITIES

Of all forms of discrimination, that against ethnic minorities has bothered the Prince most. He is determined to crush it.

"What I couldn't bear was the danger inherent to the future of not taking trouble with people from the ethnic minorities. I also recognised the challenge to make ethnic minorities feel wanted in this country. There was huge potential, I thought anyway, for conflict and unnecessary strife, which is another reason why I also concentrate on that side and try to get to know people from ethnic minorities and to visit their particular communities."

Britain in 1998 remains predominantly white and nominally Christian, but it is not the same mix as in 1948 when he was born. During his lifetime the country has changed from what was a homogenous nation to a more multicultural, multi-racial society. Rather than merely react to the requirements of a more mixed population, Prince Charles has been out in front, leading the argument in favour of tolerance and inclusion.

"I didn't want to see the tension between groups of people becoming a really dangerous issue. You only have to look at what was happening in America in the 1960s and '70s to see there was a real risk of the same thing happening here. People were feeling and becoming alienated. You only had to go to areas like Brixton and Toxteth to see that."

To be credible and make inroads into minority communities, two hurdles had to be overcome. The first was his own position. Would his intervention be well received? The first impulse of the average unemployed black teenager is not to head off to the nearest royal charity for help. The second was the structure and composition of his organisations, which had a limited history of working with ethnic minorities and where management was mostly drawn from older, white, middle-class people who had never held a proper conversation with a young coloured person in their lives.

Given his sheltered upbringing and the most traditional of British backgrounds, Prince Charles from an early age showed surprising sympathy to what many saw as an alien invasion. He is influenced by a cultural heritage of true liberalism. He once described as "marvellous" a passage in Mahatma Gandhi's writings, "tolerance gives us spiritual insight, which is as far from fanaticism as the North Pole from the South".[10]

10 Hugh Anderson memorial lecture, Cambridge Union, 3 November 1978.

He has always displayed a lively interest in other cultures, traditions and religions. He is patron of the Oxford Centre for Islamic Studies, and has read extensively about Buddhism and Hinduism. Study of these diverse cultures made an impression and reinforced an existing sense of tolerance and openness to new ideas. The culmination of this was the assertion by the Prince that he wanted to be Defender of Faith rather than Defender of the Faith. On one level, the statement was about as radical as any ever made, with its implication that one person could represent every religion in the realm. On another level it could be seen simply as a reflection of respect for different beliefs.

In a documentary entitled *Charles, the Private Man, the Public Role*, broadcast in June 1994, he said: "I've always felt that the Catholic subjects of the sovereign are equally as important as the Anglican ones, or the Protestant ones. Likewise I think that the Islamic subjects or the Hindu subjects or the Zoroastrian subjects of the sovereign are of equal and vital importance."

It is a short step from religion to race, since the two are often intertwined. The Prince believes in looking at each individual on their merits, irrespective of religion, race or any other kind of external criterion.

His remarks were not popular with many in the Church of England, but better received by other faiths. The Prince has been sincere in trying to understand all mainstream religions practised in Britain, and to find common ground with Christianity. His efforts in this area have contributed to the generally positive perception of him among most ethnic minority groups.

Prince Charles had visited 35 different countries by the time he was 30, and been exposed to an unusual degree to the diversities of race, religion and culture. His antennae were attuned to how little was being done in Britain to address discrimination against people simply because of ethnic differences. "You can't remove people's apprehensions in one night. But you can make a start by making them more knowledgeable."[11] As he said to me recently, "I thought it would help if they could see that someone where I came from was concerned and interested. I wanted to make people feel included. I'd also like to think that by identifying myself with a degree of understanding that it would work both ways."

Views held by many ethnic minorities in Britain about the Prince tend to differ from the general perception. His respect for different cultures and alternative lifestyles strikes a responsive chord. His interest in organic farming and natural medicine, which has at times attracted criticism, fits right in, and that he has not always been treated fairly by sections of the media establishment attracts empathy.

In the late 1970s resentment over potential police discrimination became a

11 *Observer*, 16 June 1974.

widespread grievance among black youths. He confronted the problem in June 1977 outside the Moonshot Youth Centre in Deptford. Arriving in his capacity as head of the Silver Jubilee Appeal he was greeted by protesters, one of them wearing a badge with the words 'Stuff the Jubilee'. Undeterred, he decided to get to the bottom of the demonstration.

The Prince had walked into a highly-charged community, where racial tensions ran high. The recent arrests of 24 alleged muggers had bought matters to a head. He listened to complaints from the protesters and a rebuttal from the police, and concluded "I'm sure there's truth on both sides. Couldn't you come together and discuss it?"[12]

This was not the way the police usually worked in high crime areas in the late 1970s and Prince Charles, not for the first or last time, was criticised for interfering. Yet a meeting was held, and there was some moderating of entrenched views. Tension did not evaporate overnight, but by bringing these people together the Prince built bridges. Since he approached the incident with an open mind, how could anyone else in his presence do any less? Recalling this and similar meetings, the Prince said recently, "the press gives the impression that all police are racist and I didn't believe it for a minute. There may be patches, but it's like on the housing estate – a couple of people who cause trouble give everyone a bad name."

The Prince's Trust was not really ready to do anything meaningful. Recognising the limitations of his own organisation, the Prince decided to go for a more personal approach. He started with David Lane, chairman of the Commission for Racial Equality, to explore ways in which he could help. Then he arranged a November 1978 meeting between George Pratt and the Commissioner of the Metropolitan Police, Sir David McNee, to share ideas on improving communications.

One problem was the gap between police policy at the top and practice at the bottom on the beat. The Prince used that potentially hot potato as a reason to call together 19 chief constables for a private seminar on how to improve community relations. He had met Asian groups in Bradford the previous month, a trip which only served to heighten his concerns. He could not intervene publicly, but he could be the catalyst in getting people who were able to make a difference together in one room and force discussion of the issues. But there was little to show for these early efforts except an increase in his determination to do something.

A typical meeting was held in Lloyds of London in February 1989, following a visit by the Prince to the Brick Lane development in Spitalfields. Anxious to ensure follow-on and in particular to encourage more participation by ethnic minorities, he had asked a number of community and religious leaders to meet him. Twenty

[12] Anthony Holden, *Prince Charles*.

or so showed up. Within a few minutes it became obvious that many of these not only were not working together but were not even known to each other. Clearly little communication was taking place in the area. Prince Charles expressed surprise. There was embarrassment round the table. His comments might have helped, because one local business leader claimed to notice a significant pick up in inter-group activity after this meeting.

The Prince has hosted receptions at St James's Palace and Highgrove. In relation to these receptions, Sarabjeet Soar, chairman of the Youth Business Trust ethnic minority advisory group, said: "Some people not exactly dashing to be seen to have any relations with the royals did turn up." And that is a start. He has also sent messages of support to a number of prominent events on the calendar of the ethnic community, such as the annual music happening hosted by Keith Vaz MP in the House of Commons and special festivals such as Jammin '85.

In what seems a particularly personal gesture, the Prince chose this, the year of his 50th birthday, to host a reception for the 50th anniversary of the first voyage of the *Windrush*, the liner which brought Afro-Caribbean immigrants to Britain after the war. Prince Charles told his guests: "The challenges we still have to meet should not lead us to dismiss how much we have achieved since 1948."

At the grass roots he has always done better. On a July 1986 visit to Birmingham, a local black radio station described him as "the caring Prince, the man who doesn't just talk, who acts". The reaction on a recent visit to Marsh Farm Estate was even more encouraging. Grace Campbell, an unemployed black hairdresser who specialises in Afro-Caribbean braiding, could not have been more ecstatic about the Prince. "Oh, he's wonderful: an officer and a gentleman! He really cares for young people; he finds time for us, there's no prejudice in him, everyone's the same to him, regardless of colour, creed and background. We really love him here for that."[13]

The Prince has made his stance plain enough on many occasions. He believes in inclusion – no exceptions. And he wants everyone to understand that inclusion embraces his work too. "I am thinking of all groups. I know ethnic minorities have special problems. The Prince's Trust is there to help. They're your trusts, too."

Multi-cultural Trusts

So the Prince instructed Pratt to make sure his Trust was addressing the issue of minority involvement. In November 1978 Pratt put forward a proposal to Checketts: "Most of our regional committees have amongst their number a member of the local ethnic minority group. We should encourage this throughout

[13] *Daily Mail*, 22 June 1998.

all our regions and perhaps invite at least one of the organised ethnic groups in a region (when these can be identified) to nominate a member, in the same way as we invite the statutory services to select their representation." Prince Charles's response was "I agree".

In 1990 he called together Trust executives and representatives of several organisations working with ethnic minorities, to try and discover why so few were applying to his self-employment programme. This meeting was a disaster. In the eyes of the minority groups the Prince's Trust was aloof and elitist. On one side of the table sat a management team that was all white and all male. The other side arrived hostile and resentful. One person present described the encounter as "trading insults and aggro".

Prince Charles suggested a different approach, a series of meetings with one organisation at a time. This was more productive. Two conclusions emerged. First, to work through established organisations that had credibility with minority constituencies, and secondly to access people with the right background who could provide advice on how to tackle the ethnic minority market.

So the Youth Business Trust set up an ethnic minority advisory group. Sarabjeet Soar, formerly at the Home Office, became chairman. The Prince wanted minority communities to feel comfortable participating in the programme. Soar recalls that "the Prince of Wales was very emphatic that we hadn't even touched the tip of the iceberg. He wanted us to find ways to increase the number of minorities we helped." He asked Soar to take on two tasks: to develop relationships with external groups who could spread the word, and to raise awareness internally of the ethnic issue.

Both were a challenge. Soar and his team set out to change the culture at the Trust, with a series of workshops and special events designed to break down myths and stereotypes. He was pleased and surprised to discover that the recommendations he made were welcomed and acted upon.

All areas brushed up on their policies and programmes. There is now a strong equal opportunity culture imbedded throughout the Prince's Trust. A pan-trust Ethnic Minority Advisory Committee came into existence in January 1998. A distinguished group was persuaded to sit on the new committee, chaired by Sir Herman Ousely, the chairman of Racial Equality. Members include Victor Adebowale, chief executive of Centrepoint, Bill Morris, general secretary of the Transport and General Workers Union, and Samir Shah, head of Political Programming at the BBC.

In conjunction with the TUC and the Commission for Racial Equality, the Prince's Trust sponsored what was the biggest event in Britain to mark the European Year Against Racism, Respect '97. Over 80,000 people visited the Trust's marquee. And not just at the Trusts. The Prince has encouraged all his organisations to lead the way in setting new standards for racial integration.

Racism still causes misunderstanding on both sides. Criticism that senior staff are white, middle-class and "not like us", continues to be voiced. Even now the profile of the Trust does not reflect its expressed aim of showing an ethnic face to minority communities. As recently as February 1997 all the same charges were levelled during a seminar at Tower Hamlets College in east London.

Open to Everyone

Even in the 1970s, grants acknowledged the special needs of ethnic minorities. One Bengali group received £250 – a useful sum then – towards the cost of video equipment which enabled housebound mothers to see films in their own language at specially arranged house groups, and strengthened cultural links for young Bengalis. But this was still an exception to the norm. The Prince raised the profile of the needs of these groups, and made sure they got more attention. July 1979 found Haywood corresponding with regional committee chairmen on this matter.

"Following his visit to Bradford the Prince of Wales has been in touch with me to suggest that we take a strong initiative from the Trust, in so far as we are able within our grants policy, to support moves made to improve relationships between the authorities and the ethnic communities. His Royal Highness is, I know, particularly concerned to support the excellent work developing in some areas between young black people and the police."

Direct grants properly placed can be a powerful tool for stimulating activity designed to reduce racial tensions. The '95 disturbances in Bradford left lingering resentment in the local Asian community. Three young people, Mohammed 'Manny' Amran, Zulfahar Hussain and Assam Javed, wanted to set up a group to arrange activities that would keep Asian young people off the streets. "There was no-one in the community to represent young people and give them a voice." Manny knocked on many doors, but with nothing to show for his hard work. "People didn't know if young people were capable of handling money, or whether anything we could do would make a difference. Only the Prince's Trust was willing to take a risk and help."

With seed capital, and the imprimatur of the Prince of Wales, doors began to open. Needing a place to meet, they found a pub that had closed after damage during the disturbances. The Trust put up £3,000. On the back of that they raised a further £72,000 from organisations such as Children in Need, Comic Relief and the Millennium Commission. "By using the Prince's Trust as an umbrella, we got others to match their funding and could get lots of people to turn up to events."

The Manningham Youth Forum moved into the former pub in June 1998. More than 500 young people and their parents are now involved, as the Forum tries to help bridge cultural gaps not just across ethnic groups but also between different generations within the same group. So much has been accomplished in such a short time that Manny has been selected to be the youngest commissioner ever, at 22, on the Commission for Racial Equality.

Ten per cent of all grants went to minority applicants in 1997 and the percentage for 1998 is likely to be higher. Some of the most successful recipients have come from the ranks of ethnic minorities, though few could rival the achievements of Julian Golding (PT Grant '94). Julian is one of five siblings, so money is tight. He had always wanted to run, so he gave up his job and devoted all his spare time to training – no easy decision. He had been employed at Willesden Sports Centre as an instructor, earning £150 working four days a week, but as he said, "to achieve a dream you have to take risks. It wasn't possible for me to train properly and maintain a full time job."

In the short term he was very hard up. A friend of his coach suggested he apply for a Trust grant. Six weeks later Julian had a cheque in his hands. "£300 at the time was a lot of money to me. The Prince's Trust helped getting spikes and a bag and clothing, which is very expensive, as well as travel expenses." Since then he has gone from strength to strength, representing Britain in numerous international meetings. Julian started in 1994 by winning a gold medal in the 4 x 100-metre relay at the world junior championships in Portugal. He returned from the August 1998 European Games with a gold and a bronze medal in regular competition. "As my coach put it, after I got the grant I kicked the door down and had my best year ever. Someone saw my ability and took an interest. It made me believe in myself and I started to believe that I could go out and achieve anything."

Jobs for the Minorities

Racism remains alive in the employment arena, even though few will admit it. Britain has had laws for decades that prohibit discrimination. Nonetheless ethnic minorities are twice as likely to be unemployed. After a briefing session at Kensington Palace in May 1983, Stephen O'Brien shared some disturbing statistics with the Prince:

- between 1973 and 1983 minority unemployment had grown twice as fast as for whites. Policy Studies Institute research 'Black and White Britain' reported that 25 per cent of men with West Indian backgrounds and 20 per cent of those from Asian extraction were unemployed, against 13 per cent of white males. In some areas unemployment among minority teenagers touched 60 per cent;
- job levels were lower, with more of minorities employed in manual labour;
- minority entrepreneurs encountered extreme difficulty in finding start-up finance.

O'Brien and the Prince concocted a rather radical idea: senior management at major companies would present their employment policies to a group of minority activists at a conference. The Prince was invited to "put your name and weight behind a simple conclusion: that redressing the unequal employment prospects of black people should become a major item of agenda for all boards of directors". This should open a dialogue between participants across the ethnic divide, creating a rare opportunity to get in the same room people who would not normally come into contact, let alone talk.

What became known as the Windsor Weekend actually took place during the week at the Oakley Court Hotel near Windsor, with Prince Charles attending, on Friday 23 November 1984.

The conference was chaired by Lord Carr of Hadley, chairman of Business in the Community, and Pranlal Sheth, a director of Project Fullemploy. Many of Britain's major companies took part, including Blue Circle, British Gas, Littlewoods and Marks & Spencer. The minority contingent came from varied backgrounds: Beverly Anderson, a freelance broadcaster and writer; Beverley Bernard from the Polytechnic of Central London; J A Lewis of Ebony Greeting Cards; Limbert Spencer from Greater Manchester Council; and Jay Mitra from the London Borough of Lambeth. This was a private conference with journalists present agreeing not to report proceedings because the Prince was interested in making progress not headlines. In the event he got both.

The conference was a real eye-opener. According to Anthony Holden, "Chastened white businessmen – unused to being laughed at when they protested that they did not discriminate in their employment policies – listened intently as the young blacks seized their rare chance with a vengeance. By the end of the conference it was his fellow bankers who raised a storm of protest when the Bank of England representative conceded that its Youth Training Scheme required a minimum of five O levels. Leading businessmen said they had no idea there was such a talent among the leadership of the black community, and the blacks themselves said that they had not expected such understanding of their problems from big business."

There were tangible results. The Windsor Fellowship, with start-up capital coming from attendees, supports young black high-fliers who are identified just prior to A level, and who are then helped through further education and on into work. Since inception there have been 495 Windsor Fellows, who have gone on to fill senior positions in the private, public and voluntary sectors.

Business in the Ethnic Community
The Prince encourages companies to find ways to match their expertise to the needs of ethnic groups, not just by changing their employment policies and the culture in the work place, but by helping in education, assisting small firms and

encouraging urban regeneration. A quick scan of a few results from Seeing is Believing visits shows the diversity.

- Granada Television made a special video to help the 'Race for Opportunity' campaign;
- companies, from British Airways through to pharmaceutical manufacturer Zeneca, took a fresh look at their employment policies and became more pro-active in employing ethnic minorities;
- a number of businesses, including Dresser-Rand and East Midlands Electric, appointed community liaison officers.

Another of the Prince's initiatives led to the launching, in June 1995, of a campaign called Race for Opportunity, chaired by Bob Ayling, chief executive of British Airways. Race for Opportunity, in the words of deputy chairman Charles Allen "combines action on negative discrimination with positive action", and aims to develop and promote business relationships with Britain's ethnic minority communities. Its campaign slogan is "Don't think what you can do for Britain's ethnic minority communities. Think what Britain's ethnic minority communities can do for you."

Race for Opportunity has teamed with Project Fullemploy to create a minority job bank. Member companies found 130 jobs for ethnic minorities in 1997, and plan to place 250 in 1998. McDonalds sponsored two unemployed minority Volunteers, and partnered with the Gujarat Hindu Society to help their 'Marketing to Asian Communities' focus group. Littlewoods has linked with U Products and after providing advice now buys peanuts from the firm. Radio XL, covering the West Midlands, broadcast advice for small businesses to its 100,000 ethnic minority listeners and received its sponsorship from RfO members.

Tangible results have been somewhat slow, though much can be gained simply by improving attitudes. The Prince has made his presence felt, attending meetings with Race for Opportunity members, encouraging companies to sign up and getting his message across. But these are early days.

Clearly one way to deal with racist attitudes in the workplace is to make sure the most senior executives understand the problem, so the Prince has encouraged more Seeing is Believing visits to ethnic minority projects, and as a result more businesses have joined Race for Opportunity, or backed special programmes targeted to be of most benefit to ethnic minorities.

Roots and Wings, a Business in the Community programme, aims to reduce racism in the workplace. Here, being the mentor to a minority student breaks down cultural barriers and prejudice among business executives. Firms, including

Bain and Random House, have encouraged employees to participate. Of the total mentors around, 60 per cent are working with ethnic minorities.

Equality has to begin with an equal education, and here businesses are particularly well placed to assist. One example is the relationship the law firm of Clifford Chance established with the Shapla School in east London in 1995. Reading is especially relevant for a student body which is 88 per cent of Bangladeshi origin. This project is still going strong, with 60 volunteers and 90 pupils. Special emphasis has been placed on including schools with high concentrations of ethnic minorities. Mulberry, one of the first Compact schools, had a student population which was 70 per cent ethnic minority. The earliest Study Support locations, as we saw in Chapter 5, included Sarah Bonnell, a veritable United Nations.

Anyone who doubts the benefits of such focus should take a look at the results of the Chapeltown and Harehills Assisted Learning Computer School. This Study Support centre is in the most deprived inner city area of Leeds, where pupils of Afro-Caribbean extraction make up about 40 per cent of the student population and Asian backgrounds add another 40 per cent. In 1996 over 80 per cent of attendees achieved five or more A-C grade GCSEs, compared to the national average of 43 per cent.

Businesses are also in a unique position to help by creating practical training opportunities designed to reach ethnic minority groups. Stanley Kalms, chairman of Dixons, formed an unlikely partnership with a local black community group, Ujima, and the Finsbury Park Community Trust, which in turn has created a model 'customised retail training scheme'. This provides training for unemployed youngsters (mainly black) to work in the Dixons shops in north London. The Bank of England, Tesco and McDonalds have set up similar schemes.

Ethnic entrepreneurs

At the Youth Business Trust, the Prince has pushed to increase the number of ethnic minorities who received start-up assistance. Some have been very successful.

In 1987 the Datoo brothers of Peterborough were desperate. Mohammed had been unemployed for over a year, after graduating from Reading University and failing to find a job. Raza had been out of work for three years. If this was not bad enough, their father, who had firm ideas about these things, would not allow his sons to sign on for benefits. The brothers decided the only way out was to go into business together, but they hardly had a penny between them. One thing they did have going for them was that Raza had qualified in the motor trade, and there seemed a shortage of good garages where they were living. They approached a local councillor for help. No banks were keen to back two untried, unemployed young Asians, so councillor Charles Swift steered them over to the Youth Business Trust.

They had found a small lock-up garage, but needed £10,000 to lease the premises and buy basic testing equipment. Their intention was to offer repairs and MOT servicing. The Trust came up with £5,000, which Peterborough City Council matched, enough to start Swift Car Care, named after the councillor.

The business plan had forecast a first year turnover of £23,000. In the event they did £65,000 and never looked back. The five-year loan was repaid in two years. In 1989 Prince Charles was presented with a seven-litre Chrysler which had been custom-built for Al Capone. Swift Car Care was chosen to do the valet work. Mohammed drove to Sandringham to deliver the car to him. Swift Car Care has been so successful that it won the Business of the Year Award in 1992. An accident crash repairs service was added. Thirty-five people now work there. The crash repair centre is being purchased this year by Nationwide. The Datoos will concentrate on service and MOTs.

Minority entrepreneurs can consider a range of ethnic markets, where special expertise helps. One caterer even attracted the patronage of the West Indian cricket team on their last visit to Leeds. Niche businesses are viable, such as meals on wheels designed for the dietary needs of elderly Asians, a funeral business for Muslims, and Eye Sharp in Blackburn, an optician's where the reading cards are in Asian languages, as is the whole consultation. Growth is the future for Nilesh Patel (PYBT '95), who manufactures poppadums. This year Shakti Poppadums will produce around 4 million, and plans to expand annual production to 30 million.

Racial stereotypes abound. For example, people often say that Asians make good entrepreneurs but that Afro-Caribbeans cannot cope with self-employment. The Prince's Trust has found that Asian young people often do make excellent entrepreneurs but success stories like Datoo and Patel are complemented by Afro-Caribbean businesses which are doing well. Alison Noyem (PYBT '96) identified a niche in the greetings card market for distinctive ethnic cards, and her line is now carried at John Lewis, Liberty's and Selfridges. Eno Erutor (PYBT '91) built up a wholesale and retail operation specialising in Lycra-type clothing.

Involving more ethnic minorities is not a one-way street. An increasing number are contributing to his work. Their contribution comes at all levels, as team leaders or as business advisors and through donations. Once Mohammed Datoo was successful, he wanted to give something back. He offers free services to local Trust businesses and has joined the regional Trust board. Tunde Adeshokan (PYBT '96), who runs a soccer school for kids, finds the time to meet MPs and talk at fund-raisers about how helpful the Trust can be to ethnic minority entrepreneurs.

Errors are inevitable when dealing with a complex and dynamic set of circumstances. A classic case relates to the suggestion, widely publicised, that the Prince should sponsor the travel of police to India to gain a better understanding of that complex network of cultures. An internal evaluation concluded that the idea missed the point. The culture of Asian communities in Britain is not the same as those of similar ethnic backgrounds living in other countries. More sensible would be for police to spend time with Asian families in places like Birmingham. This recommendation somehow got lost in channels and the initial idea was resurrected early in 1998 having been rejected by experts as unsuitable. So "them and us" suspicions still linger, and will be hard to put to rest.

In his address at the *Windrush* reception in June 1998 the Prince reflected on how far things had come. "I knew of the beginnings of organised immigration from the West Indies in the late '40s, and have watched the subsequent growth of the black community into what we have today. I grew up with the controversies surrounding the gradual acceptance not only that such a community existed but that it was here to stay. I have seen those controversies subside as subsequent generations – certainly that of my sons – have grown up knowing only a multi-cultural Britain." He will continue to push his vision of a multicultural Britain for as long as it takes. "By multi-cultural I mean not a Britain where different cultures co-exist in sealed compartments, but one inhabited by individuals whose own culture has been enriched by contact with people from different ethnic and religious backgrounds. I am proud to be part of such a Britain."[14]

YOUNG OFFENDERS

Prince Charles's interest in the problems of young offenders goes back to 1972. If you seek to help the most marginalised young people, that will include hard cases who have fallen foul of the law. It was in keeping with his thinking that his second experiment was a project run by two ex-offenders. Nearly 40 per cent of the ideas the Prince personally funded before his Trust was set up involved young ex-offenders, many of whom were banned from established youth organisations.

Show interest and encourage "idle hands" to come up with something productive, and maybe, just maybe, a life can be salvaged. The Prince stressed this aspect of his work in his 1975 speech to the House of Lords, where he gave as one of the reasons for forming a new Trust the need to find alternative activities for young people who might otherwise gravitate to crime. "The problems we suffer in society as a result of violence, mugging and general anti-social behaviour on the part of younger people, are partly due to a lack of outlets into which pent-up energy and frustration and a desire for adventure can be properly channelled."

He mentioned the 1972 Community Service Act, which he had been following closely with his Youth Group. "It is also heartening to discover how comparatively

[14] *SS Empire Windrush* reception, 25 June 1998

successful has been the scheme adopted recently for the treatment of offenders through community service rather than imprisonment, borstal or probation. Investigation has shown that in several cases the ex-offender continued voluntary service beyond the termination of the court order."

This desire to break the cycle of poverty and crime, together with his interest in the problems of rehabilitation, continued to show up in some of the more unusual Jubilee grants from that period. In the 1970s, a special unit was funded in Edinburgh Prison where five inmates provided a transcribing, duplicating and binding service creating Braille books for the blind. They received support, as did the National Association for Young People in Care, the Somerset Probation and After Care Services, and Youth at Risk.

Prince Charles was aware, and his advisors kept reminding him, that helping young offenders came with more baggage than any other area of his work. The disabled deserve our support, but the delinquent who sniffs glue and shoplifts instead of going to school does not rate much sympathy, regardless of any history of a broken home or abuse in care. If the Prince ever wants more press, all he has to do is step up the profile of his involvement with young offenders. While most of his work is unnoticed, one innocuous talk given in Dover Young Offenders Institution about the virtues of self-employment, involving a mere 11 people, generated 72 newspaper articles. Stories appeared under headlines like "Charles helps criminals".

The Prince has even had to fight his own staff, who have been concerned that he should not get too involved with people for whom most of the population has little sympathy. Why does he run the risk of associating himself with a bunch of irretrievable dead beats. "There's an enormous wealth of talent there, but you wouldn't know it was there very often unless you dug it out and helped it flourish. To me this is the important part – because ... otherwise they get depressed and annoyed and angry sometimes, and – this is counter productive. We want to help people – to overcome that inevitable period when you want a bit of challenge and adventure and aggression and excitement. If society can't provide it in some way, then I believe people will break out and go off in anti-social directions."[15]

An *ad hoc* group, headed by the late Jock Barr, Deputy Director, started to look at ways to target young offenders in 1987. The Young Offender Group was set up in 1988, to try out new and more radical ideas inside institutions.

A special committee consisted primarily of people with special knowledge, including David Williams, an ex-Section 53 offender. Section 53 covers those below the age of 18 who commit very serious crimes which carry sentences from 14 years to life.

15 The Prince's Volunteers, LWT, April 1990.

Barr set five objectives, and a detailed action plan to support them.

1. To enhance the quality of life of young people in long-term custody or secure care, by giving them an opportunity to make a positive contribution to the local community.

2. To help prepare such people for release by introducing professional support services.

3. To inform them of the range of opportunities available under the auspices of the Trust.

4. To examine schemes that offer 'alternatives to custody', and to support the research and development of selected projects.

5. To intensify the Trust's commitment to 'Young Offenders Initiatives'.

The Prince of Wales had one very simple objective in mind. "To widen their vision beyond the walls which confine them."

Activities began at 17 young offender institutions, with partial release programmes such as an exchange project with young offenders in Western France to study farming techniques, gardening at hospices in Birmingham, and a cycle ride from John O'Groats to Lands End. Barr took real risks, with individuals who badly needed support but who also might bite the hand that helped. A high failure rate was anticipated. Even deciding how to measure success was not easy. Expectations had to be realistic; but what *was* realistic? By the time it was wound down in 1992 a total of 201 recorded grants, involving on average 14 people, suggests that nearly 3,000 young offenders participated. The total cash cost of the exercise was around £450,000, which works out at £160 per head.

While it was too early to investigate the longer term impact on recidivism, there were plenty of individuals whose lives were changed. At Polmont Youth Offender Institution the Trust financed an open day to raise £5,000 for the 1990 Special Olympics for disabled people in Glasgow. This led to ten young Category 'D' offenders being paroled to assist disabled participants at Glasgow, and at Aviemore on the dry ski slopes. All concerned received very high praise for their efforts.

Swansea Prison produced a crime prevention film, *Doing my 'Ead In.* The script, written and performed by young offenders and drama students from Swansea College, highlighted the disadvantages of life behind bars. It was purchased by many other prisons, and was widely used in schools for crime prevention.

The toughest challenge was to prepare young offenders for productive employment on release. The possibility that young offenders could make the leap into self-employment seemed remote, but worth a try. A trial took place in Dover in early 1991. There were 250 eligible, of whom 34 expressed an interest. Eleven actually took the course, and started three new businesses. A success rate of 1 per cent is not anything to shout about, but the course had a cash cost of just £1,140, so preparing three young offenders to begin a business worked out at less than £400 a head.

One who subsequently kept on the straight and narrow was Maqsood Zaman. He had been sent to Dover after losing his temper with an estate agent over what he felt were racist remarks, in a dispute which went beyond a verbal exchange. Maqsood was not initially enthusiastic. "I attended the course just to get out of the cell." But by the time he was released in 1991, he had worked out a plan to set up a video business, and persuaded his unemployed brother to join him. Videocraft was duly formed. The business went well for several years, and made a decent living for the Zamans.

But in 1996 Videocraft was burgled and all his equipment stolen. Maqsood had cut costs to the minimum, and had no insurance. Five years of trading was wiped out in a single night. Even so he had no regrets. Most important, since leaving Dover Maqsood never got on the wrong side of the law again. As he said at the time, "if you've got nothing to lose, go for it", reflecting the attitude in all these schemes. The reaction of some of the young offenders involved was encouraging.

"We've played some good concerts to raise money for charity. It's helped me to think twice about the way I've behaved." *Lead Singer, Immortal Cortez (Redbrook Secure Unit)*

"Helping elderly people makes us think about caring for people, and who we're harming when we offend." *Gary (Hollesly Bay Colony)*

"I'm strong enough now to say 'No' to people who want me to commit crime when I go out on parole." *Jim (Hatfield YOI)*

"If it hadn't been for you I'd be in prison. Honest." *Scott Sheehan (PYBT '90)*

A conference took place in Pentonville Prison to assess the findings of research by the University of East Anglia into the background and behaviour of young offenders. The Prince is reported to have been deeply depressed by some of the things he heard. Young offenders claimed that people in the justice system rarely asked them why they had committed a crime. There was virtually no counselling, and little to encourage them to find a career once they had served their time – let alone practical help in making a new start. The conference was unique in that it brought the Prince of Wales and the Cabinet Minister responsible, the Rt Hon Kenneth Clarke, MP, to a prison to discuss how to rehabilitate young offenders. Prison officers and probation staff attended, as you would expect, but also Trust personnel, representatives of relevant voluntary groups and a smattering of young offenders who reported on results from their perspective.

Prince Charles reported progress arising from what had been some of the most unorthodox and potentially problematic experiments his Trust had ever undertaken. In the foreword to 'Changing Inside' he wrote:

"This objective and thorough report, produced by independent researchers, chronicles and highlights both the anticipated and less predictable consequences of providing simple pump-priming grants to those with little on their minds other than their date of release. The most important thing they have discovered is that there are more fulfilling ways to lead their lives than through crime – and perhaps for the first time they have come to believe that they possess legitimate skills and human qualities which are both needed and appreciated by their fellow men and women."

Changing Inside, both the report and the conference, was a time to reflect and evaluate whether what they were doing really did make a difference. Clarke, Home Secretary at the time, described the work as "innovatory". More of a breakthrough than any of the individual projects was the approach, as Clarke underlined in his speech.

"It is especially satisfying, from my point of view, that the Young Offender Group has, throughout its existence, operated in a real partnership with the Home Office, the Prison and Probation Services, and other statutory and voluntary agencies ... No toes have been needlessly trodden on, and decision-making has been informed by a wealth of professional viewpoints ... I am more than happy to have been provided with evidence which enables me to confirm the value of this method of working with young offenders ... Many of the Trust's initiatives have shown that offenders do not have to fester behind prison walls ... They can help the community within their establishment by undertaking projects such as the Saughton Prison AIDS/HIV peer education group. In the process they develop new skills and new confidence which, we hope, will gradually lead them away from crime and the damage it wreaks on others."

The Trust's work had demonstrated that some young offenders respond to community service. When released they had a better attitude about themselves and society. Contacts maintained since suggest that some have stayed out of trouble. But plain sailing could not be expected when dealing with a group whose sole common denominator was anti-social tendencies. Several projects suffered theft of equipment. Field trips did not always end happily. A few attempted to break away.

The Prince, of course, got little more for his pains than a few unhelpful headlines. "HRH helps inmates make jail break", *Wigan Evening Post*. "Charles helps to make bosses out of young crooks", *Daily Mail*. "Charles: I will tame tearaways", *Western Daily Press*. And of course you can always rely on the *Sun*, "Getting a lag up". He knows the score by now. "Frequently I find that, unless you have a disaster or a scandal, nobody ever knows what the hell is going on … "[16]

Why did such a promising start peter out? In a word, resources. 1993 Trust budgets called for a massive boost in Volunteers, and other projects were standing in line to take their turn. Work with young offenders did not come to an end, but disbanding the Young Offenders Group removed a vital focal point.

A 1986 survey by the Audit Commission asked young people on supervision what would stop others offending. The main answer was jobs, exactly the solution which Prince Charles is offering as his primary contribution to cutting down youth crime in this country. Social issues aside, the best way to break the cycle is by finding a young offender work, or failing that a meaningful training course or community service project.

The second and third answers were more sport or the availability of other leisure activity. The programmes the Prince uses to try and recapture young offenders, such as Recharge and Superstart, incorporate a good dose of both sport and leisure. Occasionally young offenders still serving a sentence may get a special supervised release to take part. The Volunteer programme also grafts on things which are fun, to hold initial interest before the community service aspect takes over. Extra efforts are being made to include former offenders on teams.

Disadvantaged young offenders need much the same medicine as the other alienated young people. The Trust can respond with grants, residential courses, help in starting a business, and community service programmes.

Grants

Grants, to groups as well as individuals, can give meaning to lives which might otherwise have none. About 600 will be awarded in 1998. Chief Superintendent Ted Parry of the Northamptonshire Police tells the story of 15-year-old from a broken home who was a fixture on the complaints sheet. Authorities despaired until someone noticed he had an interest in tennis. The Trust provided a grant for coaching. With a focal point for all his energy, the crimes stopped. Now 18, he leads a normal life playing at a level which could earn him a living. Parry is convinced the grant made the difference. "If the Prince's Trust hadn't helped, we would have lost him to the downward spiral."

[16] Address at launch of the 1989 Prince's Trust annual report, Livingstone, 4 September 1989.

Stories like this are commonplace. The Prince encourages local committees to take risks. Direct help to individuals is perhaps the clearest example of where intervention from the Trust can break the cycle. To turn around a life going wrong is the best possible use of its funds. Twelve per cent of 1997 grants went to people known to be young offenders or ex-offenders. The true percentage would be higher, because not all those who have done time volunteer the information, and the Trust does not ask.

Residential courses

All residential programmes include young offenders, about 500 in 1998. These one-week wake-up calls are particularly effective because their environment is completely non-judgemental and the emphasis is strictly on the future. Residential courses also work as a feeder into other organisations and Trust programmes, which carry the process of rehabilitation forward. Results for young offenders were not statistically different from those of the average attendee. One year at Caister there were six people who were serving life sentences for murder. One of them has now been working in a bank for several years.

John Salter and Tom Blake attended Caister in 1989, on release from Swinter Hall in Staffordshire. Their situation and experience was not atypical. They were 17 when they got into trouble, in a night-club when a fight broke out and someone died. Of about ten teenagers involved, 9 were charged and 6 sent to prison. John and Tom were both sentenced for manslaughter, and got 5 years each. They found prison life a shock. "Missing your family was the hardest thing."

The experience at Caister, however, was to introduce a new perspective to their lives. Tom felt much more positive about his future prospects. "The things we did at Caister were very worthwhile. In the mornings we had group discussions. We were learning about things like CVs and how to take job interviews. They were trying to help us find work. There was sport, as well as helping us think about finding employment. We've both grown up in prison. Now we're due to get out in six weeks' time. When you finish your sentence, you're just released out of the gates and that's it. They don't try and help when you get out. But the Prince's Trust is doing something."[17]

Self-employment

Home Office statistics show that 68 per cent of people who are on probation or serving community sentences are unemployed. The day the prison gates opens, a disaster is already in the making for most. Over 90 per cent have no training, let alone any kind of job to go to. For ex-offenders self-employment may be the first

[17] Prince's Trust annual report, 1989.

and last resort. The Trust had always helped young offenders on an *ad hoc* basis. A criminal background is not a consideration when assessing the proposal.

The emergence of a self-employment initiative designed to address the special problems of young offenders is a more recent development. The stated aim of the Acorn Project is "to reduce crime through employment, training and education". As one ex-offender said to his adviser: "I'm so busy with the business, I've no time to get into trouble."

Acorn set out to find young ex-offenders, rather than wait for them to turn up. Staff started to track the background of applicants. A target for more start-ups was set. Given the nature of the group, the hit rate was always bound to be lower than for the population at large. Of 370 referrals processed in 1994, only 22 received funding. But involvement with Acorn stimulated other positive outcomes. Nearly 70 applicants either found jobs, were placed on training courses or got grants for something else. Just the process of considering self-employment, and of trying for the first time to put together some sort of plan, proved to be a positive experience for many.

There is bound to be the odd slip when you put people who have a criminal record in business. Dean Benson appeared to be the perfect role model. On 20 July 1988, the *Birmingham Evening Mail* ran a nice story, "Trust Put Dean on the Straight and Narrow". Dean had been inside for 17 of his 26 years, convicted of crimes ranging from theft to armed robbery. While in Winston Green prison he discovered a talent for making matchstick models, and parlayed this in to a viable business with support from the Trust. Bryant and May, who were supplying him with nearly 100,000 headless matches a week, bought the copyright of a Harley Davison 750cc Low Rider motorcycle he created, and were all set to sign him for a bigger deal. Dean even presented the Prince with the Harley model, his pride and joy, as a token of his appreciation. But just as everything seemed to be going swimmingly Dean's marriage bust up. His wife destroyed Dean's models. Dean threw a wobbly and was last heard of back inside.

There are other stories of young offenders who started to go straight but could not stay the course. Failures cannot take away from what is more remarkable. Many do not re-offend. For every Dean Benson there is a Debbie Evershed.

Debbie feels the help she got from the Prince's Trust made all the difference. "If I hadn't had this opportunity so directly after prison I would have gone back to the same life I'd led before", which in her case had been a lifestyle dependent on money from dealing in cannabis. Debbie had not considered becoming an entrepreneur until she found herself in a cell at Bullwood Hall with someone who had a past full of problems.

Her cellmate and future business partner was in for armed robbery, the conclusion of a catalogue of catastrophes. As a child she had suffered years of sexual abuse. Summoning the strength at 17 to leave an apparently comfortable home, she did not know how to cope, and mentally she was a mess. "I was very self-destructive; unable to form any relationship, especially with men. I tried to commit suicide several times. I was desperate and had no-one to turn to." She started shoplifting, but wasn't very good at it and says now that she believes she wanted to get caught in the hope that someone would help her.

The court psychiatrist told her she was imagining her problems. At this point she went completely off the deep end, and a six-month spell in prison did no good at all. Back on the streets, she went straight back to shoplifting, and also got in with a bad lot who had a history of more serious crime. She joined an armed raid on a local post office, and received a four-year sentence.

Then she came across Debbie, and also Vivien Cockburn of the Prince's Trust who visited Bullwood Hall several times to encourage inmates to start their own businesses. Despite having a record, both women were bright, and in the case of Debbie's cellmate highly motivated. "I had something to prove to my dad: that I was better than he was."

Debbie's sister, a successful artist living in Minneapolis, produced posters and cards with social messages. She agreed to give them the UK rights. The Prince's Trust came up with £5,000. It was not difficult for them to prove no-one else would lend them money. It was even difficult to find a bank which would let them open an account and put money in.

The new company got off to a decent start by selling to specialist bookshops, primarily those with a green or feminist clientele, and to arts and crafts outlets. Turnover in the first year topped £25,000 and they were able to make a loan repayment, all accomplished even though they had personal barriers to overcome. Ironically the best seller was a card featuring child abuse.

Then the big break came. A large chain, Athena, ordered £12,000 of posters which they had printed. The big bust came literally days later as Athena hit the skids and the man who had placed their order was fired. New to business, Debbie had acted on a verbal order. Without anything in writing they did not have a legal leg to stand on. What's more, their regular customer base was going belly up at the rate of two a week, as the 1993 recession began to bite, leaving them with mounting bad debts. This could have pushed them both back into crime. Instead, "getting the business this far had given us back our confidence. We were able to deal with people again and were sure of ourselves."

They both found temporary work, Debbie as a private investigator and then as a carpenter. Her friend, who understood computers, found work in that area, casual jobs at first, but then she was taken on permanently and has done so well that she is now running an IT department for a well-known City firm. Debbie meanwhile set up a recycling programme. She also works one day a week with the probation service teaching woodwork, and at a rape crisis centre.

From the time they got out on the same day, Debbie and her friend have stayed out of prison. They attribute this in large part to the help they received from the Prince's Trust at a time when no-one else wanted to know. "They are broad minded, open and approachable. They had the foresight to see we had potential and that people can change." And it was not just about money. There were monthly meetings, advice, encouragement, and even an encounter with the Prince of Wales. During their conversation Debbie joked with him about a recent article which had appeared on their business.

"We were on the front page of our local paper."
Prince Charles smiled. "I hope that didn't ruin your reputation."
"You don't know our reputation."

Perhaps he did; perhaps not. Either way, he would have been pleased that the Trust had played a part in getting their lives back on track. Even if the original business itself merely limps along providing a small extra income, the main point is that they have gone on to bigger things. As for the Prince, Debbie says: "He is a touch of humanity within the bureaucracy of the country."

There does not seem to be any noticeable difference in survival rates between businesses started by young offenders and any other group. One explanation is that young offenders had both more motivation and greater desperation because they had fewer options. Another explanation put forward by one prison officer is: "There are a lot of entrepreneurs in prison." Acorn is not an unqualified success – how could it be – but it has enough success under its belt to justify expansion. Success, in any event, is not necessarily measured the same way. The primary goal is not self-employment as such, but to break the cycle of re-offending that is made so much stronger by the no job/no hope syndrome. The Prince wants to offer an alternative to the easy money from knocking off a couple of videos. Just to get someone to stay at home and slog away at writing a business plan represents a victory.

Community Service

Volunteers also includes offenders. Community Service is not a substitute for a more severe sentence. Attendance is optional, and the team approach ensures a very different environment, though the invitation to participate can come from a probation officer. Local authorities believe Volunteers give young offenders an exposure to alternative and more positive lifestyles. Many put their money where their mouth is, contributing to the cost of projects. There is nothing altruistic about their commitment. The Chief Probation Officer of North Wales, Carole

Moore, said: "The real 'beneficiaries' are the communities where the project makes an important contribution to community safety through the integration of offenders as responsible citizens with a stake in their community."

In 1997 about 9 per cent of Volunteers were offenders, about 700 people all told. As at all Trust programmes, having a record is no barrier as long as other team members are not put at risk. Ronnie Williams (Volunteer '98) had received a 2H-year sentence for robbery. After working at a Winged Fellowship holiday home for the disabled he has now decided he wants to become a carer. "I got my blue badge which I needed to prove I could work with the disabled. I want to go back to the Winged Fellowship ..." On the same programme was Mark Carruthers, who has been on probation. After completing his 12 weeks of work, Mark applied to go to college to complete a computing course.

Recent Developments

In 1993–97 there were few special programmes for young offenders. Resources as always were rationed, and this was the era of Michael Howard at the Home Office. His regime was one of Boot Camps, and any sentence as long as it's long. So once Kenneth Clarke, who had been sympathetic to the Trust's approach, had moved on there was no natural ally to work with. Without departmental support, initiatives which took place within prisons and secure housing were going nowhere.

The Prince has continued to show his support, visiting several of the more imaginative schemes. The Diversion of Offenders unit is a major programme for the Northamptonshire Police involving 24 people working full time with 1,400 young offenders every year. Its focus is on hard-core repeat offenders. One tactic which appears to have an effect is shock therapy, confronting the young offender with crime victims. The Prince sat in on two of these mediations in 1996, and watched a fascinating exchange.

The Trust is moving back into sensitive areas, as its work extends inside the prison system. There are a number of small-scale local activities, like support for the pre-release training course at Askam Grange, a women's prison in North Yorkshire, which provides referrals to mainstream programmes on release. The Trust acts as a jobs 'broker' at Lancaster Farm, where young offenders are trained to act as group facilitators for drug rehabilitation groups. Any ex-inmate moving to Merseyside will be helped to find suitable work. In Canterbury Prison, the Trust supports 'Comeback', which finds jobs open to ex-offenders and then trains individuals still inside with the specific skill required for the position.

Business in the Community has also encouraged companies to help, but most companies do not like to be identified with criminals, young or otherwise. Rehabilitating young offenders does not encourage consumers, most of whom

identify with the victims of crime, to buy your product. It is no surprise that little
Seeing is Believing time has been set aside for offender visits. Only a single facility
was included in all the itineraries for 1996. But an interesting concept was floated
by David Benson of Sea Containers, following that June visit to a probation service
workshop in Bristol. "Why don't we pick a skill required by industry and sentence
offenders to be trained? If they enjoy the experience, does it really matter? At the
end of the day, if they have a chance of receiving employment, they are less likely
to re-offend."

A few corporate members have done something. Volunteers from Whitbread began
prison visits to Brixton to talk with prisoners and discuss the problems which occur
after release. This stopped two years ago, because of concerns about the extra cost
incurred by wardens who were required to supervise the activity. Sedgwick employees
have set up a Job Club inside Norwich prison for those nearing release, covering all
aspects of a job search. Following an April 1998 visit to Reading Gaol, W. S. Atkins
and Waitrose will start a 'preparation for release' programme there. British Gas is
arranging special forklift truck training for prisoners on the programme.

But these remain isolated examples. Helping young offenders represents a tough
sell, even for the Prince of Wales. Lend money to an entrepreneur and a bank will
happily match funds. Put up seed money for a study centre and contributions will
flock in. Kick start regeneration of a housing estate and you can count on help
from local businesses. Put up funds so a group of young prisoners can learn to play
squash or the saxophone and ... nothing. Of the first 41 projects in prison
supported by the Trust less than half attracted any other support.

People who commit crime are not seen as deserving. But for many young
offenders anti-social, even criminal, behaviour is a cry for help. Offered
constructive alternatives to crime, they would take them. Prince Charles has heard
the cry.

There can also be the unexpected ally. Suzanne McGrail (PYBT '97), as we saw
in Chapter 6, found a niche customising clocks made from car wheel hub caps
with the colours of football clubs. Customers include Burnley, Coventry and
Sheffield United. Suzanne started on her own, but soon needed additional
employees. Rover, her prime source of raw materials, had links with Blakenhurst
Prison. Suzanne had the idea of using young offenders. Rover agreed to send the
necessary material direct to Blakenhurst where there is now an inventory of 2,000
hubs. Wacky Artists is purchasing a compressor and paint-spraying equipment,
which prisoners will use. They learn skills which should stand them in good stead
after serving their sentence. McGrail hopes to employ some herself. This unusual
partnership is one which other Trust entrepreneurs could emulate.

Prevention

Business in the Community members with automotive interests, including the AA, DHL and Unipart, are working with the Trax project in Lichfield to tackle car crime by training young people to mend and drive cars. Two hundred and fifty-six young people passed through Trax in 1997 bringing the total to over 1,000. Though lower now, in the first years 40% were offenders. Several went on to find work in local garages and specialist auto centres and at the project itself. Car crime in the region has fallen by 27 per cent since Trax started, and some of that improvement can be attributed to the project.

While one of the largest groups of its type, Trax is not unique. A similar set-up in Luton visited recently by the Prince uses car repair as a vehicle for channelling energy into productive activity. The Luton programme enables some participants to go on to technical training at local colleges, and seven were accepted in 1997.

The best way to catch potential young offenders before they offend may be in schools. Study Support is one of the unsung heroes in reducing the rate of antisocial and criminal behaviour among young people. An out of school hours activity, it keeps young people off the streets. Once in Study Support, they are likely to be engaged in useful activity. Many are convinced of its merits. Criminologist Roger Graaf believes that Study Support is one of the most valuable forms of crime prevention in the country. His reasoning is straightforward. "There are many kids who receive no attention after school. They are left to fend for themselves." Left to themselves, they may drift in to trouble. Another solution may again be mentoring. Most young people who get into trouble share a desire to be noticed. Provide positive attention, and there is less need for anti-social behaviour.

The Prince of Wales has asked his organisations to think of alternatives designed to pre-empt offending rather than research more ways to do remedial work. The grants activity has been able to respond most rapidly, scoring one notable success through support of *Prison? Me? No way!*

Three prison officers from Hull, led by Paul Wilkinson, wanted to make a video about the realities of prison, to deter potential offenders. The Trust came up with the initial funding, and helped organise the media launch. The original video has expanded to a full information pack, CD-ROM and audio tape. Ninety prisons now participate, and 1.5 million young people have seen the salutary tape.

This Work should be Encouraged

Cutting down on crime pays. Coopers & Lybrand, along with the Scottish Community Education Council and Youth Life, Scotland, recently completed a detailed study of youth crime. Coopers concluded that the average cost to society of each recorded youth crime was about £2,100. Costs outside Scotland may be more: the Audit Commission has calculated that processing a young offender through court alone adds up to £2,500. Another estimate hot off the press from NACRO comes out at £2,880.

The Audit Commission study found that the average child referred commits about three offences per year – more for persistent re-offenders. Coopers came up with the same number. And that's the numbers which are known. These averages are for the eight to 20 age group. The Prince has made the point that he wants to go after the toughest nuts to crack. For the calculation that follows, let's assume 100 crimes in a career, a number which may be conservative, and a blended cost per crime from the three studies. Working through these numbers you reach the conclusion that for each young offender who can be steered back to the straight and narrow, the quantifiable benefit to society would be at least £250,000. If you think this sounds steep, set a quarter of a million against the average yearly cost of £28,000, which was what the 1998 NACRO study came up with.

Separate statistics on young offenders have not been kept by the Trust until recently, but available information supports a conclusion that more than 15,000 young offenders have been through one or other of the Prince's programmes. Tracking them afterwards is tough, but some stay in touch. There is plenty of evidence of individuals who have done something productive with their lives after the Trust, just as there are stories of those who went off the rails again.

Anything which does not involve a return to crime is a win. Where statistics exist there does not seem to be any pattern of difference in the results for young offenders versus others, in programmes which deliver a 'success' rate of between 65 per cent and 75 per cent over the medium term. Despite data to the contrary, if we assume the young offender fall-out rate is higher, even so at least 50 per cent should have worked out. That means there should be nearly £2 billion in today's terms of benefit from less crime, attributable to the Prince's programmes.

The Prince gets involved with a lot of disadvantaged young people; young offenders may be the most desperate. In the words of one Youth Business Trust beneficiary, "I thought that, after four years out of work and with a prison sentence behind me, I'd never have the chance to make a new start." There is more at stake breaking this cycle than in any of the other areas addressed in this book, and the returns can be higher when it happens. With 150,000 young offenders, he has his work cut out. So far the impact has been limited, though there have been enough examples of things that have worked well to justify further effort. It is to be hoped that the Prince will pick up the pace again in this the most contentious area of his work.

22. Seeing is Believing in London's East End, 1987.

23. *Planting daffodil bulbs along the A55 near Colwyn Bay in 1986.*

24. Seeing is Believing on a Birmingham housing estate, 1995.

25. Seeing is Believing on the Isle of Dogs.

26 & 27. Dean Clough Mill in Halifax, before and after its regeneration (1983 and 1988).

28. Sharing a joke with 11-year-old Melanie Moseley from the Futcher School of Recovery, Plymouth.

29. Helen Tilbury (PYBT '98) shows Prince Charles what she can do.

30. The launch of Living Options, 1988.

31. Disabled drivers at Silverstone during the International Year of Disabled People in 1981.

32. Encouraging residents at the Gateway Foyer in South London, 1993.

33. *Mohammed Datoo (PYBT '88) presents Al Capone's car to the Prince of Wales.*

34. *Discussing the concerns of Smethwick residents, Birmingham, 1995.*

35. *The Dumfries young offenders' photo club at Pentonville Prison, 1992.*

36. *The Prince with celebrity ambassadors. Left to right, Jennifer Ehle, Ben Elton, Kevin Spacey, Dion Dublin and Ben Kingsley.*

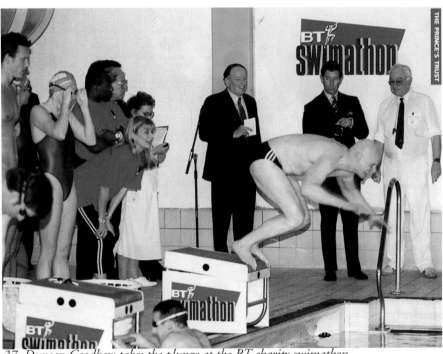

37. *Duncan Goodhew takes the plunge at the BT charity swimathon.*

38. *Prince Charles meets Status Quo at the first rock concert ever attended by a member of the Royal Family, 1982.*

39. *The masters of music: with Steve Baslemo, Billy Connolly, Roger Daltrey, Bob Dylan, Jools Holland, and Pete Townshend.*

40. *Marx and Lenin look down while the Prince of Wales extols the virtues of the enterprise culture and corporate responsibility to an audience in St Petersburg, 1994.*

41. Entente cordiale and the auld alliance at the Easterhouse housing estate in Strathclyde, with President Jacques Chirac.

42. Cultivating business support in the Gulf.

Chapter 8

PRINCE CHARLES AS CHAIRMAN

"Take risks with people"

T he Prince's management contribution compares most closely to that of chairman; executive in the early stages, non-executive as a new activity develops a life of its own. After observing him, listening to him describe what he is trying to accomplish and talking to people who have worked for him, several patterns emerge.

1. Don't be afraid to take risks. Failure can be OK.

2. Keep an open mind to change and new ideas.

3. Build partnerships wherever possible. Involve to resolve.

4. You only learn by listening (particularly to the people you are trying to help).

5. Wherever possible take the long-term view.

This list captures the essence of his management style, and reflects something of his personal preferences as well. If you watch the way he pursues his goal to help young people help themselves:, you see him in several roles: generator of ideas, catalyst, professional manager, not to mention statesman.

The one characteristic that comes though most strongly, as earlier chapters have shown, is the importance he attaches to taking risks: with people, with his own organisations and most of all with himself. In a 1989 speech he said: "The important aspect of the Trusts has been the willingness and determination to take risks and I have constantly had to go on badgering those splendid volunteers all round the country that risk-taking was very important. We mustn't end up becoming satisfied and too official, as it were, because it is obviously easy to help only those who are safe bets."[1]

Taking risks requires a certain culture, flexible and forward-looking. The Prince is adamant: "I have always tried within the Trust to keep the bureaucratic element to the absolute minimum ... There is nothing wrong with simplicity." In a 1985 letter about the proposed restructuring of Tasks Undertakings, he wrote: "I am particularly keen to avoid duplication and unnecessary bureaucracy wherever possible." The message is consistent in all his pronouncements. "Having now abolished all application forms, I think we should be proud of this particular achievement, and it is the speed of response which is so vital when so many schemes fall down on the length of time it takes to process the application, by which time the interest tends to diminish ... To make sure that you were reaching the sort of people who normally were not reached we had to react and respond quickly to people's needs on the spot."[2]

"What I like most," says Amanda Taylor, the Norfolk chair, "is the fact that we cut through all the red tape and bureaucracy to get this money to the young people as soon as possible."[3]

The Prince takes risks with his own people too. The birth of Business Leaders Forum at a 1990 conference in Charleston had all the makings of a logistical fiasco: handled out of London, with no local support structure and without any kind of organisational back-up. Until the last moment no-one knew who would turn up, and the Embassy in Washington was against the conference. Yet Robert Davies, at Business in the Community, and assistant private secretary Guy Salter, ploughed ahead and pulled off such a coup that the British ambassador, Sir Antony Acland, was one of the first to offer his congratulations. The risk had paid off.

You could say the Prince's entire programme is one giant risk. It is risky to give grants to individuals who could pocket the cash and disappear. It is risky to lend money to people with Mohican haircuts to start a business. It is risky to associate yourself with young criminals. It is risky to be on the side of disadvantaged people, those most likely to be the losers.

In one of our conversations, while discussing traditional education, he suddenly switched tack. "I said all that last year to David Frost in an interview, and got into terrible trouble. I knew I would, but I still stick by it."

[1] Address accompanying release of the 1989 Prince's Trust annual report, Livingstone, 4 September 1989.

[2] Address accompanying release of the 1989 Prince's Trust annual report, Livingstone, 4 September 1989.

[3] *Eastern Daily Press*, 17 April 1995.

He also understands that sometimes things will go wrong. "We are an organisation which has to continue taking risks and to experiment and this will inevitably involve some failures, and I don't think one should be apologetic about those because the successes far outweigh the failures."[4]

Nothing is more risky for someone in his position than challenging conventional wisdom. Being willing to challenge the *status quo* in a constructive manner is a rare talent, and many describe that as one of his great strengths. He challenges opinions, institutions and practices.

Nick Hardwick who, when Director of Centrepoint, was at the sharp end, commends his stance on the homeless. "He turned attention on the issue ... long before it became fashionable. He was there when it was still risky to be involved, because homelessness had such a negative stereotype. It took courage to get stuck into something which was not popular."

If the Prince of Wales sees something wrong in society, he does not weigh the issue in terms of whether it would help him, but solely in terms of whether or not he can help. As he said to Hardwick when they discussed homelessness, "This is one of those 'something must be done' issues."

He re-calibrates the odds and turns the definition of risk on its head. What is more risky: to make a small loan to someone who may well default but could possibly succeed in starting a business, or to leave that person without any kind of purpose to their life. Prince Charles is in no doubt. The risk to *society* is greater if nothing is done.

Risk taking *and* innovation are the two qualities the Prince uses to characterise his Trust. Yet the culture of the Trust is a reflection of its president. The March 1996 Millennium speech to a gathering of his organisations is typical: "We are able to take risks ... in a way that gives the most disadvantaged their first proper chance in life." Tom Shebbeare explains one of the reasons for their success in these terms: "We can come up with solutions to problems which are more difficult for others, because we can more easily take risks without fear of the consequences of failure."

Be Open to Change
You only have to look at the Trust today compared to 1988, let alone 1978, to see how much things have changed. All his organisations are change agents, and as such *they* must keep changing. The Prince recognises how vital it is to keep pace if you want to remain relevant. "The great thing is to constantly adapt to changing

[4] Address accompanying release of the 1989 Prince's Trust annual report, Livingstone, 4 September 1989.

circumstances because all the time the situation is altering … I keep trying to encourage all the people working for the Trust to look constantly for new and better ways of doing things …"

One essential prerequisite to coping with change is adaptability. "The Prince's Trust should remain flexible in its terms of reference because that way it is easier to respond … That's the great thing for me, anyway – remaining flexible." And not just at the Trusts, which are a microcosm of how he feels the country needs to respond. "The whole spirit and survival and regeneration of this country depend on flexibility and imagination."

These are points the Prince made obliquely in his Davos speech in 1992. "Einstein once described the problem in his own unique way. 'The world we have created today as a result of our thinking thus far,' he wrote, 'has problems which cannot be solved by thinking the way we thought when we created them.'"

On his 40th birthday Prince Charles gave an interview in which he described his own approach. "We can try pilot schemes here and pilot schemes there. If some don't work we abandon them; if others work we obviously pursue them." It's all about new ideas. The Prince's Trust excels in its ability to access, evaluate, process and test new ideas. Tom Shebbeare has described himself as running 'an ideas factory'. The same goes for Business in the Community. One of the main objectives of POWAGOD is to assess the relevance of new ideas for disabled people which others might ignore.

This aspect of Prince Charles is, for me, one of the most remarkable things about him. In spite of his background, he has resisted the temptation to dwell in the past. It is greatly to his credit that he saw the winds of change during the 1970s when all around him were oblivious. He recognised that change in the country must mean change in the royal family. The next generation would want more from the next monarch, substance as well as ceremony.

Involve to Resolve

Prince Charles has shown striking sensitivity to the need to involve multiple parties in solving serious problems. This was apparent very early. He believed progress was made by the Countryside in 1970 Committee because it "has been able to establish action groups on the ground which bring together various societies, schools, colleges, local authorities and government departments. Consequently it obtained results that could not easily have been achieved by individual bodies working in isolation."[5] His approach has been consistent ever since.

5 'Conservation and Society'.

Suggest a new initiative, and the Prince will usually begin by reeling off a long list of people who need to be involved. Before setting up POWAGOD, he took advice not only from over 250 organisations working with the disabled, and individuals with disabilities, but also the CBI and the TUC. Only when 83 per cent of those surveyed came out in support did he agree to go ahead.

Before the Community Venture was launched he was careful to float the concept past all constituencies who might be affected: businesses, emergency services, training services and trade unions. Even so, in Birmingham, Venturers were limited to arranging most work placements in the voluntary sector because local public sector union officials refused to co-operate. Volunteers also went through an excruciating process of testing the water. Over 500 copies of the position paper were circulated, and every arm of government, industry and the voluntary sector canvassed.

Consultation is the first step, followed by involvement or partnership. The Trust is always looking to link with like-minded organisations. Business in the Community has the same guiding principle.

These private/public partnerships are, the Prince believes, a panacea for many of the social ills he is trying to address. He cannot accept that people of goodwill, regardless of differing backgrounds, are unable to work together, and will use any opportunity to stress the need for more co-operation. Two key planks in every programme are individual action and building partnerships. If these elements are present, success is possible.

If you can get a group of talented people with a common interest to sit at the same table and debate a problem, solutions will emerge. And the more diverse the group the better.

This belief in a melting-pot approach manifests itself in the composition of the management board of the Prince's Trust. Over the past decade members have included the rock star, Phil Collins; Shaks Gosh, who is chief executive of Crisis; the impresario Harvey Goldsmith; the managing director of a chain of hotels, John Jarvis; Maureen Mallon, a youth worker; and David Akinsonya, a TV producer who was brought up in care.

This culture now prevails at all his organisations. At the beginning of the 1990s there were six separate initiatives, all with broadly complementary goals and all related to the Prince of Wales, but all doing their own thing and working in separate buildings. Communication was poor and such reporting lines as existed were not designed to encourage the free flow of shared information. The Prince wanted to make his organisations work more closely together. He was confident the "sum of our efforts will be greater than their individual parts". A co-ordinating committee was set up with the Prince as chair. Now all the organisations are united in one overriding objective, which is helping disadvantaged young people.

Learn by Listening

The Prince approaches problems by corralling leading experts in the field. With the 1970 Countryside Committee, he had the benefit of the collective wisdom of 32 members "able to speak with authority on almost every aspect of the environment". Specialists gave him access to informed expertise. He tried to make sure committees covered all shades of opinion.

The 25 members of the industry and commerce liaison committee in 1986 included senior executives from blue chip companies such as Shell, National Westminster, ICI and IBM, but also providing input were Gavin Laird of the Amalgamated Union of Engineering Workers, Meg Thompson from the National Dock Harbour Board and Richard Wilson from the Cabinet Office.

The composition of the 20-person advisory group on disability that same year included several people with disabilities, as well as the Earl of Snowdon, Baroness Warnock, whose expertise was education, and Jimmy Savile, the disc jockey. But experts are only one port of call for a Prince who says he is "learning all the time".

He has built a career out of listening carefully, whether the issue is how to regenerate urban communities ("the secret lies in allowing the 'ordinary bloke' to express his views and preferences …")[6] or how to deal with global deforestation ("the only way, I think, of solving the rain forest situation is to listen to the traditional people who live in those forests. They have lived with nature for thousands of years.")[7] The flip side is an aversion to unilateral solutions imposed by "outside" experts. Prince Charles has denounced professionals for failing to listen to the concerns and needs of the people affected by their work, be they architects, doctors or urban planners.

The media have interpreted this as blanket condemnation of particular professions. If anyone looks closely at what he actually said, they will see his criticism is aimed not at any specific group but at the behaviour and attitude of those who presume they know best and ignore the knowledge, feelings and rights of the community. Whether we are looking at medicine, housing, or how assistance is provided by voluntary groups, including the Prince's Trust, "people are not there to be planned for; they are to be worked with."[8]

The Prince must believe so strongly in this concept, not only because of what he says, but also from the way his organisations operate. Individuals come up with their own ideas for grants. Volunteers pick their own community service projects,

6 Address to the Institute of Directors, 26 February 1985.

7 'Saving the Ozone Layer', British Museum, 6 March 1989.

8 *A Vision of Britain.*

and think of ways to find the resources to complete them. Entrepreneurs applying for financial aid present their own business plan.

As early as 1970, the Prince wrote: "One of the most important features of the Committee's programme is to pay special attention to participation by young people. It must be remembered that decisions taken today will have repercussions many decades from now. We must, therefore, make quite certain we listen to their opinions."[9] Twenty-eight years later, his stance has not shifted. In Bro's 1998 annual report he wrote: "Young people have a particularly important part to play, for without them a community will wither. However, they are sometimes the last to be consulted, although they have the greatest stake in the future."

Strengths carried to excess can become weaknesses. Advisors suggest that sometimes he is too ready to listen, and can be taken in by the passion of an argument. Since he is so sensitive to suffering, his first reaction is to respond in some way, which also can make him vulnerable to people trying to exploit his position. Prince Charles was so concerned about the plight of the young unemployed that he was inclined to encourage help of any kind without sufficient scrutiny. In the early 1980s he was taken to see drop-in centres, whose *raison d'être* seemed to be claiming allowances rather than offering advice on getting new jobs. These visits appeared to endorse a life of dependency on state hand-outs. As Lord Young observed: "The Prince of Wales, out of the goodness of his heart, was falling in with the wrong people."

But his ability to listen and understand has been a great asset. At a time of increasing specialisation, effective managers have to be a sponge for information, able to absorb ideas, process them and make connections to see how they might be applied elsewhere. One private secretary described the Prince as a blotting paper for ideas. He has demonstrated that the world still needs generalists.

Take the Long View
In October 1992 the Prince addressed the conference on Opportunity Through Partnership. "I think it is probably fair to say that as a nation we have not always given education the priority it deserves. It is, after all, 140 years – almost to the day – since my great-great-great-grandfather, Prince Albert, wrote to Lord Derby: 'I am fully convinced that we cannot afford any longer to be the only country which gives no facilities to its industrial population for the study of Art and Science, and that the Government cannot divest itself of its responsibilities in this respect.'"

Few take the long view. This is a man who has said, "I feel history." He thinks in terms of a time horizon that most people would never consider. John Bird sees this

[9] 'Conservation and Society'.

continuity. "One of the reasons I was interested in the Prince is that he is carrying on the work of the Prince Consort, because the Prince Consort, at a time of enormous social change in the middle of the 19th century, became involved in the Artisans Dwelling Association and was involved in putting meat on the bones and getting people work and accommodation." That our responsibility is as life tenants only, since no-one owns the freehold of Britain, is constantly on his mind. Speaking at the tercentenary celebrations of the College of William and Mary, the Prince voiced his concern about concentrating on today. "Why do we so allow short-termism to dictate how we run our affairs that it prevents the longer-term strategic thinking and investment which we know is essential to safeguard our futures?"

He sees that he has a vital role to remind the rest of us of our responsibility to future generations: "Should we not be cherishing the best of what we have inherited, grateful for what it tells us about our history and conscious that in many respects the principles which govern the quality of life remain essentially the same from one generation to the next? I have said before that the paradox we face is that the 'Spirit of the Age' seems sadly to be that of an 'Age without Spirit'."

Such thinking is particularly revalent to the environment. "I am not at all sure that globalisation has been an entirely positive force, and in 25 years' time, and we have to think in these terms, we may find that there has been untold destruction and countless problems unless we think ahead today … It is clear to me and, I think, to an increasing number of people that if we and future generations are to continue to enjoy a comfortable lifestyle, we need to learn to respect the environmental consequences of everything we do."

Idea Generator

"Our last idea wasn't our best." Here is a phrase that the Prince of Wales should patent. Whenever you talk to any of his staff, they allude to his extraordinary talent for coming up with new ideas. Ideas are lobbed around like grenades. Some work well. Inevitably some do not.

"I'm one of these people who tend to come up with odd ideas and shower people like Mike Woodhouse, Elizabeth Crowther-Hunt, Tom Shebbeare and Julia Cleverdon with memoranda; and every now and again an idea is acceptable." He is aware that this is one of his great strengths. "Quite a lot of the time I think of something in the bath, literally, and write it down, and write memos endlessly to people saying 'what about this; have you thought about that? Why don't we do this, why don't we do that?' Saying 'you can shoot me down, but would you look at this idea?'"

Known as 'black spider memos', these scribbled notes are a weekly occurrence for senior management. Some, often beginning "I know you will think I am particularly potty but …" , are way out, but in many cases the connections he makes are exactly what a broadminded chairman, able to see the overview, should be sharing with staff to stimulate them to think beyond the confines of their daily activities.

It is not just his staff who know that he is a reservoir of interesting ideas. David Hunt recalls that in his last audience, when he swapped the position of Treasurer to Her Majesty's Household for Minister for the Inner Cities, the Queen steered him to her son, saying he had some wonderful ideas about how to improve conditions. Hunt was pleased that she did. "Her Majesty was quite right to direct me to Prince Charles. He had a catalogue of ideas."

In March 1992 Prince Charles was due to make a speech of thanks at a dinner for Trust donors. At his briefing the day before, he was not entirely happy with the format. He had a better idea. "Young people are the best ambassadors for our work, and we should always put them forward at every event like this. Can you find someone for tomorrow night?" This was not a lot of notice, but fortunately Manny Amadi, the Trust's fund-raising director, had a solution. Paul Gullick was underneath a car at Llanelli Radiators, a job he got as a result of Volunteers, when he got a call.

"What are you doing tonight?"
"Nothing," he replied.

So Paul borrowed his boss's dinner jacket and was *enroute* to London, arriving at Kensington Palace with a mere quarter of an hour to spare. First he was introduced to Prince Charles. "I was so nervous when I bowed I nearly head-butted him." After dinner Paul spoke eloquently for five minutes. "I made some notes on the train, but my writing was unintelligible." Then he held his own in a question and answer session.

Prince Charles asked him how he felt about giving the speech. Paul replied, "I've always liked a challenge. That's why I got married." Everyone agreed his speech was the high point of the evening. Paul had confirmed his hypothesis. Attendance by young people who have come through a relevant course, to say a few words about their experience, is now a fixture.

The Prince is constantly coming up with suggestions on how to improve the effectiveness of his Trust. This extract from a letter to trustee Mike Woodhouse is vintage Prince of Wales. At issue is how to get people to work more closely together and he has plenty of suggestions on that subject.

• "Our thoroughly professional joint presentation to Members of Parliament was an outstanding success. I look forward to repeating the exercise this year and it does occur to me that, in the meantime, you should encourage some of the regions to undertake something similar for themselves with key people in their area – such TEC Chairmen, newspaper correspondents, Members of Parliament and others.

• I was so pleased to learn at the last meeting of my Co-ordinating Committee, that we are making progress in other areas, and hope we can move towards a common database, undertake research together and (at long last!) produce a leaflet explaining the activities of the different organisations and how they fit together.

• I trust that we will soon get even better at pointing young people who have been helped by one of my Trusts in the direction of another member of the family and be able to continue the process of helping them to make something of their lives.

• Finally I do hope that when opportunities arise, we will move towards shared premises in the regions. It seems to me that all the activities I have outlined actually become much easier when people are working close by their colleagues from the other organisations."

He is so prolific that systems risk overload. One comment often made by his managers was "he gives us more ideas then we could ever cope with". The Prince said to me: "It's the bane of my existence. You see, if I read anything I want to do something about it." Staff have to be selective about what and where to follow through. One problem with a selective approach is that Prince has an excellent memory, and the disconcerting habit of asking what happened to this or that idea a year later, when everyone had hoped he had forgotten.

He also champions other people's ideas if he thinks they make sense. The name of the bright spark who suggested a directory of Trust businesses and an annual exhibition remains unrecorded, but the Prince latched on to both these ideas and pushed them along. Sometimes he is the originator of an idea, but equally he may be the catalyst.

Charles the Catalyst

One of the Prince's greatest strengths is his ability to bring together the right group to discuss issues and seek solutions. The royal rolodex comes in handy here. Initially people would show up simply because they wondered why the Prince wanted a meeting. Later his views attracted interest in their own right. Robert Davies, chief executive of the Business Leaders' Forum, explained this attribute. "He is a natural convenor and acts as the honest broker between different interest groups. It is probably his role as a catalyst that represents his greatest contribution to corporate citizenship." His importance lies in getting a new initiative started and keeping that alive until it has a life of its own. So he is something of a seed capitalist for social issues.

His drawing power is international. The two-day seminar on the royal yacht, to help reconcile conflicting positions between developed and developing nations in advance of the Rio summit on the environment, attracted President Collor of Brazil and Senator Gore from the USA, as well as many leading environmental experts. It is hard to think of many other figures who could bring together such a high-powered gathering in the first place, and then stroke so many fragile egos sufficiently to show progress. Bringing people together in this way is, as John Gummer says, "a very proper role of monarchy". Gummer goes further. "No-one else can do it the way he does. Countries without a monarchy don't have this ability, or anyone who can make this sort of contribution."

The impending arrival of the Prince works wonders. Volunteers North East got eight weeks' notice of his visit, rather a worry since they did not actually exist at the time the call came. When he arrived in Middlesbrough on 30 March 1994, the University of Teeside and the local TEC had a franchise up and running, the first team activity under way and dozens of Volunteers assembled to greet him. In the space of just 60 days, 90 people had been signed up from British Gas, the Inland Revenue, Northern Electric and Royal Mail.

The Prince also sees the importance of finding catalysts. Bringing visitor attractions to difficult neighbourhoods is one way he tries to resuscitate economic life in a depressed area. The Eureka museum has been a spectacular success in Halifax (see Chapter 6). He was also instrumental in arranging for *HMS Bronington*, the wooden mine sweeper that was his first naval command, to end up at Salford Quays on the Manchester Ship Canal, close to the Ordsall estate.

Being a catalyst may just mean shining a spotlight on an issue that is not receiving the attention it deserves. Virginia Bottomley, who when Minister of Health looked at disabled legislation, describes how his support made a difference to securing a higher priority for the disabled. "Progress on facilities and rights for disabled people and the whole empowerment drive was greatly enhanced by his backing. The issue had a following but it was not fashionable. When the Prince of Wales got involved no-one in public life could avoid the issue he identified."

From a politician's perspective Prince Charles could be an ally or an awkward cuss, depending upon your point of view, but he could not be ignored. So he was able to do great service simply by being there. Sue Stoddart, former chief executive of Provisions, believes he accelerated their expansion by getting their name in front of more companies. "I do believe that his support and opening centres really helped the awareness of Provisions among the food industry."

Penrhys is a classic case of a community where the Prince turned on the spotlight. It is a housing estate in the Welsh mountains built in the late 1960s, and not a place many people would choose to call home. When he took an interest, Penrhys was remarkable for the following:

- 83 per cent unemployment (often third generation);
- nearly every household received benefits;
- 25 per cent of households were single parents;
- average incomes were around £100 per week;
- crime was rife, and public buildings and trees had been vandalised.

In 1988 he had singled out Penrhys as exemplifying how awful architecture on housing estates can be. Quality of life there was about as low as it gets: poverty, poor education and bad health.

He went there in 1989 and was appalled. At his suggestion, Business in the Community organised a group of business leaders to make a follow-up visit. All felt a need to do something. Stephen Walls, then at Wiggins Teape, agreed to sponsor the community newsletter. Gerald Ratner made arrangements to sell clocks made locally through his jewellery chain. Bill Castell, chief executive of Amesham, committed five hours a month to helping the local community leader, the Reverend John Morgans, find ways to alleviate the worst of the problems. Business in the Community, the Prince's Trust and the Prince of Wales Committee have all been involved in a total transformation of Penrhys, drawing in corporate sponsors as well as local government. Not everything is roses but:

- a new community centre, containing a café, crèche, launderette, library and 'nearly new' shop, serves hundreds of residents each week;
- vandalism is much reduced;
- a Whitbread scholarship funds higher education for six students each year, and the first pupil from Penrhys went to university in 1996;
- a proper health centre was opened by William Hague in June 1996;
- Business in the Community member companies have donated items ranging from a minibus to medical equipment;
- an outdoor amphitheatre for meeting and events won an environmental award.

Morgans has done most of the hard slog, but he is grateful to Prince Charles for getting things going. "He was the midwife that gave birth to the vital Castell-Penrhys relationship."

Professional Manager

Prince Charles wants the seriousness of his work to be reflected in the highest professional standards. The Prince's Trust became an Investor in People in 1996. In 1997 Volunteers was the first member charity to achieve ISO 9001. Codes of Conduct and Best Demonstrated Practices have become standard management tools. Evaluation is a process of continuous assessment. Every Volunteer who takes part in a programme now fills out an exit form. Efforts are being made to build NVQ accreditation into programmes.

Rifling through files, you find all the formal documents you would expect to come across in any well-run organisation, except you do not necessarily expect the same level of professionalism in the voluntary sector. Business plans are *de rigueur*. New initiatives do not get the nod without feasibility studies. A scoring system has been devised to rate the degree of relative disadvantage from which a person suffers, to give guidance in prioritising people's needs.

Prince Charles dislikes red tape, but has been badgering his managers to maintain better records for some time. The drive for quality is on. David Cooper, director of the Prince's Scottish Youth Business Trust, recalls receiving instructions that quality should be uppermost in every aspect of their work. "He wanted us to think about the quality of our own work, and the training of our managers and advisors, as well as the quality of the businesses themselves."

He also wants the most appropriate technology employed wherever possible. "Is this a 486?" he asked of a recycled computer he presented recently to the Marsh Farm Resource Centre. The Prince's Trust is on the Net. The address has an appropriate handle: http://www.princes-trust.org.uk. Business in the Community has a separate Web site sponsored by Microsoft. http://www.bitc.org.uk went on line in July 1997.

Performance applies equally to people. Prince Charles has always pushed himself and his managers, to go one step further. When he received reports in the mid-1980s on two-year survival rates of the early business start-ups, he should have been ecstatic. Eighty-five per cent was way better than the wildest expectations. Instead his reaction was, "What happened to the other 15 per cent? Whey didn't it work out for them? Where are they now? What can we do to help them? Perhaps they were not cut out to run a business, but there must be something else we can find for them?"

In June 1996 he celebrated a milestone in the Volunteer programme. From not much more than one woman and a blank sheet of paper Volunteers had just notched up its first 10,000 graduates in less than six years. The Prince remarked, "it has taken a little longer than I would ideally have wanted ..." After acknowledging that the programme had "real quality, relevance and appeal", he then went on: "However I am encouraging my Prince's Trust to keep developing new ideas so we can make the programme even better." The man is remorseless. I exaggerate. Slightly.

One way to get more done is by judicious use of deadlines, which come about because his presence creates a key date on the timetable. Harry Fitzgibbons of Top Technology, a close advisor to the Prince, saw this act as a spur to action on several occasions during the regeneration cycle at Calderdale. "Where he's very good is in saying, 'Come on, you guys, let's get something done. I'm coming back six months from now, so show me your progress."

But the Prince also understands the power of praise. He always ensures that he is properly briefed as to who has done what, and goes out of his way to thank the person concerned. Public recognition is a vital motivational tool. Most of his speeches are peppered with references to the contribution made to the occasion by key individuals or organisations. He is always last in line himself when taking credit for things which go right. On a podium he directs all praise elsewhere. In private conversations he is consistent. "I'm only as good as the people who carry out the ideas ..." He hardly ever gives himself a pat on the back.

Striving to do more and pursuit of constant improvement does not make the Prince the easiest of bosses. He can be demanding, and insensitive to the private lives of his staff. Nearly everyone has tales of being rung very late at night. He burns the candle at both ends himself and rather expects that others will do so too.

He can be impatient at the pace of change. While he takes the long view in thinking about a social structure for the country, inside his organisations he likes things done yesterday. He can be intolerant of people who waste time, and loses interest if he feels people are only bringing him good news. He much prefers to discuss problems.

He never lets up. A letter to Antony Kenney, who ran the residential courses, is typical of the Prince constantly prodding and pushing. "Maybe I am asking the impossible, but I believe we ought to set our sights higher every now and then." Several senior figures reported constant badgering once he has a bee in his bonnet. The Prince is not unaware of this trait and has said, "I must be a real pain at times."

Statesman

It is often difficult to pin down the precise influence of the Prince on politicians and policy. Why did Margaret Thatcher announce, after the 1987 election, "and now for the inner cities"? There are numerous interpretations which overlap but certainly do not coincide. There is concensus that his speeches and high profile visits to rundown urban areas played some part.

The Prince has constantly challenged government, whether over environmental regulation, or agricultural policy, or in general. Sometimes he has called for a specific change in the law. In 1985 he made an appeal to the Exchequer in relation to housing rehabilitation. The format was a question, but the underlying intent was unmistakeable. "Will they abandon home improvement grants or estimate grants on the rateable value of a property, for instance? Will they continue with the imposition of VAT for the conversion of non-listed buildings, which merely serves to discriminate against conservation and the reuse of old buildings?"[10]

But the image of the Prince of Wales tilting at government policy like windmills is more rooted in fiction than fact. His keynote speech to the Ozone Layer Conference was discussed with the Prime Minister beforehand, and cleared with her office. Most major public statements are passed by relevant departments in advance. An accommodation is generally reached. The gossip about difficulties he has had with government departments over the years is another matter entirely.

The civil service has frequently been lukewarm towards the Prince and his plans, and is skilled at killing something off with kind words and committees. The test seems to be 'no controversy, please'. The sudden cancellation of his visit to Islington in January 1973 was the first of many interferences, just as he received advice not to go to Brixton and Toxteth nearly 10 years later on the grounds that his presence would be inflammatory. When he did go to Handsworth, his visit had another effect entirely. Equally, overseas embassy officials intervened to steer him away from poorer parts of Washington, during a 1986 visit.

The Prince of Wales has had to struggle with the civil service all his working life, even before he got his Trust going. Since then, any time he has tried to do anything of substance he seems to upset someone in Whitehall. Yet his ideas hardly constitute a threat to the nation. So why all the opposition?

Whitehall is not riddled with republicans, nor is there some malicious virus infecting the corridors of power. The difficulty comes down to the structure of the civil service, and a mentality that uniquely prevails among people who get to the top of it. The top sets the tone. The Prince does not fit in a box. There is nothing in the manual that sets out rules for dealing with him, (though I suspect by now there may be an addendum somewhere). Since his constitutional role is not set out in absolutes, there is no law to say he cannot do certain things. There are those who may wish that prohibition was possible. Worse, he is a catalyst for change and he acts outside approved channels.

As a potentially loose cannon, whose every word gets widely reported, he can cause endless problems. When Prince Charles challenges conventional wisdom, he does not accept official explanations that skirt round the issues. If your job is to

---

[10] Address to the Institute of Directors, 26 February 1985.

implement the established order, you could do without someone asking difficult questions. Unlike ministers who can often be led down blind alleys, here is someone who does not know when to shut up, and over whom the civil service has no control. But he can be blocked.

He is out there arguing the case for public/private partnerships as the solution to society's problems, which is anathema to many civil servants. They ignore reporting structures, shake up the accepted way of doing things, erode the power of the bureaucracy and ride roughshod over traditional lines of demarcation. They mean mingling money from the public purse with private funds. How will the National Audit Office track the last penny? Prince Charles, remember, did not even want to ask for receipts when giving out grants. There is a grand canyon between these two mind sets.

Nor does his lack of respect for departmental lines go down well in Whitehall, though it plays rather better in Westminster. Ministries exist to serve the people. If they can be more effective in a different structure, the answer is obvious: change the structure, or ignore it. His ability to look across departments and seek solutions that draw from every resource, regardless of narrow lines of responsibility and factional interests, is an advantage and an asset that he has placed at the disposal of the country.

The structure of government makes it extremely difficult to create *ad hoc* teams, whereas that is usually his starting point. So his role here can be extraordinarily helpful to ministers, and to enlightened civil servants often frustrated by their own bureaucracy. Take his bugbear that training seemed to get lost in the Department of Employment. Prince Charles felt it should fall under Education, where it might fare better. His comment, tongue in cheek of course, to the minister concerned: "Well, if you do manage to put yourself out of a job, you would be putting thousands of others into a job."

A final problem is that he can be seen as a competitor. The Prince comes up with ideas without having gone through proper channels. Some happen to touch on subjects that civil servants regard as their province. "How dare he suggest ..." is a frequent refrain. He might like to work through formalised channels, but they never seem open; so he goes his own way, which some find infuriating.

There is no reason why the Prince, his organisations and government departments should not enjoy a harmonious relationship. Things have come a long way since officials sat in on every meeting of his Youth Group, suspecting him of subversive political intent. The crux of the residual problem is that his work transcends departmental boundaries, yet progress may require assistance from several separate sectors of government, central and local, all jealously guarding their turf.

It was with this in mind that Michael Howard at the Home Office was approached in 1994 about the formation of an interdepartmental group to be chaired by a minister, which would simplify and expedite cross-border issues. Howard was briefed by his civil servants to decline, describing it as 'quite unusual'. The following Friday, Jonathan Dimbleby was to film a meeting with another minister, David Hunt, then Chancellor of the Duchy of Lancaster. It was suggested that the question be asked of Hunt on camera. Hunt replied, "You will have your committee. Mr Fogden will chair it. It will meet within a fortnight. And if you're not happy with the way it's chaired and led, it will be chaired by a minister." The Prince was happy. Reaction at the Home Office was allegedly less than ecstatic.

The same narrow mentality appears to prevail in Brussels. DG6, responsible for agriculture, and DG8, which covers the environment, have never made much of an effort to work together. Prince Charles has used his good offices to encourage closer co-operation. He held an informal gathering at Sandringham which brought together Raymond McSharry, the Irish Commissioner of Agriculture, and Italian Ripa di Mena, who had Environment. A relaxed atmosphere allowed for the type of conversation that would have been all but impossible in an official interdepartmental meeting. Four more similar meetings have taken place so far. Some Brussels watchers have since detected a discernible difference in the way these two departments have shown more understanding of each other's interests.

Behind the scenes influence on policy is one thing: there is also the matter of influencing the content of legislation and regulation. This is not openly discussed, and neither the Prince nor the politicians are comfortable disclosing who said what and when. As one member of the House of Lords remarked, "That's the whole point. He provides occasions when you can let your hair down, say what you really feel, and not worry about having your words repeated. If we talk about what went on, these sessions would lose a lot of their effectiveness."

Sometimes his imprimatur can be seen clearly. Trustees succeeded in inserting a self-employment option into the New Deal package. Earlier, in 1990, the Prince was able to secure support for his work in Wales due to a positive relationship with the minister, David Hunt. Doubling the funding for the Prince of Wales' Committee was a good start, as was news of support of Volunteers and £2 million for four selected urban regeneration programmes. Hunt's shift in emphasis of the programme for the South Wales valleys shows the Prince's influence. Writing in December 1990 Hunt noted that "the main elements – land reclamation, factory building, environmental improvements – will continue but I intend to switch the focus to people and community-based activities." To which Prince Charles scrawled on the letter "Hooray!"

His most visible connection with the political arena has been in the environmental field. Here we see him doing what he does best: acting as catalyst, bringing people together, prodding and pushing, plus one more vital role in the 1980s, which Jonathon Porritt feels should not be underrated. "Over a period of ten to 15 years, leadership on environmental issues had been pretty patchy and, except for a brief green period under Thatcher, there was no heavyweight political leadership in this country. It was the Prince of Wales who helped persuade people that those issues were mainstream not marginal; and what that did was to reinforce some of the progressive social movements which, up until his involvement, were largely ignored by politicians."

The Prince was always aware that there are certain things that the heir to the throne should not do and is not supposed to say. In much of his work he has expanded the scope of activities. which are considered acceptable beyond charitable gestures and gracing committees. No surprise to anyone who read a 1974 interview with the *Observer*. "Whatever cause I associate with, I want to participate in it. Some organisations would be quite happy to have me, say, patron, and just put my name on the literature. But I want to *do* something for it, with it, and through it. I don't want to be a figurehead."

There is a progression towards social issues which are inherently political. Architecture is no real problem. Medicine may be a little more touchy. When he opines on employment or the homeless, he has hit the political bull's eye, regardless of any protestation to the contrary. In the mid-1980s some political pundits were calling him the only credible opposition.

Writing in 1992, in a tenth anniversary retrospective for Business in the Community, the Prince maintained that: "Business has not sought to take over the work of government … Neither should its involvement be construed as a political statement." Not everyone would agree. Royal author Ben Pimlott called the Prince's Trust 'highly political'.

Prince Charles tends to confine his most critical comments to small meetings, rather than using the royal pulpit. He is careful to avoid overt confrontation, in spite of occasional attempts in the media to manufacture conflict, even if behind the scenes, harsh words are exchanged from time to time. Given the scale and scope of his activity, occasional collision is inevitable, but over time the Prince and politicians have learned to work more effectively together.

Ahead of his Time

"Many of his ideas, or the ideas which he took on board, were well ahead of their time." This is the view of a close associate. The career of the Prince of Wales is a series of related episodes in which he takes up a cause, goes public, often to be ridiculed or reviled. Yet as time passes his views emerge as mainstream. Education is one example. As Lord Patten says, "In many ways he was brave to wade into a debate about standards at a time when this was a very hot political potato. But ten years later on there is some measure of consensus between the political parties about the proper appreciation of spoken and written English, and the appreciation of our literary heritage, and even knowing the dates of some important historical events, which used to be thought politically incorrect."

The Prince argued for business to be closely connected to the community long before corporations accepted any responsibility. He was outspoken in his advocacy of the need for greater environmental awareness and practice long before that became fashionable. He called for cause-related marketing before the concept had a name, and years ahead of campaigns such as Tesco Computers. He started Study Support eight years before it became government policy.

So the Prince can be forgiven a slightly wry remark the other day. "It is interesting how ideas sometimes either come before their time or eventually, if you go on speaking about these things enough, you find the time becomes right and somehow everybody thinks it is a good idea when they haven't thought so ten years ago."

In a speech to the British Medical Association in December 1982 his words suggest that, for him personally, the process is not painless: "... human nature is such that we are frequently prevented from seeing that what is taken for today's unorthodoxy is probably going to be tomorrow's convention. Perhaps we just have to accept it is God's will that the unorthodox individual is doomed to years of frustration, ridicule and failure ... until his day arrives."

Perhaps the most extreme example of how far and how fast opinion can come full circle relates to Volunteers. When the initial idea was unveiled it was treated with a fair degree of suspicion and condescension. Charlie's Army or Charlie's Angels were derogatory sound bites. *The Times* accused him of being idealistic, unrealistic and implicitly critical of the Government's policies. Only six years later, the leaders of every major political party were singing its praises.

He has had to endure criticism of almost every one of his attempted initiatives, especially in the 1970s and 1980s, but he has had the satisfaction of seeing some of them becoming the law of the land. Debate he stimulated in 1982 on alternative medicine has had many repercussions. One was the Osteopathy Act of 1993. In July 1994 the Chiropractors' Act followed.

Sometimes he is too far ahead. One proposal came out of a Highgrove conference on innovation in July 1991, to start a £50 million fund for universities and industry working together on leading-edge innovative products. It never materialised. The same conference spawned his Working Group on Innovation, which won accolades from the *Independent* when its findings were announced.

"The Prince of Wales is an unlikely advocate of British science technology and industry. All the more credit then to the Prince who has, in a scant six months, produced more sense on the subject than the two main political parties have managed in six years."[11] The Government grudgingly launched a £2.5 million pilot in response.

Not least among the reasons why Prince Charles is able to achieve so much are some of his personal qualities: compassion, persistence and tenacity, an ability to put people at ease, enthusiasm and the ability to spark enthusiasm in others, and a sense of humour. These all deserve some comment.

Compassion

Stop someone in the street and ask them to name three characteristics which they associate with the Prince of Wales, and compassion is not likely to be one of them. Yet he has a genuine concern about the underclass. The only time I ever heard him raise his voice was during a dissertation on the need to break the cycle of poverty, unemployment and crime that can destroy the lives of young people before they even begin.

If there is a group of young people who need help and no-one else wants to go to bat for them the Prince of Wales will put himself and his resources at their disposal, regardless of whether the issue is popular or whether it will help or harm him personally in the eyes of the press or the public. As Rupert Fairfax said, "It was very easy to work for the Prince of Wales because you could pretty much predict how he would respond on an issue. All you had to do was to ask yourself, 'Is it morally right or wrong?'"

Almost anyone who has worked with him will attest to his true feelings His frequent and regular visits to depressed urban areas beginning in south London over 20 years ago underline the depth of his concern. People as disparate as Michael Bichard, John Bird, Lord Hunt of Wirral and the Reverend Andrew Mawson all come to the same conclusion. The Prince is a man of genuine compassion. Lord Boardman, who worked with him on the 40th birthday appeal, got to know him well. "He feels passionately that society must do more than it has and as much as it can to give the young an opportunity to make the best use they can of their lives."

He is not naturally demonstrative in public. He may not show the intensity of his feelings through physical contact, so all the world can see them. But he manages to convey them to the people who matter. Almost without exception, young people come away from meeting him with a sense that here was someone

[11] 24 February 1992.

who took a personal interest and who cared about them as an individual. Lord Weatherill sums it up: "His ideas come from the heart. He has an amazing affinity, concern and compassion for the less fortunate in society. He would have been an outstanding constituency MP, as that's what it's all about. His constituency just happens to be the country."

Persistence and Tenacity

"Once the Prince of Wales is interested in an issue, he keeps it going. On and on and on." So says John Gummer, who worked closely with the Prince to advance better environmental practice in this country. Strangely, his image is something else entirely: more like a butterfly who flits from one issue to another, quickly losing interest and then onto the next. Gummer is right and popular perception is wrong.

Staff, trustees, civil servants, business leaders, government ministers – all agree. The Prince sticks with something once he perceives a problem that needs fixing. No-one has suggested he bends with the breeze because it is convenient.

His consistency in working on the same set of problems is remarkable, as records of meetings in the mid-1970s, his own notes and letters and the few public pronouncements from the period all confirm. Though the nature of the problem may alter as society itself changes and the solution may need tweaking, the issues for him then, as now, all revolve around how to help the most disadvantaged in society.

He needed to be persistent to get anything going at all. He received virtually no encouragement; the civil service and certain courtiers were deeply suspicious of what he wanted to do. Impediments were placed in his path, but he persevered.

When he started to speak out on social issues he was criticised on almost every side for butting in. Professional organisations, the civil service, trade unions, politicians, even his personal biographers and the media, have all had a go at the Prince over the years. As he admitted: "There's an amazing amount of scepticism about any new approach, or different approach, or an approach from me at all. I've found on the whole, with any of the trusts or organisations or particular bodies I've set up, it tends to be met with immense scepticism to start with and you have to just break through it."

Putting People at Ease

The Prince may be misunderstood by many, but not by young people, who intuitively recognise his good intentions.

"The occasion was formal but the Prince of Wales wasn't." *Michael Prendergast (PT Grant '87).*

"We talked about my joinery business. The Prince joked about all the jobs that he needed doing. Said something to the effect that he had thought of doing some himself, but knew he'd make a mess of them. He put me totally at ease." *Peter Charnley (PYBT '92).*

"He is very easy-going and down to earth. You would expect it to be a fraught occasion, but it's not." *David Jones (PYBT '87).*

I have found that when you see him 'work a room', the young people soon seem at ease. He asks a question, cracks a joke and then listens as they do most of the talking. Everyone gets a chance to tell their story. Prince Charles looks interested throughout. Pupils at Acton High School seemed more nervous talking to me. Thirteen-year-old kids will not let you get away with faking it. He always seems to have some repartee at the ready.

This ability can cross both generation and culture gaps. Thirteen-year-old Teri Thompson, quizzed about his visit to the Whitney Young Magnet School in Chicago, pronounced him "a very good guy. He was very easy to talk to. He knew stuff about kids and what we watch, not like my parents."[12]

John Jarvis, chairman of Jarvis Hotels, says "I don't think I've ever met anyone who has quite the skill he has of communicating with young people in exactly the right tone." This is not the way he comes across on TV nor is it the man who is portrayed in the media. Perhaps you have to see him to believe him. Typical of the comments after he visited Superstart '96 was, "I couldn't believe that someone like him would want to meet someone like me. It was amazing." In fact this is exactly what he enjoys most.

Look at the pictures in this book. Posture shows when someone is really at ease with themselves. Prince Charles is happiest mingling with Volunteers or entrepreneurs, quizzing students in Study Support or swapping stories with young people at Caister. He makes time to meet the 'chain gang' in the receiving line. Their contribution is essential, and he is sincerely grateful for all help and support – but his eyes really light up when he can move on to mingle with the young people who are his priority.

Enthusiasm

One trait mentioned frequently is his enthusiasm. Lord Young, who has accompanied him on several occasions, says: "The Prince of Wales has an enormous ability to enthuse young people." His ability to convey enthusiasm

---

[12] *Chicago Tribune*, 6 September 1986.

makes all the difference. It is not just his staff who see this side of him, but people who meet him in the field – even briefly.

His management actually like their boss. You expect people to be cautious about what they will say when talking about any superior, especially when the boss is the Prince of Wales and, in particular, to someone who is writing a book so they know that they are on the record. Even so there is no doubt in my mind that he commands not just respect but affection. As Tom Shebbeare said, " I could not work for him if he was not for real, and after ten years I would know if he were not genuine."

It is hard to improve on the way Lakshmi V. Venkatesan describes her reactions to Prince Charles on the topic of self-employment. "He is so passionate that after one lunch I am off for the next eight years, working on the Youth Business Trusts."

A Sense of Humour

Sometimes a little comic relief lightens the load. Prince Charles has a keen sense of humour, which is not always obvious. No surprise from someone who performed skits while at Trinity, wrote articles for *Punch* and was a great admirer, and indeed imitator, of the Goons. Michael Bentine, founder member of the Goons, writing in the *Mail* on the Prince's 40th birthday, commended him on the anniversary speech that the Prince himself had written about plants predicting his future. "Self-deprecating humour is the very best way to tackle adversity ... this week he demonstrated that he possesses the very same sense of humour that is also the unassailable weapon of the put-upon, down-trodden and over-governed."

He has to hide his sense of humour often enough, but it cannot stay submerged for long and people who work closely with him describe it as one of his most valuable assets. This, after all, is the man who organised an English/German phrase book to assist soldiers stationed in Germany with their amorous exploits at local discotheques.

Prince Charles really seems to let rip when he goes across the Atlantic. Students at Harvard got the full treatment. "I confess that I have not addressed such a large gathering since I spoke to 40,000 Gujerati buffalo farmers in India in 1980, and that was a rare experience." He went on to question his invitation as keynote speaker: "I am surprised, because I thought that in Massachusetts they weren't too certain about the supposed benefits of royalty."[13] Referring to the round-the-clock demands placed on those running his residential courses, he remarked, "As I know myself, having teenage children, it is very difficult to get them to go to bed." Or one for the road, which is so in character: "I'm delighted that we're meeting in Charleston, a rather good name for a city if I may say so myself."[14] His comic

[13] Foundation Day Convocation: 350th anniversary of Harvard, 4 September 1986.
[14] *Charleston Post-Courier*, 20 February 1990.

touch has helped win over many who have met him in person, and has also stood him in good stead even during some of the toughest times.

If you accept the assessment of the last few pages, you have to wonder about the difference between this man and the Prince of common perception. You almost cannot have a conversation with a member of staff without being asked "why is the Prince of Wales so misunderstood?" He should take some comfort from the number of people who have said how different he is in reality from the person depicted in the media. Peter Charnley (PYBT '92) said: "Sometimes when I hear people saying bad things about him, I think, he's not like that … I was more nervous meeting the radio interviewer than the Prince." David Brown (PYBT '91) remarked: "he came over as very conscientious and genuinely interested – not at all like the bad way the press portray him". Mary Nightingale (PYBT '94) said: "it is all about marketing these days and less about substance; and he is about substance".

This does not mean that he is always well received. His intervention often strikes a raw nerve. If you are going to make any kind of impact on difficult social issues you cannot please all the people all the time. Problems imply criticism: someone is not doing their job properly, or proponents of a particular policy have got it wrong. Prince Charles tries not to give offence, but sometimes the choice comes down to saying nothing or upsetting someone. If a controversial statement will help the disadvantaged young people in this country, he will say what needs to be said.

Lord Sheppard, who ran one of the largest businesses in Britain for many years and has been chairman of 17 separate private and public organisations in his time, sums it up: "HRH is not an easy 'boss', and he rightly demands that his Trusts are well run and that their visions are at the cutting edge of thinking as to how society should work. He is so good at inspiring the volunteering spirit, generosity and willingness to get involved. His pulling power is tremendous, not just because of being the next king but because of the quality of his ideas."

Chapter 9

RAISING RESOURCES

"The most difficult part of life"

I n the beginning there was Prince Charles, an advisory group of eight, an answering service, £3,000 and ... that's it. Today he directs the activities of 734 full-time staff, supplemented by over 20,000 volunteers, and deploys £37 million. The first year about 60 people benefited directly from his work; this year over 60,000. How did it come so far so fast?

The two essential components have been people and money. The Prince has committed considerable amounts of time to attract the latter and recruit the former. But they are always in short supply, so to raise effectiveness he has had to go to great lengths to leverage resources at his disposal, and the single thing which has to be rationed most carefully of all – his time.

The Prince's unique position gives him a head start. Richard Beckett, a trustee for 15 years, reflects on why he felt they had made such progress. "One of the most positive sides of monarchy is that, if you do have somebody of intelligence and perception, as we do, there is a strong desire on the part of many people to help a project where the future king is involved. I don't think anybody else would have been able to make this scale of contribution." Robert Minton-Taylor, of Burston Marstellar, who ran publicity for the 1988 £40 million Prince's Youth Business Trust fund-raising, had this to say about the drawing power of the Prince of Wales: "... as a marketable commodity he is *numero uno*."

Even so nothing would happen without hard work on the part of the Prince. Since events may have multiple objectives, a precise allocation of his time is difficult, but the best estimate is that he has to spend about five per cent of each year helping to raise money for the Trust and his other primary organisations. There have been times in his life when the percentage went far higher.

Money Makes the World Go Round

If you intend to make an impact you are going to need lots of money. The Prince's Trust alone has a budget of £29 million for operating expenses. Then there's £8 million for Business in the Community. Somehow he has to find that and more every year to maintain momentum. He is only human if this responsibility gives him some cause for concern. As he said: "The most difficult part of life is to try to maintain the level of funding." He cut his teeth on what was then the largest fund-raiser Britain had ever seen: the 1977 Silver Jubilee Appeal raised £16.4 million, nearly £60 million in today's terms.

Fund-raising has two legs. 'Thank you' events are private occasions where he can express his personal appreciation to donors and voluntary workers whose contributions have been above and beyond. That could happen over tea at Sandringham, or mean a meal on the royal yacht, or something similar. Prince Charles usually fits in six such functions each year. Sometimes the line between thank your's and fund-raisers is indistinguishable. A 1997 Highgrove dinner featured violinist Vanessa Mae and fine words, but also cost £1,000 per plate, and came with encouragement to stump up more money.

There is no such thing as a royal *quid pro quo*; certainly nothing explicit. If you donate £25,000 you do not get cocktails with the Prince of Wales in exchange. That said, senior staff will perform back flips to ensure that exceptional generosity receives some form of royal thank you. The Prince tries to be flexible, because donors do prefer the personal touch. When the Bradford and Bingley Building Society agreed to give a minibus to the Community Venture, they were keen to hand over the keys directly to the Prince. Somehow a brief presentation was slotted into the schedule.

The second category consists of public events, which raise both money and the profile of the activities for which the money is being raised. There are around eight each year for the Trust alone. Prince Charles tries to attend every one. The number keeps on rising, as does the amount of money raised.

In the 1970s efforts were sporadic, with spontaneous events organised from time to time by the combined charities committee. A grand total of £7,200 came into the coffers in the Trust's first year from these events. Initial ideas tended to be typical charity dos. In December 1978 the Friends of Westminster Cathedral organised a Christmas concert. The Prince read the lesson. The occasion was suitably festive, with carols sung by Westminster Cathedral Choir School. Music from the state trumpeters of the Household Cavalry added to the atmosphere. The emphasis was more on the event itself than on fund-raising. The Trust received a donation of £7,000; not a large sum by today's standards, though sizeable back then and almost as much as had been raked in from all sources in the year before.

As we saw in Chapter 2, in 1982 something was found that would generate much larger amounts. The Prince was once asked to explain how Rock Galas came about. "After some years of the Trust's work, we had actually started off a lot of people in their own music groups. So I thought it would be rather fun to have a competition to get all these groups together and to see who would turn up. We then got together with the rock world through Pete Townshend of The Who and George Martin and they, to my astonishment, got together with the record companies and the British Phonographic Institute (which I used to think was called the British Pornographic Institute!) and put together the first show. More and more rock stars got involved. I think it fired their imaginations a bit that it was helping young characters like they were when they started."

The first really big fund-raiser was not a Rock Gala but a concert, featuring Status Quo in the Birmingham NEC, held in May 1982. At the time fund-raising was still much more of a local activity. The original idea had been for a five-a-side football tournament. A regional committee member, Simon Livingstone, suggested having a rock group play during the interval. Then the football aspect faded away, leaving the band and a date for a Prince of Wales visit, which happened to coincide with a Status Quo performance. This was the first time any member of the royal family had ever attended a pop concert, and it reinforced the image of the Prince's Trust as a more progressive charity, in tune with the people it was trying to help. The Trust received the largest donation in its six-year history – £72,283 – a staggering sum for a single event.

Following the 1982 Rock Gala, the Prince fired off a letter to Peter Smith thanking him for his work as chairman of the organising committee. His letter ended with the suggestion "… Perhaps we can try a similar recipe for next year and take advantage of any goodwill that may now exist in the pop music world?" The first Rock Gala raised £21,520, the second £49,084, and things got steadily better from there. Annual Rock Galas are now an integral part of the campaign calendar, drawing in top talent from all over the world.

No-one has been more helpful than Phil Collins, one of those who sang in the first Gala. He has played in no fewer than six charity concerts, including a Genesis special, and has attended numerous other fund-raisers, donated personal items for auction – such as a box containing a complete set of signed Genesis CDs – and led musical workshops at many of the residential courses. Then he agreed to become a trustee and ambassador. The Prince expresses enormous gratitude for what Collins has done. "I greatly admire Phil Collins. He has done fantastic things. Without him I don't know where we'd be. He is a genius." There have been others who appeared repeatedly. Few deserve more credit than Pete Townshend, another loyal and long-standing supporter.

If rock concerts worked, why not films? No reason at all. They worked every bit as well. The sum of £68,880 came in from a showing of *Indiana Jones and the Temple of Doom* in 1984 – the first royal premiere to benefit the Prince's Trust. One year the choice came from a chance encounter with Michael Douglas and Melanie Griffiths, who were filming in England when they were invited to join Prince Charles in the royal box for a Shirley Bassey concert at the London Palladium. By the end of the evening, the Prince had been so persuasive in extolling the exploits of his Trust that their film *Shining Through* became the 1991 charity screening. When Al Pacino came to stay at Highgrove, the conversation soon turned to his work. By the end of the weekend Pacino was volunteering the UK release of *Seeking Richard* for the 1997 premiere.

Concerts, galas and films now form the backbone of fund-raising events. Over the years, stars such as David Bowie, Neil Diamond, Dire Straits, José Carreras, Michael Jackson, Mick Jagger, Rod Stewart and one of the Prince's personal favourites, Tina Turner, have sung. Comedians, from Rowan Atkinson to Barry Humphries, from Michael Palin to Jennifer Saunders, have cracked jokes; and a roster of royal premieres, including the James Bond movie *View to a Kill* and *Back to the Future* have been screened – all in aid of the Prince's Trust. The 1986 Wembley Rock Concert was the greatest single success story in the fund-raising history of the Prince's Trust, grossing over £1 million from attendance proceeds and the subsequent sale of music rights.

A comparison of two fund-raisers, each typical of the period, is illuminating. The Mayfair Ball, held on 29 October 1982, assembled as distinguished a group of patrons as ever a charity bash could hope to find, including Leon Brittan, Lord Carrington, Lord Delfont, Sir Derek Ezra, Michael Heseltine, the Duke and Duchess of Marlborough, David Steel and Margaret Thatcher. Diners enjoyed *Filet de dorée* and *Suprême de canard à l'orange*. Fifth prize in the raffle was a champagne dinner for four at Stringfellows. This glittering evening netted £2,495. Fast forward to September 1995. Employees at 30 McDonald's restaurants in London designated the Prince's Trust as their charity for the Smile campaign. As a result of several weeks of smiling, some of it by people on not much more than a minimal wage, the Prince's Trust received a cheque for £100,000.

The range of sporting events roped into service as an excuse to collect cash runs the gamut. Swims and walks top the bill, but name almost any sport and someone, somewhere, will have staged a contest, with the winner being the Prince's Trust. There have been car rallies, cricket matches, cycling, golf, regattas, riding and squash and more exotic events like bungee jumping, bus pulls, go-karting, judo, mountaineering, obstacle races, rafting, sky diving and simulated mountain climbs on ladders. Occasionally the Prince himself gets roped into these exercises. He cycled the last kilometre for a team of Prince's Trust Volunteers from Newport, who were raising money to renovate a fish farm in Romania, and raised £430 from cycling a distance equivalent to Wales from Romania.

Sporting and entertainment celebrities have pitched and putted, played tennis and run marathons. Manchester United played a charity football match against Fluminese of Brazil. The Prince even converted his love of polo into an opportunity to raise funds. With up to three matches a year raising £25,000 a go, his polo provides a useful sum.

Some sporting events were small-scale local affairs, raising modest amounts. Others brought in sizeable contributions. In 1996 he attended the Tesco Charity Pro-Am Classic Golf Tournament, and collected a cheque for £250,000. The BT Swimathon of 1997 galvanised over 40,000 swimmers nationwide, and raised £1.3 million. Sixty-five per cent of that went to the Trust.

Sedentary activities like bingo, quiz shows and auctions have also played their part. He watched as the original orchestral score of Eleanor Rigby, donated by George Martin, and a chess set from world champion Gary Kasparov, went under the hammer at Windsor Great Park. Over £57,000 came in from the sale of those and other items.

Then there are the way out, wacky and even the rather revolting, unless you fancy sitting in the stocks on the receiving end of wet sponges and custard pies. The more daring have taken part in a sponsored head shave, and offered themselves out for rent on Tarzan nights. One team of Volunteers locked themselves in a police station overnight. Another team dressed as transvestites went around Birmingham with collecting tins. The winner in the category of Monty Python madness is David Crawford from Shepherd's Bush, who lay in a cold bath of eggs and baked beans for three and a half hours to raise £268.

Prince Charles Leads by Example

The Prince has used his personal talents to raise money for his causes. Autographed copies of his book on Highgrove have been sold. Michael Parkinson purchased one in a charity auction where his winning bid was £250. A special limited edition of three signed lithographs based on his water-colours went on sale to benefit the Trust. He has recorded a TV special. He has given lectures. Duchy Originals make a useful contribution through the sale of beverages, biscuits and preserves.

The Paint a Mask campaign was one of the most original and successful fund-raising events. Celebrities were asked to decorate a mask, which would then be auctioned. The Prince painted two himself. The first arrived, still suspiciously wet, to grace the press launch. A picture of his mask was then enclosed with every invitation. A thousand masks were sent out. A staggering 498 came back. Celebrity painters came from the worlds of acting, business, fashion, music, politics and sports: household names such as Mike Atherton, Tony Blair, Richard Branson, Danny de Vito, Neil Diamond, Placido Domingo, Nick Faldo, Charlton Heston, Tim Henman, Christian Lacroix, Gary Lineker, Mary Quant and Ringo Starr. The pick of the bunch were from Sir Alec Guinness, Rolf Harris, Janet Jackson, Stella McCartney, André Previn and Paul Gascoigne. When bidding began, the two masks painted by the Prince sold for £10,000 and £6,500 respectively. The total raised, when all was done and knocked down, came to £259,000.

People now approach the Trust with proposals. Recognition of its work has attracted the attention of businesses. Companies want to cash in on its cachet, rather like a charitable licence with the royal imprimatur at one remove. If you buy Newby Teas, or use a special affinity credit card from MBNA, or order flowers from Earthworks, the Prince's Trust will benefit. Edge Hill Candle Lanterns produce lanterns for the Highgrove collection. These are on sale in shops at Windsor Castle and Holyrood, with royalties going to the Trust.

One-off corporate sponsorships have also been useful. Doc Marten boots launched a promotion whereby 25p went to the Trust for every pair sold up to one million. The sum of £250,000 was gratefully received. One of the most original ideas must be the Easter egg hunt sponsored by Thorntons chocolates and Goldsmith's jewellers: £25,000 worth of diamonds were hidden in eggs in the run up to Easter 1997. The Trust received a royalty on every egg sold.

The Prince's Trust has developed a range of merchandise. The catalogue features badges, pens, mugs and clothing with a suitable logo. As part of the celebrations for his 50th birthday the Royal Mint is issuing a special anniversary crown featuring the Trust. Fifty pence of the purchase price goes to swell the coffers.

Even funerals have been an occasion for fund-raising. The late Jock Barr, former deputy director of the Prince's Trust, asked friends to make contributions in his memory. They pitched in for £6,500. The Scottish law firm of McGrigor Donald has produced a guide entitled *Make it Count* to get people to think about making a will, hopefully to include a legacy to the Trust.

Some events can attract negative publicity, as happened over the Palm Beach dinner organised in aid of the United World College in 1985. Armand Hammer, the international oil man who sponsored the event, had a mixed reputation resulting from allegations of dubious business dealings with communist Russia. The chairperson for the evening had been a belly dancer before becoming a regular on the Florida social circuit. But as Prince Charles said, "How on earth do they expect us to get anything done without money?"

Success could not hide the two inherent flaws in the way fund-raising evolved. First, the whole exercise depended very heavily on the Prince. This was especially true in the early years. So if he suddenly had to go away, say, to be Governor General of Australia, income could drop dramatically.

Of possibly greater concern was that most money was coming in large but irregular dollops through special events. There were personal donations, but they were relatively few and tended to be small. Intriguingly the first *recorded* donation of size in the accounts was from Sir Paul McCartney, who gave £1,000 in 1981. So worried were the Trustees about forward planning in the mid-1980s that they squirreled away the equivalent of one year's budget in case the whole money machinery came to a grinding halt.

The Prince too was keen not to remain the sole focal point. Diversification in the sources of funds was required. That meant either finding donors who could be relied upon to contribute sizeable sums on an annual basis, or creating a pool of capital which would provide a reserve should donations or other special sources go through a dry spell. The solution came through a massive one-off exercise designed to set the Trust, and in particular the Youth Business Trust, on a sound financial footing. This was the grandfather of all fund-raisers.

The Prince took up the tale in a speech-cum-solicitation to the US Chamber of Commerce in London. "Rather rashly, encouraged by the success of the Trust's work in its first four or five years or so, we decided to launch an appeal to last for a year. My people in the Trust said, 'Because it is your 40th birthday, let's opt for £40 million.' I said, 'You must be mad. How on earth are we going to raise that much money?' Anyway, it is a very bad reason to use my advancing decrepitude as an excuse. However, that is what we decided. But the great, the encouraging factor about this is that we also managed to persuade the Government – though they may be rather regretting it now – to match whatever we raise in the private sector on a pound for pound basis. So it is possible for people who give money to see their contribution doubled, which I think is quite a useful incentive."

Activities around the £40 million campaign during 1987–89 were the most intense of any period. Aided by Lord Boardman and Sir Angus Ogilvy, the Prince found himself seeking serious money from individuals for the first time. He did not get involved in direct solicitation, but he was the star attraction. Some surprising people turned out to be the backbone of the appeal. One unsung hero was Gerald Ronson, who gave the first £1 million donation which set the tone. Ronson also worked hard to butter up other potential donors.

Among those who came up with serious contributions were: the Barclay Brothers; property developer Tony Clegg; Peter de Savary; Stephen Griggs of Doc Marten; Donald Gosling of National Car Parks; Captain J. Latsis; and Robert Maxwell. The Prince met every one of these heavy hitters to thank them personally. Many gave anonymously. Even Maxwell never made public mention of his donation. And in case you are wondering, his cheque cleared. The actual amount raised was very close to £40 million and, with the Government doubling the total, the Prince's Youth Business Trust could go on to bigger and better things.

Less glamorous, but very significant in fiscal terms, has been government support. Getting money out of the Treasury has never been easy. The Prince has friends and supporters around Whitehall, and in all the main political parties, but there has always been a hard core of resistance when it came down to cash rather than kind words. The results achieved in the self-employment initiative won over a number of senior people in government, and a regular income now comes by way of restricted funds linked to actual jobs created. The success of Volunteers has silenced sceptics, and has led to direct subsidy payments. Government funding also comes in for Study Support centres. The Exchequer is now a significant source of the required annual funding, and the Prince of Wales takes great care to cultivate the co-operative spirit he wants to see between relevant departments and his priority programmes.

All these activities over the past 22 years have raised something in the region of £250 million for the Prince's Trust, and considerable sums for other charities who often shared in fund-raising events. The sum of £250 million may not seem huge, given the effort that has gone in, but the Prince has leveraged that money many times over, as his Trust's achievements show.

Good People Count for More than Cash

Recruiting at all levels is another constant requirement. For many, personal contact with the Prince, however fleeting, can make all the difference. Anne Lavery, the Norfolk area manager for the Youth Business Trust, in a special supplement published by the *Eastern Daily Press*, encouraging people to become advisors, wrote: "There are possibilities of meeting the Prince of Wales … We have had various local events he has attended." Prince Charles will say repeatedly that he does not want people to get involved for his sake, but because the goals of the programmes are good. The reality is a mix, but he is the trump card.

Prince Charles's work also attracts people who are not drawn by the royal angle, and his personal commitment keeps them involved, regardless of their views on the monarchy. Professor Anthony Clare, an Irishman who chaired POWAGOD for the best part of ten years, describes the honours system as "a clever way the British have of getting people to work for much less than would otherwise be the case". Yet when it comes to the Prince of Wales, he says: "… what is so engaging about Prince Charles is that he is very serious about what he does". Dr Neil Caldwell, who now runs the Prince's Trust – Bro in Wales, was once a republican radical. "In my younger days I could see no value in the monarchy, and even demonstrated against it. But I've come round to see that it is important, and I'm keen to help it evolve and play a suitable role in the new millennium."

You do not have to work for him to feel this way. Carolyn Brown, head teacher at the Sarah Bonnell School, says: "We're not natural royalists in the east of London. We have a strong republican streak and a particular view of royalty, but we found him quite disarming. He was very aware of what is happening in schools. One could see that it was not just platitudes. It was genuine concern."

Where the Prince makes the approach, he has a very high conversion rate. In 1993, the north-east region needed an infusion of senior management. At short notice a slot was carved out for a 'recruiting' event on the royal train. A group of businessmen and Trust personnel assembled on 20 June outside Hexham railway station, where a special stop was scheduled. As the party boarded, they were greeted by Prince Charles and then had to squeeze sideways along a corridor into a small carriage. The day was very warm, and air-conditioning came from open windows. Furnishings were on the Spartan side and rather too many people were crammed into an area designed for smaller gatherings. The Prince was oblivious to his surroundings, and in his element hearing about results of recent Volunteer projects and the benefits of their work to the community.

Sitting directly opposite him was Richard Maudslay, managing director of the Industrial Power Group at Rolls-Royce. Maudslay (Seeing is Believing '91), had been fingered by the incumbent chairman as his designated successor. The Prince went round asking each in turn what their company was doing to help, leaving Maudslay until last. "Rolls-Royce is the largest organisation in the area. What are they doing?" Maudslay's reply was not satisfactory, so the Prince continued: "I don't recognise those names. No doubt they are good causes, but why not get involved in one of mine?" Maudslay remembers: "I realised I was in a corner with nowhere to hide, but I was happy to help." By the time the train returned to Hexham, Maudslay was on board as the next north-eastern chief of Volunteers. In addition, all nine other executives present, who had been on the receiving end of princely enthusiasm, followed suit and subsequently signed up to support one or more activities under the Trust's umbrella.

There is a ritual associated with how Prince Charles usually asks for help. It may seem convoluted but shows his sensitivity. The routine is that someone on his staff will send a letter which says something along the lines of: "The Prince of Wales is thinking about doing this. Would you consider coming on board?" It is simple to say no to this sort of invitation, if the person approached is reluctant. Equally, if the response is positive then the Prince can write a personal thank you note, saying he is delighted to hear that they will be helping.

On the whole he seldom approaches people directly, except in special circumstances, or where he has a good personal relationship; or where he bumps into someone at a specific event, when he is quite likely to let his enthusiasm get out of hand. At the October 1996 conference of the Institute of Personnel and Development, chatting to the director general Geoff Armstrong after the formalities were through, the Prince eulogised about the many merits of participating in his programmes – especially for developing personnel. The next year, staff from IPD were helping at the Recharge residential course, and became Volunteers.

In meetings with business leaders to receive Seeing is Believing feedback reports, he is famous for turning to the presenter and saying something like "Could you let me know what happens after this? I do so hope you will keep me in touch." I watched recently as he finessed a donation of washing machines out of Granada with an exquisite sense of timing. And when the occasion demands, and something specific is wanted from a particular individual, he has perfected the art of the indirect approach which does not place him in the embarrassing position of personally soliciting, but which leaves the individual in question almost no way out. Having secured washing machines, he did not stop there. "I dare say there are lots of training needs, too," he added, looking around the room to nods of agreement from the voluntary organisations. "Like bookkeeping for the voluntary shop in the estate." This with another meaningful glance at the table where the business leaders were congregated.

During a discussion with the Prince on how to sell more products at retail, I mentioned that my wife was a buying director for the House of Fraser. His eyes lit up. "We are trying to find other suitable outlets for the Trust Shop," he said. "Something in the West End would be most helpful. We had thought of Liberty's." I took the hint. My wife promptly called up the general manager of Dickins and Jones to make the necessary arrangements, and within weeks of that conversation the Trust got the go-ahead to open a concession in the Regent Street branch. Two years on, and having proved that Trust merchandise can move, the arrangement is being expanded to other stores in the group.

Let's Do Lunch

And not just lunch: tea, cocktails, dinner, all could become an occasion for the Prince of Wales to suggest, sometimes with subtlety but on occasion with bluntness, what a particular person, company or organisation could do. These invitations can be quite costly for the unwary. Lord Young testifies to his effectiveness. "He was quite shameless in the way he would use invitations to lunch or dinner. People would come in from all over the world to go to Highgrove."

The Prince has a thorough grasp of how to press the buttons of senior people across the spectrum, from the highest echelons of government to chief executives of the largest companies. A seminar at Windsor, a garden party at Highgrove, an invitation to a show with a seat in the royal box, a reception at the Palace; all have been called on to serve the cause. That over 80 of the *Financial Times* top 100 companies are active in Business in the Community is a telling testimony to his pulling power. All across government, every department is now committed to produce personnel to take part in Volunteers.

Prince Charles always tries to set aside some portion of an 'Away Day' to meet groups of existing and potential advisors. By 1996 he was able to see the results. "In the early years I spent an awful lot of time begging people to become advisors. I used to go to the Institute of Marketing one day and British Nuclear Fuels the next, trying to persuade them to help. As a result of talking to these people, writing to them, thanking, pleading and cajoling, we built up over 5,500 advisors." John Pervin confirms this assessment. "Whenever he was giving a speech or at an event, and he saw people there who might help, he would always slip something in about the Prince's Youth Business Trust, encouraging them to get involved. This produced a steady stream of recruits."

Recruiting in the early years was daunting. He was peddling a concept that had no credibility, to an audience which was suspicious or even hostile. He proved equal to the challenge in large part because his sincerity was so palpable. Rupert Fairfax, who went with him to several such sessions, remembers that he would turn sceptics round by using their own poor opinion of the idea as a reason to help. "It would be thoroughly irresponsible to give money to people who, on their own, probably wouldn't stand a chance. You might raise their hopes only to dash them, and destroy what little self-confidence they might have. It's up to us to make sure that it works out, so we can confirm that they are not useless."

In 1994 Prince Charles wrote personally to every advisor then active, asking them each to sign up a friend. Over one third produced a qualified candidate, and 1,400 new advisers were added to the roster. The magnitude of this achievement cannot be underestimated. As Sir Angus Ogilvy says: "To get a voluntary army of 7,000 people all working for nothing is remarkable, and it really was down to him." And not just business advisors but team leaders for Volunteers too. Prince Charles recalls: "I remember going round the country begging marketing people to help, or accountants. We had groups all over the shop trying to encourage … more employers to send volunteers – but you have to go into rooms endlessly with people sitting looking furious, and trying to convince them that it is a good idea."

There are never enough assistants for Study Support, mentors for children at risk or people to work in homeless centres. Young people who have been on the courses and come out with a new approach to life can be very powerful advocates. "The best people to do the persuading are the people who have already been helped."

Since the Kensington dinner, when he had watched former Volunteer Paul Gullick do so well (see Chapter 8), the Prince has insisted that representative graduates should talk whenever possible. He believes strongly in their effectiveness: "Going round different parts of the country and meeting employers to try and encourage them to release more employees to go on these courses, I would say, 'well, there's no point listening to me, listen to the Volunteers. They're the ones who can really explain what it all means … and what it's actually done for them in terms of giving extra confidence and improving their own potential.' What has impressed me listening to the employers is their reactions to the Volunteers who've returned … we always get ex-Volunteers in to describe what it has done for them, and that usually makes a huge difference."

Recently, a room of business leaders and celebrities sat enraptured as a girl who had been a virtual prisoner in a hostel told how she had turned her life around with the help of the Prince's Trust. Ben Elton was seen with tears in his eyes. The Prince was moved. "The other day we had a presentation for about 300 movers and shakers at St James's Palace about the work of the Prince's Trust Action, and they produced three or four extremely good young people who had had their lives transformed. They stood up and spoke in such a way that most people ended with a lump in their throat. I did. There was one particular girl, only about 17, who was quite astonishing. I could not believe how much presence she had. Do you remember she walked on in an incredible way? Quite something. Anyway most people couldn't resist. Of course it doesn't work with everybody."

Star Quality

On an *ad hoc* basis, sports and entertainment personalities have been helping since the late 1970s. In 1983, public relations adviser Bryan Tate was seconded by ICI to work on publicity, and start a systematic attempt to harness the goodwill of celebrities. For a young person on voluntary service, to receive a visit from a star was a bit of a rush, and added glamour to the whole experience. Frank Bruno gave his reasons for being at Caister. "I come because, if I weren't in boxing, I would have ended up like the kids – unemployed and struggling to get jobs. I feel I can give something by being here."

Phil Collins explained why he supports the Trust. "It's all about young people who need help. They've left school and haven't got jobs to go to. They lose their direction. They lose their conviction in themselves. Then of course they start drinking or taking drugs, and it's a very long tunnel after that. The Trust really does … help them to believe in themselves."[1]

---

[1] The Prince's Volunteers, LWT, 25 April 1990.

In 1991 the need to clone the Prince of Wales was the driving force behind the idea to create the special category of celebrity ambassador. Everyone understands that Prince Charles cannot be everywhere, but people would really like him to fit them in somehow. Most who give time or money to one of his causes would like to meet him but for some Pierce Brosnan or Gary Lineker or Diana Rigg can be equally exciting. The first 12 who signed on were a strong cross-section of the top media and sporting personalities in Britain:

Clive Anderson, Frank Bruno, Will Carling, Phil Collins, Nick Faldo, Gareth Hale, Martyn Lewis, Gary Lineker, Simon Mayo, Annie Nightingale, Norman Pace, and Kevin Whately.

Their first official duty was a briefing and lunch at Sandringham, hosted by the Prince of Wales in early April 1992. There are now 100 ambassadors, and a further 200 celebrity supporters who can be counted on to do their bit from time to time. The list covers the worlds of the arts, literature, music, theatre, films and sport. Their varied background makes them that much more effective. Melvyn Bragg, Jasper Conran, Dion Dublin and Susan Hampshire tend to appeal to different audiences. But celebrities can only be used where they will do the most good. For nuts and bolts stuff the Prince needed to look elsewhere.

Service from the Services

He believes that the training received by the members of the armed forces instils many of the skills needed to be especially effective as team leaders for Volunteers. And since he is Colonel in Chief of seven regiments, when casting around for recruits he naturally thought of his own regiments. During the first half of 1993 the commanding officers were contacted. Then Elizabeth Crowther-Hunt visited all seven regiments, and signed up not only team leaders but full-time secondees as well. She went on to see Sir Peter Inge, at that time Commander in Chief of the Armed Forces. Taking her request right to the top was a more daunting proposition, so she was relieved to hear him say "Elizabeth, there is much more to the army than the Prince's regiments." During 1997, 42 members from the forces gave their time. There have been a total of 142 service secondees at Volunteers alone during the past five years.

If this targeted recruitment programme worked for the army, why not other national organisations such as the emergency services? A new fire device had won a Prince of Wales innovation award, which he was to present at a fire service college in Gloucestershire on Maundy Thursday 1994. The head of the college had been involved in Volunteers in Birmingham, and suggested that he might like to use the occasion to pitch to a larger group of fire chiefs. Getting an instant go-ahead, ten chiefs from other areas were invited. All ten were won over. Fire brigade participation is one of the most vital assets at Volunteers. In Strathclyde, where the local fire department became a partner in one of the most deprived and toughest areas of Glasgow, the involvement of no nonsense fire-fighters proved indispensable.

All the emergency services have been co-opted. In March 1996 the Prince asked a bunch of ambulance bosses to Highgrove to discuss first-aid training for Volunteers. By the end of that meeting, several more areas had signed on. David Hill of Lancashire, and vice-president of the Ambulance Service Association, liked what he heard from the Volunteer speakers. "We were very impressed by their confidence, and the real sense of achievement and satisfaction they had clearly derived from working on their projects." Also music to the Prince's ears was to be told that the ambulance service saw Volunteers as a source of potential recruits.

Next was the police. Extra sensitivity was required here, but the Prince was determined to include them. He saw benefits in getting both officers and alienated young people, often enough the same ones they saw in their official capacity during their day job, to meet in an environment where prejudice could be set aside. This has not always worked, but by August 1998 police team leaders numbered 23 at Volunteers. Again Prince Charles reveals his willingness to take risks.

See It and Believe

The struggle to get corporate Britain on side has been tougher. He has had to battle scepticism in the business community. One executive put it like this: "The voluntary sector still has little credibility. They are seen as a bunch of 'lefties' with earrings, looking after a bunch of social misfits with self-inflicted problems."

He overcomes scepticism in two ways. Field visits confront business executives with social issues, and ram home the message that they are in a position to be part of the solution. The Prince believes direct experience is much more effective than anything he could say. In a 1997 Business in the Community video, he claimed that there was no magic about the approach. "By being taken to see things for yourself, you very quickly overcome natural preconceived notions about other people or the way other people do things ..."

Seeing is Believing has been crucial. "I have spent a lot of my time ... dragging reluctant and sceptical business leaders ... to see for themselves successful examples of how this approach works. A good many are transformed into enthusiastic practitioners almost overnight, and it is not just because they think they may end up with a knighthood, either!"[2]

Nowadays Prince Charles can demonstrate results that could feed back to the

[2] Addresss to the World Economic Forum at Davos, Switzerland, 4 February 1992.

benefit of the companies concerned. The appeal changes from 'do this because you should care' to 'do this because it will help you too'. At its most basic, the largest business in town should be keen to make sure that the next generation of employees are literate.

Reaching the Target Market

The Prince was concerned that grants were going only to organised groups who were good at filling in forms. "The money from the Trust must reach young people who are not members of established youth organisations and who are not used to all the paraphernalia of the so-called establishment. I know that this is an extremely difficult thing to achieve but ... I want to show everyone what the young can do, given half a chance."[3]

He is still searching for more and better ways to get to those who slip between official cracks. Support from the likes of Zoe Ball and Fatima Whitbread adds credibility to his work among target constituencies, and may ring a bell with exactly the young people the Prince wishes to attract into his programmes. After all, if Jools Holland thinks it's cool, it must be cool. Phil Collins explained his involvement in just these terms at the launch of Volunteers. "One of the reasons I thought maybe I might be able to help, is to help people say, 'Well, he's involved, and if he's involved it must be all right.' And then they see people like me and Clapton, and they see Elton John and Mark Knopfler and all the guys who do the concerts."[4]

The right people spreading the word will do more than any number of ads or mail shots. In April 1990, the celebrity video at the launch of Volunteers had this message: "We manage things, and you'd better manage to volunteer and help out homeless people with the Prince's Trust, "cos if you don't ... I'm gonna saw your leg off and kick you to death with it." – Hale and Pace. "You kids out there, go and help others. It doesn't cost too much and it doesn't take too much time to help others if you know what I mean." – Frank Bruno. "So listen, don't just sit there. Get off your arse and get involved, all right, because it really does make sense. Do it! Now!" – Phil Collins.[5]

The Prince recently launched a special initiative in conjunction with seven of the leading football clubs. Kick off was on 19 September 1997. Manchester United's leading lights expressing their support, included Alex Ferguson, David Beckham, Ryan Giggs and David May. Sporting celebrities can be every bit as

3 *The Prince's Trust: The First Ten Years*, July 1986.

4 The Prince's Volunteers, LWT, 25 April 1990.

5 The Prince's Volunteers, LWT, 25 April 1990.

effective as musicians in encouraging disadvantaged young people to take up what the Prince has to offer.

By salting workshops with celebrities who young people want to see and meet in person, you ensure programmes will be oversubscribed. If Pete Townshend or Phil Collins will be taking a session, an invitation to Ayr or Caister becomes a pleasure not a chore. Access to computers that were not always available at home, both for games and the more serious stuff, has helped attract people into Study Support and similar programmes. Inclusion of special sports such as rock climbing and abseiling has bolstered the attraction of the Volunteers. Grants need no special inducements. The offering is spiced up with programmes like Go and See and Go and Help, which give disadvantaged young people an experience they normally could not expect – visiting a foreign country.

Help in Kind

Time and money are the two most vital resources, but other contributions are also in demand. In the early days many of the fledgling groups went from one squat to another. The Prince's Trust started life rent-free in a room at the Drapers' Hall. POWAGOD began in an annexe of IBM, and then found shelter courtesy of British Rail. Grand Metropolitan, chaired for some years by Lord Sheppard, had space in St James's Square. Because of Sheppard's support, the Youth Business Trust enjoyed two years there. Office equipment and supplies are often donated. Even the annual audit by Coopers and Lybrand is free.

The main beneficiaries, however, are not so much his organisations as the people they are trying to help. Business in the Community members are active in Gifts in Kind and Provisions. The Professional Partnership Group is also a valuable resource. Accountants, architects, lawyers and surveyors all provide free advice to voluntary organisations and schools, on problems requiring special expertise.

Leverage, Leverage Everywhere

Outside the Duchy of Cornwall, the Prince of Wales does not control any resources. Unable to endow his Trust with more than a nominal sum, and unable to provide staff out of his personal budget, the Prince has had to resort to begging, borrowing and begging again. This makes it all the more impressive that he has come so far. Even now, what he has at his disposal does not add up to enough when set against the problems he is determined to tackle. Progress on anything substantial can only come through leveraging the pot, and by getting government or businesses involved.

Leverage makes it all work. People leverage adds up through networks of voluntary helpers who give time to supplement full-time staff. Partnering with other organisations can leverage specific projects. Seeding a scheme with a small sum, but with the Prince's prestige, can attract sizeable donations from other sources. Then there is his personal time: used well, a little of the Prince of Wales can go a long way.

There are approximately 15 full-time staff in his private office – but this is just the tip of the iceberg. At the Prince's Trust there are a further 434 employees. When you count the numbers at all the organisations profiled here, from Business in the Community to Volunteers, you find there are over 20,000 people making some contribution to his work in his 50th year. At the Youth Business Trust 39 full-time secondees supplement employees. Then there are the advisors, 7,089 of those in 1998. So here in just one slice of activity there are 7,439 people of whom only three per cent are on the payroll.

Similarly at Business in the Community, a small central staff of 30 are responsible for 11 regional offices with 184 people. They in turn are linked to 1,500 business executives at 400 companies who are active supporters and an estimated 5,400 employees who volunteer at one or more BITC-sponsored initiatives. It does not stop there. Regional staff build partnerships with local authorities, Training and Enterprise Councils, indeed any body with similar goals where resources can be harnessed. There were 900 active in 1997.

Financial leverage is also an absolute necessity. An evaluation of grants given out during 1997 has shown that for every £1 contributed by the Trust, £7 is raised locally. In early projects leverage was limited. When the Community Venture was set up in 1985 funding was almost entirely internal, with the training agency topping up only the last ten per cent. Times have changed.

As little as £1,000 has been known to bring in a further £60,000. In Halifax the Trust gave £5,000 to a tenant association to convert an empty house into a youth club. This attracted other funds, including £10,000 from the local authority and £25,000 from a charitable trust. So £5,000 multiplied into over £50,000. A run-down neighbourhood without any facilities acquired a club attracting young people off the street, with just a little pump priming. The Young People's Forum in Bradford may be the best example, starting out with £3,000 from the Trust, and still rising some £250,000 later.

Leverage is practised across all the Prince's organisations. The ten-year review of POWAGOD makes the point that "by utilising the concept of partnership … achievements have been made which are significantly greater than might have been expected, given the group's size." A full-time team of only four, plus four advisory committees of a further 49 people, has influence which belies their numbers. The development of that code of conduct on medical treatment of people with disabilities shows how far their reach can be.

Another way to look at the leverage that the Prince can stimulate is to trace the ripple effect. Only about 900 business leaders have been on sponsored visits, but the right 900 can trigger an awful lot of activity. Many top managers of Britain's most successful companies have taken part, Gregory Hutchings of Tomkins, Neil Shaw of Tate and Lyle, Dominic Cadbury of Cadbury Schweppes and Archie Norman of Asda, for example. Several highly effective initiatives have followed directly from walkabouts with senior business executives. The entire head teacher mentoring programme was started by KPMG, the accountancy firm, because Michael Fowle was struck during one school visit by the administrative burdens that hampered that position.

A classic case of leverage at work in the community is the story of the Granada Challenge, originated by Charles Allen. When he was managing director of Compass, Allen went on a 1990 Seeing is Believing visit to Coventry. There was follow-up of sorts, but Allen felt the results were less than satisfactory. "We have done Seeing is Believing. Now we need to go on to Seeing is Doing," he declared.

The opportunity arose when he became CEO of Granada. He envisaged a programme that would completely revitalise a chosen community. Then he raised his sights. He found five companies to provide five middle managers for five hours a week to identify and solve problems on five housing estates in the north-east. The companies enlisted their suppliers to help provide resources required to fill gaps in local community facilities. The communities were invited to specify precisely what was needed. The exercise was bottom up, not top down. The wish list produced some rather bizarre requests, including one for a shelter where gun carriage races could be staged. Over 18 months all the wishes were fulfilled. These five estates became better places to live. One person going on one visit had led directly to mobilising an estimated £6.7 million in materials, which went on to those five housing estates.

Without the Prince

The work has now grown to such an extent that potentially the greatest barrier to expansion is Prince Charles himself. In the early stages of a new initiative, his participation is vital. The trick is to get to a critical mass as quickly as possible and then sustain something, once things are moving, without making excessive demands on his time. This is tricky, because so many people do join up, work very hard indeed and would rather like a little recognition from the Prince, and preferably in person.

Technology can help. The old approach was to have a foreword from him in a programme stating his support. Alternatively, a 'wish I was there' message could be read out. These days it is possible to show a video, which comes closer to a personal appearance. Video conferencing and the internet have opened up new possibilities. Now he really can be in two places at once.

There has never been any attempt to come up with a complete list of his activities. Even now I am not sure that I have tracked down every last area, but he plays a part in at least 263 organisations. How can one person, however disciplined at time management, possibly give enough of himself to all these good causes and make them all work?

The short answer is that he cannot. The Prince has done his best to replicate his personal appeal through the celebrity Ambassadors. The spirit of Volunteering which enthuses all the programmes also comes to his aid. Many of the people who work full time are there because they are believers and care about making a contribution. They will go the extra mile if that is what it takes, so his task becomes easier.

The second answer is focus. Some causes matter more than others, and the Prince has had to take decisions about his priorities. Priority projects change and evolve in response to progress, new problems as they are identified and the changing needs of the country. So the Prince's focus must change in line with them.

Meetings and events must maximise his exposure. One-on-one is rarely an option. He has little choice but to work through groups, however much he misses the personal touch he prefers. The restructuring of Seeing is Believing was forced on him for this very reason. There was a time when he went on almost every one. Now over 100 executives from a dozen separate visits come together to present their findings to him. Meeting and thanking helpers has to be done *en masse*. Garden parties at Highgrove have grown from small gatherings. The format of 16 July 1993 is now the norm. Then he joined over 350 volunteers from the Prince's Trust, the Prince's Youth Business Trust, Business in the Community, the Prince of Wales' Committee and the Business Leaders Forum and thanked them, all in the space of two hours. Minutes matter when you add up all the demands.

It all comes down to effectiveness. Personal leverage at its best operates when you get the right people in one room. The Prince has enormous personal pulling power, and has become more comfortable about exerting that power to move his agenda on. But leverage is not so much a matter of quantity as of quality. The Prince pulls from the top drawer.

Unlike the chairman or chief executive of a large corporation, Prince Charles cannot borrow from banks or sell shares to expand the capital base. Given the nature of a voluntary organisation operating in his name, there are many tasks that cannot be delegated without careful consideration. When he starts off a new programme, part of the formula that makes it come alive is his involvement, so he has to be visible and accessible. The Prince is almost certainly correct when he says, "the most difficult part of life is to try and maintain the level of funding". He is the lifeblood of his organisations. It is greatly to his credit that so much has happened so quickly, but to maintain momentum will not be easy and the challenges that lie ahead remain daunting.

Chapter 10

INTERNATIONAL ACTIVITIES

"Spreading information, innovation and best practices"

T he Prince of Wales has always tried to introduce an international aspect into his work wherever it made sense. There are five types of activity. Grants I call direct foreign investment. In Outward Bound programmes people living in Britain get to go overseas. With exports, the Prince of Wales transplants something which has a proven track record in Britain to another country. Imports mostly spring from ideas brought back by the Prince from a foreign visit. Finally there is free trade, problems that are global and where Prince Charles has made a contribution to the general good.

Direct Foreign Investment

Grants to groups outside Britain grew out of the 1977 Jubilee appeal, and beneficiaries had to come from Commonwealth countries. Projects in 1979 included a workshop in the Cayman Islands, the Kirinyoga Project in Kenya which involved construction of grain and water silos in a remote village, and a scheme to make special sandals for leprosy patients in India. To the extent any strong theme emerges, the way grants were directed put strong emphasis on community service. The Cobham Outward Bound School in Anakiwo, New Zealand, was given funds to help young people from the Pacific Islands to train for community service.

The international selection process appears to have been more haphazard than at home. The 1982 choices were in Fiji, Ghana, St Vincent and Swaziland. Others were tacked on to royal visits. When the Prince went to India in 1980, a £10,000 grant was given to the National Orthopaedic Institute. In March 1984 in Zambia, he was able to use a dinner at the State House in Lusaka to announce a £15,000 award to the Wildlife Conservation Society of Zambia.

International activities consumed about ten per cent of Trust disbursements each year through the 1980s. Commonwealth grants in the 1990s mirror priorities in Britain more closely. There has been a shift towards practical projects that emphasise employment and education. Piet Ramosale of Botswana received £1,000 to buy photographic and silk screening equipment, so he and two deaf colleagues could start a business. The ILA Youth Group in the Solomon Islands received £2,300 to buy equipment for honey production. Mighty Gully Youth Project of Jamaica used £3,750 to build wood carving workshops. Grants helped refurbish schools and buy educational materials all around the Commonwealth, from Pangbourne College in Kenya to Bakau, Gambia.

Outward Bound

Go and See is a straightforward illustration of Outward Bound in operation. The programme provides grants specifically for young people who would not otherwise have the opportunity to go overseas and experience a change of culture, and learn something useful in the process. In the spirit of adventure, two participants from Ayr '95 went to Italy to study cooking. Many grants emphasise cultural exchange between artists, theatrical groups, clowns, jugglers, mummers and musicians. Such contacts could have educational and even employment outcomes, but the principal goal was to encourage the development of personal skills.

Others were set aside for applicants with a clear business objective, such as Sue Daly, whose grant allowed her to exhibit decorative enamel mirrors and frames at a trade show in Limoges, France. Grants also help Trust businesses learn more about overseas markets, get ideas from similar firms in other countries, and make contacts for import or export. Tom Rees, a cabinet maker, got an award to travel to Amsterdam and look at how cabinets were being constructed by craftsmen there. Gilli Hoy went to Poland to study techniques of working with amber. Marc Inglis, who managed the band Blind Justice, travelled to Germany to arrange gigs. Puppet designers Teresa and Catherine Grimaldi went to Romania, where there is a long tradition of pantomime and theatre, to learn new techniques. Wheelchair-bound Stuart Dunne, who designed a new lightweight model that could be adapted for sports (see Chapter 7), got £500 to go to Spain, where he was able to visit a highly-ranked disabled tennis player who agreed to promote his design.

A more altruistic version is Go and Help, where the overseas experience includes a couple of weeks of work. It is now the predominant Outward Bound grant. Recipients who go abroad might work on a conservation project or, like Tracey Gibbings, work in an orphanage in Romania where many children are HIV positive.

Enroute is a new idea lasting many months rather than a fortnight. Taking some of the most disadvantaged young people, their experience is enlarged with a language course, followed by community service in Germany, France and Spain.

The first intake presented a few logistical problems. Very few had passports, and almost no-one had a birth certificate, but these obstacles were overcome in time to get them on a plane. This was fortunate, especially for Lisa Metcalfe, who had been mooching around, living in a hostel and going nowhere. She had left school at 14 with no qualifications, and was more or less unemployable. "I didn't have a job, and didn't know what to do with my life. I saw this ad for volunteers and I thought, 'Well, why not go for it?'"

Lisa found herself working at a home for the mentally disabled in Reutlingen, Germany, while living with a local family. "I was so nervous to start with. I'd never been in another country, but it was brilliant." Enroute has changed Lisa's life. "I've grown up. My life's together now. I didn't think I was capable of anything before I went, and now I think I can do anything. I've got my confidence back." On returning to England Lisa got a job working with the elderly at a home in Stoke-on-Trent. Her experience and positive approach secured the position. She moved out of the hostel and into her own flat in May 1998.

Grants also take young people to Commonwealth countries to broaden their outlook and, where practical, to make a useful contribution. The Commonwealth Youth Exchange Council has been the main driver for these arrangements. Schools from South Wales sent students to do voluntary work in Antigua and Sri Lanka. A recent grant of £4,000 went to a project involving young disadvantaged people from Birmingham, to build a day centre for the elderly in Belize.

Grants enable young people to carry out community service projects all around the world. A group of 18 students at the Archway School in Stroud were given £1,000 to refurbish a refuge for battered women in the Himalayas. Kate Armstrong of Newtown travelled to Bombay to work in orphanages for nine months. These and future schemes will continue to provide an international component to the UK grant giving.

Exports

The Youth Business Trust has spawned international imitators. The idea of encouraging self-employment has travelled, and this is especially evident in Eastern Europe. Speaking in April 1994 in Budapest, the Prince of Wales said, "There is an urgent need for us to consider the aspirations of young people to find meaningful work, opportunities for self-employment and enterprise, and to play a part in their communities." Shades of Toxteth on the Danube. Economic conditions similar to those that prevailed in Britain in the early 1980s – particularly very high youth unemployment – are all too common elsewhere, and the Prince promotes solutions that have shown tangible results. The Youth Business Trust becomes 'életp àya' in Hungary.

In 1987 Sir Harold Haywood went to Australia to see how funds raised locally during the 1978 Jubilee appeal were being managed. He found that, while there was plenty of activity, grants tended to be going to young people who made the most articulate applications – which was the reverse of what was going on at the Prince's Trust. Haywood suggested that a portion of the funds should be siphoned off into something similar to the self-employment scheme. He contacted Professor John Ewen, a lecturer on youth affairs at the Philip Institute of Technology in Melbourne, and asked him to take charge.

The Prince of Wales then telephoned Ewen, who started a local version in 1988 in the state of Victoria. Its initial survival rate of businesses was even higher than had been seen in Britain. One of the first people to make a donation in support of the Australian Youth Business Initiative was Rupert Murdoch's mother Dame Elizabeth. Australia, however, has largely ploughed a furrow separate from Britain.

The story of how the Youth Business Trust concept began its international expansion really starts in April 1990, when Lakshmi V. Venkatesan, daughter of a former President of India, met the Prince while staying at Buckingham Palace during a state visit with her father. During an official lunch, the Prince told her about the Trust, and in particular about the self-employment scheme. "I was just describing to her what we had been trying to do over the previous six to seven years, and she is a very good listener."

Venkatesan recalls their conversation. "What impressed me was the extent to which the Prince's Youth Business Trust had done work at the grass roots level. Charles had stories about these young people he knew and with whom he had interacted in person – drug addicts and high school drop-outs with no qualifications and people with no hope who had made a success of nothing. He told me about this young Asian chap who had started with £5,000 and become a millionaire. And I thought, here are Asian young people doing well in Britain ... why not transfer this back to India?"

Prince Charles had information sent round immediately, so that by the time Venkatesan returned to her room that night the table was piled high with books and brochures, and a meeting with chief executive John Pervin was squeezed into her diary for the following day. The Prince of Wales remembers "describing things to her in a rather boring fashion", but his enthusiasm really is infectious. Venkatesan says of her involvement in expanding the self-employment scheme overseas, "one lunch with Charles, and I have spent the next seven years doing this!" He returns the compliment. "She was one of those extraordinary people who gets on and does something. She is incredibly enthusiastic, and those sorts of people do not grow on trees."

Owing to a technical restriction on use of funds, the Youth Business Trust could not support any effort to start up something similar outside Britain, but the Prince suffered from no such constraints. He became Venkatesan's personal conduit over the next 18 months, writing letters and telephoning. He suggested she try out a small-scale pilot first, to see if the model really would transplant to India and to make sure that the Indian version included the vital business advisor or mentor.

He also stressed the need to secure commitment from leading figures in the local business community before scaling up, both to provide financial help but, more importantly, as a source of mentors. Senior business executives, ncluding J.R.D. Tata, Rahul Bajaj and Mantosh Sondhi duly joined the Indian board. Venkatesan gives the Prince full credit for seeing her through the early stages. "He was not a hands-off guru with a bird's eye view. He had lots of ideas and personal experiences to share. He was my mentor."

A pilot began in 1991, at the end of which results were sufficiently encouraging to justify a national organisation: the Bharatiya Yuva Shakti Trust. The Prince attended the launch in February 1992, and met some of the nine young Indian entrepreneurs who had been the first pilots. They included Asha Kohli, who had started in catering, and K. P. Pandey, who ran a printing and bookbinding business. He was also able to address over 200 of the top executives in India, so helping to cement business support for the new venture. "Circumstances in India and Britain, I know, are somewhat different, but I do think the concept is, on the whole, applicable. I hope we keep close relations and I shall take a very close personal interest to see how the graph continues in the years to come."

With India off the mark, Prince Charles was convinced that his model could be transplanted elsewhere, even in very different economic environments. Other countries agreed. While the only working example was Britain it was one thing, but if the concept could succeed in India it opened up many potential new countries. The Prince promoted international expansion wherever possible. A November 1995 dinner at merchant bank Robert Fleming's, for a group of business leaders with interests in South Africa, gave him the opportunity to urge their involvement in the infant Nation's Trust.

Nowadays the Prince tries to use every overseas visit to show his support for these international offspring, thanking mentors and encouraging entrepreneurs as if he were at home. So he was able to include a meeting with executives of the Hambantota Youth Business Trust when he went to Sri Lanka in February 1998. Occasionally other members of his family are roped in to help. Princess Anne was asked to do her bit on a trip to Sierra Leone. The Queen played a pivotal part in launching the Nation's Trust in South Africa, and the Duke of Edinburgh met local representatives on a visit to India.

In some respects the Prince has designated Venkatesan as his international ambassador – acting in his stead to promote the story which she took on with so much success herself. When the Prime Minister of Mauritius expressed an interest after his visit to India, the Bharatiya Yuva Shakti Trust took over the training and support role to help start a programme there. And when he travels to new countries and wants to promote self-employment he often asks her to tell her story. In February 1997 they both spoke at a seminar organised by the Business Leaders Forum in Dacca, Bangladesh. Prince Charles described the British experience, while Venkatesan presented evidence which would seem more relevant coming from a next-door neighbour. "You've seen the success they're having in India. They took back the model, which was very useful, then made it their own. You can do the same here," were his closing remarks.

Almost any venue will do. "Often when I sit next to someone at a state occasion, I have conversations about what we are doing and send them the bumf. I am sending something to the President of Portugal after sitting next to him at a dinner last week. I suspect eight out of ten drop it in the wastepaper basket – but sometimes it falls on fertile ground."

A three-country itinerary to the Gulf in 1997 gave him a further chance to show his wares. Among the people who met the Prince in Oman was the Minister of Commerce and Industry. As is his wont, Prince Charles waxed lyrical about the Youth Business Trust and how it was spreading. A couple of weeks later faxes began arriving in London. Not long after, Soliman Demir and Ahmed Tahous Al-Rashed arrived at Park Square East because the Prince had converted the managing director of the Kuwait Investment Authority. A feasibility study followed in both countries.

Some country start-ups are very small. Others put Britain's early days in the shade. The Youth Business Initiative got £68,155 from the Prince's Trust for its first full year. The Omani version began life with capital of 40 million rials – or £60 million.

Just as in Britain, some get off to a strong start. Rock Water Adventures, in St John's, Newfoundland, is a scuba diving store and tour operator, providing cold water diving to over 400 wrecks, with local club membership approaching 100. It is only in its second season, but has already won the Canadian Youth Business Foundation Award for 1997. In 1998 turnover should top C$150,000, with five people being employed for the summer. There are failures. During the pilot phase in Belize, one applicant was given a loan to buy a taxi. Seeing greener pastures elsewhere, he promptly drove off into Mexico, and was last heard of living in the USA.

The Prince of Wales has special personal links to the Nation's Trust in South Africa, and particular affection for its co-chairman, Nelson Mandela. In addition to providing the inspiration, the Prince's Trust contributed to its initial funding with donations of £222,000 in 1996. The Prince also attended a concert to benefit Nation's Trust, featuring the Spice Girls, which raised over 550,000 Rand. In its first year, Nation's Trust gave birth to 43 new businesses. It is focusing its efforts on the most disadvantaged young people, seeking out shanty town inhabitants in its attempts to broaden the appeal of entrepreneurship. Bathobile Zulu (NT '98) has set up a book-keeping service for small businesses in Katlehong, while Jabulani Maphanga (NT '98) has opened a general store in Etwstura West.

There is now an International Association, with members from 11 countries across six continents. Pilots are underway in another ten countries, ranging from Argentina to Senegal. Local members overseas will tie in with a global micro-credit movement, which has a goal to reach 100 million of the world's poorest families by the year 2005.

Not every organisation is exactly alike. In India, applicants qualify up to the age of 35, while in Belize people as young as 17 can apply, the lower limit designed to match the cut off point for existing poverty programmes there. In India, a mobile mentor clinic extends the reach to rural entrepreneurs in remote villages. In Barbados, the loan size is larger, the local equivalent of £6,000 first time around, and rising to £30,000 for businesses that usually start off with an average of two and a half people. This reflects a slant towards the need to build local businesses which will employ others, rather than emphasising self-employment for individuals.

But there are more similarities than differences. One Prince's Youth Business Trust area manager who went out to Bombay in 1997 reported that "sitting in on a board meeting there was exactly the same as attending one in the UK, except hotter".

These are very early days, and the programme in many countries is still in its infancy, but over 2,000 businesses have already been started outside Britain, with estimates of those employed topping 9,000. The current run rate is 12 new businesses a day, targeted to rise to 15 next year. In separate but parallel developments, the Business Leaders Forum can take credit for having spread the culture of entrepreneurship, especially in Eastern Europe. Over 2,000 potential entrepreneurs have received training and advice on how to set up in business.

The Prince of Wales was in Hungary in May 1990, the first royal to visit a former Communist Bloc country. Included on the itinerary was the old army barracks at Kecskemet which was being converted into a small business incubator for young entrepreneurs such as Zoltan Kosa. To Kosa, Kecskemet made all the difference. "I would never have had the confidence to run my own business had it not been for the Incubator House." The Prince was able to motivate a team of experts from the UK, including Alex De Gelsey from Kent, who has enterprise agency expertise, to work on this as a model for transferring new ideas. By the time Prince Charles and President Göncz officially opened the converted barracks in 1994, it already contained 20 companies and 50 employees. These totals have since more than doubled. The barracks became home for businesses as diverse as a telephone maintenance operation and a supplier of tropical fish. Kecskemet was helped by the commitment of companies such as ARCO, BP and Cable and Wireless, who shared the views of the Prince and wanted to bring a culture of entrepreneurship to Hungary.

Self-employment has been the most successful Trust export, but other schemes will follow. Nelson Mandela showed strong interest in Study Support as something that could work in schools in South Africa. The first centre was opened by the Queen in March 1995 at Vukuzakha High School in Umlazi (Durban). The Prince's work on urban regeneration has attracted attention from closer across the Channel. In 1996 he said: "It is also very encouraging that President Chirac of France has asked if, when he comes to Britain on a state visit, he can spend a day looking at the work of the Trust and of Business in the Community, because he wants to see how our experience in peripheral estates in Glasgow might help tackle some of the challenges facing young people in France." Subsequently, Chirac took Prince Charles to visit even worse areas in the suburbs of Paris, as they shared ideas on how to bring hope into depressed communities.

The Business Leaders Forum

The other main way in which the Prince spreads his ideas in the international arena is through the Prince of Wales Business Leaders Forum, which got its start at a 1990 conference convened by Prince Charles in Charleston. 'Stakeholders: The Challenge in a Global Market' was an attempt to develop international links between businesses, to address global issues. The focus was on the environment and education – both areas in which business can make a difference. After two days of talks and workshops with over 100 business leaders, a four-point charter emerged:

- to form an international group of leading entrepreneurs to promote enterprise in other economically developing nations;
- to encourage senior managers of multinational companies around the world to become personally involved in community initiatives;
- to assist in the transfer of successful educational initiatives involving business;
- to encourage the business leaders of tomorrow to examine and understand the increasing public expectations for higher environmental standards of business operations, services and projects.

The formation of the Forum put the Prince in a position to help promote employment, community service, education and the environment, the four themes that matter most to him, in other countries. Again he was pioneering a holistic approach, combining economic, environmental, and even spiritual dimensions in international regeneration activity. The emphasis, as in Britain, is on the most disadvantaged, though here prioritising tends to be countries rather than groups. Some of the world's poorest nations, such as Bangladesh, Egypt, Peru, the Ukraine and Zimbabwe, benefit.

The Forum started with a strong Eastern European orientation, though the global remit is much broader. The Prince is breaking new ground, involving himself with change in its broadest sense, not just of a community but of a whole country. Stephen O'Brien says, "He's seen that a principal engine for change in society can be the private business sector. Before him no-one assumed that this was possible" – or at least not on such a large scale, and in respect of massive social issues such as creating a culture of entrepreneurship and urban regeneration. The Prince's challenge to the business community everywhere was: "You have the potential of promoting great improvement in the quality of life in communities around the globe."[1]

The Business Leaders Forum has responded to that challenge with what could be seen as a global extension of similar activities in Britain. There are certainly areas of overlap with Business in the Community. Both organisations encourage a sense of corporate responsibility to the community, and emphasise training and education. The three main global programmes are Investing in People (which emphasises youth), Investing in Communities (human development in local communities), and Partners in Development (which focus on the contribution of business). All are linked through INSIGHT, which is a sort of international Seeing is Believing.

When INSIGHT takes business leaders to projects, the emphasis, like that of Business in the Community, is on the blending of business excellence with social advancement: the Grameen Bank in Bangladesh is a pioneer in micro credit, which lends to over three million women every year – sums so small you could barely buy a round of drinks in Britain; and Bantai, a hats manufacturer sets aside five per cent of its budget for staff welfare, running a crèche and a family planning clinic.

One disappointment to the Prince is that voluntary service which, in many respects, is what he has championed longest, has not found favour elsewhere. "Funnily enough, no-one has tried to imitate Volunteers, but then I felt I was trying to imitate what they were doing in Europe."

[1] Stakeholders: The Challenge in a Global Market, Charleston, 2 February 1990.

Imports: Technology Transfer with No Royalties

Ideas travel in two directions. Importing ideas which have worked elsewhere has plenty of precedents. Whenever he goes overseas, the Prince looks for new ways to increase the effectiveness of existing programmes in Britain, or for new initiatives. "One of the things I have been able to do, when I find examples of good practice in other countries, is to encourage their adoption here in a particularly British way, so we adapt the concept for this country." Some of his greatest successes have grown out of ideas he has brought back from foreign travels, like the visit to Lowell which spawned the Calderdale One Town Partnership in 1987, and the conference in Madrid which introduced him to the Foyer concept in 1991.

He operates a bit like an intellectual vacuum cleaner, sucking up new ideas everywhere he goes, and a few turn out to be real gems. The Prince is curious as well as open-minded. He would rather ask a question than answer one. Of Gifts in Kind he said, "I picked up this idea called Second Harvest on a visit to Canada, which is recycling surplus goods. We have extended the concept to office equipment, furniture, things which companies are frequently getting rid of but which young firms can't afford. I want to have a proper database to enable people to pass on useful things."

In Toronto, Second Harvest had a narrow focus, distributing perishable food. Prince Charles asked Julia Cleverdon and Tom Shebbeare to look into this, saying, "get on to it and see what we can do here". Shebbeare tracked down a programme called Provisions which was still at the concept stage. He helped set up a meeting in Manchester involving the Salvation Army, Age Concern and several keen local charities. Hays, a logistics company, offered a warehouse at Trafford Park. Food began to come in and then out again, to day centres and groups such as Lifeline and the Wood Street Mission.

But the Prince saw the need for something that covered more than just food. Several companies were running schemes to recycle surplus products, but there was no general co-ordinating body to make existing efforts more effective. This was where Cleverdon and Business in the Community came in. By expanding into multiple product categories, Prince Charles increased the value of existing efforts, creating a vital role for a new programme. Gifts in Kind helps companies who want to offer community organisations surplus products and equipment. Many corporations participate, including Disney, which uses Gifts in Kind to distribute 'seconds' toys which, while not saleable, are still perfectly good. In its first year, Gifts in Kind found homes for products at over 800 charities in Britain.

Free Trade

Some problems are truly global. The Prince's environmental work, though anchored at home, inevitably has international ramifications. When he calls for a ban on CFC gases, his voice is heard and his support cited in other countries. Dealing with ozone depletion requires international efforts because every country is involved. Whenever he campaigns for change in environmental practices, it makes news.

Outside the UK, the Prince speaks of general global issues where his early warning system compels him to express concern. In April 1996 he addressed a Round Table Meeting with Canadian business leaders in Toronto and outlined his concerns about the pattern of global development. "I am thinking in particular of three pressing threats to ourselves and future generations:

- the pressures of environmental degradation and urban pollution;
- the undermining of communities, particularly in rural areas in much of the less developed world;
- the gap between better off and have-nots widening."

His approach has coloured activities at the Business Leaders Forum. There are echoes of regeneration à la Calderdale, in the Kecskemet conversion and others of that ilk which followed in Hungary and Russia. Some of the young international entrepreneurs are already lining up alongside. Rockwater Adventures helped fund Oceannet, a Newfoundland group which carries out beach clean ups.

The reputation of the Prince of Wales is spreading. The former mayor of St Petersburg, Anatoly Sobchak, approached him in 1993 for assistance with the post-Soviet transition of the city. Not only did the Prince meet a visiting delegation, but following their discussion he went to St Petersburg in 1994. This led to the formation of the St Petersburg Partnership Initiative. The Prince recalls how urban regeneration began. "I was told by somebody who had met Anatoly Sobchak that he wanted my help. He sent three people over. I thought to myself, 'what can I do?' I suddenly thought 'One Town Partnership [Calderdale]'. Perhaps we could try the same sort of approach in St Petersburg. Anyway, in a minor way we got people to help, and gradually, I hope, there was a difference to some areas of life. It certainly introduced them to a few thoughts about how you could do these things." It did.

Much of the early work has been educational, exchanging ideas and management practices. There was the legacy of 70 years of communist repression to overcome. Tangible results are emerging. Directors of almost 100 museums have been learning how to survive state cut backs and to attract visitors in a new and more commercial environment. One director's conclusion is: "We've learned that lack of ideas is worse than lack of funding."

A task force has been showing local hospitals how to manage pharmaceutical and medical supplies. Some $2 million worth of material and management assistance has been mobilised here. PLD Telekom has offered placements to first year students at technical training institutions. In small steps the quality of life is being improved, partly through proven concepts from Calderdale.

Target Markets are Better in Britain

When you come to examine his international work in terms of the beneficiaries, things begin to get murky. Who is disadvantaged? What is an ethnic minority? Even if you could come up with a workable definition the field is dynamite. Helping young offenders may be seen as an implicit criticism of the host country's justice system, especially in countries where crime and politics overlap. In too many emerging economies the homeless form a majority not a minority.

One area that is never controversial is encouraging aid to people with disabilities. While the Hoteliers' Forum on Disability has centred on Britain, there is a pan-European component to changes. Given the reach of chains involved like Choice, Hilton, Holiday Inn and Novotel, the potential could be global. In January 1998, Prince Charles received the 'Access to Freedom Award' at the International Congress for Travellers with Disabilities, in appreciation of his efforts to encourage better treatment of disabled customers by the hospitality industry.

The globalisation of corporate responsibility is a massive movement, and the Prince is only one important player in what is now an established trend. Business in the Community was a pioneer, so its members are also exporting practices learned in Britain. Most British companies at the Charleston Conference were already converts.

The Prince of Wales has criss-crossed the globe, meeting groups in every continent, but always with the emphasis on those countries with the greatest difficulties. Since the Charleston conference, he has taken part in 45 meetings in over 20 countries. Business Leaders Forum now has active partnerships from Warsaw to Delhi, from Hong Kong to Mexico City and Johannesburg. Efforts in individual countries are supplemented by exchange programmes. Students and trainee managers from Eastern Europe have gone for work experience in Japan, and executives of British Steel, who had experience in helping former steel workers find new careers, have visited areas in Eastern Europe where similar dislocation patterns were inevitable.

His speech in Budapest in April 1994 might as well have been delivered in Halifax, because he was advocating the same process: coalition and partnership. "All sectors of society, local communities, government, business, churches and voluntary organisations, can work together to rebuild healthy economies and civil society." A stronger sentiment emerges later in the speech. "Where such great hope is placed upon the free market to deliver benefits to all society, business surely inherits special responsibilities ..." and these include a "long-term commitment to play its part in a safe and ethical way, in building healthy communities", which in turn "requires more than talk and high aspiration. It demands leadership ..." No-one in a civilised society could possibly take exception to his message, but the tone comes close to going beyond a call for voluntary contributions.

Foreign Currency
In assigning a value to the impact of the Prince of Wales I have tried to quantify only those benefits where there is a direct link to his work. International activity is at one remove. The Business Leaders Forum sees itself as operating rather in the same way POWAGOD works in Britain; influencing and encouraging behind the scenes to get others to act and when they do the right thing, they take the credit.

The Prince of Wales Business Leaders Forum and many members of the expanding family of Youth Business Trusts owe their existence directly to his encouragement. When the Charleston Conference closed the editor of the local *News and Courier* wrote, "It remains to be seen whether it ... adds up to more than a snappy public relations gimmick and a splurge for the rich and famous."

We can see the answer already, in improvements now unfolding in St Petersburg, or the Czech Republic, where education and training in environmental management has been estimated to have a value in excess of $10 million, or Shanghai, which saw $350,000 of support including the assistance of 94 experts for Chinese state enterprise managers; and just about every country in between. It adds up to hundreds of millions of pounds of incremental investment. Some 11,000 business executives have participated in Forum activities, and at least 9,000 people work outside Britain in businesses that would not exist without the Prince's support for expanding self-employment schemes internationally.

For the Prince of Wales it is sufficient that people feel his work is sufficiently valuable to be worth replicating in other countries. "I am flattered and delighted if people in other countries think what we are doing is worth emulating."

Chapter 11

THE WAY WE ARE

"A Britain where everybody has a part to play"

B efore we look at where the Prince of Wales may try to take his work in the future, it is essential to sort out two things. The way forward is a function of what has been accomplished and why. The Prince's personal philosophy will colour what comes next.

So Far So Good

In an interview given on his 40th birthday, the Prince revealed low expectations. "We would reckon that a five per cent success rate would be good going." Ten years later all the main programmes have positive outcomes for over 50 per cent of graduates.

- Business start-ups: 60–80%+
- Residential camps: 50%+
- Study Support: 65%
- Volunteers: 70%+

In each case a disillusioned individual has broken out of a negative cycle and gone on to achieve something positive – be that higher grades, further education, training, volunteer work or employment – and is usually still on an upward cycle some time after participating in the programme. On that basis, even grants rate 50 per cent. Nearly every person has something to show for the experience. 'Soft' outcomes can be just as important. If, after the help of the Prince, a person is more employable or more self-confident, that does not get classified as a success but is still positive. The Trust's results are good by any standards, especially since these people have failed in life: at home, at school or in a job. Lives that had been marked by failure and rejection are now more fulfilled.

In earlier chapters I have made a detailed compilation of the main areas of activity. Record keeping was not the top priority, particularly in the early years, so it is impossible to produce a definitive total. The quality of tracking has taken huge strides in recent years, ensuring that enough hard data exist to quantify the impact of much of his work. Volunteers has always been meticulous, as have the self-employment schemes. The tally that follows may not be 100 per cent accurate, but it comes close enough and gives a sense of scale.

Cumulative number of individuals in Britain aided by the Prince of Wales (to June 1998)

Grants	258,000[a]
The Prince's Youth Business Trust and The Prince's Scottish Youth Business Trust	49,000[b]
Training	78,000
Study Support	92,000
Compact/Compact Plus/Compact Plus and Jobs	55,000
Mentoring and Reading Assistance in schools	38,000
Volunteers/Venturers	27,000
Residential courses	9,000
The Prince's Trust: all other	9,000[c]
TOTAL	**615,000**

[a] Does not include Jubilee Trusts pre-1989 merger.

[b] Based on number of businesses started with 1.25 people on day one. No allowance made for subsequent hirings.

[c] Includes Enroute, Go and See, Go and Help, Rock School, Youth Break etc.

A few people participate in more than one programme, but double counting would be very low, probably less than two per cent. Take out possible overlap, and you get a total of around 600,000.

It is important to be clear about what is in this total and what is left out. Study Support only includes students in a year when the Trust gave assistance. Once up and running, a centre drops out. Since the Trust was the catalyst and continues to monitor the network, perhaps all children should be counted. This interpretation would add approximately 20,000 so far, and many more in future years. The Compact is a more extreme case. The Prince of Wales came to be known as 'the Compact Prince' because he promoted the scheme so actively. Many local Compacts were created at his urging, but the number receiving direct assistance was small. The movement grew to cover over 140,000 students. Only the first five Compacts that were active or in formation before others got involved are counted, a fraction of the eventual number.

Also excluded are local initiative grants, which have benefited 28,000 young people over the past two years alone. I have left out everyone better off because of urban regeneration programmes, even where he has clearly contributed. All 195,000 inhabitants of Calderdale have enjoyed some uplift in living standards because of the One Town Partnership. Llanelli is a better place for the 60,000 who live there, but I am restricting the computation to where we can trace a direct benefit – a filter that also screens out all the excellent work in the area of disability. Programmes where the Prince has made a big difference but which do not come under one of his main organisations, like Foyers and Gifts in Kind, have also been excluded. Taking a broader definition would add hundreds of thousands, if not millions, to the total. Even under my narrow interpetation, the number is rising rapidly as many programmes shift into high gear. Between June 1998 and his 50th birthday, a further 44,000 young people should have benefited from one or other of his activities.

If 640,000 is a starting point for 14 November 1998, then by his 50th birthday the Prince of Wales will have directly helped over one per cent of the population of this country. The multiplier effect would imply that, for each one who receives help, two others should see a positive knock-on effect. So say 1.9 million. When you start talking in millions of lives, the message can get detached from the meaning. The Prince keeps his eye firmly on the ball, and continues to count his successes one individual at a time.

Measure Success One Individual at a Time

It gives him pleasure to meet and hear about individuals who have made a success of their life and who have been helped by his organisations, even in a small way. Each year there are more of them. Those who have not yet heard of Steve Balsamo (Rock School '96) soon will. A solo album is scheduled for early 1999. Only three years ago Steve was desperate. He started singing at 18 and wrote songs, too. Music had been fun but financially unrewarding. In his own words: "I had been unemployed for about two and a half years. I was working in a band but you don't get paid at all, so we were all on the dole as well. Just as thousands of bands up and down the country are. At the time I was toying with getting real, getting a job and discarding those dreams that I've had all my life."

Steve prepared a business plan and arranged an interview with the Prince's Trust to request funding for a greetings card company. Then he got into Rock School. "The course was brilliant. All the tutors were established musicians. They'd been playing for years. It was invaluable to me at that time, particularly because having been unemployed for so long, your morale starts to fade a little bit and you tend to lose faith in yourself. And what the course did was to instil a little hope and give a little bit back."

He decided to give the singing one more shot. "On our course we had a fantastic group of musicians. We formed a band, and the Rock School was so impressed that we were asked to play at the Masters of Music Concert which was held in Hyde Park. So of course we jumped at the chance. We were among all these fantastic, big, huge megastars who were playing: Eric Clapton, Bob Dylan, The Who. And we opened the concert for them in front of 150,000 people. That in itself was a magnificent achievement and a great opportunity."

Charged with new confidence, Steve went on to audition for a part in *Jesus Christ Superstar*. After 14 auditions and in competition with over 1,500 candidates, Steve won the lead role. In the process he attracted the attention of Sony, who signed him to the Columbia label in July 1997. Steve was last heard of travelling the world assembling songs for his album.

He has met the Prince of Wales over half a dozen times, including at a special charity preview, where he sang, and at a gala event for the Trust. And an added bonus: Steve now dates someone he met while she was working at the Trust, and his brother, who also attended Rock School, acquired a partner on his course.

Steve is only one example. There are many others.

- Heather Craig (PT Grant '92) had a place at the Rambert School for Dancing, but needed money for point shoes, leotards and tights. Two years later, Heather appeared in *Phantom of the Opera*.
- Douglas Gordon (Go and See '90) won the 1996 Turner prize, the highest accolade that contemporary art can bestow.
- Gareth Marriott (PT Grant '90) won a silver medal for canoeing at the 1992 Olympics.
- James Purrock (PT Grant '89) was a member of the British swimming team at the Seoul Olympics.
- Spencer Scott (PT Grant '95 and PYBT '96) was helped with the cost of hairdressing tools. He won many awards, including in 1995 the prize for best male stylist at a national hairdressers' competition.

Every time the Prince still seems just as pleased to come across another young person whom he has helped. "After seeing Steve Balsamo's performance I was meeting some of the musicians, and this chap from Wales comes up and says, 'Did you know you started us off with equipment?' Sometimes the Prince's Trust is like an octopus."

The number of people is the most powerful indicator of his achievements, but there is another way to measure the impact: cold, hard cash. The table below summarises the main areas with a monetary impact.

	Cumulative value of the work of the Prince of Wales (£ billion)
Self-employment	4.3
Job creation	2.4
Voluntary work	0.4
Education	2.0
Environmental projects	0.4
Incremental impact on homelessness	0.2
Incremental impact of crime prevention	2.0

Added together, the total in the plus columns rounds up to £12 billion, give or take a few million. This computation is far from complete. It does not take into account the full span of his work, only what is covered in Chapters 3 to 7, and then only those activities I could quantify. So £12 billion is a massive understatement of the total uplift Britain has received as a result of the work of the Prince of Wales.

He is not unaware of the economic impact of his work. "Helping just one person to start their own business, thus taking them off unemployment benefit, saves the country thousands of pounds each year."[1] What can follow is more important. "But the benefits of our work go far beyond the merely financial. As I often see, starting a business not only restores the self-confidence of the individual but can also play a part in helping to shore up the fabric of the community in which they live and work." The Prince never loses sight of the grand design, even though his vision of a better Britain can only be achieved one person at a time.

Who Cares Anyway?

Would these things have happened without his involvement? It is hard to say. It is absolutely certain that much of what has been documented here would never have come to pass if he had not decided to spend part of his life helping others to help themselves. Without the Prince there could be no Prince's Trust. Business in the Community would exist, but all involved agree they would have made a much smaller impact had anyone else been at the helm.

With over 20,000 people committed to the cause, Prince Charles now has a

[1] The Prince's Youth Business Trust annual report, 1994.

sizeable machine at his disposition – but its sheer size could become a threat to the spirit which lies at the heart of its success. He is acutely aware of the importance of maintaining the culture. Writing in the Trust's 1998 annual report, he says: 'There is always the danger that the Prince's Trust, now a substantial group of high profile charities, could play safe, failing to take the risks which have to date characterised our work and style. We have continued to innovate so that we remain relevant to the needs of disadvantaged young people in the late 20th century … We remain as exciting and relevant as we were 20 years ago." Pioneering into even tougher situations will continue to be the hallmark.

"The Prince of Wales does doesn't have to do this. It is because he cares. I have not only an occupation but a future. I have a chance." Stephanie Richards (PT Grant '88).

Stephanie makes a valid point. He doesn't have to do this, so why does he? Over the years he has been accused of wanting to meddle in politics, of being bored, of having deep-set guilt because of his own upbringing, and of hustling in defence of his right to succeed the throne. The truth is that the Prince of Wales cares about other people, and wants to help the less fortunate. Listen to him talk about the pleasure he gets from hearing his work really does make a difference. As he explained, "I get the most encouragement from seeing people develop, be successful and manage their lives. It's also getting letters from them, saying thank you or whatever, which is the most heartening thing. I always try and write back."

Private letters provide further confirmation. He wrote to Antony Kenney: "I can't tell you how rewarding it is for me to hear and discover what an effect the Caister experience has on so many of the young." It is the knowledge that he can make a difference that keeps him going. In a 1984 letter to Sir Alcon Copisarow, he wrote of meeting a group of young entrepreneurs after which "I came away with my morale restored".

More and more people are beginning to rally to his support:

"The Prince's Trust is one of the most under-praised, under-written about success stories in the country." – Joanna Lumley, actress.

"Some people are of the opinion that it's just putting some new clothes on an old model, but it's actually about social involvement and social responsibility on the part of the royal family." – John Bird, *Big Issue*.

"Tell you what we want, what we really, really want, is for the Prince's Trust Volunteers to grow in the community and take over Britain." – The Spice Girls.

"I got involved with this programme when I saw the enormous impact it had on the lives of young people throughout the country." – James Naughtie, BBC Radio Four presenter.

Politicians have picked up the Prince. It is now permissible to quote him and his organisations. Writing in *The Times* on Good Friday 1998, on the subject of role models and mentors, Margaret Hodge MP, chair of the House of Commons Select Committee on Education and Employment, cited the work of the Prince's Trust. The Rt Hon David Blunkett MP, Secretary of State for Education and Employment, commends the Prince's role in Study Support. At long last the bandwagon seems to be rolling. The Prince accepts accolades with only a hint of irony. "I've noticed that if you keep going and persist whatever is said, then sometimes people turn round and think they invented it."

For a long time no-one in the media seemed to notice. There almost seemed to be a conspiracy to ignore what he was doing if it meant highlighting a positive story. Reporters went AWOL when the Prince visited a Study Support centre or a housing estate, but stand him next to the Spice Girls and front page coverage was assured. Prince Charles would never complain publicly at this treatment now, but he has been less circumspect in the past. "It is easy to become irritable and to feel that it is only when things go wrong … that the gentlemen of the press are interested, that it is only when you are upside-down or halfway up a tree that photographs appear in the papers or on TV."[2]

It is astonishing that the impact of his work has not been analysed until now, and that the Prince receives so little credit. Perhaps it is because, as Hugh Merrill, a former assistant private secretary, said, "He will not play to the press. He'll do something because it will help, not because it's popular."

Of course there have been real problems, failures and the occasional blooper. The original publicity brochure for Volunteers had to be reprinted because the raised hand logo was considered to have connotations of the Hitler Youth. When you set out to help the most marginalised elements of society, a fair share of things will go wrong. People remember reports of the Prince's prostitutes, abused animals, community entrepreneurs who are exposed as drug dealers or misapply money, Volunteers shacking up with married team leaders, entrepreneurs who abscond with their loans and offenders who simply cannot stop and are at it again just when you think the cycle has been broken. If you work for the Prince of Wales, you have to accept that these things have happened and will happen again. The number of wins is what matters at the end of the day.

2 *Observer*, 16 June 1974.

The Prince will always return to one measurement: improvement in personal skills. "An awful lot of people suffer from never having any kind of motivation in life. School doesn't provide it. Very often their parents haven't helped to provide it. They feel, I suspect, low self-esteem. The low self-esteem problem leads back to things like drugs: the awful spiral of drugs, crime and prison."

More than the success rates or all the value created, the thing that matters most in the long term is breaking that cycle. The right way to look at his work is not only in what the Trust and others have accomplished, but also in the example set. When a new idea works, the path is there for others to follow. The Prince is not directly responsible for what follows, but deserves credit for pointing the way.

Imitation is the Sincerest Form of Flattery

Lately Prince Charles must feel well and truly flattered as government department after department incorporates his ideas in its programmes. Business Links, supported by Barbara Roche MP, the Minister for Small Firms, has been looking closely at the Youth Business Trust. "Promoting role models is a very important way of widening people's perspectives. Trust-supported business can play a vital part in this. In fact they played a key part in a Treasury initiative – Alan Sugar's tour of schools." She plans to bolster business advice and similar support available to small businesses in Britain.

The present government is moving down a parallel track, and though he would never say so because he must not be seen to support any political party, the Prince must be pleased. The government is making unrealistic goals a reality by backing his ideas. Reading about the New Deal for the young unemployed, one is reminded of Volunteers – but with a stick as well as the carrot. As several staff said, "We rather feel we've won this particular argument." Look at what is happening in 1998:

- Volunteers – official subcontractor to the New Deal.
- Study Support – £200 million New Opportunities Fund to boost expansion.
- Education – a national numeracy hour; a new literacy programme.
- Self-employment – offered as an option in the New Deal.
- Homelessness – a Foyer in every city.
- Urban regeneration – incentives to boost house building in inner cities, £800 million for the New Deal for Communities.

To balance this picture, it is important to point out that as the Prince's work grew he received support from the previous administration. John Major chose to highlight the achievements of Volunteers when speaking to the One Percent Club. He committed the Conservative Government to assisting with its expansion, and also supported the activities of the Youth Business Trust.

And it is not just government. The British Chamber of Commerce intends to launch a 'new' scheme in April 1999 to do exactly the same thing that the Prince's Trust already does for entrepreneurs. The only difference is a willingness to back people up to 35.

When it comes to helping young people, Prince Charles is always delighted if other organisations with greater resources pick up on one of his programmes. For other organisations, also read government. The Prince believes in an open operating system. Anyone who wants to help themselves to any of his software is welcome. Since he believes that an open system works best, the latest watchword at the Prince's Trust is: 'Big enough to make a difference; good enough to be copied!'

Lord Young, who has watched the Trust mature and saw the Prince in action, says: "What the Prince of Wales is doing today is more effective but less important." Young is not belittling the current effort. Rather the reverse. He has every admiration for the Trust's performance, with programmes that today reach ten times as many people as they did ten years ago. His point is that Prince Charles is no longer a renegade. Ideas that were once radical and risky are now conventional wisdom. All of which rather begs the question, "what should he do for an encore?" The answer lies in a more detailed understanding of his philosophy.

Philosophy

Of paramount importance is his passionate belief that every person is capable of living a useful life. People who pitch up at the Prince's Trust often have a horrendous history of rejection by everyone they have approached, are all-round failures and are used to being judged and discarded as worthless. They walk through the door expecting more of the same, and instead they hear, "You're just the kind of person we want."

The Prince wants every young person in the country to have a fair shot at a life – no matter how many problems and how ghastly the history. A fair shot starts with a decent education, and goes on to advice and assistance in the transition to adult life. Writing in the second issue of *Working Together* in autumn 1993, he reaffirmed the reasons for his work. "Just as it was nearly 20 years ago, there are still too many young people who are simply not getting the chance to make a 'go' of their lives. That waste, and frequently despair, is something that the whole of society ends up paying for, either through lack of skills, through alienation and apathy or through petty crime and worse."

In a speech delivered to the Institute of Personnel and Development in October 1996, one sentence stands out. "We also want to live in a country which gives all its inhabitants the opportunity to fulfil their potential and to fulfil their civic obligations as good citizens." Tom Shebbeare says much the same about the Prince's Trust. "The aim is to help create a society in which everybody can perform to the best of their abilities and live up to their full potential." To do that you have to disentangle three separate but interrelated elements: the individual, the community and the past.

The Importance of the Individual

When Prince Charles says that it is reward enough if all this effort improves the life of just one person, it is not perhaps meant entirely in the literal sense. What is important to grasp is that the war against disadvantage will be won by victories clocked up one individual at a time. During a 1978 speech to the Cambridge Union he talked about "the importance of the individual and his lone individual needs, however humble and small". He went on to say that "only in a remobilisation of the energy of man in smaller units, where everyone is recognisable as an individual and contributes as an individual, can those creative energies be realised to renew modern society".

The Prince goes on to quote from the Dorothy Sayers detective, Peter Wimsey: "People ... must understand their salvation is in themselves and in each separate man and woman. They must not look to the state for guidance. They must learn to guide the state."

The Prince addressed this theme again in a speech to the Institute of Directors, in February 1985. His concern was deteriorating urban environments, the prescription was the same: people power. Quoting the architect Mies Van Der Rohe, he said, "The individual is losing significance; his destiny is no longer what interests us." Prince Charles went on to argue against this trend and stressed that the individual was key. "It is high time ... we concentrated our collective efforts on unleashing the vast, transforming and regenerative potential which lies within the individual as a member of his community." Again, the emphasis is on the individual – but *as a member of his community*.

The Importance of the Community

Balance can only be achieved if the goals of individuals and the community are in harmony. The Prince has often said that only by balancing individual needs at the local level can a community break out of a downward spiral. A strong, regenerated community cannot subjugate the aspiration of individuals, but individuals should not pursue goals without regard to the impact on their community.

The Prince sees the community as something of a cocoon from the slings and arrows of a increasingly competitive world. "It seems to me that in such a turbulent world people's sense of place matters more and more. That place – the community

– is where people live and work, where their children go to school, where friends and neighbours meet. It is familiar and understandable and it is where individuals can believe they have some control over their own destinies."[3]

It would be difficult to overestimate the emphasis the Prince places on the community, and on dealing with problems at the community level. The reason he believes the community must be the focal point of all effective problem solving was articulated in that same speech. "If we think nationally, the problems of urban blight, of homelessness and alienation, of unemployment, crime, drugs, health and the environment can seem overwhelming and intractable. But viewed locally, they can become far more manageable. At the community level it is the individual firm that counts; the individual school; the individual housing estate or neighbourhood."

The community is not an abstract concept that can spring up overnight. It is coloured by everything that has gone before. Its future viability is influenced by its inheritance.

The Importance of the Past

The Prince describes himself as an historian. "I just happen to believe that you can learn a lot from the old and you can't have anything new without having some reference to what happened in the past."[4] Historians respect the lessons of the past. They also appreciate that progress requires new ideas to be tried, risks to be taken, and are more tolerant than most of mistakes since history shows that mistakes are inevitable – all of which does sound rather like the Prince of Wales, who has said, "Tradition need not rule out progress."

His sense of history may be one reason he feels so strongly about the need to balance respect for our heritage in its broadest sense against the benefits of development. Connection to an accumulated store of wisdom should give each new generation not just a sense of continuity but also the advantage of building on the past. He saw this during a trip to Japan in 1986. "The most intriguing thing is the extraordinary relationship between the ancient, traditional past and their new, highly efficient technological existence."

He has also cited Edmund Burke in support of his position. Burke wrote that a healthy civilisation exists when three relationships remain intact: a relationship with the present, a relationship with the future and a relationship with the past. All form part of a natural continuum. There is a paradox to the Prince of Wales. On the one hand he represents a continuity of tradition as next in line to the throne. "I have no professional qualifications to speak on this subject – other than a degree

[3] TEC Conference, Birmingham, 14 July 1994.

in history and the strange nature of my position, which I like to think occasionally allows me the luxury of a somewhat dispassionate view of certain aspects of life."[5] This comes out most strongly in his work on education and the environment. He embraces the teaching of traditional values, morality and ethical behaviour.

To understand his goals for the future, it is important to grasp the core beliefs which coalesce into a personal creed and which influence his work. Here is the consistency his critics have failed to find. These beliefs explain why he has chosen to emphasise some areas rather than others, as well as explaining the way he goes about his work. The Prince of Wales believes that:

- every individual, however unpromising, has some talent;
- each individual has the power within to change for the better;
- it is the responsibility of society to bring out the desire in every individual for self improvement;
- to realise his or her potential, each individual needs to learn a set of skills. Basic literacy and numeracy should be taught in schools. Acquiring personal skills, such as self-confidence, may need out-of-school-hour supplements;
- an individual cannot be complete without serving his or her community;
- it is the obligation of government to provide the wherewithal to enable an individual to take the action necessary to achieve self-improvement. To the extent government cannot, or will not, business should take up the slack;
- the more disadvantaged an individual's circumstances, the greater should be the effort to include him or her.

Time and again he reminds his staff how important it is to go right to the bottom of the barrel. Half way down is not far enough. While things are getting better for many, improvement is not running all the way through the community. Unemployment is down, but 250,000 in the age group 16–24 still have no job. These are amongst the most marginalised and disadvantaged in our society, and that is where the Prince will continue to concentrate his efforts.

The Prince thinks highly of Melanie Phillips, a journalist who writes in the *Observer*. He says she "understands the essential features of a liberal society. She sees what has happened over the last 30, 40, 50 years and understands all the things which are under threat: things which underline the foundations of a liberal democracy." He has read her book *All Must Have Prizes*. Some of the views expressed by Phillips, especially in the area of education where she favours an emphasis on literacy and numeracy and alternative skills such as vocational training, are similar to his own. Of course Phillips does not suffer from the same

[5] Address to World Economic Forum in Davos, Switzerland, 4 February 1992.

constraints. She can make her point as forcefully as she likes, and is free to argue policy.

Phillips believes teachers should teach, and opposes the idea that "teachers should merely act as a facilitators to allow what is already inside a child to come out. This approach has left children bereft, struggling to make sense of the world and without the tools to do so." The missing tools are judgement and a value system, which children can only acquire if they are taught them. It is essential that they learn how to make judgements, because "a liberal society has to be based on judgement" and "if you didn't have boundaries constraining behaviour, both formal and informal, you cannot have freedom, or tolerance or liberalism". Phillips is a strong proponent of traditional teaching methods.

Where this gets more interesting is when the analysis extends beyond education. Phillips sees the erosion of standards in schools as part of a larger pattern, in which society as a whole has lost the capacity to make judgements, and "social policy is predicated on the belief that every way of living a life is equally valid", whereas in reality "there are hierarchies of values and we cannot pretend they do not exist". What bothers Phillips is that the losers in such a society are those labouring under the greatest handicaps, precisely the people who need the most help.

In a society where individualism rules, "the ideal of service is nowhere because it cannot be measured. You damage yourself as well. People feel more alone and not attached to anything. Either the family or the community." Phillips wants to reverse that syndrome, and believes we need a better balance between the needs of the community and complete freedom of expression for the individual. "If everyone acts on their own behalf people lose the attributes of generosity and responsibility for others which are part of a tolerant society. If individual values dominate then we can end up losing the general inherited values which are part of our common history and tradition: values of democracy, fair play and tolerance. We should all work in a common cause. We need to rediscover the missing attributes." There is every reason to believe that the Prince would endorse all these sentiments.

In practical terms, that philosophy translates to policies that start in school and extend to re-shaping attitudes all across society:

• Teachers need to transmit the common culture.
• There should be more emphasis on looking after each other.
• Since so many problems in life can be traced to the breakdown of the family, government should promote more measures to help families.

The emphasis on individuals as part of a community is of course central to the whole approach of the Prince of Wales, who also ties in business to complete the concept. "Companies could perhaps try to re-establish that strength of commitment to the local community that was taken for granted in Victorian England."[6]

How would this philosophy translate to Britain in the 21st century? What would the country be like if it were governed by Prince Charles? Of course he has never set out his prescription for a better Britain in its entirety, but bits and pieces are there just waiting for someone to put it all together.

Trying to put the Prince of Wales in a political box will not work, because he straddles several strains of political ideology, but conforms to none. *The Economist* has tried to label him "... a mainline Social Democrat ... the meatier parts of his speeches might have been lifted from an SDP manifesto."[7]

But he defies labels. Regardless of whether or not he gets involved in political issues, he could never align himself with one party. His whole attitude to life is inclusive – he is concerned about the welfare of everyone. His belief in the community and the need for individuals to subjugate personal gain to its good suggests socialist tendencies. The doctrinal element of socialism, however, is at odds with his emphasis on developing individuals, not organisations, and his expressed preference for pushing as much power as possible down to the local level. Maybe he would have been at home in the ranks of the old Liberal party, whose values included self-help and volunteering, alongside a healthy scepticism about what central government could accomplish. The Prince has said on many occasions that "governments can't do it by themselves".

Perhaps he is a caring capitalist. He implied as much at Davos. During the conference in Charleston he said, "I believe we need a new day when capitalism wakes up as a somewhat more humane expression." A similar theme can be found in the December 1987 Mansion House speech.

Perhaps there is a third way, involving a participative approach, with the public and private sector co-operating to mutual benefit. The speech to the World Economic Forum may have been tailored to an audience containing some of the most influential international business leaders. The Prince chose to emphasise corporate responsibility. "Like it or not – and most of us like it very much – business is the core of modern society. But with that privileged position goes a special responsibility." He went on to expand on that responsibility. "Business can only succeed in a sustainable environment: illiterate, poorly trained, poorly housed, resentful communities deprived of a sense of belonging or of roots provide a poor workforce and an uncertain market. All this means looking somewhat beyond the interests of traditional stakeholders – in other words the customers, employees and shareholders – to a broader church including neighbours, the wider society, community groups and of course governments. Working in partnership with these groups ... "

[6] Address to the Institute of Directors, 26 February 1985.

[7] 19 July 1986.

Maybe political labels do not matter. Phillips, who has been described as half stereotypical *Guardian* woman, half average *Daily Mail* Sloane, believes that "the old political division between right and left is obsolete. The division ... is between people who, rooted in the traditions of the past, believe in the future and those who don't."[8]

If there can be such a thing as a communitarian, then I believe that description comes closest to capturing his position. He believes in the right of communities to determine their own destiny, and in the right of individuals to develop their own talents, though consistent with building a better community. Take a fresh look at the much publicised speech of 30 May 1984 to the Royal Institute of British Architects. The press seized upon the "monstrous carbuncle" criticism, but the bulk of the text was a plea for community involvement in projects on behalf of those whose quality of life would be affected by the buildings in question. Or, as any good chairman might suggest to management, the route to success starts with consulting the customer – and the community is the customer.

The Prince of Wales's Britain would be a more compassionate, inclusive and community focused society. The country would pay more attention to the environment and have greater respect for its heritage. The pace of life would probably be slower. Sustainable development would be the way forward. "We in the West have suffered in recent decades from a surfeit of visionaries worshipping the gods of growth and progress."[9]

The community would be largely self-governing in all internal matters of importance. Decision making would be primarily at the local level, with central government acting as catalyst rather than imposing legislation on the basis that one law fits all. There would be participation in decision making for all affected – a true town hall meeting with every resident entitled, or even obliged, to vote. The emphasis, however, would be on building coalitions, not on 51 per cent takes all. With decision making decentralised, administration would be minimal. Bureaucracy and red tape would largely melt away. Those managing the community would do so at the pleasure of the residents. The power vested in the executive would be limited.

Interestingly, technology makes such a vision much more feasible. Local communities as integrated units taking control of their own destiny become a realistic proposition when people working from home by computer becomes the norm. Small businesses can be competitive for most services, so self-employment is increasingly viable. This is not a rural utopia. In *A Vision of Britain*, the Prince of Wales writes: "Good communities are usually small enough for people to get

[8] *All Must Have Prizes.*
[9] Charles University, Prague, May 1991.

together to organise the things they want." He adds: "This is possible in the inner cities as well as in smaller towns and villages."

Society would be centred around smaller, self-contained communities that had a sense of place. Mixed use communities should provide a full suite of facilities, with accessible shopping for everyday necessities, offices and all essential services available on a shared basis, such as launderettes, libraries and more community-based transport – ideally non-fossil fuel buses.

The Prince has described the true urban village as "… developments in which business as well as residents can feel at home, where a mix of people of different income levels live side by side rather than in socially segregated ghettos; where the juxtaposition of schools, shops, homes and workshops can help to forge living communities through a more appropriate and imaginative design of the urban environment, drawing on some of the ageless principles which somehow echo an inner imperative in all of us."[10]

He has used Montparnasse in Paris as an example of what he has in mind. "The physical side complements the psychological side. It reinforces a sense of place and a sense of community and belonging."

In spite of his well-known love of buildings, the emphasis would not be on the physical but on the spiritual welfare of the residents. The Prince is concerned that, as we approach the next millennium, a society that increasingly measures success in material terms may overlook one whole side of life. "Should we not be asking ourselves pretty carefully where scientific materialism has been leading us – and, indeed, what kind of society it has been creating?"[11]

The Prince worries particularly that young people may grow up without balanced judgement or a value system which recognises mutual obligation. "In the last 20 years or so the emphasis has been on individualism rather than realising that we are individuals but also part of a community … I believe that what may be missing in too many young lives is a sense of community, a sense of what we share with others, what we owe to others and what we can do for others. In short, a sense of belonging."

Such a society requires significant changes in the way things work at the moment. Attitudes would have to shift quite radically, especially in respect of acceptance of more responsibility for others. Yet there is something appealing about this hypothetical country, which combines the best of the past with an open mind about what the present has to offer, and optimism that the future may yet deliver something better.

[10] Address to World Economic Forum in Davos, Switzerland, 4 February 1992.

[11] Lecture to the Royal College of Psychiatrists, 5 July 1991.

Chapter 12

A BETTER
BRITAIN FOR
THE FUTURE

"A chance to develop their full potential for every single individual"

In March 1996 the Prince's Trust held a conference, 'Towards the Millennium'. The Prince of Wales spoke about those areas which he felt would need the most attention in the years ahead. His overall message was familiar: we must not fail the young people of the country at the most important moment in their lives.

"As we approach the celebrations to mark the year 2000, people throughout the country are planning millennium initiatives covering many spheres of our national life. But just as important as all these – at this point in our history – is what we do for our most vital resource of all, the young people who will actually be living in the next millennium."

As the millennium approaches, there is still a depressingly long list of problems confronting young people "Whether through unemployment, or difficulties at school, or lack of qualifications, or – in too many cases – problems such as drug abuse or even homelessness, the reality is that hundreds of thousands of young people are finding they cannot play their full part as citizens."

Having reminded his audience of their *raison d'être*, the Prince of Wales went on, "Even more worrying, in my view, is the social impact on communities of 345,000 people aged between 16 and 25 who have left school and been out of work for six months or more. And the most alarming figure of all relates to the young people who simply 'disappear'. Based on the Labour Force Survey of spring 1995, there may be as many as 100,000 unemployed 16- and 17-year-olds with no visible legal means of support. They have left school but are neither in college nor higher education, nor in work, nor involved in youth training. They seem to have vanished. They, ladies and gentlemen, are our primary concern."

Addressing that concern will come through formulating concrete goals for all of his organisations. In the early 1990s Prince Charles agreed specific long-range targets with senior Trust management for all of his most important programmes. Each was part of a five-year plan, responding to his goal that the Trust should be "this country's leading organisation for enabling disadvantaged young people to achieve their potential".

• Volunteers to create a structure to allow 25,000 young people each year to experience community service by the year 2001.
• The Youth Business Trust to start 6,000 new businesses in 2002.
• Study Support, to have 1,000 active centres all across the country by 2000.
• Residential camps – to increase from two a year to 12 by 2001.

As of April 1998 Volunteers is operating at an annualised rate of nearly 10,000 from a standing start in 1990. The Youth Business Trust expects to set up over 4,000 businesses this year, more than double the total in 1990. Study Support already runs to 580 active centres.

The plan had two overall goals. By the year 2000 the Prince's Trust should be within reach of all disadvantaged young people in the UK. Everyone in the age bracket 14-25 would be aware of its work and the opportunities offered. Ten per cent would receive practical support or advice, while five per cent, estimated at 75,000 individuals, would take part in one of the programmes. The Prince signed off on the plan, which went on to balance numerical targets with a commitment to quality. "Our first priority will be to maintain and enhance the quality of all that we do." No-one could possibly be under any illusion that raw numbers alone was an adequate way to keep score.

Numbers do, however, provide a benchmark against which to measure progress. The total for Britain should come out comfortably above 80,000 in the year when the Prince of Wales turns 50, exceeding the 75,000 target two years ahead of plan:

Programmes	Number of participants estimated for 1998
Study Support	55,000
Volunteers	9,000
Grants to individuals	6,000
The Prince's Youth Business Trust and The Prince's Scottish Youth Business Trust	5,000
Training	4,000
Residential camps	2,250
All other	1,000
GRAND TOTAL	**82,250**

The year 1998 is just one stop on the line. Add up the goals for the year 2001, and if they are all met, then in just three years the current number will need to nearly double again. A tall order, but not out of line with the rate of expansion that has been achieved in the past three years.

Extend Activities Everywhere

The scale of the Prince's vision for Britain is mammoth. It includes everybody and every organisation in the country. "The difficulty, as with so much of your work, is that you are literally changing a culture," is how Guy Salter saw the situation in a memo written to the Prince of Wales in January 1991.

Prince Charles does not go public with the grand design, but occasionally some aims are aired. With community service, for instance, the long-term agenda is that everyone – every single person in the country – should perform community service at some point, whether through the Prince's Trust or some other structure. That may not happen this decade or next, or even the one after that; but that is the goal.

The Prince will not be satisfied until every last, run-down urban area has been revitalised. Business involvement should increase: it is an enormous accomplishment that over 80 of the top 100 listed companies are now active in community work, but that is not enough. "I look forward to the day when every business in Britain, regardless of its size, will play an active role in creating a sustainable society where everyone can prosper ... Business in the Community is now working to extend this activity even further, particularly to more small and medium-sized firms. I am always heartened when I go to see new examples of companies using the ingenuity and skill which have bought them commercial success to make a difference on local community."

As with companies, so with people within companies. "Managers at all levels have the potential to be catalysts for improvement of the communities in which they are based."

His Own Role

One dilemma that has not been fully resolved is exactly how he should participate in the work carried out by his organisations. He has played down his part, saying merely, "I have tried to make my own modest contribution by bringing together people from different walks of life who can work in partnership to create real social change."

To the Prince of Wales, 'real' must mean something fundamental – a massive sea change in the way people think and behave in the context of their community. His vision for Britain does not envisage nationwide programmes imposed from the centre and applied uniformly around the country. Guidance and suggestions, sharing of ideas and codes of best demonstrated practice – all this should emanate from the centre; but leadership, if social change is to succeed, must come from individuals at the local level. "Solving social problems depends not only on the large-scale actions of politicians and others but also on the day-to-day collaboration of individuals in local communities."

EMPLOYMENT

In 1987 he had said he wanted the Youth Business Trust to become "the biggest voluntary seed corn finance operation in the world". The plan was to help start 25,000 new businesses by 1997. That happened a year early. In a speech to the US Chamber of Commerce around the same time the Prince explained some of the spin-off benefits he hoped would follow. "I am convinced that in 15 to 20 years' time, we shall see very successful large companies which will have developed from the original Youth Business Trust enterprise." That is also happening only 10 years later. Dylan Wilk (PYBT '94), a distributor of computer games who parlayed £2,000 into £6 million, is an extreme example, but there are several other self-made millionaires in the ranks.

"I hope then that we will have an army of people really keen to help put back something into their communities, and into their country, at the end of the process." That, too, has begun to happen as businesses which have prospered have helped the next generation of entrepreneurs. Wilk, for one, pays part of the salary of the local Trust manager in West Yorkshire.

Wallace McCracken and James McDonald of Mac's Bakery (YBIS '83) may have started a trend when they presented a cheque for £1,000 to the Prince of Wales on 14 May 1987 – enough to make sure one more new business would see the light of day. More frequently, support has been in kind or time. Julie Dedman of West Riding Laboratories (PYBT '86) now runs the West Yorkshire Prince's Youth Business Trust Association, as well as sitting on the regional board. Stuart Dunne (PYBT '89), a disabled entrepreneur, has become a member of the Disability Steering Committee. People who once needed help can now begin to put something back. Stuart Copewell (PYBT '90) provides a free jewellery cleaning service to local charity shops. Mark Davis (PYBT '96) raises funds for Pennies From Heaven, a hospital charity, and runs free fitness classes at his local community centre in Batley, West Yorkshire.

The primary focus for the self-employment scheme is to combat unemployment. With over 23,000 active businesses, many of whom are taking on new staff, the Prince has within his own stable the potential to find jobs for thousands of young people every year. This is the realisation of an ambition he shared with Alistair Burnet during a TV interview in 1986. "We need a new industrial revolution because only that way, through starting off small businesses, can you eventually arrive at a situation where the small businesses become bigger and employ more people."

He is optimistic that a virtuous cycle is being created. "I am rather hoping that all the investment we have put into the businesses will feed back in 20 or 30 years' time in terms of how those people feel about society. I've always felt that what we're doing with the Trust is, more than anything else, an investment for the future, and I hope some of these people that we've helped will want to, in return, help in the future with the many things that need to be done to help others.

"I also want to find ways of coming back to the people who didn't quite succeed in achieving the business start-up, who applied but who needed further training or, what I still feel is possible, an apprenticeship to a master of a particular trade so that they learn how to do the job properly before they go on to set up in business. I still believe there are ways of developing that, but it is not easy. If someone wants to set up a business but they don't quite make it because they haven't entirely got the necessary skills and need more skills developed. And that means learning from somebody else – somebody older."

He has been on this tack for some time, toying with ways to attach training to established Trust businesses. "There's an idea that we will pay apprenticeship fees for someone to go and work at one of our businesses where they only need a part-time person. This is a sort of marriage of two separate needs."

The drive to raise quality should see more training modules. In Scotland essential skills training, such as keeping accounts, is mandatory for every entrepreneur whose application is approved. Training courses at Threshold teach spreadsheets and word-processing. The Prince picked out marketing as needing particular development. "We have to help them become efficient in their marketing and more effective in their packaging and presentation." Hence the need to continue to develop the Trust brand and retail concept, and so give extra opportunities for entrepreneurs to learn about the consumer through Trust shops, as well as offering more market access and pre-start up test marketing grants to help find flaws in a plan before resources are wasted.

The Prince also believes more could be done to build up businesses that show promise and have growth potential. He wants to extend existing support mechanisms to enable more rapid expansion for those with that ambition. "I also wanted to try and find a means of providing help for some of the most successful businesses who wish to have more venture capital support."

Scottish Equity Finance for Youth aims to bridge the gap between seed capital and traditional venture capital. The fund, managed by a secondee from Murray Johnstone, will invest between £30,000 and £50,000, with a support package of cut-price legal and accounting help and a non-executive director who replaces the business advisor. The first company to receive funding was Gordon Ross Welding Services (PSYBT '97), which specialises in pipe work for the semiconductor industry and which already has 19 employees after just over a year.

Estimates for the number of unemployed between the ages of 18 and 30 are around 600,000. The Prince's Trust intends to help over three per cent of that group into self-employment over the next three years. Any acceleration will not be at the expense of the survival rate. "We are not doing anyone a favour to put them into business to fail. I also think we are restricted in what we can do by the number of advisors we have, and one has to be realistic about that. It depends on how many we have as to how many young we can start up."

He is also keen to increase help to disabled people who can sustain self-employment. The Trust intends to increase the number of disabled applicants from the five per cent level where it stood in 1996 to eight per cent by 1999. Three dedicated managers are committed to attracting applicants with disabilities and increasing the Trust's visibility within that world. The Prince described BOOST as critical to his goals in a recent speech, when he met several disabled entrepreneurs. Similar and equally ambitious targets were set for increasing the number of ethnic minorities and young offenders to be helped into self-employment.

After the success of the residential camps, Prince Charles asked that these should increase to one every month. The Trust had a working model, but the constraints were money and the right voluntary workers for what is always a very intense week. Moreover, suitable sites are hard to find. To meet the target, changes will be necessary in the format. Specialist schools, such as one devoted to IT, are under consideration. Current courses cater for 400 attendees. To get around the shortage of locations, group size will vary from 150 upwards. Graduates from previous camps will be asked to come back and help run teams and the funding will be found somehow. There has been concern over the low that can follow the high of a week at camp. Weekend reunions to maintain momentum were tried successfully in 1996. That may become a regular feature in the future.

COMMUNITY SERVICE

The Prince of Wales has never lost sight of his original idea: community service in some shape for all.

"My ultimate vision was that we should end up with a national community service exercise which everyone could take part in or, in many ways, I think should take part in when they finish school just for a short period ... There is ample opportunity for those who are particularly interested in what they discover as a result of doing the 12-week course, if they then wanted to go on, you could develop a citizens' service which would be applicable to all sorts of different aspects of life, whether it's environmental work, or work with the elderly, or with handicapped people, or whatever."

There is no longer anything controversial about the Prince's call for community service. Disagreement remains over whether it should be compulsory. Prince Charles is firmly in favour of compulsion, but compulsion is not an option for now so he is pressing for the largest voluntary coverage possible. In this, as in all the programmes, he will continue to concentrate on providing opportunities to people who many might feel are in need of help themselves.

For Volunteers there will be more money available through the New Deal. The role of 'subcontractor' to a government programme will be a first for the Trust. There is no reason why the relationship should not flourish, but the Prince, paradoxically, owes some of his success with young people to the perception that he is outside the political establishment.

Parameters of existing programmes could come under review. The New Deal covers ages 18–24. Prince Charles is likely to devise something tailored to the needs of those outside that age range. He also wonders whether some form of community service could be helpful for children identified as problem personalities – by pushing high and low achievers together, could pre-16s be redirected before things go badly wrong? Peer pressure, plus a change of environment, might be just the ticket over the summer holidays. Just an idea for now ...

EDUCATION
The Prince of Wales's goal in education is simple: zero defects. Implementing it is not so simple. Much has happened over the past few years, particularly in respect of out-of-school-hours support, but some struggles never end, they merely ebb and flow. Sadly education is one of these.

In June 1998 he talked of fundamental failings. "Some of the more traditional approaches to education are the most likely to provide people with the necessary equipment to face the difficult challenges of life. Businesses are always saying that they are going to need more people who are flexible and adaptable. They want people who could cope with life in the future of a high powered and fast changing world. To me, the only way you could produce adaptable, flexible people is by having a more disciplined approach to life. If you don't have some sort of structured discipline, how can you ever be adaptable? The idea that you have to produce ever more progressive approaches to learning, leaving students to find out for themselves, just seems quite idiotic because then you end up with people unable to cope. So I believe in the reintroduction of time-tested methods of education. It is very interesting to see how somebody like the chief inspector of schools has gone full circle from being a very enthusiastic, progressive educationalist 25 years ago to having seen the damage that has been done."

So traditional teaching methods, with continuing efforts to strengthen the role of basic literacy and numeracy in the core curriculum, will be encouraged. Here he may be pushing on an open door. The new numeracy hour announced by David Blunkett will mean junking calculators until students know their tables. Awareness of low levels of literacy has never been higher. Yet problems persist. One additional programme from the Prince is Business in the Community's millennium initiative, 'Time to Read' which aims to improve literacy standards through more business investment.

Another area which will remain a high priority will be out-of-school hours study. In January 1998 the Secretary of State for Education, David Blunkett, wrote to the Prince's Trust: "You have encouraged schools and young people to explore different learning methods outside the classroom to the extent where we are on the verge of fundamentally changing attitudes to learning and education." Prince Charles has articulated clear goals: a national network. "My aim is to make Study Support Centres a permanent and integral feature of the UK educational system." By the year 2000 he wants 1,000. With around 120 pupils in each, that would take the movement well above 100,000.

The New Opportunities Fund, bringing lottery money to help this movement, should take the tally much higher once the funding process has been finalised. The Trust will continue to be the linchpin, both in ensuring standards of delivery and improving codes of conduct across all centres.

The Prince of Wales reserves his biggest push for the growing role of mentors in schools: both as an aid in academic achievement and also more generally in getting more out of school for students, especially the most disadvantaged. If it works for kids of 15, why not at 13 or even earlier? Forward thinking schools are already running experimental sessions, and the Prince is taking a close interest. One pilot involving Prince's Trust mentors at Acton High School is working well. Prince Charles liked what he saw. "Many teachers could identify the people who have low self-esteem, the ones who are most difficult. These are the people who therefore need the mentoring. I am sure more could be done through mentoring."

Prince Charles will turn to corporate UK to encourage more employees to mentor. As always, his emphasis will be on the most difficult areas which need help most. The Roots and Wings programme should see a rapid increase, from around 500 active today to 5,000 early next century.

Much of his work in the past has focused on achievement: better exam results, alternative qualifications, making students more employable and smoothing the transition into employment. That will continue, but the focus could shift to the underlying causes of poor performance, particularly truancy. The relationship between truancy, poor results and low socio-economic status is recognised, as is the link between truancy and criminal activity among young people. The challenge the Prince has set the Trust is how to sever that link. Youth Cohort data suggests that around 100,000 children are absent from school in England and Wales on any one day. There are about 26,000 persistent truants. They are the primary target; underachievers who require a different balance in education to unlock their potential.

The Prince has begun to argue that secondary schools are not set up to address the most disaffected young people. Too many secondary students still need education in basic literacy and numeracy, yet their teachers are mostly subject specialists not trained to provide basic skills support. Prince Charles has also been pushing to boost the vocational component for those who do not score well academically. He has called for a vocational curriculum, with more structured work experience. According to people close to him he is particularly disappointed at the lack of interest schools show in vocational alternatives for those who do not display academic ability.

The Prince is still searching for the best way to raise esteem and place alternative training on a par with academic courses. He hopes the national skills contest in the year 2000 will improve the climate. Millenium awards will be given to winners in categories from hairdressing to metal work, starting with local heats whence the winners will go on to a national final. The debate on the role of vocational education mirrors his main concern about current trends in schools. Too much attention is focused on achieving A to C at GCSE. Not enough is done for the bottom 20 per cent.

Recent research by the Trust identifies those most likely to be truants as coming from families where the parents are unemployed, have a history of local authority care, and certain ethnic minorities, particularly boys of Afro-Caribbean origin. There will be much more emphasis on those young people across his work in education.

The Prince is questioning whether there should be a modified curriculum for the bottom 20 per cent in academic ability. He is likely to be ahead of his time. His belief that everyone is good at something remains as strong as ever. People do better at subjects they enjoy. This is simply common sense. Who better to consult than the truants themselves? When schoolchildren are asked why they truant, one quarter cited irrelevant lessons as the main reason. Make lessons relevant and you fix that. Course work problems and subject difficulty came second in the survey. That argues for curriculum adaptation. One education does not fit all.

In *The Sunday Times* on 26 July 1998 Chris Woodhead, chief inspector of schools, suggested that many pupils between 14 and 16 would be better off out of school in a different sort of education environment and training for a job. Teaching unions are opposed, but the idea is gathering support. Margaret Hodge, chairman of the Commons Education Select Committee, has argued for a part-time apprenticeship alongside English and Maths GCSEs. "What do you do with this group of disaffected children for whom school doesn't work? There is no point in banging your head against a brick wall."

Nearly all work so far has been with students, but a good teacher makes a huge difference. Teacher training colleges may now receive more attention from the Prince. Head teacher mentoring is now judged a success, and aims to go from 800 pairings in 1998 to 5,000 by 2001. Mentoring's relevance to other key staff members is under consideration. The Prince believes teachers deserve more support and recognition. "We have many outstanding and committed teachers, some of whom work under conditions of great stress in deprived communities. They need our support. Equally, we do need to rebuild respect in society at large for our teachers."[1]

One new initiative will commence this September. Business in the Community, working with selected primary schools, has developed a practical training course for post graduates which will result in qualified teacher status. This School Centred Initial Teacher Training will last a full intensive year, in stark contrast to the short supervised blocks of classroom experience (usually about five weeks) which are part of the current teacher training curriculum. Some 90 trainees will take part in the first year, including four at Berrywood Primary School, which the Prince visited in April. If this is successful, many more schools will offer the option in 1999.

All efforts prioritise schools located in socially and economically disadvantaged areas. Some formal definition for selecting these areas might be helpful. Environmental action areas have been identified. Next up, education action areas?

ENVIRONMENT
In April 1998, Business in the Community announced a list of 47 locations which would be special targets for future efforts. These 47 action areas are the urban regeneration priorities of the next decade. The Prince has stated that "my Seeing is Believing project will focus on these areas".

Familiar names appear on the list, places where the Prince has been before, such as Great Yarmouth and Balsall Heath, and many others are already receiving help community where the quality of life falls below the national average. Some areas are being left behind, and more needs to be done.

[1] Aim High Awards, 11 July 1996.

The Prince hopes that progress will be made over the next 10 years to create more urban village neighbourhoods. "I would also hope that a very large number of historic sights which the Phoenix Trust will have rescued and converted into entire villages, would by then have prevented the necessity to build four or five million new homes in green belt areas. So that we end up with regenerated communities in different parts of the country, utilising former 19th-century hospitals or whatever as mixed use communities with employment facilities, which is perfectly possible considering that so much industrial activity is now hi-tech. Clean industries work extremely well in converted buildings, providing a much, much more civilised environment."

Seeing is Believing visits will continue, alongside efforts to step up the support from corporate UK for social programmes in their local areas, and into the 47 action areas in particular. An intensive effort is being made to raise the profile of community entrepreneurs, who the Prince knows are vital to the success of meaningful urban regeneration. "I admit that this is not an easy process. We must start by giving greater attention to developing the capacity of voluntary organisations, and individual community leaders, to become active members of local partnerships. As I go round the country, I never cease to be amazed by what some remarkable individuals are able to achieve, often in the most difficult circumstances and against all the odds. I think we have a responsibility to nurture and develop those community entrepreneurs, who often have a pivotal role."[2]

Business in the Community is developing a fellowship programme, to support 100 community entrepreneurs each year, linking them to a national network, so they can share best practices and raise the profile of the work. Other support will come in the form of new, customised information and communications technology for community applications. The ultimate goal is a total support package for a community entrepreneur, combining all the tools that so far have been unavailable, and enabling more rapid change.

DISABLED PEOPLE

The Prince spoke of his long-term goal in the realm of disability in a message sent to the World Council of Partnerships in Awareness in January 1998. "We are all now striving for a culture change, whereby there are no special allowances made to accommodate people with disabilities because all service becomes special for everyone … A positive change of attitude and acceptance can overcome almost any barrier."

[2] TEC Conference, Birmingham, 14 July 1994.

The restructured Disability Partnership reaffirms the strategy of encouraging existing organisations to take the lead, while the Prince lends his name to provide prestige, attract resources or help in other ways. The complexity of many of the problems requires goodwill, and contributions from many sources, if real progress is to be made. And, as Professor Clare points out, "He's still invaluable with his way of bringing people together on an issue which straddles a number of fields. It's amazing that people who are very difficult to get together will respond when the Prince of Wales asks, and so he becomes the catalyst for progress."

Prince Charles will continue to support established initiatives, but going beyond the basics. Firms now hire disabled people for entry level positions, but the glass ceiling seems very low. He encourages the Leadership Consortium, which takes disabled people with above average potential and provides bursaries for career development. BOOST is another initiative for which he has great enthusiasm.

HOMELESSNESS

During much of the 1990s Prince Charles played a less public role in helping the homeless than previously. This has been attributed, not to any lessening of his concern, but to a reluctance to do anything which might be seen as competing with the work of his late wife. During the next decade he is likely to revisit this problem, which still attracts little popular support.

The current Trust offering has proved its effectiveness, but the homeless are hard to reach. What is needed is not new programmes but more effective routes to recruit homeless people into existing courses. Business in the Community has homelessness high on its list for more action.

One promising partnership brings together Business in the Community and CRASH, the construction industry charity, and key voluntary groups such as Centrepoint, Crisis, Foyers and Shelter. A joint conference in October 1997, The Challenge Is On, led to a new Executive Forum announced in July 1998. The aim is to generate more support for an issue which ranks way down on corporations' list of social priorities. Research on what might work is under way, alongside a study into how to 'market' helping the homeless to businesses. A programme to move people off the streets into a home of their own should be announced soon. Another possibility is prevention, by helping those who can be identified as at risk of becoming homeless.

ETHNIC MINORITIES

The Prince of Wales is keen that ethnic minorities receive a fair share of Trust resources. Everyone who works for him is well aware that he wants to see more emphasis on the most depressed areas, partly to make existing programmes more ethnic friendly. Self-employment, Volunteers and Rock School work equally well for young people of every extraction. The challenge is to convince more ethnic minorities that the programmes are right for them. Race for Opportunity is also developing a range of new initiatives to help make businesses more ethnic minority friendly.

YOUNG OFFENDERS

About 40 per cent of the prison population is under 25, and once in prison the probability of reoffending is frighteningly high. Nearly 90 per cent of those released from young offenders' institutions commit crimes again within two years. They need guidance and support, quite apart from the watchful eye of officialdom. Few show any interest in helping: perfect Prince of Wales territory. The Prince knows that the most effective way to reduce re-offending is to find employment. He has already set goals for recruiting young offenders into self-employment. The emphasis in other programmes is also likely to rise.

Historically, with the exception of the 1988–92 period, the Trust has done more post release. The Prince's work is increasingly taking him inside again. Rehabilitation should start pre-release. Links have already been forged at a local level. The aim is to formalise a relationship with the Prison Service Welfare to Work programme, itself a pilot, but involving over 2,000 young offenders in 11 institutions. This eight-week period of training and preparation for work could hook up with Volunteers, as a second stage of social reintegration. Alternatively, Volunteers could import its own team-based programme into the prison environment. These ideas are still on the table, and the outcome is not yet certain.

Also getting another hard look is the whole area of prevention. Crime prevention would not be a new activity. Grants have long been given out to groups and individuals working to prevent crime. Nearly 20 years ago £300 was given to the Tameside Crime Prevention Panel in Manchester, to organise a summer football league designed to keep 900 11- to 14-year olds out of trouble. Now a much more comprehensive look at the causes of youth crime, and how to intervene, is planned.

At the Pentonville conference in December 1992, the Prince said, "I wonder whether the notion of recompense to victims, whether direct or indirect, could be more systematically built into many of the ventures undertaken." Apart from anything else, highlighting victims' rights helps balance work that could otherwise be perceived as rewarding the wrong party. Criminals, young or otherwise, need to be confronted with the consequences of their actions. Prince Charles has indicated that he may take a new look at an old problem.

"Crime is always going to be with us, obviously, but I still believe that there are ways in which we can look a bit more imaginatively at some of this. I am a sort of hopeless romantic about these things. How you break this cycle, I think, is one of the great challenges, and is one of the things I would like to try and do. I have always felt that it requires a different psychological approach, a different approach to prison."

Another approach is to try and catch young offenders early in life. Recent research carried out by the accounting firm KPMG for the Prince's Trust suggests that half of the young offenders could have been 'saved' if there had been the right sort of intervention when an early crisis precipitated antisocial tendencies. The event most likely to turn youngsters down the wrong path is the separation of parents, and the Trust is trying out some ideas to ameliorate the consequences. Mentoring has been mentioned in this context. "I do believe that there is huge potential in mentoring in the whole area of prevention. We have seen it to be effective, not just in business advising but in schools and generally. I think the Trust's involvement could be enormously effective in finding good mentors who can provide help, advice and encouragement at an early age."

OTHER AREAS

Looking forward a decade or so, the Prince has a broad perspective about creating a better quality of life. "I would hope that, in the healthcare field for instance, we would have by then a more integrated approach to medicine to the benefit of the whole patient – which is another thing I have been working at for years – which would make a big difference to people. How they manage their own health. I envisage the cost becoming ever greater unless we do more to integrate the best of the traditional, the best of the orthodox, and the elimination of the worst of both."

Prince Charles may start to address issues that could court greater controversy. Single parents is contentious territory. At Recharge '95, nearly ten per cent of attendees were single parents. A programme in Suffolk arranges special child care grants – up to £2,000 per month – so single parents can continue education. Working at home and self-employment are compatible, and could be practical for single parents of either sex. They already have priority status at the Youth Business Trust, though no formal programme caters for the extra hurdles they face in becoming entrepreneurs. Recently the Trust linked up with Launchpad '97 to develop a course customised to the needs of young lone parents. Child care facilities allowed participants to focus fully on the workshops.

Substance abuse – be it alcohol or drugs – is also coming in for closer scrutiny. Government statistics indicate that 30 per cent of 14- to 16-year-olds have taken some form of drug, and 55 per cent of 16- to 19-year-olds. The police believe that as much as 50 per cent of all crime is drug related. The Trust is already funding awareness activities, including a stage play on drug misuse, *Don't Trip or You'll Fall*. The Business in the Community Partnership Against Drugs Project is collating case studies of good practice, and in particular examples of how corporate investment made a difference. The Prince is taking a hard look.

Ecstasy, glue and alcopops are all endemic among disadvantaged young people. The residential camps too have seen their quota of people with addictions. Even mentors in schools come across examples, especially when working with excluded children. The Prince of Wales recalled: "The problem can even be on our own doorstep. The Prince's Trust in Gloucestershire recently organised a public meeting in Tetbury, the small market town near Highgrove, to talk about young people at risk from drug and alcohol abuse. Almost 300 people came, which just shows the relevance of the Prince's Trust work even in a small and relatively prosperous place like that!"[3]

Of course the drug culture collides with the legal system which can have unpleasant consequences for all concerned. The Prince has picked up on this point and sees another cycle which must be broken.

"Obviously lots of people do marvellous work in this field, I know. But when I went to a drug rehabilitation centre the other day, the Phoenix House, of which I'm patron, I was talking to all these characters who had been detoxed and everything else. The vast majority of them would have been people with low self-esteem. How do you tackle that one? I've been trying to tackle it through the various things we have already talked about, but I still believe there are ways of looking at it earlier, and bringing in the adult mentor who's not a parent, because very often the problem with parents is that home is a disaster and it may be a criminal family anyway. Prison officers will say it goes on until it becomes a hereditary business."

Another social black hole is the question of child abuse, which all too often involves family members or close 'friends'. Stories of parents falsely accused make this subject more than usually messy. Anyone who joins the debate, let alone proposes to get involved, runs real risks. Yet this ghastly problem does exist, and there have been horrendous failures on the part of the social services. Abused children need the right sort of high profile, non-political spokesperson to bring

[3] Prince's Trust conference, Towards the Millennium, Manchester, 11 March 1996.

together a private/public partnership to tackle the problem. Someone, in fact, just like the Prince of Wales.

Prince Charles became more concerned after reading papers prepared by Dr Gwyneth Boswell of the University of East Anglia. Not everyone accepts her research, which confronts extremely unpleasant events, but one finding is that the overwhelming majority of young offenders have suffered some form of abuse as children. In the case of young murderers it has been suggested that the true figure is 100 per cent. This is disturbing stuff; and how best to go forward, or even whether the Prince should get involved, remains unresolved.

He believes he could make a contribution. "I've never forgotten when we did a study seven or eight years ago of young offenders, and we discovered that over 90 per cent may have been physically or sexually abused children. It goes on in terrible cycles. I was talking to some prison officers, and one of them was telling me he has worked in 11 prisons over 30 years and he is now seeing the grandsons. I believe my Trust is in a position to be able to pioneer an experiment in areas in which perhaps it is not easy for others. I think we could learn from some of my experiences in the Trust, as to how one might devise an approach which is a bit different."

Funding for one project, 'Damaged in Childhood', was made available in 1996, to provide help for young people mentally scarred by abuse in their childhood. These are early days, and the work is still exploratory.

Child abuse at home is impossible to ignore for other reasons. Mental anguish, often exacerbated by physical damage, is a lethal cocktail. Abuse is one of the prime reasons for homelessness among young people, and swells the numbers in care. Around 160,000 young people come into contact with the child protection process each year. Thirty-two thousand were actually placed on a protection register in 1996. This is a large constituency, without a powerful representative. Part of the problem is that local and central arms of government often disagree over what to do. A few small steps have already been taken, and ideas were debated at a conference the Prince attended in February 1997.

There have been care leavers on programmes in the past. Forty per cent of the young people aged 15 to 17 at Superstart '96 were not living with their parents, and 20 per cent had been in care. The Prince's early warning system has been activated. The number of young children once in care who show up on Trust programmes is a data point that has alerted him to the significance of this problem.

Michael Bichard, Permanent Secretary at the DoEE and someone whose judgement the Prince respects said, "Young people in care is a national disgrace. The likelihood is that they will have lower educational qualifications and a higher probability of offending. The reverse should be the case." So the Prince has begun to make space in his calendar for groups like the National Foster Care Association. The NFCA has a membership of over 13,000 carers. It is active in two areas that would meet with his approval: developing the first nationwide standards for foster care, and the 'My Place' scheme, which involves the young people themselves in devising better ways to meet the needs they will have when they leave care.

As Prince Charles delves deeper into one of the most disturbing areas of the social services, he is looking for new and better things to try. Too many children shuttle between multiple homes with separated parents, residential care and a foster family. This lack of continuity had him wondering whether stability in a personal relationship might make the difference. "The more I see of the surrogate parent research, the more places I see where it can be successful. These young people need someone who is not the parent and not in their school." Of course, as the Prince pointed out, carers in the foster families could be mentors, if only the child stayed still long enough for a relationship to be established. This seldom happens. The majority leave within 14 days, and are back where the problem began.

Soon there will be a Trust programme tailored to care leavers and their specific problems. An initial test started at the end of 1996 assessed the impact of mentoring a person leaving care. As I write, a project manager is training potential mentors, who will establish a one-to-one relationship as a trusted and caring adult friend, and fill the gaps left by the current support system. These mentors will assess the personal skills of their mentees, and may link with other parts of the Trust that could help, such as Volunteers, or training. Some 8,000 young people leave care each year, usually very poorly prepared for life's challenges. Within six months of leaving, 25 per cent of them get into some kind of difficulty. Twenty per cent of young women are pregnant or already mothers. Over one third of the young homeless come from a care background. The Trust plans to provide mentors for 2,000 of these young people between now and the year 2000, or nearly ten per cent of the total.

Then there are those whom the Government does not track at all. At Caister in 1992, he told the crowd "You may think that people have forgotten about you, but the Prince's Trust has not." They are meat and drink to Prince Charles. As Bichard pointed out, this is a gap which someone needs to fill. "Who are the people who even now are still falling through the net? There is a role here for an organisation like the Prince's Trust."

Where next for Prince Charles? Look in the tea leaves today, and it would be realistic to expect that within a few years the Prince's Trust will have established formal new programmes to help young people leaving care, school truants, young people suffering due to substance abuse, victims of child abuse and young single parents. I also expect to see more resources going to revive the pioneering work of the Young Offenders' Forum. If there is one group of young people who present the toughest challenge and who attract the least sympathy, these are they.

Younger May be Better

For all his success in remedial work, the Prince is thinking more about how to catch people before they go off the rails. The trick may be to start even earlier: begin with young offenders when they are still inside; catch people leaving care before they go. In education, the age limit in mentoring and out-of-school-hours work keeps coming down. More Business in the Community activity covers primary schools.

The Prince's Trust research department is working to identify points of intervention before the rot sets in. The same thrust is apparent in residential programmes. He has stressed this issue recently, encouraging his team to be more aware of younger people. Recharge was created out of these conversations, specifically for 16- to 18- year-olds who might have been smothered by older and more assertive characters at Superstart.

With the New Deal covering a good chunk of the 18- to 24-year-olds, that leaves the 16 to 18 bracket needing extra attention. Might streaming make sense in the context of Volunteers? Section 53 offenders are by definition young people below the age of 18. There is a growing sense across all the activities that reaching towards ever younger people is the right way to go.

As the programmes start to create a continuum, it is possible to see how someone could find support from a very young age, say six, all the way through into their first job. The Prince will have something to offer for well over ten years during the most critical phase of child development. The positioning of his safety net is almost complete: right at the bottom, the net of last resort to catch those who fall through all official ones.

Making More Things Happen

Three constituencies get the lion's share of the Prince's attention, simply because they can bring about the greatest change: government, business and the voluntary sector. He knows help is needed from each. The starting place is more co-operation, sharing and partnership. The Prince has challenged each group in turn.

"I would like to see as much co-operation as possible between different agencies and bodies, voluntary organisations and the public sector to try and tackle many of these problems. It seems to me that there are a large number of very worthwhile and extremely competent voluntary organisations who would be very effective, if given help and encouragement, perhaps from government, to carry out many of these tasks."[4]

When the Prince says "perhaps from government", he means "government should and must". After all, "the Prince's Trust is one of those bodies which now has a lot of experience and a very good track record. We've a lot of volunteers and helpers ... and we are known about now in every part of the country. We can deliver the goods, I think, if given more support."[5] Again, the Prince is being too polite. "I think" here means "I am absolutely certain".

What is new is the scale. Whereas he used to think in terms of small, local projects, a few thousand here, a few thousand there, now he is talking about national programmes – still administered at the local level – but requiring millions of pounds annually to maintain momentum; hence the need for government to be a more active partner.

One great advantage the Prince has is that he is not a government department and can do pretty much as he pleases. One disadvantage is that he still has to maintain a fine line between involving the government and enlisting their help whilst staying detached. This may become a more difficult balancing act, as his ideas become mainstream and more substantial, and it could become even trickier if the future focus of his work is with the most difficult young people, such as school truants, those leaving care, offenders or addicts. Prince Charles understands the constraints of the constitution, but he holds discussions with politicians – of all parties – and sometimes influences policy and, indirectly, legislation.

To limit direct involvement, 'Recess' was set up along similar lines to Seeing is Believing. Recess takes MPs to see his activities in their constituencies. Sixty MPs participated in 1997. He held a feedback session with them in December. There is now a dedicated individual mandated to strengthen existing ties with government and put across the Trust's point of view, usually a reflection of the views of its president.

He cannot fulfil his mission without getting involved at Westminster, and perhaps these days in Brussels as well. There has never before been a closer working relationship between government and any Prince of Wales. As Prince Charles continues to stake out strongly held positions on critical social issues, the risk of his becoming embroiled in a partisan debate will increase.

The Prince is uniquely placed as a non-partisan figure of sufficient status to build bridges between senior executives from the private sector and key figures at the highest levels of government. The two groups are not natural allies, coming

[4] TEC Conference, Birmingham, 14 July 1994.
[5] Anniversary interview on Radio 1, October 1996.

from different cultures and with conflicting objectives. Yet contributions from both are vital.

Further progress also requires his own organisations to become more efficient. Change must occur not just in activities but also in administration, to ensure resources are effectively directed, and to encourage comprehensive evaluation of results. He is constantly questioning whether improvements are being attained. Internal cost/benefit analysis is now applied, right down to individual projects. Much of the work may be voluntary, but that does not mean it can be sloppy. Alongside this, he is pushing for the sharing of good ideas to become institutionalised at all levels and in every organisation, in the drive to deliver more services to disadvantaged young people.

Generational Transfer: A Concept for the Next Millennium

The Prince regrets that the young of today miss out on the accumulated wisdom that historically has been handed down through the family. This problem exists partly because the traditional family unit, closely knit across three generations, has been replaced by the nuclear family or no family at all. New methods in education, an indifference to tradition, and a culture which prefers change to continuity, have made matters worse.

The greatest void is when a young person has no caring adult to turn to, who can give support and help them avoid or overcome the problems of growing up. Mentoring of young people at risk may be the answer. "I recently saw the remarkable results, where mentoring is making a really big difference to those teenagers in Acton. They've never had anything like it before, with someone taking an interest. Now they have someone who has encouraged them to go to school, to get there on time – and that's more than before." He is not alone in his praise. Keith Ajebo, head teacher at Deptford Green, said of its value at his school, "The mentoring helps build that sense of self-confidence that they can achieve."

The Prince wants to use mentors with young people on a much greater scale. This will require a pool of suitable people who have time to give and will not drop the ball when the inevitable crisis erupts. "Nowadays people my age – 50 – are considered to be on the heap, aren't they? It is ridiculous. And all that experience and, one hopes, a bit of wisdom could be utilised much more in the volunteering and mentoring approach. I am sure this is something which will develop much more before too long at the Prince's Trust, and through Business in the Community as well."

He asks, "is it possible to galvanise millions of retired people all across the country to take up the challenge of setting the life of one child on the straight and narrow?" As patron of a number of organisations which are devoted to assisting senior citizens, he has access to a powerful forum. His idea is not a one-sided deal, where the old put in all the effort and the young suck out all the benefit, but an extension of the concept that by helping others you help yourself. In the case of active older people who need a fulfilling challenge, what could be more rewarding than mentoring a child who needs guidance and maybe more?

As early as 1974, the Prince stressed the importance of a human relationship in personal development. "To bring the best out of people it is essential to take a real interest in them."[6] He is keen to test the waters for what could be the most far-reaching innovation ever to emerge out of the Prince's Trust. "I have been very impressed by the results obtained from adult mentoring of young people who are at risk while adolescents at school, because they then find they have somebody who is intelligent and organised enough to give them another look at life. I think that is an area where we can develop a lot more, and that is another reason why I want to use my patronage of Age Resource, Age Concern, Help the Aged and all these things, because I feel there is a huge potential pool of retired people out there."

With people pensioned off ever earlier, yet able to live full and productive lives ever longer, there is an enormous gap opening up between the full extent of an individual's ability to contribute to the community and opportunities offered through traditional work. If a national mentoring programme became a reality, it might need three million volunteers: a massive and ambitious undertaking, but one that deserves serious consideration. In effect, what Prince Charles is proposing is that for every child in the country who needs help due to disadvantaged circumstances, "you have a surrogate parent". Perhaps now that he has proved his worth as a pioneer of solutions to complex social problems so many times, this idea may get rather more respect than the customary raspberry.

Overseas

International expansion, particularly the self-employment scheme, could also come in for increased attention. The current goal is to add two new countries a year. Lakshmi V. Venkatesan has suggested altogether more ambitious targets. If the programme can work in 14 countries, why not 40, and why not in four years? This is not entirely unrealistic. After all, if even Yasser Arafat wants one after his recent visit to Delhi, then there can be no doubting the breadth of its appeal.

Argentina and Ghana are likely to begin operations in 1998. A representative from Argentina spent June 1998 in England learning how it works. By the time this book is published Buenos Aires will be in business.

[6] *Observer*, 16 June 1974.

The opportunities overseas are almost unlimited. The Prince could be the right person to head an international movement to establish Youth Business Trusts in many more countries: discussions held inside the World Bank stemmed indirectly from conversations the Prince had with James Wolfensohn about business partnerships, and from direct contacts between international funding groups, such as IFC and the International Association of Youth Business Trusts. However much he might like to, it seems unlikely he would have time to add such a major international undertaking to his portfolio, but it is an interesting expression of the regard in which his work is held in other countries and by international experts at the highest level.

The Prince spoke of a personal vision during a meeting at Highgrove in July 1992. While referring to Eastern Europe, his invocation could apply anywhere. "If every international investor took some measure, supported at least one project to help the wider community to assist the transition to the market economy, and played their role in partnerships with local communities and business leaders, just imagine what could be achieved."

What next?

You can count on the Prince of Wales to keep on with his work. He told Jonathan Dimbleby, "I've had to fight every inch of my life to escape royal protocol. You're suggesting that I go back and play polo. I wasn't trained to do that. I have been brought up to have an active role." The fight continues, even now that it is clear he has carved out a role that takes him far beyond what might have been predicted back in 1972.

The Prince has made his work on behalf of young people the cornerstone of his career. As early as 1978 Anthony Holden estimated that what he called Prince Charles's "social work" consumed something approaching one third of his working hours. Today he has a host of official engagements to fulfil, and is currently patron, chairman or president of 263 separate organisations – yet he still manages to allocate over half his professional time to helping disadvantaged young people. It is the view of his advisors, and also I believe of the Prince, that he should prioritise 'emerging issues' where he has the most impact. Once he has drawn attention to a problem, and resources have been mobilised, there is less need for direct assistance.

The next generation of Windsors will soon be able to consider helping. As Prince Charles passes 50, Prince William is 16 and Prince Harry 14. His staff regularly receive requests that his sons might accompany him on visits to Prince's Trust projects. Already the Thomas brothers – Gary, Ian, David and Glyn – who all found work through their local Prince's Trust, have sent the Prince an application form for Prince William to join the Llanelli Volunteers.

Prince Charles disarmingly deflects such interest, as he protects his sons' privacy in their formative years. In an interview on Radio One broadcast in October 1993, he said carefully, "I don't know. But it would be nice to think that one of my sons will show an interest and, perhaps, take it on."

Though he prefers not to comment publicly on any future role for his sons, it would be strange if he did not harbour hopes that they might get involved. When I asked him whether his sons might work with him at the Prince's Trust, he was again reluctant to be drawn. "You mean with an apostrophe at the end? I don't know, we'll see. It's a long way to go yet, and they've got an awful lot of other things to do. At some point, if I am to succeed, then I hope that one of my sons might take it over. In which case it can still be the Prince's Trust."

So one day perhaps the Prince's Trust will become the Princes' Trust. Or maybe it will pass from one Prince to another. For now, he wants to give his sons space to grow up in conditions which are as near to normal as possible. If there is one thing that will take precedence over his commitment to his work, it is his desire to be there when they need him. Whatever his private ambitions, he, who did not always choose his own way in the world, wants his sons to make up their own minds. If they are to follow in his footsteps when they are older, then the choice must be theirs. They must truly be volunteers.

Why does the Prince of Wales work so hard? A few cynics say he feels guilty about his inheritance and needs to bolster his popularity. But Prince Charles has never courted popularity. Rather the reverse. He has never looked at anything from the point of view of "what's in this for me?" He has been entirely selfless in his work, except perhaps for taking some satisfaction from knowing that he has helped people improve their lives when no-one else would.

He has been described by close associates as having a passionate belief in the essential goodness of people and of human nature, and an equally passionate loathing of its waste. If you accept that description, it is easier to see how his apparently disparate activities are part of a pattern. Unemployment is wasteful and loathsome; young offenders have essential goodness and need a second chance; community service can express people's essential goodness if given the opportunity; racism is wasteful and loathsome; and even architecture, when bad, is wasteful and destructive. Injustice and waste make him angry. In the past he has been criticised as being something of a cold fish. Up close it is impossible to miss just how passionate he is when talking about young lives going to waste.

The Prince works so hard because he cares, and he knows he can make a difference. Now everyone should be able to see and understand. All his work chronicled here stems directly from the fact that he cares about the country, about the people who live in it and their communities, not only now but also for future generations. He is not given to public displays of emotion, but anyone who spends any time with him and listens to what he says and the way he says it cannot be in any doubt about his feelings.

His overall goal continues to be that of helping others help themselves. For young people in particular he has a special aim. "To enable them to become socially and economically independent, and to make a success of their lives." That goal, simple but powerful, is at the heart of everything he has tried to do, and will remain there as long as young people need his help.

I cannot think of a more appropriate ending than the consistent refrain from people who have received his help, through the Prince's Trust and other organisations: "He didn't have to do anything."

APPENDIX 1

A List of Programmes

Prince Charles: Breaking the Cycle is peppered with programmes. As the Prince's work evolved, names often changed. Residential programmes, for example, went through several incarnations, sometimes called by the location of the camp where the course took place and at other times by the name of the course itself. Thus Work, Sport and Leisure, and Caister, are interchangeable. This brief listing should help avoid confusion.

The Acorn Project   Prince's Trust programme to increase the number of young offenders entering self-employment.

BOOST   Targeted programme, under the Prince's Youth Business Trust umbrella, which helps disabled people into self-employment.

Business in the Community   Founded in 1982 to encourage companies to do more to help communities, both through donations and by employee volunteering.

Centrepoint   Pioneering organisation in the field of helping homeless people, which operates a central London hostel and drop-in centre.

Changing Inside   Research by the Young Offenders Group into experimental projects between 1988 and 1992, primarily inside institutions. Also the title of a conference.

Community Service Volunteers   Leading national organisation promoting community service, not affiliated with the Prince's Trust.

The Compact   Private public partnership created in the USA, whereby businesses agree to provide part- and full-time jobs to students, usually from inner cities, who fulfil certain undertakings relating to school attendance and performance.

The Employers Forum on Disability   An organisation which specifically focuses on employment issues for disabled people.

Foyers   A French concept: *Foyers pour jeunes travailleurs*. Special residences offer room, counselling and training in a package designed to reintegrate young homeless people into the community.

Gifts in Kind	A conduit for companies, often Business in the Community members, to transfer excess equipment such as computers and furniture to the voluntary sector.
Go and See/Go and Help/Enroute	Trust programmes which give grants to disadvantaged young people to go overseas for educational, work or community service purposes.
KAPOW (Kids and the Power of Work)	An American idea which began in Britain in 1992: introduces students to the work environment so they can see the relevance of school lessons to their future.
The King George's Jubilee Trust and the Queen's Silver Jubilee Trust, collectively 'The Jubilee Trusts'	Charitable trusts set up to mark the 25th anniversary of the accession to the throne of King George VI in 1935 and Queen Elizabeth II in 1997.
Middleton-on-Sea/ Caister/Ayr	Locations of holiday camps where Prince's Trust residential courses have been held.
The New Deal	1998 Government welfare-to-work programme for 18- to 24-year-olds who have been out of work for more than six months.
The Phoenix Trust	Charity which converts old buildings, particularly mills, to new uses.
Prince of Wales Advisory Group on Disability (POWAGOD), now The Disability Partnership	The body set up in 1982 after the International Year of the Disabled to advise the Prince on issues relating to disabled people.
The Prince of Wales Business Leaders Forum	An international organisation which encourages multi-national companies to play a positive role around the world in community service, education, employment and the environment.
The Prince of Wales Committee/Bro	The umbrella organisation for the Prince's work in Wales. Started in 1970 as a separate body and subsequently folded into the Trust.
The Prince of Wales Community Venture/ Venturers	The first community service programme set up by the Prince in Sunderland in 1985.
The Prince's Trust Volunteers/Volunteers	The second generation community service programme at the Trust, which commenced in 1990.

Professional Firms Group   An affiliate organisation of Business in the Community in which professionals, such as accountants, architects and lawyers, commit to work free of charge, and through which their skills are matched with needs in the voluntary sector.

Provisions   A programme to 'recycle' food, such as unsold sandwiches, or cereals with wrongly labelled boxes, to charitable organisations.

Rock School/Sounds Live   A Trust course for disadvantaged young people interested in a career in music.

Roots and Wings   Business in the Community mentoring programme coaching students aged 14 to 18, to help reduce their chances of being excluded from school.

Seeing is Believing   Visits which take senior business leaders to see voluntary and public sector activity, usually in depressed areas, where corporate support could be helpful. The international equivalent is INSIGHT.

Study Support   Out-of-school hours centres set up to help students study in a supportive environment.

The West Midlands Training Initiative/Task Undertakings/ The Prince of Wales Training/Threshold   All names for technical and vocational training activities affiliated with the Trust between 1982 and 1998.

Work, Sport and Leisure/ Recharge/Superstart   Residential courses run by the Prince's Trust at different times between 1987 and 1998.

The Young Offenders Group   Task force started in 1988 within the Trust to try new ideas to help young offenders, primarily those in some form of custodial institution.

The Youth Business Initiative (YBI)   The original name for the 1982 self-employment programme.

The Prince's Youth Business Trust   The programme formed out of the merger of YBI and YES, which helps young people unable to find support elsewhere to set up in self-employment.

The Youth Enterprise Scheme (YES)   A similar programme to YBI set up by Sir Angus Ogilvy in 1983 through the National Association of Youth Clubs.

APPENDIX 2

Chronology of Main Events and Key Organisations

1935   King George's Jubilee Appeal

1968   Chairman of Welsh Steering Committee for European Conservation Year (1970)

1971   The Prince of Wales' Committee (Pwyllgar Tywysog Cymru)

1972   Meeting with George Pratt, John Rea Price, Norman Ingram Smith, Jon Snow, and Inspector Collie, which led ultimately to the formation of The Prince's Trust

1974   President of Administrative Council of King George V Jubilee Trust

1976   The Prince's Trust

1977   The Queen's Silver Jubilee Appeal

        Moonshot Club meeting between police and ethnic minority members

1981   Patron of UK Chapter for United Nations International Year of the Disabled

        Riots in inner cities, notably Toxteth

        West Midlands Training Initiative

1982   Youth Business Initiative

        First Rock Gala

        The Prince of Wales Advisory Group on Disability

1984   The Windsor Conference on discrimination in employment

1985   Launch of Living Options on planning and providing disability services

        President of Business in the Community

        1000th new business start-up

        The Prince of Wales Community Venture

        Visit to Centrepoint

1986   The Prince's Youth Business Trust

        First residential camp

        Community Enterprise Award

        Visit to Lowell and Boston Conference: 'Futures for Youth'

        One Per Cent Club

1987   United Kingdom Patron of the European Year of the Environment

        The One Town Partnership in Calderdale

        40th birthday £40 million fund-raising for the Prince's Youth Business Trust

        Appointment of Tom Shebbeare as Executive Director of all the Trusts

1988   The Prince's Scottish Youth Business Trust

        Nationwide Anglia Design Award for house builders responsive to the needs of people with disabilities

        Young Offenders' Forum

1989   The Royal Jubilee Trusts (comprising King George's Jubilee Trust and the Queen's Silver Jubilee Trust) merge with the Prince's Trust

1990   The Charleston Conference: 'Stakeholders – the Challenge in a Global Market'

The Prince's Trust Volunteers

The Employers' Forum on Disability

The Prince of Wales Business Leaders Forum

First Study Support Centre

1991   Seeing is Believing

The Prince's Trust Ambassadors

Co-ordination committee across all main organisations

First Foyer

Environment seminar in Brazil

The Bharatiya Yuva Shakti Trust

1992   The Prince's Youth Business Trust Ethnic Advisory Committee

The Leadership Consortium

Aim High: Business in the Community education initiative

Provisions

Pentonville Prison Conference: 'Changing Inside'

1993   St Petersburg Partnership Initiative

1994   Hoteliers' Forum to encourage better practices in dealing with people with disabilities in the hospitality industry

The first meeting of all the Prince's main organisations in Sutton Coldfield

Project Acorn for young offenders

1995   The Prince's Trust Administrative Council

Race for Opportunity

Head Teacher pairing programme (mentoring)

Invest in Futures (homelessness initiative)

KAPOW: Kids and the Power of Work

1996   Trust activities concentrated in Park Square East

10,000th Volunteer: programme endorsed by all main political parties

25,000th new business start-up

Annecy: first foreign residential camp

Gifts in Kind

Index of Corporate Engagement

1997   500th Study Support Centre

BOOST: special programme for potential entrepreneurs with disabilities

Enroute: community service in Europe

1998   The Disability Partnership created as an umbrella group for all activities relating to disabled people

47 environmental action areas named

Executive Forum on homelessness

Scottish Equity Finance for Youth

School-centred initial teacher training for primary school teachers

APPENDIX 3

Letter of Endorsement for Study Support

10 DOWNING STREET
LONDON SW1A 2AA

THE PRIME MINISTER

I have a vision of an energetic, compassionate and highly educated Britain fully equipped to maximise the opportunities of the 21st century. Realising that vision depends crucially on our education service ensuring that all our young people achieve their full potential at school, combined with wider opportunities to learn outside the classroom.

The Prince's Trust has been championing study support over the past five years and you have provided new opportunities for tens of thousands of young people in disadvantaged circumstances to enjoy learning, acquire skills, and gain confidence.

I am delighted to endorse The Trust's Study Support Code of Practice which is being launched at your National Conference and which has been supported by the Department for Education and Employment. I am confident that the Code will do much to ensure the development of good standards in schools, libraries and youth organisations. I welcome the Code's structured but flexible approach to helping local centres to reflect on their practice and to meet the particular needs of their pupils and communities. I am also delighted that The Trust is closely involved in DfEE's work to develop a national framework for motivating pupils outside the classroom. Together these contributions will help to create a network of provision which offers extra learning opportunities and challenges for all our young people.

The Trust's work in this area is a good example of partnership involving central and local government, the business community, voluntary and statutory bodies, teachers, teaching assistants, youth and community workers and volunteers. The Trust's concept of a co-ordinated framework, allowing for local diversity, will ensure that Study Support Centres can select the most appropriate programmes from the numerous available initiatives, multiplying the benefits for pupils and everyone else involved. Indeed one of the most remarkable things about Study Support is the opportunity it offers young people to develop their key skills as mentors or peer tutors while helping others.

I send the Trust – and all those attending this third national Study Support conference – my best wishes for a successful and enjoyable day and a fruitful year ahead.

Tony Blair

November 1997

APPENDIX 4

How Can You Help?

This book has been about the work of the Prince of Wales and his vision for the future of Britain. If, like me, you have been touched by these stories of individuals whose lives have been changed for the better, and if you share his desire to do something, please call one of the following organisations, all of which are involved in this great enterprise. The scope of their activities is so broad that there should be something here for everyone; and everyone who can read this book could help in some way.
If you want to celebrate Prince Charles's birthday, please sign up now. There is always more to be done.

The Prince's Trust   **– Action**
                  – Volunteers
                  – Youth Business Trust
                  – Fund Raising
                  – Special Events
18 Park Square East, London NW1 4LH
Tel: 0171-543 1234

The Scottish Prince's Youth Business Trust
Mercantile Chambers, 53 Bothwell Street,
Glasgow G2 6TS
Tel: 0141-248 4999

The Disability Partnership
60 Gainsford Street, London SE1 2NY
Tel: 0171-403 9433

Business in the Community
44 Baker Street, London W1M 1DH
Tel: 0171-224 1600

Gifts in Kind UK
PO Box 140, 4 St Dunstan's Hall,
London EC3R 5HB
Tel: 0171-204 5003

The Prince's Trust – Bro
Empire House, Mount Stuart Square,
Cardiff CF1 6DN
Tel: 01222-471 121

Scottish Business in the Community
30 Hanover Street, Edinburgh EH2 2DR
Tel: 0131-220 3001

The Prince of Wales' Business Leaders Forum
15-16 Cornwall Terrace, London NW1 4QP
Tel: 0171-467 3600

APPENDIX 5

**International Affiliates of The Youth Business Trust
(as of June 1998)**

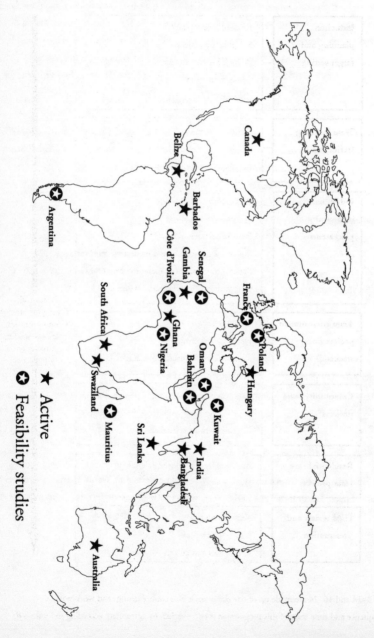

APPENDIX 6

Typical Volunteer Programme

Sample 60-day part-time programme – a mix of short blocks and day release

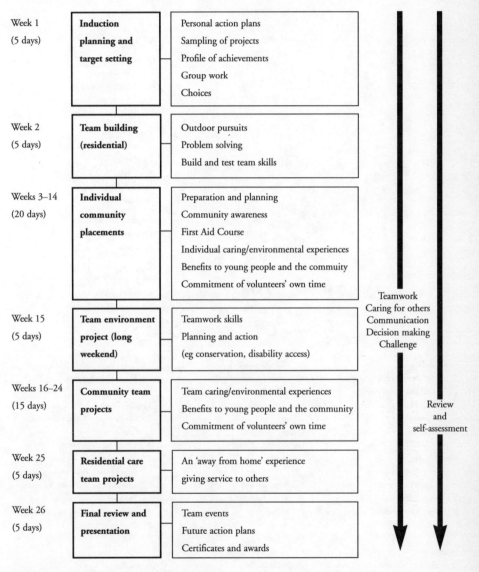

Week 1 (5 days)	**Induction planning and target setting**	Personal action plans Sampling of projects Profile of achievements Group work Choices
Week 2 (5 days)	**Team building (residential)**	Outdoor pursuits Problem solving Build and test team skills
Weeks 3–14 (20 days)	**Individual community placements**	Preparation and planning Community awareness First Aid Course Individual caring/environmental experiences Benefits to young people and the commuity Commitment of volunteers' own time
Week 15 (5 days)	**Team environment project (long weekend)**	Teamwork skills Planning and action (eg conservation, disability access)
Weeks 16–24 (15 days)	**Community team projects**	Team caring/environmental experiences Benefits to young people and the community Commitment of volunteers' own time
Week 25 (5 days)	**Residential care team projects**	An 'away from home' experience giving service to others
Week 26 (5 days)	**Final review and presentation**	Team events Future action plans Certificates and awards

Teamwork
Caring for others
Communication
Decision making
Challenge

Review
and
self-assessment

Notes

1 Weeks 3–14 and 16–24 are made up of one day a week plus some evenings and weekends

2 The sequence and time scale of this programme may be varied, by agreement, according to local needs

APPENDIX 7

Action Areas for Regeneration

The 47 Priority Areas for the Prince of Wales

(Neighbourhoods or housing estates in brackets)

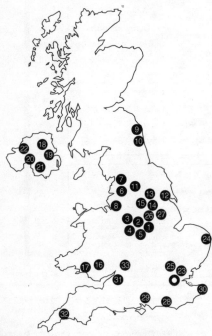

London
North West:
Brent (Carlton)
Hammersmith and Fulham
Kensington and Chelsea
Westminster and City

South:
Gtreenwich/Bexley
Lambeth
Lewisham
Southwark
Wandsworth

North:
Camden/Islington
Haringey

East:
Newham
Tower Hamlets
Hackney (Holly Street)

West Midlands
1 Coventry: Foleshill (Pridmore)
2 Birmingham (Lee Bank)
3 Balsall Heath
4 Ladywood
5 Wolverhampton

North West
6 Bolton/Salford (Little
   Hutton/Farnworth)
7 Preston (Deepdale)
8 Merseyside (Speke, Garston, New
   Wallasey, Granby, Toxteth)

North East
9 West End of Newcastle (Benwell)
10 Sunderland

Yorkshire and Humberside
11 Bradford

12 Hull (Gypsyville)
13 Leeds: Halton Moor
14 Rotherham
15 Sheffield

Wales
16 Rhondda Valley
17 Neath

Northern Ireland
18 North East: Ballymena
19 Belfast

South East
20 South West: Enniskillen
21 South East
22 North West: Strabane

Eastern
23 Basildon

24 Great Yarmouth (Middlegate)
25 Luton (Marsh Farm, Bury Park)

East Midlands
26 Derby (Sinfin and Castleward,
    Osmaston,
    Chaddesden/Derwent)
27 Nottingham (NG7, Radford,
    Forest Fields, Hyson Green and
    Lenton, The Meadows) Leicester,
    Belgrave
28 Brighton and Hove (Whitehawk)
29 Portsmouth
30 Thanet

South West
31 Bristol (Knowle West)
32 Plymouth
33 Gloucestershire (Hesters Way)

INDEX